Traders' Tales

D1454089

Traders' Tales

Narratives of
Cultural Encounters
in the
Columbia Plateau,
1807–1846

By Elizabeth Vibert

University of Oklahoma Press
Norman and London

Also by Elizabeth Vibert

(ed. with Jennifer S. H. Brown) *Reading Beyond Words: Contexts for Native History* (Peterborough, ON, 1996)

Library of Congress
Cataloging-in-Publication Data

Vibert, Elizabeth, 1962–
  Traders' tales : Narratives of cultural
encounters in the Columbia Plateau,
1807–1846 / by Elizabeth Vibert.
      p.   cm.
  Includes bibliographical references
and index.
  ISBN 0-8061-2932-8 (alk. paper)
  1. Indians of North America—
Columbia Plateau—History. 2. Fur
traders—Columbia Plateau. 3. Acculturation—Columbia Plateau. 4. Indians
of North America—Columbia Plateau—
Public opinion. 5. Public opinion—
Great Britain. I. Title.
E78.C63V52 1997
979.6'100497—dc20   96-42235
                                                    CIP

Text design by Cathy Carney Imboden.
Text typeface is Cheltenham.

1 2 3 4 5 6 7 8 9 10

To my mother, Isabel Vibert Moffitt,
and in memory of my father, James C. Vibert

Contents

Illustrations

Maps

Preface

Traders' Tales is a study of European perceptions of colonized peoples. More specifically, it explores the images conceived by British fur traders to describe the Native American societies of the Plateau region of the Pacific Northwest. The book began life with a rather different mission: my intention was to produce a study of Native American responses to colonization in this little-studied region. As in so many other regions of North America, fur traders were the first Europeans to establish a presence in the Plateau; they arrived early in the nineteenth century. Their journals and log books, trade-post records, and published narratives provide the earliest written historical record of the indigenous societies. The documents of the fur trade are many and varied, offering rich insights into a fascinating era of cultural encounter.

It is precisely their place at the meeting of distinctive cultures that makes the fur-trade documents so intriguing. Not long into my project to uncover evidence about Native responses to the fur-trader presence, I found myself wrapped up in the documents themselves. What began as an uncomfortable sense that these sources were not entirely to be trusted, when it came to depictions of Native peoples, soon became a need to understand why the traders wrote what they did. Not that I thought the traders told untruths: the stories they told, so far as we can tell, were related faithfully—they were the traders' truths. But it quickly became clear that one's truth is another's tall tale. Native people undoubtedly had very different understandings of their own motivations and practices. The point here is not to censure the traders for misreading what they could not be expected to understand. These men arrived from Scotland, England, and the eastern colonies carrying a heavy burden of cultural baggage. Like any of us when we travel to unfamiliar places, the traders' view was colored by ideas and assumptions derived from their own background and experience. In time many would come to appreciate aspects of Native culture; some would even be accused by their peers of "going native." But none, it seems, could entirely let go of the cultural notions they had carried with them—notions about the "civilized" way of life, the proper economy, appropriate social roles for men and women. These assumptions formed a kind of coordinating grid in the travellers' encounters with Native people.

Much of this discussion may seem obvious. However, a little research into the scholarly and general literature reveals that all too often traders' accounts have been treated as the whole truth. A British Columbia Supreme Court judge, drawing on trader writings in his recent decision on a major land dispute, held up the documents as "fact," declaring that he had "no hesitation accepting the information" contained in them. Anthropologists and historians have frequently taken a similar tack, albeit with a little more scholarly sophistication. The documents of the fur trade constitute the earliest "ethnographic" record of the indigenous societies of northern North America, a record scholars of many persuasions have been eager to tap. Trader texts have shaped subsequent understandings of Native histories in ways as profound as they are unacknowledged. Very few who have used these texts have considered in detail the ways in which the traders' cultural lenses molded and refracted their view of Native societies. The more I read of trader accounts and of studies drawing on those accounts, the more convinced I became that these were the questions that most needed asking: Why did the traders produce their particular images of Native American societies?

What ideological, social, and economic forces shaped their vision? How were the traders' preconceptions influenced by their experiences on the ground—their relationships with Native communities, their activities as fur traders? Is it possible to "read through" the thicket of contradictory meanings and ambiguous images to get at some historically accurate picture of people and events over a century ago?

Those looking for confident assertions of historical truth may be disappointed in the chapters that follow. The primary focus is on the traders, the primary project to unpack their cultural baggage and attempt to understand the preconceptions, pressures, and forces that caused them to see Native American societies as they did. Their writings are treated here as constructions of indigenous lifeways rather than faithful *re*constructions. Yet colored as they are, the accounts do bring into the light aspects of Native life, and of the encounter between Natives and newcomers, that would otherwise be lost from view. When read with a critical eye, when compared and contrasted with the range of traders' accounts from the same period and the same setting, and when considered in the context of linguistic, anthropological, archaeological, and biological evidence, certain strong images begin to emerge. These images are presented in the chapters that follow not as definitive statements of historical fact, but as speculations on the nature of historical realities.

This brief discussion of rationale glosses over many important and difficult issues of methodology and approach. I have a good deal more to say about these matters in chapter 1. There the reader will find an introduction to the cast of characters, the setting for the study, and the larger historical context of British travellers abroad in the early nineteenth century. The chapter also provides an extended discussion of the theoretical underpinnings of my approach. Some readers may find the theory tedious, and some will see it as an unnecessary diversion. But in my view theoretical positioning is a basic part of any historical analysis. Every such analysis is shaped by its author's philosophy of history; some simply choose to be more explicit about their position than others. I often remind my students of the words of theorist Hayden White: "[E]very historical discourse contains within it a full-blown, if only implicit, philosophy of history." My aim in the pages that follow is to shed light on the philosophies shaping trader discourse, and to be explicit about the philosophy informing my own approach.

Acknowledgments

Traders' Tales started life as a doctoral dissertation, and after three summers of reconsideration and revision, it now ventures forth as a book. In the nearly eight years that I have been engaged in research and writing I have accumulated many debts. I would like first to acknowledge those who supported me through the sometimes harrowing and always challenging business of dissertation writing.

My first debt of gratitude is to my doctoral supervisor, Terence Ranger, whose enthusiasm for this project and for my efforts went well beyond what I had a right to expect. The dissertation bore the mark of his careful criticism; I hope the book reflects my ongoing respect for his wisdom, insight, and gifts as a historian.

The late John Vincent was very supportive in my first year of research. John Dunbabin and Phyllis Ferguson provided helpful commentary on portions of the thesis, and much-needed moral support. My examiners, Megan Vaughan and Glyndwr Williams, provided suggestive comments and encouragement that have stayed with me through the long period of revision.

On this side of the Atlantic, I have leaned heavily on the enthusiasm and support of my friend and colleague Wendy Wickwire. I am very grateful for the steady encouragement and excellent models provided by Jennifer Brown, Julie Cruikshank, and my mentor at Dalhousie, Kenneth Heard. Countless others have been generous with advice and time over the years, among them Rick Stuart, Nancy Turner, Cole Harris, Richard Mackie,

Kaye Lamb, John Lutz, Laura Peers, Robin Fisher, Paul Tennant, Jim Troup, Sylvia Van Kirk, Victoria Wyatt, and Anne Yandle. My colleagues at the University of Victoria have provided a supportive research and teaching environment and welcome diversions. I especially thank Lynne Marks, who has acted as sounding board, thoughtful critic, and kindred spirit since I arrived at UVic; Gregory Blue; Eric Sager; Annalee Golz; Peter Baskerville; Phyllis Senese; Pat Roy; Karen McIvor; and my students. South of the border, I am very grateful for the contributions of Bill Swagerty and Alan Marshall. My editor at University of Oklahoma Press, Sarah Iselin, has made the process of final preparation quite painless. Finally, I owe much to Editor-in-Chief John Drayton, whose faith in this project provided inspiration from the early days.

The staffs of the following institutions have been very helpful: Hudson's Bay Company Archives; Provincial Archives of Manitoba; British Columbia Archives and Records Service; University of British Columbia Special Collections; Suzzallo Library, University of Washington; Public Archives of Canada; Rhodes House Library, Oxford; and Public Record Office, London. I thank the Hudson's Bay Company for granting permission to consult and quote from the extraordinary company archives in Winnipeg. I am grateful to Stuart Daniel, Starshell Maps, for his fine mapwork. I have benefited from the financial support of the British Council, under the Commonwealth Scholarships program; the Social Sciences and Humanities Research Council of Canada; St. Edmund Hall, the Beit Fund, and the Committee for Graduate Studies, Oxford; and the University of Victoria.

The most important tribute is often saved for the last. I wish to thank my family for getting me started and getting me through. My mother, Isabel Moffitt, has been a constant source of moral support and grounding. My sisters and brother helped me keep a sense of humor; special thanks to Ann for showing me how to be a "toad." My grandfather, Harley Hatfield, provided the initial inspiration and has been an enthusiastic reviewer. My son, Will, who arrived in the throes of copyediting, provided fresh eyes to see the world and the best possible reason to get the book done. Finally my partner, Todd Hatfield, has been my expert critic, patient counsellor, and best friend. I can hardly begin to express my appreciation.

ELIZABETH VIBERT

Editorial Procedures

Every effort has been made in this study to remain faithful to the original documents. Phrases and passages from original sources are quoted unedited, with the single exception that ampersands have been changed to "and" (except when used in &c, for "et cetera"). Where clarification or amplification is called for in the midst of a passage, square brackets denote my editorial inserts. Brackets in the original documents are rendered as parentheses.

As is so often the case with historical documents, spelling in fur-trade documents can be varied and creative. In direct quotations original spellings are preserved. Several confusing usages in the text should be noted: Colville is spelled with two ls when in reference to the trade post or district, named for Andrew Colvile of the Hudson's Bay Company (HBC), although traders were not always consistent in *their* spellings; the conventional spelling of the name of the Sxoielpi people also has two *ls*: Colville. Traders generally referred to the Thompson River as "Thompson's," hence "Thompson's River Post." The Canadian spelling Okanagan is used throughout this study except in reference to the post, for which the American spelling Okanogan is used, since the historic site stands in the United States. Kutenai is the accepted spelling for the people, Kootenay for the river, and Kootenay for the post. Sahaptin refers to the people of the middle Columbia River and their language, while Sahaptian is the name of the larger language family.

The choice of collective names by which to refer to particular
Native American peoples is a difficult issue. The names by which
they are known vary in different segments of Canadian and
American society and from region to region; the names by which
the people know themselves can also vary from community to
community. Ideally, I would have chosen to call each people by
its own preferred name—for example, the Salish Flathead would
be simply the Salish. Ultimately, this would entail retrieving the
local names for individual communities—a practice that would
lead to an almost endless proliferation in a region as broad as the
Plateau. (For more on problems of labelling, see discussion in the
introduction.) The real difficulty is that few such names appear
in the historical record of the fur trade. To use the traders' labels,
in all their varied forms, when quoting trader texts, and an
entirely different set of labels in my own narrative, would be
hopelessly cumbersome and confusing to most readers. Recognizing that ethnic designations have shifted with the tides of
history, and continue to do so, I have chosen to use the names
that I believe to be most familiar to readers in the present day.
I apologize to those who do not recognize themselves or their
ancestors in these labels. By choosing labels of common use and
convenience, I do not discount the work that has been done in
many communities to reinstate culturally meaningful names. The
return to traditional ethnonyms is not simply a swipe at scholars
and bureaucrats (those great purveyors of labels), nor a gesture
at political correctness. It is a political act, a move to regain a
measure of self-determination through the power to name. I
regret that in this book, a historical account with a daunting
geographical and cultural sweep, it is not always feasible to make
reference to the names used by Native Americans today.

Traders' Tales

CHAPTER ONE

Introduction

George Simpson was not amused.
Ever the uncompromising businessman, on his first tour of the
Columbia Department in 1824–25, the Hudson's Bay Company's
overseas chief dismissed the Native people living along the
Columbia River as "indolent and lazy to an extreme." The source
of their vice was clear to him: the river and nearby root grounds
provided such abundant provisions that these people had no
need to hunt, whether for their own food or—more to the point
for Simpson—for trade. To make matters worse, the governor was
informed that these "salmon tribes" had shown little interest in
British trade goods, and less in trapping beaver. The latter
activity, he sardonically noted, they considered "a wonderful
exertion."[1]

Simpson's views were widely shared by fur traders in the
Columbia-Fraser Plateau region of the Pacific Northwest. The
British traders who arrived in the Plateau early in the nineteenth
century found the indigenous peoples living in an "unhallowed
wilderness," sustaining themselves by fishing, hunting, and
gathering—living, as one trader phrased it and all presumed, in
a "rude state of nature."[2] The contours of that state were not new
to these observers. The British had been encountering "natives"
abroad for centuries, inscribing them as savages both noble and
ignoble.[3] The British fur trade had been underway in North
America for well over one hundred years by the time traders with
the Scots-dominated North West Company had crossed the Rocky

Mountains to the Plateau; some of the Pacific-bound North Westers already had years of experience in the "Indian Country" east of the mountains.

As travellers abroad British fur traders produced their own voluminous, and in many ways distinctive, cultural commentaries. Naturally these writings were informed by the ideological baggage the traders carried with them from their British or colonial homes. The content of that baggage was a complex of assumptions, conceptions, and other ideas that derived from particular historical circumstances and that functioned as a kind of coordinating grid in the travellers' encounters with "the Indian." The outline of the grid was defined by an imagination that was white, male, British, and middle-class. On this grid traders attempted to order and account for difference; on this grid the Native was described. In the language of the new cultural history, the coordinating grid was a "web of significance," a complex of enshrined cultural meanings to be read as a text.[4] The British traders' webs are the subject of this study. The project is to read these webs as they are revealed in traders' writings from the Plateau and to try to understand why the writings took the forms they did.

My approach is informed by the trend in cultural studies most often identified as poststructuralism. Where once upon a time many scholars working with historical documents might have viewed those texts as purveyors of objective truth, a truth that could be revealed through the application of proper scholarly methodology, many now reject the notions of "objectivity" and "truth." In cultural and literary studies, anthropology, geography, and other fields, it has become increasingly common to characterize meaning, value, and knowledge itself as unstable, uncertain, and open to multiple understandings. It is often said that historians are resistant to this postmodern turn in the humanities and social sciences; however, of late a growing number of scholars trained in this field have begun to apply methodologies that start from the premise that meanings in texts are not transparent.[5]

Texts—whether written, spoken, or pictorial—are not some carved-in-stone body of raw facts. The "facts" are socially constructed; they are products of the social and cultural forces in place when the texts were created, and of the forces in place as the texts are continually interpreted and reinterpreted.[6] The notion that historical documents can be treated as objective eyewitness accounts is an illusion. Trader texts, like any others, are never objective; rather, they present their reader with multiple subjectivities, multiple ways of knowing the world. This is an important part of their fascination. A text's many voices can be listened for, balanced with one another as best we can, read alongside the voices in other texts, but they can never be melded into one single, indisputable truth. Nor can we ever silence our own voices as readers or scholars. A highly educated, white, middle-class woman in the 1990s, I can never remove myself from the social, cultural, and intellectual contexts in which I am embedded—from my own "predicament of culture."[7] What I can do is to be alert to the ways in which my predicament shapes my reading of fur traders' texts, just as I seek to be alert to the forces that shaped their writing of the texts.

Language is the medium that conveys cultural meanings in the texts under study here. It is not a neutral medium: the language of any cultural or social group, in any epoch, reflects and helps to constitute that group's view of the world. When we read texts, one of our main tasks is to analyze closely the work of language. That work—the ideological functions that language performs in speech, in writing, in action—is generally referred to as discourse.[8]

Ten years ago, before most students of Native American history were talking in such terms, anthropologist Mary Black-Rogers provided a searching analysis of a particular strain of fur-trader discourse. In an essay entitled "Varieties of 'Starving': Semantics and Survival in the Subarctic Fur Trade," Black-Rogers unpacked the notion of the "starving Indian," an image that crops up with alarming frequency in trader writings. Closely connected with the word "starving" was "indolent"; Black-Rogers showed that both concepts carried with them a range of cultural and specific fur-trade connotations that often had little to do with either a shortage of food or idleness. Her study was a revelation to me as I attempted to find my way through the thicket of contradictory meanings and ambiguous images that color Plateau traders' texts. Black-Rogers's essay underscores the point that concepts like "starving" and "indolent" need to be sharply interrogated. Scholars consulting historical documents must be vigilant to the ways in which such concepts are culturally shaped and contextually bound. The unpacking of these notions can be of far more than dry academic interest. As the earliest "ethnographic" records of the indigenous societies of northern North America, fur traders' accounts have been extensively—and far too often uncritically—mined for data. These days the documents are regularly pillaged for information about historical patterns of Native American land use, by those involved in land-settlement cases before provincial, state, and federal courts.

In a controversial 1991 court ruling, Chief Justice Allan Mc-Eachern of the British Columbia Supreme Court, finding against the Gitksan and Wet'suwet'en plaintiffs of north-central British Columbia, privileged the contents of fur traders' accounts as "fact." McEachern drew on the writings of British traders in the 1820s and 1830s to support his conclusion that life for the Gitksan and Wet'suwet'en people was "primitive," indeed "nasty, brutish, and short."[9] A fundamental assumption informing this view was that fishing-hunting-gathering societies occupy the lowest rung on a ladder of social evolution—a discourse that came into full flower in eighteenth-century Europe and influenced trader perceptions of the "rude state of nature." It is a fundamental premise of this book that the process by which historical texts such as these were constructed is in dire need of close historical analysis. The texts have shaped subsequent understandings of Native histories in ways as profound as they are unacknowledged.

To return to the web metaphor, my aim is first to identify the strands of inherited meaning that are woven into trader discourse about the Plateau and its peoples. But there is necessarily much more to the project. Our attention is captured not only by the traders' webs of significance but also by the process of their spinning; not only by culture, but by history. If we are to "read" the traders' ideas, literally and figuratively, we must do so fully apprised of the social and historical *processes* in which those ideas were embedded. This is not to imply that cultural meanings are caused by, or merely reflect, the material world; ideas and symbolic systems have a momentum quite their own. Categories of meaning are partially autonomous, partially constrained components that at once condition and are conditioned by social forces, local and beyond.

The concept of "culture" itself needs to be unpacked. It is used here, warily, for lack of a better alternative. Culture is not invoked in the sense in which the word has been used for much of the twentieth century, to refer to a package of more or less distinctive traits of which every society on earth claims ownership: culture so conceived takes on the shape of a material entity, frozen in time and reduced to a checklist of essential elements—a list defined, in the end, by Western experts. Nor is the concept used strictly in the sense of symbolic anthropology, to refer to systems of representation, classification schemes, and metaphors: in this formulation, culture often appears somehow to transcend its social and historical context. At the risk of sounding pat, culture is conceived here more as a process in history. It does involve, centrally, systems of meaning or ways of knowing to which individuals collectively subscribe. But such a collective identity is inventive and malleable, and subject to pressures and processes beyond its permeable borders. Culture is taken here to be a system of representation that is constantly being reinvented. In the words of one of its recent critics, culture lives "by pollination, by (historical) transplanting."[10]

A large part of the project of analyzing traders' narratives is to assess how traders' cultural knowledge of "the native" was produced, reproduced, and reordered in the setting of the Plateau fur trade. The traders' purpose was to carry on a profitable—and therefore peaceable—trade with Native peoples. In many cases the traders lived for years on end, in small numbers, in the "Indian Country" (if generally behind insulating walls). They married indigenous women. Their links to the home country were often tenuous. The cultural meanings of such a group were surely open to inventive refashioning. Traders were subject to that "jarring of meanings and values" that one cultural theorist so convincingly portrays as the consequence of inhabiting the liminal spaces of interacting cultures. The images they chose were shifting and contradictory as the writers vacillated between what was already "known" about the Indian and what was in need of anxious repetition.[11] With these observations in mind, I will attempt to place the traders not only in the context of their own shifting ideological heritage, but firmly in the flow of the events and processes of which they were a part. The process of particular interest is the establishing and carrying on of trade relations with the indigenous peoples of the Plateau, the region known in fur-trade parlance as the Columbia Interior.

Suddenly, as readers of trader texts, we are enmeshed in a global historical process, the expansion of Western capitalism (initially of the merchant form) to "new worlds" of economic opportunity. We are enmeshed in that expansion, but not overwhelmed by it: the history of the expansion of Western capitalism is not given. The outcome of that expansion has been enormously varied, making clear that the outcome "depends as much on [local] cultural mediation as on colonial and postcolonial domination for its explanation."[12] Even within the realm of the North American fur trade, there was much variation across cultural, ecological, and temporal landscapes.

At base, the fur trade was the process by which furs and hides produced by indigenous peoples were exchanged for manufactured goods supplied by Europeans. Beginning in the late 1500s, the trade brought French, British, Dutch, Spanish, Russian, and other mercantile interests to the North American continent.

Beaver pelts were the principal inducement; the wool provided the felt so sought after in the European clothing and hatting industries. After a long history of imperial and commercial jockeying for power, by the early nineteenth century the fur trade of British North America was presided over by two arch-rival enterprises, the London-based Hudson's Bay Company (HBC) and the Montreal-based, Scots-dominated North West Company (NWC). The NWC, having established itself west of the Rocky Mountains ahead of its rival, was able to monopolize the trade of the Plateau and the larger Columbia district until economic necessity forced the companies to amalgamate in 1821 (which they did under the name Hudson's Bay Company).[13] Until the early 1840s the Hudson's Bay Company was to remain the only effective non-native presence in the region.

The fur trade cannot be reduced to the economic exchange of manufactured goods for furs and hides. There was no single fur trade, but many. The importance of historical specificity, and of local cultural mediation in larger processes, are exceptionally well illustrated through the example of the fur trade of the Columbia Interior.

With important exceptions, most Plateau groups were less involved in the trade than were Native peoples in other regions of northern North America. The findings presented here indicate that this was in large part because the economic strategies of most Plateau societies were based on gathered vegetable foods and fish rather than the products of hunting and trapping. Given these strategies, which generally provided amply, many communities took little interest in trapping furs for trade. Naturally this had repercussions for traders' views of Native subsistence methods. The emphasis here is on traders' representations of those methods in their writings on Plateau land and resource use. There is a pragmatic reason for this focus, in addition to basic intellectual curiosity: traders, being traders, had a good deal more to say about matters of Native "economy" than about religion, social organization, and so forth. However, matters of spirituality and kinship are not readily fenced off from resource use in these societies, and it would be artificial and ethnocentric to attempt to do so. Such issues often come to the fore in this study. Chapter 2, which sets the backdrop to the traders' arrival, is explicitly concerned with indigenous intellectual responses to what was undoubtedly the most catastrophic outcome of the early encounter between Native Americans and whites, epidemic disease. In chapter 4, systems of marriage (about which traders had a good deal to say) and kinship lead to discussions of the gendered nature of traders' views of women's productive activities. However, in the main, the focus generally is on the traders' writings about Plateau land and resource use.

Despite the relatively limited nature of the Plateau fur trade as an economic venture—and the limitations should not be overstated—the trade was nevertheless a profound cultural encounter. Cultural meanings on both sides were challenged and subtly adjusted, though seldom transformed. The reciprocal influences of European and indigenous trade practices in the context of the North American fur trades has been the subject of considerable historical interest over the past two decades. In the face of overwhelming evidence to the contrary, few students of the fur trades have found it possible to sustain an older view that Native Americans were pawns in the trade, rendered "utterly dependent" on superior European goods, their economic and social systems rapidly and radically transformed.[14] That interpretation was part of a larger metanarrative, a descending plot line that cast Native Americans as the inevitable losers in a contest between civilized and primitive worlds.[15] Much of the research of the past two decades has been concerned to overturn such "fatal confrontation" reasoning and to demonstrate the crucial influence of indigenous demands and motivations on trade relationships. In the words of two contemporary scholars, Native people were "partners" in the trade.[16]

The new approaches of fur-trade scholarship have never before been turned to the Columbia Interior. This particular fur trade has scarcely been touched on by historians. While there has been a growing interest in the trade west of the Rockies in recent years, most studies have focused entirely on the Northwest Coast. Those that have looked to the Interior at all have tended to treat it as an adjunct to the trade on the coast rather than as a region with its own distinctive fur trade.[17]

Native American agency in the fur trade is no longer a subject for serious debate. Debate continues to percolate, however, over Native motivation: is it to be ascribed to universal notions of economic rationality (the so-called "formalist" position), or is it better explained with reference to indigenous institutions, values, and relationships (the "substantivist" position)? In 1930 Harold Innis was one of the first to look in depth at Native demands for European goods. For Innis those goods were unquestionably superior to anything available locally; that assumption was sufficient to explain Native motivations in the trade. By the latter 1960s such views were being questioned. Anthropologist Wilcomb Washburn, for example, drew attention to indigenous cultural logics, demonstrating how "noneconomic" factors drove exchange within Native societies. Washburn argued that gift exchange as a means of marking status and prestige, and of forging relationships, became as important in the cross-cultural fur trade as it had long been in indigenous trade and diplomacy. Furthermore, Washburn showed how European goods that might be seen in their home societies as "utilitarian" could be put to unexpected "nonutilitarian" uses in Native communities. Cornelius Jaenen, a historian of New France, picked up this theme in a 1974 study in which he demonstrated the culturally specific uses to which European goods might be put—uses that were "aesthetic, magical, or purely decorative," not merely economic.[18]

In his monumental history of the Huron people, Bruce Trigger tied their early interest in French trade goods to a desire for "magical" properties. While they made use of European metal goods for subsistence activities, the Huron also buried large quantities in their Feast of the Dead, indicating that the goods were accorded some religious reverence. Trigger concluded, however, that the special powers of Europeans and their goods tended to be set aside as Native people became more familiar with both. In a recent essay he restates firmly his position that while "cultural beliefs" were important early on, "in the long run rationalist calculations came to play a preponderant role" in the Native American response to foreign trade goods. By "rationalist calculation" Trigger means the calculation of economic benefits and costs according to the logic of some "universal human reason."[19]

A particularly influential counter-interpretation of the value of European goods to Natives has been developed in recent years by Christopher Miller and George Hamell. Focusing on the early years of cultural encounter, they argue that the impact of "utilitarian" goods on the practical subsistence strategies of peoples of the eastern woodlands and eastern plains was insignificant. However, metal goods and glasswares were incorporated with relish into Native ideological and symbolic systems, alongside indigenous copper, crystal, shell, and other items. The most prized European goods were not those that were unusual or unique, but those that could be adapted to ritual uses; in other words, those that were akin or equivalent to prized Native goods.[20]

In a close reading of French accounts, historian Bruce White has come up with a still more complex analysis of Ojibwa and Dakota responses to European trade goods. White argues that, while much of the very early documentary record indicates that these groups viewed the French as supernatural beings, the evidence is that it was in fact French merchandise that was believed to possess special power. The term "spirit" (*esprit* in the documents), frequently applied to the French, arose from Native peoples' appreciation for the goods the French offered. A central tenet of White's argument is that the Ojibwa and Dakota valued French technology for its many applications to their daily lives— applications that ranged from the prosaic to the spiritual, and that could shift over time. He emphasizes that the attempt to set up a dichotomy between "utilitarian" and "nonutilitarian," "economic" and "noneconomic" uses, is spurious. Rather than thinking of trade goods as slotting into one or the other of these binary categories, White calls for an analysis of the cultural trajectory of things, of the way goods pass "successively and sometimes simultaneously through a variety of cultural contexts." To ascertain the meanings of European goods for indigenous peoples, it is necessary to consider the range of possible uses, and the stages through which seemingly fixed objects might pass in their lives.[21]

While there are many shades to these culturalist or substantivist lines of argument, and subtle differences well beyond our concern here, scholars who subscribe to these approaches share certain assumptions. First, they reject the notion that the introduction of European goods necessarily led to upheaval and rapid cultural change in Native societies. In more general terms, they may be seen as rejecting the descending plot line that casts the onset of colonialism as producing a sharp break in the histories of indigenous peoples. In crudest terms, the latter view of cultural change implies that there was a time of pure tradition (the often-invoked "ethnographic present") prior to the colonial incursion, and that colonialism—symbolized here by the introduction of foreign goods—upset the balance. Such an approach concentrates on externally induced change; for White and the other scholars canvassed here, the focus is on cultural continuity and on change directed to some extent by indigenous values, institutions, and relationships. Without discounting the enormous effects of the European incursion into Native worlds, scholars like White adopt analyses whose great strength is the light they shed on the internal logic of Native behavior and motivation in the colonial encounter. While focusing on the trader side of the equation, this study also attends to indigenous meanings and motivation. Particularly in chapter 2, which is a kind of prelude, but also in later chapters, I explore the conflicting realities and divergent cultural premises that inform both trader and Native actions and responses. Yet, at base, this is not so much a study of cultural encounter as an analysis of trader perspectives on that encounter. The subject, to restate, is trader perceptions of land and resource use by the peoples of the Plateau. What were those perceptions and how were they produced in the fur-trade setting of the Plateau? What were the traders' inherited cultural notions about the "civilized" way of life and the "proper" economy, and what were the impacts of those notions? How were traders' perceptions influenced by their experiences in the field—their experiences of the Plateau, the fur trade, and their evolving relations with Plateau peoples? How were the traders' received notions reordered over the course of the Plateau fur trade?

Studies of European or Euro-Canadian and -American imagery of "the Indian" generally have focused on the inherited, derivative content of notions of noble and ignoble savagery.[22] Such scholarship stands at one pole of what historian James Clifford has described as a typically bipolar approach to the study of cultural encounter. At one pole a "dominant" culture imposes its vision on, and ultimately absorbs, a "weaker" one; at the other pole there is resistance to absorption, and cultural persistence. Studies of Western imagery of the Indian or "the other," while not necessarily speaking in terms of dominance and subordination, have tended to highlight Western impositions on the identity of the colonial other. The only other extensive study of traders' narratives certainly takes that approach, perhaps not surprisingly since it was published nearly thirty years ago, before Native agency became an intellectual issue.[23] In many settings— and the fur trade of the Plateau is eminently one of these—it makes more sense to look at reciprocal contributions to cultural meanings and identities. This is the approach now favored by many scholars writing in a postcolonialist vein, who seek to demonstrate the role of the colonized in shaping colonial discourse. As Gyan Prakash has written, if those in the position of colonizer "enacted their authority by constituting the 'native' as their inverse image, then surely the 'native' exercised a pressure on the identification of the colonizer."[24] Such an approach does not deny that things got lost in the encounter, that cultural change occurred. The point is that the process is reciprocal. Cultural meanings on either side are neither forced expressions nor stubborn survivals. They are products of a kind of cultural negotiation. The process is messy: in the inflated jargon of literary criticism, Clifford describes it as "radical polyphony," "unruly dialogue," "heteroglossia." Identity, he argues persuasively, is a "nexus of relations and transactions," an "ongoing process, politically contested and historically unfinished."[25]

It is important to consider how the peoples of the Plateau, and the "reality" of their way of life, influenced traders' narratives. The contention that there was some material reality to which traders' writings referred puts this study on contested terrain, since the dominant tendency of the new cultural history is to conceive of everything in narrative as constructed. The narratives are indeed treated here as constructions of indigenous lifeways, rather than faithful reconstructions. Traders viewed these societies through the refracting lenses of their own cultures, and of their own immediate purposes. Yet in the chapters that follow, we will see how those lenses could bring into focus aspects of Plateau life, and of the initial encounter between Plateau peoples and Europeans, that might otherwise be lost from view. The traders' narratives are, in a sense, the earliest "ethnographies" of these groups. Like all ethnographies, they are highly fictionalized accounts;[26] it might be argued that given their authors' purposes, they are narrower and more contrived than many. But when the texts are read with a critical eye, compared and contrasted with the range of traders' accounts from the same period and the same setting, and considered in the context of linguistic, biological, archaeological, and anthropological evidence, certain strong images begin to emerge. These images are presented in the chapters that follow, not as definitive statements about Plateau realities—which could only be another construction of the past—but as speculations on the nature of those shifting realities.

Personal Insights and Reconstructions

Who were the traders? The backgrounds of these predominantly Scottish sons are considered later in this chapter. To this point they have been represented as an undifferentiated group. Yet there was considerable diversity among them. Some were born in fur-trade country. A few others were trained as physicians before taking up officer positions in the companies. For some the Plateau was their first exposure to alien cultures; others had spent many years in Indian country east of the Rockies. Differences in experience and personality are duly noted where they seem relevant. Nevertheless, there are sufficient commonalities among the traders considered here that I find it appropriate to conceive of them as a social segment or group.

Social theorist Pierre Bourdieu provides a useful analytical framework for understanding the emergence of shared dispositions in a group like the traders. The parameters of an individual's personal identity he sees as structured into the objective environment. As one lives one's daily life in a particular spatial and temporal setting (house, village, city; following particular rhythms of work and leisure), one comes to embody the assumptions or "dispositions" of that setting—assumptions about social hierarchy, gender, age, race, and so forth. These dispositions Bourdieu calls a habitus, meaning "a way of being, a habitual state . . . a predisposition, tendency, propensity, or inclination." Thus, habitus has at once psychological and sociological dimensions. For Bourdieu historical actors are instances of a type, members of social segments who occupy particular structural positions in the larger setting. This is not to suggest, however, that an individual's actions are simply structural reflexes, or the enactment of "roles." Action is rooted in habitus, but it is, after all, an act: it is behavior shaped by and answering to the needs of the moment.

There is room for innovation in Bourdieu's formulation, but not limitless room. The relation between structure and practice, structure and event, is dialectical. Structures "are themselves products of historical practices"; at the same time, those practices are conditioned by structure.[27]

This seems a particularly useful way to conceive of the position of individual traders in relation to one another and to the larger strain of colonial discourse that I term "trader discourse." Traders thought and acted for themselves, but those thoughts and actions were grounded in something we might call trader habitus—ways of being and knowing the world that derived from their historical backgrounds and life experiences and, most immediately, from their position in the social environment of the Plateau. This theme is taken up later in this chapter.

For present purposes, one of the most significant individual differences among Plateau traders was the degree of interest each showed in the cultures in whose midst they found themselves. Alexander Ross lived for several years among the Southern Okanagan and married an Okanagan woman he called Sally. Ross was a close observer, and he devoted a long section of his first published narrative to "Manners and Customs" of the Okanagan.[28] This reflects in part the demands of his anticipated audience, but Ross's accounts reveal a genuine interest in his subject. The writings of an individual like Simon McGillivray, chief trader at Fort Nez Percés in 1831–32, betray no such intellectual curiosity. The only extant records of his time in the Plateau are his entries in the official post journal that he was required to keep. Granted, the post journal was a very different vehicle from the published narrative and offered much less scope for description and speculation (see discussion of sources, below). However, even in comparison with other such journals, McGillivray's sets him apart as an uncommonly short-tempered and unsympathetic observer.[29]

The ways in which even the ill-humored commentaries of a Simon McGillivray can contribute to the speculative *reconstruction* of Native American history will become clear in the chapters that follow. A few examples are in order. In chapter 4 the phenomenon of "begging" is examined at length. At Fort Nez Percés, McGillivray was fixated on the habits of the "beggarly sett" who came to the fort any hour of the day or night to ask for food, tobacco, and other small items. He saw the demands as "extortions," motivated entirely by a desire for property. If we place McGillivray's accounts of begging in the context of other traders' similarly scornful accounts, the behavior begins to take shape as something more than a "beggarly" plea for a handout. Linguistic and anthropological analyses provide suggestive insights into the indigenous meanings of actions that looked to traders like abject begging.

The "beggarly" and "indolent" behavior of many Native men was frequently contrasted with the heavy labor burden of the women. In contemplating this seemingly unnatural state of affairs, Samuel Black came to the conclusion that women in the Sahaptian communities of the southern Plateau were responsible for the main nutritional support of the family (chapter 4). Like his colleagues, Black had little taste for the roots and other vegetable foods produced by women; but unlike many of them, he saw roots as a key staple. Passing observations by other traders, together with biological and anthropological evidence, lend support to Black's conclusions. Evidence in the fur-trade record of the central importance of gathered foods in Plateau subsistence strategies challenges the still dominant view that these were societies of "hunters" and "fishermen."

Those were precisely the labels traders used: they categorized Plateau peoples as either hunting or fishing "tribes." As is demonstrated in the chapters that follow, a great weight of moral and material meaning attached to the categories. In essence, the groups that traders labelled as fishermen were considered the poor and lowly of the region; hunters were the brave, wealthy, and heroic. The wealth of the hunters was marked by many things, not least their possession of horses, firearms, and the other products of the white presence. In the early days of the Plateau trade it was widely assumed that, if provided with the necessary means—guns—fishing peoples would become hunters, and hunters would become more productive. Despite their constantly reiterated faith in European technology, there is ample evidence in traders' writings to indicate that indigenous tools and weapons were preferred for some purposes.

The belief that as hunters and fishermen, Native peoples wasted the land and its resources held powerful sway over traders' perceptions of land use in the region. Yet here again, a careful reading of the sources uncovers much information about Native American methods of resource management. Traders' commentaries on indigenous burning practices are a good example. Indigenous burning of the woods and plains was universally denounced as careless and wasteful. Accounts of that burning often crop up in the context of descriptions of rich grassland, open meadows, and parklike woodland. Traders did not make the connection, but a link is easily made between those landscapes and the indigenous use of fire, especially if the traders' accounts are considered in light of recent research by forest ecologists and others on the historical impact of fire on landscape (chapters 3 and 6).

Humans in Nature

Implicit in traders' narratives about Plateau lifeways are Western ideas about human domination of nature. This set of ideas is much too complex to explore here in any depth; the concept of nature is itself an enormously elaborate, and shifting, imaginative construct (see chapter 3). For the purposes of the argument at hand, what is important is the ascendancy by the late-eighteenth century of the notion that humans—read "men"—had the capacity to dominate the natural world. The shift away from an ethos that conceived of humans as passive actors, or even helpless victims, in the face of natural forces over which they had no control was gradual and incremental. The possibilities for the manipulation of nature had long been explored, but during the seventeenth and eighteenth centuries the development of the powerful analytical tools of science and the practical tools of technology greatly enhanced confidence in the particular powers of humans over nature.[30]

By the early eighteenth century the dominant philosophy of nature was one that emphasized the interrelationships among the components of the natural world, and the influences that the earth, the atmosphere, and all aspects of the physical environment exercised over living things. Increasingly during the 1700s it was assumed that if the systematic features of the relationship between environment and organism could be understood, they could also be manipulated. For example, climatic theories made direct links between cutting down trees and air moisture and quality (and therefore also human health), and made prescriptions for forest management on that basis. The scientific study of the processes of nature was seen as the essential first step toward controlling it.[31]

These developments in scientific thought were buttressed by the growth and popularization from the mid-eighteenth century of theories relating social development to environmental influences. The by-now-voluminous record of European encounters with "new worlds" was the basis for a ferment of philosophical activity. In response to the vexed question of why peoples in different parts of the world differed so markedly in moral and physical attributes, came the answer "environment." The concept implied that a cluster of factors—not just climate and geography, but also diet, activity, family, social organization—determined the attributes of human beings. The prevailing view in educated circles was captured by Samuel Johnson's correspondent, Mrs. Thrale, who wrote at mid-century that her great desire was "to see how life is carried on in other countries, how various climates produce various effects, and how different notions of religion and government operate upon the human manners and the human mind." It was put more succinctly by the London Committee of the Hudson's Bay Company in a query directed to its traders: "What influence does the climate seem to have upon the mind and body of the inhabitants?"[32]

The philosophical currents of the eighteenth century have been exhaustively analyzed, and need not be rehearsed here. For present purposes, what remains to be remarked is the pervasiveness of hierarchical and progressivist notions about the development of human societies. In the 1750s and 1760s, Adam Smith in Scotland and A. R. J. Turgot in France marshalled prevailing ideas to found what amounted to a new social science on the theory that societies develop through four successive stages. The stages were defined by physical circumstance, and more specifically, by methods of subsistence: "1st, the Age of Hunters; 2dly, the Age of Shepherds; 3dly, the Age of Agriculture; and 4thly, the Age of Commerce." The framework was clearly hierarchical. The hunting stage was "the most rude and barbarous of any"; illustrations drawn from the exploration and missionary literatures from North America supposedly proved the point.[33]

Hierarchical as it was, however, an essential aspect of the thesis was its progressivist assumptions. Societies could progress from the first stage to the fourth, for differences were derived from environment, not from innate human qualities. The four-stages theory did not hold monolithic sway, of course; it stood in opposition to Rousseau's influential thesis that the stage of hunting and fishing was a "golden mean" between the indolence of the original state of nature and the "petulant activity" of self-serving commerce, and to other primitivist appeals to the glories of the simple life.[34] Nevertheless, by the turn of the nineteenth century "Enlightenment" notions about the stages of social development and their crucial relationship to the physical environment had achieved something very like orthodoxy.[35]

The influences of Western discourses of environmental determinism, human domination of nature, and the progressive potential of human society, on the views of British fur traders in the

Plateau are not difficult to discern. Fundamental to their observations was the evolutionist four-stages theory, which figured the "hunting" stage as the unreformed state of nature and implied that a society practicing the "civilized arts" of agriculture and commerce was making better use of the land—despite the fact that indigenous hunting was the traders' bread and butter. The essential difference of Native peoples was located in their relationship to the larger environment; in their methods of subsistence.

Also underlying traders' narratives, however, was the belief that progress out of the state of nature was possible, perhaps inevitable. Traders' responses to the success with which Native people adopted firearms, for instance, are considered in chapters 6 and 7. In the minds of the traders, mastery of that technology was the first imperative of progress. Here the distinction between "hunters" and "fishermen" comes into play: those they viewed as hunters appeared to be better disposed to successful adoption of the gun than their fishing cousins. Such notions of progress were certainly bound up with material concerns. They reflected as well contemporary notions about the masculine domination of nature, a theme explored in chapter 7.

The basic distinctions that traders drew between "fishing" and "hunting" peoples illustrate well the power of contemporary discourse concerning the influence of environment on society. As is made clear in the chapters that follow, the identities these labels describe are in large part inventions of the traders. All Plateau peoples included a range of subsistence strategies—fishing, gathering, and hunting—in their seasonal round. Traders overemphasized fishing and hunting, predominantly the activities of men, as many scholars continue to do.[36] Distorting as such labels may be, they do speak to some material reality: different Plateau communities emphasized different aspects of the seasonal round. The emphasis itself was seasonally and historically variable, however, and communities described as "hunters" at other times gathered and fished. Perhaps the most consequential distortion in traders' writings is their tendency to overlook variations among individuals within communities. Beyond the basic gender division of labor, they had little to say about the productive activities of individual women and men in Plateau communities. This bias in the reporting is inevitably reflected in the chapters that follow. As for the influence of environment on "hunters" and "fishermen," the groups that occupied the banks of the Columbia River were cast as hopelessly indolent, supposedly because the river "afford[s] an abundant provision at little trouble for a great part of the year."[37] Those who lived in areas that were richer in animal life, and particularly those who hunted on the buffalo plains, were judged far more industrious. Clearly, the traders' material interests figure prominently in imagery that casts fishing peoples as lazy and hunters as hard-working. The complex, and often contradictory, interplay between the inherited "webs" of meaning and more immediate material needs is explored throughout the following chapters.

Boundaries

The boundaries of this study have been difficult to define. The Plateau exists as a geographical entity, a historical realm of the fur trade, and, more problematically, as a "culture area." In geographical terms the Plateau is that region carved out by the main trenches and tributary valleys of the Columbia and Fraser river systems of the Pacific Northwest (map 1). It is generally conceived to be bounded by the Rocky Mountains on the east, the Cascade Mountains on the west, the Blue Mountains and Great Basin on the south, and more ambiguously, the bend of the Fraser River on the north. It is an enormous area (approximately 360,000 square kilometers), and it is far more diverse geologically and ecologically than the term "Plateau" suggests. It comprises four distinct ecological provinces; the topographies run to broad valleys and rolling highlands in the central region, steep slopes and impressive mountain peaks on the east and west. The climate in the valleys is semiarid steppe. On the Columbia plain (the

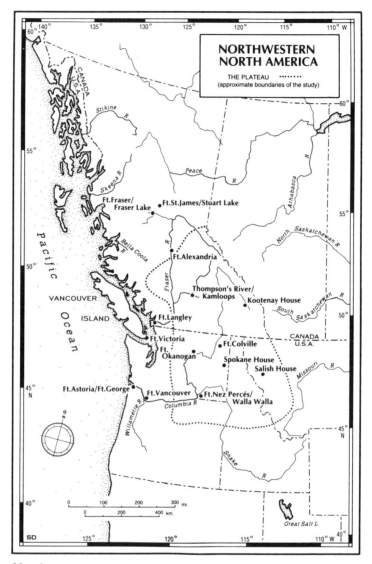

NORTHWESTERN
NORTH AMERICA

THE PLATEAU ·········
(approximate boundaries of the study)

Map 1

southern Plateau) the indigenous vegetation is predominantly sagebrush and bunchgrasses, while the valleys of the Fraser-Thompson plateau are cloaked in bunchgrass and sparse ponderosa pine cover. The higher hills, with their fir and spruce forests, have a slightly more humid continental climate, and in the mountains the alpine tundra regime prevails.

The geographical Plateau coincides very neatly with the Columbia Interior of the fur trade. This portion of the larger Columbia Department comprised the Fort Nez Percés, Spokane/Colville, and Thompson's River districts (map 2). Fort Nez Percés stood alone in its district, although the mobile trading and trapping campaigns, known as the Snake Country expeditions, were usually run from there. Spokane House and its successor as the Interior headquarters after 1825, Fort Colville, were headquarters to a series of outposts, the most significant being the Flathead and Kootenay posts. Kamloops, or Thompson's River Post, was head of that district, with Fort Okanogan as outpost.

These diverse districts (excluding the Snake Country) overlap with the Plateau "culture area" as defined by anthropologists in the early twentieth century. A. L. Kroeber in 1939 styled a culture area as a "regionally individualized type of specific growth of culture." Use of the concept has evolved over the years, but it now seems to be hopelessly compromised, not least by the way it reproduces essentialist notions of culture.[38] It is impossible for a concept that fences off communities into bounded domains to accommodate the movement, tension, and "radical polyphony" that mark the histories of communities like those of the Plateau. While most anthropologists now accept that culture areas are in many respects arbitrarily defined, it remains widely assumed that the term denotes a once-stable relationship between a range of cultural traits and a particular environment. It need hardly be said that environment influences culture; one wishes that it were equally transparent that the relationship is historically constituted and shifting. In the decades just before the onset of the fur trade, for example, Plateau populations moved and merged and

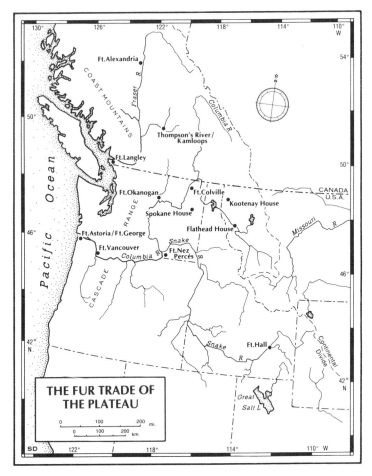

Map 2

were weakened by epidemic disease. During the eighteenth century adoption of the horse by many of these peoples dramatically
accelerated patterns of mobility, trade, and communication.

The only relationship even approaching stability among the
indigenous peoples of the Plateau is language: most of the indi-

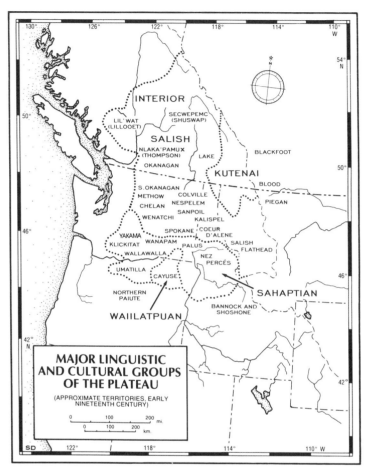

**MAJOR LINGUISTIC
AND CULTURAL GROUPS
OF THE PLATEAU**

(APPROXIMATE TERRITORIES, EARLY
NINETEENTH CENTURY)

Map 3

genous languages of the region fall into two families, Interior
Salishan and Sahaptian (map 3).[39] Fur traders and other early
travellers in the region named peoples according to language and
a range of other criteria having to do with "habits," "customs,"
and "manners." It quickly became apparent to the earliest visitors

that Plateau societies were not organized like the "tribes" they had encountered east of the Rockies.[40] In any case, the term "tribe" is not used in this study except when quoting traders. Nor does "band" accurately represent social, economic, and political arrangements in the region. Admittedly ambiguous terminology like "people," "community," "society," and "group" is used where collective identification is called for. "Native," a political and ethnic designation in common use in both Canada and the United States, is used in preference to "Indian," which is not only an etymological nonsense but can have pejorative connotations in Canada. ("Indian" is adopted, however, when quoting the traders.) "Aboriginal," widely used in Canada, is avoided for its stigma in the United States. "Native American" is also used, the "American" referring to peoples of the Americas, not merely the United States. "First Nations," an evocative label now well accepted in Canada, is too cumbersome and too country-specific for regular use here.

The difficulties traders had in conceptualizing these societies are captured in Alexander Ross's detailed account of political organization among the "Oakinacken" (Okanagan). He used that label, as traders often did, as a shorthand for all those peoples of the central Plateau who spoke dialects of the Okanagan-Colville language. Subsumed under the label were groups known to linguists as the Northern Okanagan, Similkameen, Southern Okanagan, Methow, Sanpoil, Nespelem, Sxoielpi (Colville), and Lake. Ross identified "twelve tribes" in the Okanagan "nation," and he compared them to states in a union, all largely autonomous but ready to unite against a common enemy. When it came to describing the actual functioning of their political systems, however, Ross shifted without notice to the level of the winter village. Identifying the village as a "tribe," he explained that each village had a hereditary "head chief" who determined seasonal movements and other important matters. There was also a council of adult men, and when circumstances required, a "war chief" was elected. The power of the village chief was strictly circumscribed: Ross concurred with other traders that chiefs exercised "merely a nominal superiority." They never interfered in the affairs of families or individuals, he noted, the maxim being that "Indians were born to be free."[41]

Clearly Ross conceived the village to be the largest autonomous unit in the Plateau. Nevertheless, he would join other traders in enumerating the "national characteristics" of the Okanagan as against the Sanpoil or the Colville. The very naming of these groups is a vexed issue. Often traders took the name of a particular village and applied it far and wide to those who spoke the same language with the same "accent" (a reference to dialect). In the early twentieth century a Chinook woman described to an ethnographer how the naming process unfolded on the coast: "Chinook" was the name of a single village until the whites came and "spread it all over."[42] Some Plateau designations are more difficult to explain. The Salish Flathead, for example, are not known to have ever practiced head-flattening. For that reason among others, they now call themselves simply the Salish. Early French trappers in the region left no clue why they called the Salishan peoples west of the Flathead the "Coeur d'Alêne" (the "awl-heart" or "pointed-hearted"). Arbitrary as they may be, such are the names by which the traders knew Plateau peoples, and where they have come into general currency, the names are adopted here. The one exception is that Nlaka'pamux, the self-designation of the Salishan peoples of the northwestern Plateau, is used in preference to the more widely known "Thompson," because the latter would be too easily confused here with the name of trader David Thompson. On the other hand, Lil'wat (Lillooet) is used in preference to the less widely known Stl'atl'imx for the western neighbors of the Nlaka'pamux.

What did it mean to be Nlaka'pamux, Lil'wat, or Salish Flathead in the fur-trade era? What was the locus of such identities, and how did people differentiate themselves from others? As is shown in the chapters that follow, the village appears to have been the main reference point, although village affiliation was very flexible. Individuals could put down at any number of villages or camps where they had kin, for the purpose of food gathering, seeking a spouse, or visiting. Marriage routinely brought together people of different villages, and frequently of different languages, and the exchange of goods helped maintain the bonds among kin groups so united. The fluid and extended nature of kin groups, and the corresponding fluidity of residence patterns, accounts for the problems traders faced in trying to determine family relationships.[43]

Native American self-designations often mean something like "the people" (e.g., the Nez Percé term *numipu*). Names for others are frequently based on descriptions of their habitat (for example, the Nez Percé call the Cayuse *waylatpu*, "people of the rye grass place").[44] Given the fluidity of social and political boundaries, language is the descriptor most commonly invoked by students of these societies. Yet traders' accounts make it very clear that bi- or multi-lingualism was commonplace in the Plateau. Intermarriage among language groups and extensive travel for trade, resource gathering, gambling, and other activities required facility in more than one language. On their travels traders seldom had trouble finding people to act as interpreters as they passed from one linguistic domain to another. While at the posts, traders who spoke little of the local tongue could rely on the skills of their Native wives or on company interpreters, many of whom were the métis sons of traders and their wives.[45] Ross, who lived several years at Fort Okanogan, came to speak the Okanagan language fluently. His colleagues had varying levels of proficiency. On occasion, traders carried on conversations with Native people "by signs."

Widespread multilingualism in the Plateau raises questions about the utility of maps such as map 3, a standard ethnographic scheme of the Plateau. Not only did language not coincide with culture, it did not coincide nearly so neatly with territory. Language was little obstacle to the movement of people, goods, and ideas in the Plateau. As will be seen in later discussions of inter-ethnic gatherings at resource sites, the maps are misleading for the way they evoke "tribal" boundaries to be defended. However, the maps are roughly indicative of dominant regional linguistic affiliations in the early years of the fur-trade encounter. And they represent well the traders' views of where particular "tribal characteristics" prevailed and where particular languages were spoken. Perhaps it is too much to expect two-dimensional, fixed maps to capture the flexible and shifting nature of the seasonal movements and winter residence patterns of Plateau peoples.

The Sources

If "things got lost" in the cultural encounter on the Plateau, it goes without saying that things got lost in traders' recording of the encounter. To this point the focus has been on what might be called mental constraints. We turn now to logistical constraints. The selectiveness of traders' accounts of indigenous lifeways is in part an artifact of the physical arrangements of the fur trade. Historian Jennifer Brown provides an intriguing statement of the problem. Traders' worlds were largely confined to the posts and their environs, and they had "great trouble imagining that any history was being made or that anything significant was happening" beyond the orbits of these posts. Brown compares the attempt to study the history of northern North America from the 1600s to the mid-1800s from the vantage point of the fur trade, to an attempt to study the history of the continent in the late-twentieth century from the vantage point of McDonald's fast-food outlets.[46] Yet the point is not to throw into question the whole project of examining fur traders' writings as a way into Native American history. The point is to underline the limitations of retrieving Native histories from the records of so confined and specialized a sphere of cultural interaction.

Clearly it is no longer acceptable simply to read trader and other "eyewitness" accounts for content, presuming them to be more or less accurate representations of a moment in time. Another very pertinent logistical issue is the authorship of traders' writings. The evolution of a text from its original to its published form is an aspect of the process of representation all too often neglected in textual studies, critical though it may be to situating a text in its proper historical context.[47]

Traders' writings from the Plateau come to us in a variety of forms, from daily field notes and log-book entries written in their own hands to posthumously published narratives complete with illustrative plates and editors' introductions. Published narratives must be relied on particularly heavily for the period before 1821, the North West Company era. Few original documents survive from the NWC years in the Columbia Interior, most having been destroyed or lost during the years of violent competition with the Hudson's Bay Company east of the Rockies. When the companies merged in 1821 to form a restructured Hudson's Bay Company, there was little change in personnel in the Columbia posts. However, certain differences in company policy did reveal themselves in traders' writings. For one thing, the London Committee of the HBC required its officers to keep daily post journals and to file annual reports on their trade districts. These journals and reports, together with post correspondence and travel journals, are the key resources for the study of the HBC era. Even with all these sources, there remain enormous gaps in the documentary record of the Interior. This is not such a problem for a study of representation and imagery, but it goes some way toward explaining why the Columbia Interior has so long been ignored by historians.

In general, daily journals are concerned with matters immediately affecting the business of the day, which they record in often-tedious, repetitive detail. Descriptive passages are few and terse. Annual district reports entail more ample description, and speculation on matters of "natural history." The traders' attention to matters economic was to a large extent dictated by guidelines set down by the London Committee of the HBC. The company's "Standing Rules and Regulations" required that senior officers in each district provide annual reports including "complete and satisfactory accounts of the business thereof" and "every requisite information in regard to the present state, resources and mode of conducting the Trade." However, the company's requirements did not stop there. In the mid-1820s the Committee issued a set of "Queries Connected with the Natural History" of HBC territories. The 253 queries were divided into four categories: "Of the Geography," "Of the Inhabitants," "Of the Natural Productions," and "Of the Climate, &c." The section "Of the Inhabitants," which ran to seventy-seven questions (considerably fewer than the series on natural productions), opened with questions about economic activities and demography. What were the "particular occupations" of the members of each "Tribe"? What were their numbers? How did they subsist? These were followed by queries about other aspects of culture, including the material (dress, tools), the social (systems of government and marriage), the moral ("virtues and vices"), the ideational ("superstition" and religious practice), and finally, the Natives' physical attributes.[48] The detailed nature of the questionnaire, and the timing of its appearance, may well reflect the growing influence of scientists on the activities of trading companies like the HBC; certainly, the questionnaire speaks to the contemporary zeal for collecting and cataloguing the masses of new information being generated by the colonial encounter.[49] Traders' annual reports from the districts take on new meaning when read in conjunction with the queries. The questionnaire set the agenda for what are, alongside the published narratives, the traders' most detailed accounts of Native peoples.

All the textual forms under consideration in this study raise issues of narrative strategy. What did the author of the logbook omit, in the interests of time? How did his perception of his audience (the governor and committee in London) influence what the trader recorded in the official daily post journal? And what was left unsaid? To what extent were the original journal entries tidied or abbreviated by the clerk whose job it was to render the records into standard legible form? These are not insignificant issues. But the real problems arise with the published editions of original accounts. This is not the place for a detailed discussion of issues of authenticity and mediation of text by editors or ghostwriters.[50] However, some of the problems must be highlighted so that they may be kept in mind when considering traders' published accounts.

Literary scholars have devised a useful framework for analysis of the evolution of travel texts like those of the traders. The first stage is the field note or logbook entry (and in some cases, the letter), written en route and representing the traveller's first attempt to mediate her or his experience into the written word. The second stage is the journal, the write-up of the travel notes after the fact. Retrospection allows the writer to invest the text with continuity and purpose. The point cannot be made too strongly that the writer's awareness of potential readers conditions the writing in important ways.

The third stage is the draft manuscript of the book, and the final stage the published narrative. The reading public in Britain by the late-eighteenth century had high expectations of works in the travel genre. A good many travellers and their publishers, daunted by the specter of commercial failure, opted for ghostwriters and editors with a record of delivering what the audience sought. As explorer and North Wester Alexander Mackenzie (or perhaps his editor) explained it, travellers like himself were "much better calculated to perform the voyages, arduous as they might be, than to write an account of them."[51]

The published narratives of North Westers like David Thompson, Ross Cox, and Alexander Ross bear certain of the hallmarks of literary editors. All are problematic for being written years after the fact. In such cases the author's own headnotes and embellishments may be almost as inventive as an editor's. Cox's narrative presents a particular problem, since it is all we have from his time on the Columbia; for Thompson and Ross, there are logs, post journals, annual reports, letters, or some combination, to compare with the published work.

Cox, who came to the Columbia with the Pacific Fur Company in 1812 and remained for five years (four as a North Wester) was the first of the Plateau traders to publish his narrative in Britain.[52] *The Columbia River* appeared in London in 1831, by which time Cox had been back in his native Dublin working as a postal clerk and correspondent for the *London Morning Herald* for over a decade. The book was a great success, achieving a third printing within a year. His modern-day editors find Cox's experience as a journalist sufficient explanation for his often florid style.[53] It does seem perfectly plausible that Cox himself prepared the manuscript for publication. The self-aggrandizement that pervades the text might be taken as further proof. Cox frequently put himself in the midst of adventures at which he could not have been present, and placed himself in charge when he was more likely an assistant. Confronted by a party of Nez Percés who sought restitution for the murder by a trader of one of their kin, for instance, Cox became commander and diplomat. When Spokane hunters offered to take the traders' side, he responded with exemplary restraint: "I thanked them for their friendly offer, which I declined, assigning as a reason, that we wished to live on good terms with all the nations."[54]

In fact, the question of whether Cox was final author of the narrative may be far more complex than it first appears. Literary critic Ian MacLaren stresses that aggrandizement or "elevation" of the narrator was a key device of editors and ghostwriters of the day, and was applied to both the narrator's persona and language. Thus the individual could be swiftly transformed from adventuring explorer or trader to high-born gentleman on a New World version of the Grand Tour. The device served strategic purposes. Most obviously, it brought the narrator closer to his audience in class and social background, making him a more credible witness. More insidiously, elevation could alter the vantage point of the observer so that he was now "looking rhetorically *down* on the objects of his enquiry." The device cast him as an agent of the civilized world, in a position of dominance over the "uncivilized," and beyond reach of "the taint of savage custom."[55]

MacLaren's careful study of the evolution of Captain James Cook's writings into published form in the late-eighteenth century has valuable lessons for students of published narratives. The problem with MacLaren's analysis, however, is that it is based largely on what appears to be an extreme example of editorial manipulation, Dr. John Douglas's disfiguring of Cook's journals. Douglas, who published after Cook's death, indulged in extensive use of elevation, exaggeration, and other flights of fancy to fit Cook's activities to the loftiest imperial motives. The editor cast Cook in the role of hero of the empire, lording his power over the "uncivilized nations" and "bestowing" the gifts of a superior culture in a way that bore little resemblance to the experiences of either Cook or the indigenous peoples he encountered. Those peoples played a prominent role in Douglas's rendering—though a singular one. In a few strokes of the editor's pen, cultural and historical chasms were erased: from the South Pacific to Vancouver Island, indigenous peoples were uncivilized, un-Christian savages. The impressions so carefully rendered by Cook were obliterated from the text.[56]

The published narratives about the Plateau consulted here certainly bear some of the marks of editorial meddling. However, the effects appear to be more decorative than determining. Comparison of the journal Alexander Ross kept as leader of the Snake Country expedition in 1824 with the published account of the expedition that appeared in his *Fur Hunters of the Far West* thirty years later, reveals more amplification than outright alteration of content. It is not clear whether Ross or a London-based editor worked the journal into a narrative; quite possibly both were involved. The original account of the ordeal of finding a route for the expedition through the snow-blocked passes of the Continental Divide concludes like this:

Thursday [April] 15th. This day we passed the defile of the mountains after a most laborious journey both for man and beast. Long before daylight, we were on the road, in order to

profit by the hardness of the crust. From the bottom to the top
of the mountain is about one and a half miles. . . . The delay
[clearing the road] has cost the loss of one month and to the
freemen [trappers] 1,000 beaver.[57]

In the published work the journey across the Rockies becomes
a classic confrontation of man against man and man against
nature. It opens with Ross in the role of enterprising team
captain: "'Pass we must', said I to them!"; the published Ross is
much given to exclamation. The journey was indeed laborious
for human and beast. A day's toil might see the men clear a
quarter mile of track, only to have their efforts undone by drifting
snow. After fourteen pages, Ross (or his editor) comes to the final
day:

> It was a new scene in the wilderness. Nothing appearing above
> the surface of the snow, of all that was moving, but the heads
> and shoulders of the riders! Children calling out with hunger,
> men with thirst, women afrighted, dogs howling, a scream here
> and a scream there; yet amidst all this bustle, anxiety, and
> confusion we pressed forward and got safely across after fifteen
> hours' exertion . . . perhaps few men in the ordinary routine of
> their lives ever suffered more anxiety or laboured harder to
> accomplish a task they had undertaken than was our lot during
> the month past.[58]

Whether Ross achieved these narrative heights on his own—
and his letters and journals suggest he was equal to the feat—or
with the help of an editor, the effect is the same. He is elevated
to the leading role, and the original passage to the status of
Gothic adventure. None of this is surprising, but it is somewhat
unsettling, given that for long periods of the fur-trade era in the
Plateau, such embellished accounts are the only sources
available.

Comparisons of HBC Governor George Simpson's original and
published accounts of his 1824–25 and 1841 visits to the
Columbia turn up a few more disturbing discrepancies. However,
with regard to imagery associated with indigenous peoples, it is

generally a matter of brief passages omitted or ornamented; there appears to be no parallel with the kind of wholesale rewriting to which Cook was subjected. The most puzzling incongruity between the 1841 journal and the 1847 published version is in Simpson's scornful description of the Lower Kutenai he encountered. In the journal:

> [T]hey were a miserable looking set of beings, small decrepit and dirty, of the men there were but two that could be called handsome, and of the women none, in fact the more venerable members of the fair sex bore a striking resemblance to the famous Chimpanzee which delighted London of late, most especially so when they shut their eyes and scratched their heads.[59]

In the published version:

> Though of the men there were two that might be called handsome, yet of the women there were none; and, in fact, the more venerable members of the fair sex, particularly when they shut their eyes and scratched their heads, hardly bore the semblance of human beings.[60]

This case provides an interesting contrast with the Cook-Douglas accounts. Here the editor deliberately softens the blow of the governor's pen. Paradoxically, the decision to excise the reference to the chimpanzee performs a similar function to Douglas' hardening of Cook's delivery: it serves to dignify the writer. Simpson's reputation as a gentleman officer of the "Honourable Company" might well have been tarnished by such an unseemly attempt at humor.

The published Plateau narratives were molded to the demands of a discerning British readership in much the same way that other successful travel accounts were. However, in none of the cases examined did editing for publication become the trans-formative process that it did in Douglas's editions of Captain Cook's journals. Most important for present purposes, as will become clear in the chapters that follow, indigenous peoples appear in the published accounts much as they did in the journals. They remain distinct peoples, distinguishable from one another in at least some "national" particulars (although gender, generational, and other social differences are often disregarded). It is true that in the published accounts narrators are more likely to find themselves in near-death danger, lost in "unhallowed wilderness" and "surrounded by savages." Yet for all the rhetorical flourishes, the accounts are far more nuanced in their treatment of indigenous peoples than the Cook volumes and they have an important niche in a study such as *Traders' Tales*, where part of the project is precisely to uncover the imprint of British cultural assumptions on representations of indigenous peoples. The limitations of the narratives as historical sources must be kept in mind, but by reading the published works in conjunction with their author's original letters and journals, where available, we can gain a sense of an author's voice, and can ascertain whether the published version speaks in that voice. By carefully reading each of the Plateau accounts in the context of all the others, we can gain some sense of the reliability of the published works.

Who Were the Fur Traders?

The fur traders whose writings are the subject of this study were the "gentlemen"—the chief factors, chief traders, and clerks—of the North West and Hudson's Bay Companies. This focus on the elite is regrettable, but inevitable: few of their subordinates left written records. Much has been made of the distinctiveness in personnel and practice of the two companies; those distinctions blurred to insignificance in the Columbia Interior.[61] The Hudson's Bay Company became active in the region only upon merger with the NWC, at which time it absorbed not only North West Company personnel but also many North West Company practices. The continuity in personnel is striking: even John McLoughlin, chief of the Columbia Department from 1824 to 1845, was an old North Wester. Only six of the approximately thirty traders who

left records of their time in the Interior were with the HBC at the
time of the merger, and of those, half had been Bay men for fewer
than five years.[62] Many of the North Westers, by contrast, had
served with that company more than ten years by 1821. Continuity in company recruitment practices is discussed below.

The North West Company emerged in final form in 1804, the
product of a series of alliances and mergers among the mostly
Scottish merchants who had come to dominate the Montreal-
based fur trade since the fall of Quebec. The interaction of rank,
class, and ethnic divisions created a distinctive and taut hierarchy
in the North West Company, one which persisted in the Columbia
Interior throughout the era under study. Promising Scots and
Englishmen and their colonial counterparts were recruited in
their teens at the rank of clerk, their advancement all but assured
by the patronage of a real or fictive kin member in the position
of senior officer. Many of these young clerks appear to have come
from tenant-farming or trades families. The fur trade offered
them opportunities that simply were not available at home. Not
only could the thrifty among them put aside sufficient funds to
return to Britain or the eastern colonies much wealthier than
when they had left; within fur trade society itself, they achieved
a social rank far beyond that from which most had come. They
cultivated this status with some finesse, as we will shortly see.

Those of other ethnic backgrounds were principally French
Canadians, peripheral Scots,[63] métis, and "Iroquois"—a blanket
term used to refer to eastern Natives in the service, who might
be of Iroquois, Cree, Nipissing, Abenaki, or some other Native
background. Their prospects tended to be less attractive. They
entered as boatmen and laborers, the "servants" of the trade.
Most remained in such positions, although some went on to more
remunerative jobs as interpreters and guides. The difficulty of
recruiting laborers for the distant Columbia led the North Westers
early on to adopt the practice of contracting Sandwich Islanders
(Hawaiians) for the service. The result was a complex ethnic
milieu, at least in the servant class. The ethnic complexion

established before 1821 persisted, so that by 1835 there were 218 Canadians, 138 Scots and other Europeans, 55 Hawaiians, and 47 métis and eastern Native men on servant contracts in the Columbia and New Caledonia.[64]

The pattern of promotion based principally on personal and familial ties, a hallmark of the North West Company, also persisted into the HBC era. Governor Simpson and his close colleagues adopted recruitment practices very similar to those of the North Westers, such that individuals with links to Simpson or his Ross-shire connections were consistently favored for promotion.[65] This was at the root of John Tod's complaint in 1840 that the service was so "swarming" with Finlaysons, Simpsons, and McKenzies "that few others, no matter what their qualifications may be, stand any change [chance] of promotion."[66] Tod's remark was inspired by bitterness over not only his own slow progress to the rank of chief trader, but what he saw as the unfair treatment of Columbia colleagues like John Work and Francis Ermatinger.

Members of the officer class, the clerks included, styled themselves the "gentlemen" of the trade. Their most immediate referent for this self-identification was "the men," the company servants, but it will become clear that there were many others against whom the gentlemen defined themselves. Rituals to mark off their exclusive social space were highly formalized. Dining arrangements, for example, spoke to class, ethnic, and gender hierarchies. This theme is developed most fully in chapter 3.

The one personality who had the greatest impact on the defining of social hierarchy in the nineteenth-century fur trade was HBC overseas governor George Simpson. A proud Highland Scot with solid London connections, Simpson cut a very manly figure. He was precise in defining the qualities expected of his officers: "zeal," "hard work," "firmness," and "restraint" were pet phrases. Simpson's own zeal is legendary. He was a tirelessly competitive man, who earned both notoriety and reverence among fellow traders for his habit of pushing his canoe brigades to eighteen-hour days as he travelled about the region under his control—all the while clad in top hat and dress coat.

Contemporary notions of the manly behavior befitting fur-trade gentlemen are spelled out in the officers' narratives. Intriguingly, such notions also form a strong undercurrent in their commentaries on Native men. Much more will be said about this later (see especially chapter 7); for the moment, one example will suffice. In the midst of a passage praising the clean and handsome dress of Plateau hunters, John Work drew attention to a lapse: "The young, and especially the males . . . occupy no inconsiderable portion of the morning decorating themselves[;] in point of time, and the degree of pains taken to ornament their hair, paint their faces &c they compete with the more accomplished fops in the civilised world."[67]

The resonance with early-nineteenth-century middle-class notions of respectable manhood is striking. For the new man of enterprise such affectations were a waste of time and invoked the decadence of an idle and self-absorbed aristocracy. The alternative model implied here would seem to be one of serious manhood, modesty, and self-restraint—Simpson's zeal, firmness, and restraint. The emergence of this new man in Britain, in an era of burgeoning urban capitalism and ascendent Evangelical religion, has been convincingly portrayed by Leonore Davidoff and Catherine Hall. In this shifting social context masculinity was defined in a new way, with the emphasis on a harsh work ethic (for "man's work was God's work"), independent enterprise, piety, sobriety, and dedication to family.[68] This model of manhood had more significance, perhaps, for the traders' self-image than for their imaginings of Plateau fishers and hunters. However, the two are closely intertwined. While the texts considered in *Traders' Tales* are explicitly about Native Americans, and especially Native American men, there is a constant undercurrent of comparison to British middle-class men.

A "Liberal Education"

The vast majority of the traders whose writings are considered here were of Scottish background, fifteen of them born and raised in Scotland. Six grew up in Lower Canada, and one in Vermont; two were raised in the colonial service abroad but schooled in Britain. Ross Cox and John Work were Irish, while David Thompson was born of Welsh parents but spent his childhood in London. Little is known of the early years of many of these men. All had some formal education, although it ran the gamut from instruction in basic literacy in private homes, to grammar school, to specialist training in navigation, surveying, or medicine. Most entered the fur trade in their teens or early twenties at the rank of clerk, a position that required some proficiency at writing and basic accounting.

Donald McKenzie's educational experience may be typical of many of the Scottish-born traders. McKenzie was born in 1783 near Inverness. Nothing is known of his parents' occupations, but he is reputed to have had a good education.[69] By the late eighteenth century there was a well-established network of parish and burgh schools in the settled countryside and towns of lowland Scotland, and in the larger settlements of the Highlands and islands. The result was a peasantry and working population that was literate in more than a merely functional sense.[70]

To get his "good education," McKenzie would have spent several years in the parish school. The curriculum for younger children consisted of reading, arithmetic, grammar, "good manners," and depending on the resources of the schoolmaster, perhaps an extra subject like geography. Money was ever a problem for parish schools because the "heritors," the local landowners, often proved distinctly reluctant to meet their duties of financial support. Books were limited, and lessons frequently consisted of a large dose of "the Book and Carritches" (Bible and Catechism). Where human and financial resources permitted, those who stayed on at the higher levels undertook studies in Latin, Greek, and additional courses such as bookkeeping and practical mathematics. At this stage gender roles hardened: while the boys studied Ovid and Cicero, the girls learned needlework.[71] McKenzie probably remained in school until he was seventeen, at which point he joined three older brothers in the North West Company.

David Thompson's schooling at the Grey Coat Hospital, a London charity institution with a mandate to provide a moral and practical education for the poor, stands as something of a counterpoint to the experience of educated Scottish children like McKenzie. Thompson would have had little exposure to classical learning. After a firm grounding in basic literacy and numeracy and liberal rations of religion, his higher-level studies entailed training in rudimentary navigation. When Thompson was thirteen, the masters of the school responded to a call for apprentices from the Hudson's Bay Company by volunteering the boy for service. He would soon have the opportunity to hone his navigation skills under the tutelage of a company explorer.[72]

Many traders, whatever the details of their formal education, showed themselves to be very literate men. The importance attached to basic literacy in the officer class is reflected in John McDonald's remarks on the performance of his brother Finan in this regard. The senior McDonald, himself a North Wester, regularly sent money to the family in Lower Canada to see to it that Finan got a "liberal education" before joining the fur trade. Finan joined without completing his schooling, with the result that, to his brother's dismay, "he cannot rise higher than the charge of a single post for the want of education."[73] Sure enough, Finan spent nearly twenty years at the rank of clerk in the Columbia Interior, his inimitable prose betraying the deficiencies of his education.

Beyond functional literacy, many traders were lovers of books. Ross Cox's narrative is laden with literary allusions. This was the fashion in travel writing, and as we saw earlier, editors were often to thank for such embellishment; in Cox's case, the references may well reflect his own wide reading. Alexander Ross and Francis Heron discussed philosophy and religion, among other matters, in their personal correspondence, and John Tod showed himself to be versed in the burgeoning "Mental Science" of phrenology.[74]

Tod delighted in the well-equipped little library he found at his early posting in New Caledonia.[75] Book collections at posts developed in a number of ways. The HBC had a tradition of supplying books of a technical or religious nature, as a measure to "Promote Virtue" among its employees. Newspapers and periodicals were included in inventories from London, and while hopelessly out of date, they were read voraciously. Numerous traders built up personal libraries through orders and visits to London or Montreal; David Thompson was one such bibliophile. A recent study of fur-trade libraries uncovered titles like Milton's *Paradise Lost*, Voltaire's *Dictionary*, and Gaelic editions of crofters' tales alongside the Bibles and technical manuals.[76] No details of the collections of the Columbia Interior have been found, but there is no reason to doubt that there were books about, particularly at larger posts like Spokane and Colville. Indeed, by 1836 the Columbia had the first lending library in fur-trade country, based at Fort Vancouver. The library stocked newspapers, periodicals, and books acquired through London dealers.[77] This would have been a welcome supplement to the scattered and oversubscribed personal collections of bookish traders. It is doubtful that Columbia traders consistently had access—or that more than a few wanted access—to the works then in vogue in the literary salons of the metropolis; however, should they seek exposure, traders were not as remote from those currents as geography would suggest.

For young men, like Donald McKenzie, who had familial links to the fur trade, and for those, like Thompson, who were actively recruited by one of the companies, the fur trade promised adventure and economic opportunities not available at home. For those growing up in Lower Canada, the choice of career was even clearer: the fur trade was at the center of commercial life in the colony, and a part in it was the dream of any adventurous young man.

The Companies in the Columbia Interior

The years 1807 and 1846 mark the beginning and the beginning of the end of the fur trade of the Columbia Interior. In 1807 the first British traders, a North West Company party led by David Thompson, penetrated the Rocky Mountains to the Plateau; in 1846 the Columbia District (and therefore the Plateau) was divided at 49° north latitude into British and American jurisdictions (see map 1). The year of the boundary settlement is taken as the end point of *Traders' Tales* because it represents an important transition in the history of the Native-white encounter in the Plateau. At this time missionaries and settlers became the dominant white presence in the southern half of the region; just over a decade later, gold miners would displace fur traders in the northern third. By 1846 missionaries had been active in the eastern and southern Plateau, albeit sporadically, for a decade. Problematic as it may be to ignore the missionary presence in these latter years, it would be far more complicating to consider them. Missionaries are left entirely to another study.

After a period of rivalry with the New York–based Pacific Fur Company (1811–13), for which several prominent North Westers initially worked, the North West Company had the trade of the Interior to itself until the merger with the Hudson's Bay Company in 1821. Despite the monopoly, the NWC was plagued by problems of transportation and communication, marketing, and relations with Native peoples. The reorganized Hudson's Bay Company faced all those problems as well as some thorny diplomatic issues: of most concern in the Interior was the unresolved question of the international boundary west of the Rockies.[78] Given that the most lucrative Interior trade regions—indeed, all but one of the permanent Interior posts—fell between the Columbia and the forty-ninth parallel, the company had an enormous vested interest in a southerly boundary. It was not to be.

When HBC Governor George Simpson first visited the Columbia in 1824, he was appalled by the legacy of "wasteful extravagance" the company had inherited from the North Westers. Convinced that the department could be profitable, Simpson devised a program of retrenchment and rationalization. A new depot for the Columbia trade, Fort Vancouver, was established on the north bank of the river some 130 kilometers (80 miles) from its mouth; and a new Interior supply depot, Fort Colville, was established near Kettle Falls on the upper-middle Columbia. Both sites had fine agricultural potential, a key concern of Simpson in his campaign to slash the costs of imported supplies. The country south and southeast of the Columbia, the so-called Snake Country, was to be rendered a "fur desert" as a means of quelling American commercial interest in the region. John McLoughlin was appointed chief factor of the Columbia district, and was given the charge of implementing the strategy.[79]

Details of the fur-trade history of the Interior are discussed in the chapters that follow. It remains to mention the events that signalled the end of the fur-trade era in the region. The demise of the Pacific Fur Company in 1813 did not eliminate the American threat. A joint-occupancy agreement assured both Britain and the United States open trapping and trading rights in the region, and American fur interests resumed activity in the southeastern Interior in the early 1820s. In the 1830s, American trappers and traders were followed by missionaries and by military officers on official survey duties; by late in the decade small parties of American settlers were arriving on the Oregon Trail. The trickle became a torrent in 1843, by which time the Hudson's Bay Company had seen the writing on the wall. In that year it began construction of a new company headquarters in the more secure British territory of Vancouver Island.

By the early 1840s fur returns in the Interior were only a fraction of what they had been a decade before. As a trader at one Interior post put it in 1844, "There appears to be no longer any prospect of either profit or pleasure here—a general scarcity of furs prevails at present all over the country."[80] The Colville district and New Caledonia (the huge region north of the Columbia district) remained profitable, but returns were at half their earlier levels. The company probed new areas in Utah, California, and on the north coast; however, declining production was paralleled by a big drop in the price of beaver on the world market. The HBC increasingly turned its attention to ventures originally intended as adjuncts to the fur trade—production of grain, livestock, other agricultural goods, timber, and fish for export to Russian Alaska, Britain, and the East.[81] The boundary treaty recognized the company's rights to the lands it had long occupied in the newly christened Oregon Territory, and to transit on the Columbia River. As a result the fur trade continued in the region for a few more years. But by 1846 the end was in sight, and the Hudson's Bay Company had begun a slow exodus northward. In much of the region covered in this study the fur trade had all but come to an end.

Overview of the Chapters

The logistics and historical details of the fur trade are not the focus of *Traders' Tales*. This is principally a study of perception and representation. Chapter 2 sets the stage by establishing the backdrop to the encounter on the Plateau. The chapter looks at the most consequential aspect of early contact between Europeans and indigenous peoples, epidemic disease. In some senses this inquiry is peripheral to the main issue of traders' representations of Plateau economy and resource use; after all, the most disastrous early epidemics preceded the arrival of traders in the region by some years. In another sense, however, it is absolutely germane. The communities that traders were observing in the early-to-mid-nineteenth century were communities already profoundly affected by the white presence in North America.

Chapter 3 begins to set the scene for the study of imagery associated with Plateau peoples by sketching out the imaginative space of the Plateau as traders conceived it. The chapter looks at the complex interplay of symbolic and material meanings in landscape, exploring the tensions in traders' representations and the methods they devised to reproduce familiar physical and social surroundings.

Chapters 4 and 5 focus on those the traders called the "salmon tribes," and chapters 6 and 7 detail the traders' perception of the "hunting tribes" of the region. The aim in the first chapter of each pair (chapters 4 and 6) is to consider the state of the societies in question as represented in traders' texts, drawing on relevant evidence from other sources to illuminate their accounts and to fill in the gaps. In chapters 5 and 7 the project is to consider how those images were structured by the traders' culture, gender, social class, and background; by their purposes in fur-trade country; and by their relations with the local peoples. Throughout there are two central objectives, closely interwoven: to analyze traders' narratives with a view to unpacking their images of Plateau peoples, to interrogate those images and to reveal their contradictions; and to find glimpses of alternative visions. To reiterate, these alternatives are presented not as definitive statements about Plateau realities, but as speculations on the nature of shifting realities.

CHAPTER TWO

"The Natives Were Strong to Live"

Plague, Prophecy, and the Prelude to the Encounter

The most important consequence
of the early encounter between Europeans and the indigenous
peoples of the Plateau was epidemic disease.[1] The available
evidence indicates that by the time the first fur traders reached
the region early in the nineteenth century, two recent smallpox
epidemics had already dramatically reduced the population.[2]
This chapter considers the impacts of smallpox and other introduced disease in the Plateau from the precontact period to 1846,
and looks at the nature of indigenous responses to disease.

The history of introduced disease is a kind of prologue,
standing apart from the main issue of traders' representations of
Plateau economy and resource use. In another sense, it is absolutely germane: the societies that traders observed in the early
nineteenth century had already been profoundly affected by
epidemic disease brought by Europeans. The traders were the
first to record the effects of depopulation in the region. They
found that in some areas whole communities had been lost to the
ravages of disease. However, they did not find societies that had
succumbed. Drawing on a range of evidence, some of it by necessity from sources other than the traders' accounts, I will explore
the links between the early epidemics and fervent prophetic
activity in the Plateau, pointing to the ways in which Plateau
peoples responded intellectually to this terrible moment in their
history.

The early epidemics demonstrate how the contours of the encounter between Europeans and indigenous peoples depended to a significant extent on local cultural mediation. To argue, for instance, that the prophetic movements of the early 1800s were an intellectual response to the catastrophe of epidemic is not to suggest that the movements were simply reactions to the pressures of colonialism. On the contrary, in order to understand such movements, it is essential to consider their internal logics—the systems of beliefs and practices that gave them resonance in Native American societies. Native people dealt with even the most cataclysmic consequence of the early colonial encounter, the smallpox epidemics, from within a framework of indigenous beliefs and practices.

Early Smallpox in the Plateau

There is evidence of one or possibly two smallpox epidemics in the Plateau just before the coming of European fur traders, but the record is scattered and sketchy at best. As the first people to record in writing the visible aftereffects of the epidemics (pockmarks), as well as snippets of oral reminiscences, traders provide critical nuggets of information. Although the full disease history of the Plateau may never be written, historian Robert Boyd has gathered much of the available documentary, ethnographic, and epidemiological data in a careful, if preliminary, study that indicates that the effects were devastating. Here Boyd enters a thicket: the topic of disease contact and native population decline is one of the most contentious in Native American history. Nevertheless, most current estimates point to an indigenous population decline of 90 percent in the century or so following the arrival of Columbus in the Western Hemisphere.[3] In a recent study of smallpox around the Strait of Georgia, just west of the Plateau, historical geographer Cole Harris argues that such a figure is probable for the first century of contact in British

Columbia as well.[4] The findings presented here, while not quantifying the impact, tend to support such assessments.

The first epidemic in the region to enter the historical record was an outbreak of a lethal Variola major (classical smallpox) strain sometime between the late 1770s and 1782. Variola major's fatality rate has been estimated to be at least 30 percent in virgin populations.[5] A probable second outbreak, in 1800–1801, appears to have been somewhat less destructive. Basing his projections on local documentary and oral accounts, combined with extrapolations from better-documented epidemics elsewhere in North America, Boyd contends that by 1802 smallpox alone had reduced the Plateau population by a staggering 45 percent. This was three years before the first direct encounter with Euro-Americans in the region (the Lewis and Clark expedition arrived in 1805). Complex factors contributed to the high mortality. The lack of physical immunity would almost certainly have been exacerbated by the often-counterproductive responses of people with no experience of such disease—responses that worked well against other illness. These would have included fleeing the infected area and thereby spreading the disease, sweatbathing, and plunging into cold water. The general overload of the health-care system in a time of epidemic would have been a factor, as would the interruption of normal subsistence activities and consequent nutritional stress.[6]

Constrained as he is by the sources, Boyd nevertheless constructs a picture of smallpox epidemics as complex interactions of people, pathogens, and environment. A classic crowd disease, smallpox generally depends on dense populations for its maintenance. It becomes endemic only where such populations provide a constant supply of susceptibles (newborn babies).[7] One might expect that the low population density of the Plateau would have hampered spread of the disease, but an accurate "political ecology" of smallpox requires consideration of the patterns of human activity in the region. The precise nature of human settlements—their location, form, and duration—has recently been posited as a key factor in establishing rates of contagion.[8] The nature of social interaction is also important. The intricate web of intergroup relations that characterized the aboriginal Plateau, and the extensive mobility of its peoples— patterns that will be demonstrated in later chapters—may well have neutralized the effects of low population density. It has been amply demonstrated that smallpox will "spread throughout entire regions where there is no significant discontinuity in settlement or *intergroup contacts*" (my emphasis); therefore, Boyd's contention that the late 1770s–1782 epidemic would have swept much of the Plateau appears persuasive.[9]

Boyd departs from Henry Dobyns's hypothesis of a North American smallpox pandemic continuing from 1779 through the early 1880s, suggesting that there were two or possibly three regional outbreaks over several years, with distinct origins in the plains region, Spanish ships on the coast, and perhaps the Russian colony at Kamchatka.[10] Boyd contends that northern groups—in particular the Lil'wat, Nlaka'pamux, and Secwepemc—might then have been exposed to the disease from two directions, the Northwest Coast and the Great Plains. The Lil'wat and Lower Nlaka'pamux, for instance, may have served as vectors between the coast and the western Plateau (map 3). Okanagan-Colville groups may likewise have carried the disease from the east. On the other hand, Harris, in his study of the coastal epidemic (which he dates to 1782), cites convincing evidence that it proceeded from the plains and Great Basin to southeastern Plateau communities, and then through trade contacts to the coast.[11] If the question of provenance remains a vexed one, so does that of the evidence more generally. There is no documentation of visible aftereffects (pockmarks) from this earliest outbreak in northern regions of the Plateau. Possibly, this lack of evidence is simply a function of the scattered nature of documentary evidence of any kind before the 1830s and 1840s. This point will be returned to shortly.

The earliest account of the 1770s epidemic in the southern Plateau is found in fur trader Ross Cox's published narrative:

About thirty years before this period [i.e., before 1814] the smallpox had committed dreadful ravages among these Indians, the
vestiges of which were still visible on the countenances of the
elderly men and women . . . the disease first proceeded from
the banks of the Missouri. . . . It travelled with destructive
rapidity as far north as Athabasca and the shores of the Great
Slave Lake, crossed the Rocky Mountains at the sources of the
Missouri, and having fastened its deadly venom on the Snake
Indians, spread its devastating course to the northward and
westward, until its frightful progress was arrested by the Pacific
Ocean.[12]

John Work's 1829 report from the Hudson's Bay Company's
Fort Colville provides insight into the impact on the peoples of
that region: "Immense numbers of them were swept off by a
dreadful visitation of the smallpox, that, from the appearance of
some individuals that bear marks of the disease, may have
happened fifty or sixty years ago [ca. 1769–79]. The same disease
committed a second ravage, but less destructive than the first
about ten years afterwards."[13]

Subsequent missionary accounts suggest that the first epidemic
cut a wide swath in the southern Plateau. Asa Smith, writing
from the Kamiah Mission in Nez Percé country in 1840, recorded
this testimony:

Twice during the remembrance of the most aged among this
people has the smallpox been among them. The first time it
visited them must have been 60 or perhaps 70 years ago
[1770–80]. Some very old people . . . relate that when they were
children a large number of people both of the Nez Perce and
Flatheads wintered in the buffalo country. In the spring as usual
the people from this region went to buffalo. Instead of finding
their people as they expected, they found their lodges standing
in order, and the people almost to an individual dead. . . . From
thence it followed the people to this region and swept through
the whole country, very few surviving the attack of the
disease.[14]

In his 1847 "Recollections" from Flathead Mission, Jesuit Father Gregory Mengarini recorded that by the calculations of the elders, the Salish Flathead had once numbered at least four thousand. He recalled being told by the elders that about seventy years earlier (ca. 1777), a devastating outbreak of smallpox had killed a large camp of Salish Flathead, sparing only a few children. At the same time the epidemic destroyed an "entire nation" living five days' journey to the north. This nation was very likely the Kutenai Tuna'xe, an eastern band of Kutenai who, like the Salish Flathead, travelled annually to the plains to hunt buffalo.[15]

These accounts leave little doubt about the impact of smallpox on the southern and eastern Plateau. As noted earlier, no such accounts have been found for the northern Plateau; however, epidemiological and social considerations strongly suggest that the disease reached there as well. John Work was told that "immense numbers" died in the vicinity of Fort Colville in the first epidemic. Trade, marital, and other social links were very extensive among the peoples of the Colville and Okanogan areas. Indeed, the Northern Okanagan, Similkameen, Southern Okanagan, Colville, Sanpoil-Nespelem, Lake, and Methow all spoke dialects of the same language, and adjacent groups closely interacted. Those more distant often came together to fish and trade at Kettle Falls.[16] Given such extensive interaction, it is almost inconceivable that a virgin-soil smallpox epidemic would not have had some impact in these northerly regions.

Contrary evidence is contained in the oral accounts collected by ethnographer James Teit at the turn of the twentieth century. Teit's informants told him that the Upper Nlaka'pamux, Secwepemc, and Northern Okanagan were spared the effects of smallpox until the 1850s.[17] That they were entirely spared appears questionable, in light of the characteristics of the disease and of Plateau social networks. In view of the shifting nature of oral narrative,[18] it is reasonable to suggest that memories of the major outbreak of the mid-nineteenth century may have eclipsed those of the earlier one. The lack of documentation of pockmarked faces is not conclusive, given that the earliest extant records, in the form of scattered correspondence, date from at least three decades after the fact. More systematic accounts were not recorded until some forty years afterwards, when few survivors would remain.[19] On the other hand, the telltale signs noted by Cox and Work to the south were recorded equally late. Lack of documentation and negative oral accounts introduce doubt about a 1770s outbreak in the northern Plateau, but epidemiological and social data would seem to present a strong likelihood.[20]

The Second Outbreak and Other Illness

In 1808 Simon Fraser noted the effects of smallpox in a Lower Nlaka'pamux camp on the Fraser River, commenting that "several of the Natives were marked with it."[21] These may have been the marks of the "second ravage" alluded to by Work, an epidemic dated by Boyd to 1800–1801. This visitation, which apparently spread from the plains through Interior Salish groups to the coast, was far more confined in its effects than the first.[22] Fraser saw no signs of it among the Upper Nlaka'pamux and Secwepemc, for example, and Teit's informants agreed that it did not reach there. It may have been a less virulent strain of the disease, although high mortality among the Salish Flathead and Lower Chinook suggests otherwise. The more compelling explanation is that the effects of this outbreak were curtailed because in this region of the northwestern Plateau many adults, at least, were now immune. Boyd suggests that demographic changes arising from the first epidemic may also have been significant. Desertion of some regions and concentration of populations in more restricted areas may have hampered spread of the disease. If the Lower Nlaka'pamux still had a high population density at the time of this second outbreak and were hit hard by it, this may indicate that the local impact of the 1770s epidemic had been less severe than in some areas of the Plateau.[23]

If the Upper Nlaka'pamux were spared the second strike of smallpox, they were certainly suffering from some illness at the time of Fraser's visit. At Kamtci'n, the big settlement at the fork of the Thompson and Fraser Rivers, the explorer noted that "[m]ost of the children were really afflicted with some serious disorder which reduced them to skeletons." The identity of the disease is a mystery, but it may have been the same one David Thompson had witnessed among the Kutenai a year earlier, a "violent distemper" that struck the Lower and Upper Kutenai and the Salish Flathead. Thompson recorded that the disease "brought the major part of them so low, as to prevent them from decamping"; many children died, and the ill were "reduced to mere skeletons."[24] The potentially disastrous effects of such a disease are hinted at in Thompson's remark that the people could not decamp. Illness prevented them leaving their fishing camps to move on to the next phase of the subsistence round; hunger would be the inevitable result, no doubt compounding the illness.

Winter illnesses of various kinds broke out regularly around Interior posts throughout the period 1807 through 1846. The gathering of large numbers of Native people in the vicinity of the posts, where it occurred, created the conditions for the spread of many viral infections. People were particularly susceptible in late winter, when, as will become clear in later chapters, food was often scarce. Winter illness—cold and influenza being the main complaints—may have been an almost annual event in the Interior during the fur-trade era. At Colville in December 1830, for example, Chief Trader Francis Heron noted that many of the Indians about the place were ill. He attributed the sickness to "such numbers being crammed together in large tents—their filth and bad food, which consist of rancid dried Salmon and unwholesome roots."[25] Close winter quarters would certainly have encouraged the spread of viral infection. As for "rancid" and "unwholesome" food, the cultural meanings bound up in such valuations will be probed in the coming chapters. For the moment, it should be noted that Heron's comments on "bad" food are somewhat puzzling, given that in several earlier journal entries he had been expounding on the great abundance of salmon the local people had laid away that year.[26]

Malaria is not at issue here, as it was largely confined to the lower Columbia and Willamette valley regions, with isolated cases perhaps as far inland as Walla Walla. The dreadful impact of the malaria outbreaks of 1830–34 must be noted, however. Traders' accounts recorded the horror. Boyd provides evidence to indicate that by the mid-1830s the population of the lower Columbia–Willamette region had been reduced to one-twelfth its pre-1770s level. Earlier smallpox epidemics were significant in the decline, but malaria probably had the most devastating impact.[27]

The demographic effects, quite apart from the broader cultural impacts, of these epidemics will never fully be understood. In hard-hit regions the changes wrought by disease were underway long before the first fur traders arrived. Families were ravaged, and villages lost their leaders and their doctors. It must have seemed a "spiritual apocalypse."[28] But, except for such tragic examples as the Kutenai Tuna'xe, these societies did not succumb. The remainder of this chapter is concerned with the likely social impacts of, and local responses to, the crisis of epidemic. The focus is on the prophetic response.

Plateau Prophecy: The Prophet Dance Complex

The first detailed study of Plateau prophet movements was anthropologist Leslie Spier's 1935 monograph, *The Prophet Dance of the Northwest and Its Derivatives*. The controversy that it sparked was a local expression of a larger scholarly debate: whether prophetic movements have indigenous origins and motivations, or are to be explained as reactions to the pressures of colonialism. The argument advanced here is that in order to understand such movements, it is essential to consider their internal logics—the systems of beliefs and practices that give them resonance in indigenous societies. To link the prophetic movements of a particular era to contemporary epidemic is not necessarily to cast them as reactions to the colonial incursion. In the case of the first two contact-era Plateau epidemics (late 1770s–82 and 1800–1801), there is much to indicate that illness and death were not interpreted as a consequence of contagion by outsiders. Instead, the peoples of the region turned inward for an explanation. Like all serious disease, smallpox was read as a sign of imbalance or power struggle among the personal spirit partners that animated the spiritual universe of the Plateau. The scourge of smallpox was read as a sign of spiritual crisis *within* Plateau societies, and the prophetic movements of the time were an attempt to stem that crisis.

The set of religious beliefs and practices known to scholars as the prophet dance complex was described concisely by Spier:

[A]mong these peoples [of the Plateau] there was an old belief in the impending destruction and renewal of the world, when the dead would return, in conjunction with which there was a dance based on supposed imitation of the dances of the dead, and a conviction that intense preoccupation with the dance would hasten the happy day. From time to time men [sic] "died" and returned to life with renewed assurances of the truth of the doctrine; at intervals cataclysms of nature occurred which were taken as portents of the end. Each of these events led to the performance of the dance with renewed fervor, only to have it fall into abeyance again when their expectations remained unfulfilled.[29]

Spier enumerated the following core elements of the complex: (1) the central figure of the prophet, an inspired leader who had dreams or visions involving "dying" and travelling to the land of the dead; (2) reference by the prophet to unusual events foreshadowing the destruction of the world; (3) prediction of imminent destruction, paving the way for world renewal and the return of the dead; and (4) urging of the people to demonstrate their belief and hasten the day by dancing, leading a righteous life, and otherwise preparing for the apocalypse.

The potency of the prophetic injunction to dance is intimated by the deep symbolic significance of dancing in Plateau societies.[30] At the most significant large-scale religious ceremony of the year, the annual winter dance, people affirmed and displayed the power of their personal guardian spirits. Dancing in a euphoric or trancelike state while possessed by the power of the spirit was a principal means of "paying it proper regard."[31] No one dared ignore the spirit's injunctions for this kind of display; illness, or even death, was sure to result. The prophet dance appears to have been an entirely separate phenomenon: people danced under instruction of the prophet—in imitation of "the dances of the dead"—rather than in a state of possession. However, the weight given to dancing in prophetic ritual very likely related to the centrality of dancing in routine Plateau religious observance. As anthropologist Raymond DeMallie has argued in another context, the dance itself was a ritual means of "spiritual and physical betterment."[32]

Spier believed that the prophet dance complex, as it manifested itself in the early-nineteenth-century Plateau, was an aboriginal phenomenon, a long-established response to extraordinary happenings—volcanic eruptions, earthquakes, and the like. To demonstrate that the Plateau was the source of this particular religious movement, he provided evidence of a "more or less coherent complex" from the Babine and Sekani in the north, to the Paviotso (Paiute) of western Nevada in the south. Later "revitalization" movements such as the 1890 Ghost Dance of the Plains derived from Plateau traditions, according to Spier. For the purposes of this study, "Plateau" refers to the more confined region of the Columbia-Fraser Plateau, which is loosely, if problematically, designated the Plateau "culture area."

Spier offered a tale, recorded among the Nespelem by ethnographer Teit, to illustrate the "common doctrinal background" on which Plateau prophets drew. Almost identical tales have been recorded among the Nlaka'pamux and Secwepemc. The Nespelem narrative finds Old One, the creator figure, having just completed the task of preparing the earth for human habitation. He tells the people:

> I will send messages to earth by the souls of people that reach me, but whose time to die has not yet come. They will carry messages to you from time to time; and when their souls return to their bodies, they will revive, and tell you their experiences. Coyote and myself will not be seen until the Earth Woman is very old. Then we shall return to earth, for it will require a new change by that time. Coyote will precede me by some little time; and when you see him, you will know that the time is at hand. When I return, all the spirits of the dead will accompany me, and after that there will be no spirit-land. All the people will live together. . . . Then will things be made right, and there will be much happiness.[33]

The tale speaks of the initial creation, impending destruction, and ultimate renewal of the world. This notion of creation as an ongoing process—as opposed to a one-off enterprise accomplished in seven days—is central to Native North American worldviews.[34] Beyond this, it is problematic to speak of a "common doctrinal background": there is much variation in such tales, over space and time, across the Plateau. In the final analysis, creation stories are, like all narrative traditions, expressions of an active, shifting cultural process.[35] Nevertheless, the Nespelem tale highlights elements that appear again and again in Plateau prophecy narratives. Creation, destruction, and renewal are portrayed as components of a continuum; prophets are depicted as messengers from Old One, or some other creator or transformer figure from the mythological age. Finally, there is the foretelling of the return of these creator/transformer figures (represented by Coyote and Old One), and of the dead, at a time when the world is renewed and things are "made right."

The Prophet Dance Controversy: Thesis and Antithesis

Spier's aboriginal-origins hypothesis challenged head on the views of those like James Mooney, student of the Ghost Dance, who saw such prophetic movements as a response to an immediate need for a messiah—a need inspired by the special pressures and transformations resulting from the encounter with Euro-American society.[36] Over the years, Spier has been challenged in turn by others who would locate the impetus for such movements in the pressures of colonialism. Indeed, as late as 1989, in a review of the literature on the Ghost Dance, Alice Kehoe demonstrated that theories of deprivation, acculturation, and revitalization in the face of the colonial incursion continue to dominate analyses of such movements.

Among well-known counters to Spier was Vittorio Lanternari's 1963 volume, *The Religions of the Oppressed.* Lanternari proposed that the Ghost Dance, like all messianic movements among Native peoples, derived from "the problems that had come to beset [these societies] under colonial rule," and especially from the conditions of "antagonism between two different cultures, one striving to dominate the other."[37] Here he drew on Ralph Linton's earlier formulation of nativistic movements as conscious attempts to revive "neglected" aspects of a culture when confronted with threatening contact with another culture. Anthony F. C. Wallace extended the definition of "revitalization-type" movements to include a wide range of movements for social reform, all of which aimed to "construct a more satisfying culture."[38] One of the enduring strengths of Wallace's analysis is its emphasis on historical specificity—the need to attend to the particular historical context of each society engaged in such movements. The literature on the contact origins of these movements is too vast to canvas here; the focus must now shift to those studies dealing explicitly with the Plateau.

Here Spier's critics have been measured. Anthropologist David Aberle, for example, argued that although definitive statements were impossible, one could not reject "deprivation" caused by direct or mediate contact as the source of movements like the prophet dance and the Ghost Dance. Deprivation came in several forms, namely, a general worsening of conditions, exposure to new wants, differential shifts in the status of various groups, or some combination of such externally induced pressures.[39] In the late 1960s anthropologist Deward Walker offered perhaps the most persuasive argument for the contact origins of the prophet dance. Walker assembled ethnographic, ethnohistorical, and archaeological evidence in support of his thesis that the pressures arising from indirect contact in the late eighteenth century were sufficient to account for the emergence of prophetic movements. He did not reject Spier's notion that an aboriginal bedrock of beliefs and practices informed the Plateau movements, pointing out that cult movements everywhere embrace at least some elements from antecedent religious beliefs. Walker argued, however, that prophet activity was a new phenomenon, a response to the "extraordinary, crisis-ridden" conditions of the eighteenth century—conditions created by the as-yet-indirect influences of newcomers of European descent.[40]

The most recent contribution to the Plateau debate comes from Christopher Miller, whose 1985 work, *Prophetic Worlds*, essentially follows a contact-origins line. Like Walker, Miller locates in the period of indirect contact the stresses that paved the way for Plateau prophetic activity. Like Walker, he believes that the introduction of the horse—with its attendant cultural impacts—and epidemic disease were crucial. More curiously, Miller goes on to argue that extreme climatic conditions—the Little Ice Age—during this period resulted in disastrous resource shortages. The cumulative effect of all these pressures was to destroy the "delicate balance" between the physical and spiritual worlds of Plateau peoples and to force a new "thought pattern" or "mazeway" by which they could comprehend their changing circumstances. For Miller, Plateau prophecy was a "new religion," born de novo of the stresses of the era.[41]

Toward a New Synthesis: Theoretical Considerations

The central weakness of the contact-origins theses is their narrow focus on colonial penetration as the spur to prophetic movements. Miller offers a partial corrective by incorporating local environmental factors, but his thesis of disastrous resource scarcity appears highly dubious in light of evidence of flourishing indigenous trade networks (map 4) throughout the period when resources supposedly were so few.[42] Miller's argument is further diminished by his insistence on the novelty of the prophetic idiom, and by his characterization of it as an expression of a completely revamped mental "mazeway." It is instructive that in the vast literature exploring similar spiritual movements in Africa, arguments that treat contact-related factors as causal have not stood the test of time. Lanternari exemplifies the shift. In the nearly thirty years since publication of *Religions of the Oppressed*, he has abandoned most of his original propositions about the colonial roots of African religious movements, in favor of an analysis of the *internal* cultural and psychological forces shaping the creation of sects.[43]

Lanternari's work is reflective of a tendency among Africanists to try to understand indigenous religious movements on their own terms, and not merely as reactions to external forces, however profound. Similar approaches in Northwest scholarship include studies by Wayne Suttles on the Coast Salish and Robin Ridington on the Dunne-za (Beaver) of northeastern British Columbia.[44] Suttles argues that although white influence was not insignificant in the eighteenth century, aboriginal factors—specifically, crises arising from what he casts as the poverty of Coast Salish political institutions—more likely account for the periodic rise of prophets. Ridington depicts prophecy as an integral part of the ancient mosaic of meaning through which the Dunne-za organized their relations to one another and to their environment, both in the aboriginal period and after the onset of European colonialism. In Ridington's analysis, the turn to prophets

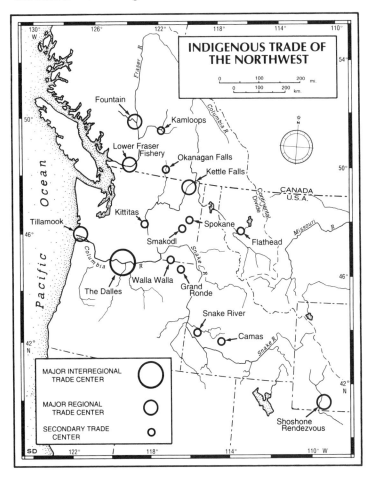

Map 4

after the intrusion of European-derived influences was not a harbinger of a "new religion," but a "traditional" and "distinctively
Indian" reaction to the human need to organize a changing reality.[45]

Scholars who subscribe to such approaches, while differing on
many details, share certain common assumptions. They reject the

notion that indigenous religious movements of the "protohistoric" and colonial periods are to be explained in terms of anticolonialism—that everything that happened under the influence of colonial penetration must somehow be a result of it. In the same vein, they reject the view that there was necessarily a sharp break in the histories of indigenous cultures at the time of the onset of colonialism. In crudest terms, such a sharp break would imply that there was a time of pure tradition before the onset of colonialism, that colonialism "upset the balance," and that prophetic and other movements were efforts to define a new balance.[46] Miller's theory falls into this category, the very language he chooses making clear his allegiance: "dynamic pressures from outside . . . turned many central aspects of Plateau culture upside down"; the "delicate balance" between the physical and the spiritual was upset; pressures combined to "require the formation of a new thought pattern that could bring some order to the changing scene."[47]

Suttles, Ridington, and many of their counterparts in African studies, without discounting the enormous effects of the European incursion into Native worlds, adopt analyses whose great strength is their emphasis on the *internal* logic of prophet cults. The key question implicit in these analyses is why the prophetic response seemed a natural and rational one to the prophets and their followers. Those who consider prophecy as a "new religion" (Miller), or who consider the "extraordinary, crisis-ridden" circumstances of the protohistoric era as sufficient to account for the emergence of a new cult (Walker, Aberle), would have some difficulty answering this question.

Far from depicting prophetic movements as attempts to forge "a new thought pattern," those who focus on internal logics are concerned with the deep roots of the movements in the encompassing culture. Indeed, they see the movements as meaningful to their adherents precisely because of their ability to tap all of the ambiguous power of enduring symbol and myth and ritual.

This is not to suggest, however, that prophecy was merely a reiteration of age-old patterns; it could be innovative. In some settings, the very act of prophecy was a new twist: J. B. Peires argues that this was the case in Xhosa society in the early nineteenth century, when the people were "driven to desperation" by a conjunction of forces including epidemic, military defeat, eviction from natal lands, and the pressures of the white colonial economy. It was in this context, Peires contends, that Xhosa prophecy arose for the first time.[48] At first glance this sounds much like Aberle and Walker's theses of the "crisis" roots of prophecy, and similarities do exist. Yet there are crucial differences in emphasis.

Walker shares Peires's view that extraordinary circumstances trigger the act of an individual who "dies" and returns to earth with a prophecy. As noted above, Walker readily accepts that certain critical beliefs in the prophet dance cult had "aboriginal analogues." What is troubling about his analysis is the way he downplays the importance of these analogues. For Walker, the fact that cults like the prophet dance "happen to resemble former religious systems conceptually is a truism of only limited significance." What matters is the unusual circumstances that "produced" the cult. For Peires, by contrast, that conceptual resemblance is fundamental. The content of Xhosa prophecy was acceptable to a wide cross section of Xhosa society precisely because of that resemblance, precisely because the prophecy was "compatible with bedrock common beliefs."[49] The extraordinary circumstances of the time before the rise of the prophets did not *produce* the prophetic response. The response could not have emerged in the absence of that bedrock of belief—and one might extend this to argue that given the bedrock, the prophetic response *could* have emerged in the absence of epidemic, land loss, or the other particular circumstances that impinged at the time. These insights are enormously valuable in analyzing Plateau prophecy.

Plateau Prophecy: The Eighteenth-Century Context

Although emphasis on the internal logic of prophet cults is a welcome counter to the tendency to view them simply as reactions to colonialism, it must not come at the expense of attention to the larger context in which the cults arose. As Walker's and Miller's accounts make clear, and as will be demonstrated in later chapters, the late eighteenth century was a period of cultural and social upheaval in the Plateau. The rise and spread of horse culture, particularly among the peoples in southern and eastern areas, enhanced mobility and communication and increased intergroup raiding and buffalo hunting. Horse pastoralism and buffalo hunting brought eastern and southern groups into the midst of the violent competition that characterized the mid-eighteenth to the mid-nineteenth century in the western Great Plains and Rockies. However, those forces did not affect all Plateau peoples equally. For example, the communities of the upper Columbia—the very ones most prominent in early prophecy accounts—had only limited experience with horse culture by the early nineteenth century. They were more profoundly affected by another foreign element, the smallpox virus.

Plateau Prophecy: The Narratives

The first documented Plateau prophets were active around the turn of the nineteenth century. Southern Okanagan oral narratives illustrate the framework of early prophecy. One account, from the time "before the whites came but after the fall of 'dry snow'" (volcanic ash, as explained below), tells of a goose with two heads appearing from the southeast. The prophet had warned the people to be on the lookout for this messenger bird, which would herald the time to dance. The people were frightened:

> They said, "The world must be coming to an end.". . . As soon
> as they saw the bird they began to dance, standing in a circle

around the dreamer. . . . As they danced they sang the prayer song which the dreamer had taught them. . . . While dancing the dreamer exhorted the community not to fight, steal, lie, commit rape, or sin in other ways. . . . As a result of this preaching, some of the people became so righteous that they did not allow their children to run about after dark lest they do evil things.[50]

As noted earlier, the prophet taught a dance that was supposed to imitate the dances performed by the dead, who inhabited the land of souls. David Thompson recalled seeing dancing at villages all the way down the Columbia River in the summer of 1811. The precise form varied from place to place, but in general, Thompson reported, men and women danced separately, singing and moving in a restrained manner, following the lead of a figure he took to be a "chief."[51] This restraint differed strikingly from the often-frantic dancing of people displaying their spirit powers in the winter festivals. Although he called the dancing "strictly a religious ceremony," Thompson interpreted it as a form of greeting, and as an expression of the people's desire for the European goods he believed they coveted.[52] Given that there is no known tradition of a greeting dance in the Plateau and that the trader would soon learn of the activities of prophets in the region (see below), he must have been witnessing the prophet dance. His account of the Nespelem dance is vivid:

> The Chief [prophet?] made a short prayer, after which the dance commenced of the Men and Women, each separate, to the music of their singing, which was pleasingly plaintive . . . each line of Men and Women had a clear space of three or four feet, within which they danced; at first the step was slow, and the singing the same, but both gradually increased, the step of the dance very quick as if pursuing, or being pursued. This lasted for about eight minutes, when a pause of two minutes took place; a prayer was made [by the leader], and the dance and singing repeated twice: the whole was strictly a religious ceremony, every face was grave and serious, almost to sadness.[53]

Prophecies dating from the opening years of the nineteenth century have been frequently linked in oral accounts to a fall of "dry snow," as was the Okanagan account cited above. Scientists have dated a heavy fall of volcanic ash in the region to 1800, give or take a year or two.[54] Sanpoil and Nespelem informants told Teit that in their area, people were very frightened by the ash fall and were afraid that it foretold evil. Accounts of the prophet dance are common for this period. There are many stories of people dancing so fervently and constantly that they neglected their usual activities and suffered food shortages the following winter. In the words of an Okanagan woman, "the people just danced and danced until they had nothing stored away for the winter." A Sanpoil man recalled his grandmother's account that the people "prayed to the 'dry snow', called it 'Chief' and 'Mystery', and asked it to explain itself and tell why it came. The people danced a great deal all summer." Among the Kalispel, "the Indians supposed that the sun had burnt up, and that there was an end of all things."[55]

In the 1840s a Spokane man known to whites as Cornelius told members of a U.S. surveillance expedition (the Wilkes expedition) that when he was a young boy, he was awakened suddenly one night and was told by his mother that the world was falling to pieces:

> He then heard a great noise of thunder overhead, and all the people crying out in terror. Something was falling very thick, which they at first took for snow, but on going out they found it to be dirt: it proved to be ashes, which fell to the depth of six inches . . . causing them to suppose that the end of the world was actually at hand. The medicine-man arose, told them to stop their fear and crying, for the world was not about to fall to pieces. "Soon," said he, "there will come from the rising sun a different kind of man from any you have yet seen, who will bring with them a book, and will teach you everything, and after that the world will fall to pieces."[56]

Anthropologist Eugene Hunn has suggested that the reception accorded David Thompson in the Plateau reveals that people took him to represent the fulfillment of their prophetic expectations.[57] Perhaps he was, indeed, received as the "different kind of man" whose arrival their prophets foretold. At least one prophet known to be active in this early-contact period spoke of the whites as miraculous providers (see Ross's account of Kauxumanupika, below), and several later prophets did so. If Thompson's arrival inspired hope for material gain, as he believed it did, it also inspired fear. Near the mouth of the Umatilla River, he and his brigade put ashore at a small village where people were terrified at their appearance. The villagers sent forward two old men, who approached in what Thompson described as "the most pitiful manner; crawling slowly . . . imploring mercy."[58] Thompson had no idea why they behaved in this way. He would soon learn of the prophecy of deadly plague.

Prophecies of Epidemic

The association of prophecy and epidemic disease is explicit in several oral narratives dating to the early nineteenth century. Among the earliest is a story of a Yakama man who visited the afterworld. The informant dated the occurrence to about 1800, the time of the second smallpox epidemic in the Interior:

> There was an epidemic of smallpox among the Yakima and people were dying and leaving the country. One old man, a chief, took sick and was left behind. He died. In his dream he travelled and came to a place where people were gathered eating lots of good things. He was awfully hungry; he was weak he was so hungry. He came to a kind of gateway and asked for food. The people turned him away and told him it wasn't time for him to come in yet. So they directed him to another place a long way off. He travelled and finally he reached there. They told him when he asked for food that they didn't eat there. They

looked thin and raw-boned and didn't say much. They said, "We
are people called angels". They told him to go back where he
came from. "We can't take you in", they said. He felt bad and
went back. When he came to his place he came to life again.
But his people thought he was dead. He followed them. He
surprised them. The first place he went to was Hell. The second
place was Heaven.[59]

A Wishram account, recorded in the 1930s, linked epidemic
to the coming of the fur traders. In this account the whites were
said to have been angered by the theft of a silver powder horn,
which, from the details given, appears to refer to a theft from
American traders in the region in 1812. A white doctor "got
mad and turned some kind of medicine loose to make disease.
The Indians all got sick with a fever."[60] This part of the narrative echoes accounts of Dr. Marcus Whitman's presumed role
in the spread of measles in 1847. The Wishram narrative highlights how later events can reshape remembrances of earlier
ones.

These accounts of disease and world destruction bring us to the
prophecies of Kauxuma-nupika. Her career as the one-time wife
of a North West Company voyageur who declared her sex
changed and became a renowned warrior, compelling as it is,
need not concern us for the moment.[61] Dressed as a man and
accompanied by her wife, Kauxuma-nupika arrived at Fort
Astoria on the lower Columbia in early June 1811. Thompson,
who arrived at the coast soon afterward, knew Kauxuma-nupika
from her earlier association with the voyageur, and from an
encounter east of the Rockies. He described her as a woman who
had "set herself up for a prophetess, and gradually had gained,
by her shrewdness, some influence among the Natives as a
dreamer, and expounder of dreams."[62]

Kauxuma-nupika and her partner accompanied the Astorian
brigade on its first journey to the interior in the summer of 1811.
The traders soon learned of her prophecy of the imminent end
of the world in a great plague. Thompson, who travelled partway

upriver with the Astorians, heard about it from four Native men in the Columbia Gorge:

> [T]he four men addressed me; saying, "when you passed down to the sea, we were all strong in life, and your return to us finds us strong to live, but what is this we hear," casting their eyes with a stern look on her [Kauxuma-nupika], "is it true that the white men" (looking at Mr. Stuart and his Men) "have brought with them the Small Pox to destroy us; and also two men of enormous size, who are on their way to us, overturning the Ground, and burying all the Villages and Lodges underneath it: is this true and are we all soon to die"... the Natives were strong to live, and every evening were dancing and singing.[63]

Thompson recalled that he did his best to reassure the men that the traders had not brought smallpox and that the world was not about to end. He surmised that they might have killed this messenger of doom, had the traders not been present. Despite Thompson's skepticism about her "lies," that the people "every evening were dancing and singing" intimates that Kauxuma-nupika's prophecy had profound resonance on the lower Columbia. Farther upriver, Thompson found people "eager to learn the news"—news of Kauxuma-nupika and her partner being of particular interest.[64]

Alexander Ross, a member of the Astorian interior brigade in 1811, recalled in his narrative how the influence exercised by these "bold, adventurous Amazons" extended all the way to the Okanagan:

> The stories they gave out among the unsuspecting and credulous natives, as they passed, were well calculated to astonish as well as to attract attention. Brought up, as they had been, near the whites ... they were capable of practising all the arts of well instructed cheats; and to effect their purpose the better, they showed the Indians an old letter ... and told them that they had been sent by the great white chief, with a message to apprise the natives in general that gifts, consisting of goods and implements of all kinds, were forthwith to be poured in upon

them; that the great white chief knew their wants and was about to supply them with everything their hearts could desire; that the whites had hitherto cheated the Indians, by selling goods, in place of making presents to them as directed by the great white chief. These stories, so agreeable to the Indian ear, were circulated far and wide, and not only received as truths, but procured so much celebrity for the two cheats that they were the objects of attraction at every village and camp on the way . . . [the local people] loaded them for their good tidings with the most valuable articles they possessed—robes, horses, leather, and *higuas* [dentalium shells]; so that on our arrival at Oakinacken they had no less than twenty-six horses, many of them loaded with the fruits of their false reports.[65]

Ross was silent on the epidemic and world-destruction elements of the prophecy emphasized by Thompson, focusing instead on predictions of a coming time of plenty. It is hard to imagine why the traders reported such divergent accounts in such close proximity. But to propose, as one scholar has done, that the differences reveal nothing more than a calculated change of heart by Kauxuma-nupika is to follow Ross a little too closely.[66] The suggestion that a negative response to her prophecy of destruction prompted her to abandon it in favor of a happier outlook removes Kauxuma-nupika's activities from the larger context of prophecy, and depicts her as nothing more than an opportunistic spinner of tales. Kauxuma-nupika's messages may well have contained ambiguities and inconsistencies; in the nature of prophecy, they could hardly be expected to be fully formed orthodoxies. Yet it seems very clear from both traders' accounts that the people who heard her words took them very seriously.

Perhaps the traders heard only partial versions of her message. Quite plausibly, each, for his own reasons, focused on different aspects. Ross's fixation with the material expectations embodied in the prophecy comes as no surprise. As a trader charged with establishing a profitable trade post in the region, he stood to be directly affected by such ideas. The common denominator of the Thompson and Ross accounts is the stress each lays on the aspects relating to the whites. Thompson focused on the Natives' perception that whites were responsible for the smallpox; Ross stressed the notion that the whites had a duty to make up for "cheating" the Indians by giving them "everything their hearts could desire."

As white newcomers to the region, both men could be expected to be paranoid about a woman who travelled through the very country where they hoped to establish trade relations, prophesying the imminent end of the world. If Kauxuma-nupika incorporated them into her pronouncements, so much the worse. The traders saw her activities as a threat to their own. That she had so receptive an audience would only heighten their unease. The perception of a threat may well have led both men to exaggerate the antiwhite elements of the prophecy.

The same interpretation may apply to the Wilkes account of the Spokane prophecy ("soon there will come from the rising sun a different kind of man . . . and after that the world will fall to pieces"). The narrative underscores the importance of recognizing the influence of postprophecy developments on accounts collected some years after the fact. Whether the Spokane prophet in 1800 predicted the coming of the whites and their "book," and linked them with world destruction, or whether this was a spin put on things by Wilkes's 1840s informant—and perhaps further emphasized by the white recorder of the account—can never be known. The Christian cast of many later narratives is another aspect of the problem. To argue that white commentators may have exaggerated the aspects of prophecy that related to themselves is not to suggest that they invented them from thin air, however. Although prophecy in this era was not antiwhite in its motivations, it could and often did incorporate the white presence into its prescriptions.

Ross's account of Kauxuma-nupika hints at an entirely different explanation for such prophecy: the possibility that it expressed the people's desire for the myriad wonderful goods introduced by Europeans. Plateau communities had been exposed to that great wealth through flourishing intertribal trade networks with plains and coast in the eighteenth century. Such an interpretation does not sit well with the argument here, that to understand Native religious movements, we must look first inside Native cultures. Still, these movements did respond to changing circumstances, and the introduction of European goods to the region was a critical change. This is the subject for another study.[67]

The Basis of Belief

Perhaps, in the final analysis, Thompson's and Ross's accounts of Kauxuma-nupika's prophecy were not divergent at all. As the Nespelem tale quoted earlier implies, creation and destruction are elements of a continuum in Plateau cosmology. As aspects of the ongoing process of creation and transformation, the two are inseparable; they were expressed as such in Plateau prophecy. The predicted destruction of the world was a necessary phase on the way to world renewal. During his time among the Okanagan (1811–18), Ross learned of their conviction of the coming destruction: "They believe that this world will have an end, as it had a beginning; and their reason is this, that the rivers and lakes must eventually undermine the earth and set the land afloat again, like the island of their forefathers, and then all must perish. Frequently they have asked us when it would take place—the *itsowleigh*, or the end of the world."[68]

At the various times in recorded Plateau history when prophets declared the moment of destruction to be near, the people, far from surrendering, demonstrated their belief and their desire to hasten the process through fervent dancing and singing. Their actions did not indicate a desire to die, but signified that they were, in Thompson's words, "strong to live." In an era of devastating epidemic, perhaps more than at any other time, people were eager for renewal. Epidemics confirmed both the imminence of world destruction and the renewal that would follow.[69]

There was more to the widespread appeal of the Plateau prophecies than their coincidence with beliefs about creation and destruction. Other aspects, too, had deep aboriginal roots. Most obvious is the striking parallel between the journey of the prophet to the land of the dead and that central aspect of Plateau religious experience, the vision quest. Initiates on the quest sought the partnership of a guardian spirit, who would bestow on them the supernatural powers that were the basis of an individual's special talents. The child in search of a spirit partner made the first quest sometime before puberty. Long training in the myths of the culture, together with isolation, fasting, and other means of spiritual and physical preparation, prepared the ground for visionary experiences. The child who achieved a spirit vision returned from the quest with a song, a dance, a name, and a medicine bundle of sacred tokens bestowed by the spirit partner, all of which were generally not revealed until adulthood; the details of such practice varied a good deal from society to society. Prophets took their place within this system as individuals who had acquired the extraordinary ability to dream their souls to the land of the dead and back, and to communicate with the spirits there. Similar to initiates in the spirit quest, they returned with songs, dances, and supernaturally inspired instructions.[70]

Orphean tales of visits by the living to the land of the dead appear frequently in Plateau traditions, as they do in Native North American traditions more generally. The Nez Percé tale of Coyote and the Shadow People is a good example. In this tale the culture hero Coyote visits the place where his wife's spirit went after her death. A spirit guide leads him through a kind of preparation-by-deprivation, after which Coyote is able to visit with his beloved wife and all his dead friends. He is told he may bring his wife back to the land of the living, provided he follows certain instructions. Most important is that he is not to touch her until they have completed the arduous journey home. During the journey Coyote's wife gradually appears more and more real to him, and finally he is overcome by the desire to embrace her. The indiscretion marks the end of the quest. The death spirit berates Coyote for his folly, and tells him: "You, Coyote, were about to establish the practice of returning from death. Only a short time away the human race is coming, but you have spoiled everything and established for them death as it is."[71] The tale is just one of many to raise the possibility that the dead might one day return, a notion fundamental to the early-nineteenth-century prophecies. Coyote may have "spoiled everything" for the people of an earlier time, but as the Nespelem tale promises, there would be another chance.

Prophecy and Epidemic

Indigenous conceptions of illness were integral to the ideological underpinnings of prophecy in the era of the early epidemics. Plateau concepts of disease causation were complex, but they may be organized into two broad categories: disease due to physical disorder, which was treatable with practical medicinal cures; and disease due to spiritual disorder, which required the skills of a gifted specialist. Serious illness—and epidemic smallpox certainly qualified—was spiritually based. Such illness was believed to be the product of an imbalance or a power struggle among the personal spirit partners that animated the spiritual universe of the Plateau. Thus it might result from the intrusion of a malevolent spirit or the injury or loss of one's own guardian spirit through wandering or desertion.[72] It is impossible from this vantage point to do more than speculate on how the cataclysm of smallpox epidemic was interpreted. But it is clear how people responded.

   All the prophets decreed that at the declared time people were to dance and sing devoutly according to the prophet's teaching. The record indicates that people followed the instructions scrupulously, often to the exclusion of their usual routines. "Do not fight, steal, lie, commit rape, or sin in other ways," the Okanagan prophet said; so zealous were people to follow the order that they kept their children at home. So earnestly did people follow the injunction to dance that they neglected their food-production activities. The proposition here is that their fervor derived from their belief in, and their urgent desire to attain, the positive expectation embodied in the prophetic message. Prophets offered an agenda for release: by avidly following the prophet's injunctions, people believed they would hasten the end, and subsequent renewal, of the world. Promises of world renewal and return of the dead must have had special poignancy in an era when the world appeared sick to the core and people had lost many of those they held most dear.

Prophecy as Challenge

Smallpox posed an insurmountable challenge to indigenous Plateau systems of public health control. As outlined above, serious illness was seen as a symptom of deep unease or imbalance in the spirit world. Shamans were individuals who had acquired extraordinary spiritual powers that enabled a person to cure the ill; they healed by using their more potent spiritual prowess to restore powers that had been lost, or to conquer invading powers.[73] Naturally, success in curing or controlling disease was essential to legitimate the practitioners' claims to medical, and broader religious, authority. Fur traders frequently commented on how quickly shamans might lose respect when their cures failed.[74]

Smallpox proved utterly unresponsive to the shamans' powers. It was and is a terrifying disease. After a benign incubation period of less than two weeks, symptoms take the form of high fever, headache, and body pains. The rash appears after about two weeks, starting with red spots and developing quickly into raised lesions, blisterlike sores, and finally, pustules. Fever persists throughout, and in the final stage there is extreme itching. In surviving patients, scabs fall off to leave telltale pockmarks. In severe cases lesions become confluent, and there may be hemorrhaging and sloughing of the skin. The patient is infectious from the first appearance of lesions until pustules fall off; corpses remain infectious for up to three weeks. Complications of the disease include pneumonia, encephalitis, and blindness.[75]

In populations that experienced regular outbreaks (say, every generation), or in which smallpox became endemic, indigenous medical orthodoxies could adapt to include various protections against the disease—the most obvious being isolation of victims and, eventually, inoculation.[76] The Plateau epidemics from the 1770s through 1782 and in 1800–1801 were unexpected and capricious. The disease completely overrode existing control systems. It was bound to give rise to intense speculation, and to challenges to prevailing medical orthodoxies. The rise of prophetic movements in this era was one such challenge.

Implicit in all this discussion is the assumption that the principal aim of prophecy was *internal* cleansing and renewal. Prophecy was not an antiwhite response. Smallpox was not, in this early period, interpreted as a consequence of contagion by people of European descent: the causes, as with all serious disease, were believed to be spiritual. Some of the early prophets did incorporate the contaminating influences of whites into their larger program of cleansing and renewal. In the Spokane prophecy the destruction of the world was slated to follow the coming of the whites with their new religion. In the Wishram narrative a white doctor got mad and Native people got sick. In Thompson's version of Kauxuma-nupika's prophecy, the white men brought smallpox. Later in the century, Smohalla, the renowned prophet of Priest Rapids, would blame a measles epidemic on the "poison" of missionary Marcus Whitman.

Yet the presence of whites was not a necessary ingredient of the early prophecies. The first contact-era epidemic, after all, occurred some three decades before the arrival of the first whites in the Plateau. Certainly, European influences had begun to penetrate the region. But as has been stressed throughout, it is shortsighted—and one is tempted to say, arrogant—to view everything that happened in the time of colonial penetration as a reaction to it. Plateau societies had their own motivations. In an era of smallpox epidemics prophets offered an agenda for the most pressing of motives: the need to cleanse and renew a filthy world. Admonitions "not to fight, steal, lie, commit rape, or sin in other ways," and to perform the prophet dance, were aspects of this agenda. So eager were people to demonstrate their adherence to the decrees of the prophets, and their desire for world renewal, that they neglected their food-production activities—apparently even to the point of hunger.

Issues of authenticity and "contamination" of accounts aside, the narratives point to the capacity of prophetic movements to innovate. Much as prophecy drew on long-established religious idioms, it was no mere restatement of old ideas. It transformed itself to changing conditions. Prime examples are the incorporation of whites and, before long, of Christian elements. Thompson's sketch of Kauxuma-nupika's prophecy is telling: the prophet foretold the coming of white men with smallpox, and also of "two men of enormous size . . . overturning the ground." The two men sound much like Coyote and Old One, who, as the Nespelem tale promised, were to return at the time of destruction. This juxtaposition of old and new speaks to the dynamic potential of prophecy.

It should be clear by now that epidemic was not a necessary condition for the rise of prophetic movements. They may well have arisen at other times, in response to other inexplicable happenings. Many of the earliest accounts of Plateau prophecy link it to an extraordinary fall of volcanic ash, for example. The proposition here is that the ash fall may indeed have triggered a round of prophetic activity, but that epidemics provided the context for the frequency, wide distribution, and intensity of response in this era. Epidemics created a deep spiritual unease,

and prophecy tapped it. The vision of the imminent destruction
of the world, followed by its renewal and the return of the dead—
a vision deeply rooted in Plateau cosmology—had an eerie
cogency in a time of smallpox epidemic. Prophets held out the
last and best hope for an end to the horror and a return to peace
and prosperity.

Concluding Remarks

The communities encountered by British fur traders in the
Plateau at the start of the nineteenth century were communities
already heavily marked by the European presence in North
America as a result of earlier smallpox epidemics. We can never
know the extent of the ravages, but given that the disease was
the virulent *Variola major*, and in light of patterns of mobility
and intergroup communication in the region, John Work's assertion that "immense numbers . . . were swept off" seems modest.
Given the difficulty of estimating pre-epidemic population levels,
there is no way to test Boyd's contention that fully 45 percent of
the Plateau population had perished as a result of smallpox by
1802; equally, given much higher hemispheric estimates, there is
little reason to consider it excessive. Nor does it appear likely
that populations rebounded in the fur-trade era. The Jesuit priest
Mengarini, for example, writing in the 1840s, recounted Salish
Flathead oral testimony that their numbers remained much lower
than before the arrival of smallpox. Elsewhere in the region
subsequent outbreaks of smallpox, measles, and other introduced
disease would have forestalled any such rebound.

    The social, economic, and psychological impacts of epidemic
in the pre-fur-trade era have been considered as closely as the
sources allow. Villages lost their elders, their youngest members,
their doctors; people neglected their subsistence activities; a
deep spiritual unease overtook many communities. There is little
more detail than this in trader and oral accounts. Perhaps, in
the final analysis, the detail is less significant than the broader

implications. British fur traders, the first non-Natives to visit the Plateau, encountered societies already seriously affected by the European presence. Yet these societies responded to the new stresses and transformations according to their indigenous categories of knowledge. This is not in the least to suggest that those categories were static and unchanging, nor that Plateau societies were so. That Plateau communities had suffered the trauma of epidemic disease, and had changed in irrecoverable ways in the face of it, serves to underline the point that these societies had histories—that they had experienced the pressures of social and cultural change long before the coming of the whites. By the early nineteenth century smallpox was embedded in those histories.

CHAPTER THREE

Landscaping the Wilds

Traders Imagine the Plateau

Wilderness—"a desert; a tract of solitude and savageness."
Samuel Johnson (*Dictionary*, 1755)

According to Dr. Johnson's definition, the Plateau as fur traders saw it was quintessentially wild. As if to illustrate Dr. Johnson's point, Alexander Ross portrayed the region as boundless, rough, and barren, and bemoaned his fate at being "alone in this unhallowed wilderness, without friend or white man within hundreds of miles of me, and surrounded by savages."[1] The image of the desert was endlessly invoked to describe the central plain of the Columbia Interior.[2] David Thompson wrote of "the sterile, sandy plains," a country "rude and hilly without woods for several miles, and destitute of deer, or the wild Sheep of the Mountains." George Simpson initially found the place to be "nothing but a sandy desert." Nor was the desert metaphor restricted to the plain. In the deep forests of the northeastern mountains, "[t]he aspect was gloomy, scarcely the chirping of a solitary silence. In all this extent of desert through which we had passed not a human being was to be seen, nor the traces of any."[3]

Human beings are indeed remarkably absent from the textual landscapes depicted by these early travellers to the Plateau. But solitude appears to have been a common feature of landscape writing in the era of European expansion. Mary Louise Pratt, surveying the works of early British travellers in southern Africa, finds it was a routine textual strategy to separate the land from the people who inhabited it. This is not to suggest that such travellers did not write about people at all; rather, their ethnographies tended to be removed from their writings about the land. Representations of landscape were just that—characterizations of place, prospect, resource. To make these landscapes available for possession and improvement, the people who inhabited and claimed them had to be written out (or nearly so). In Pratt's words, "[t]he European improving eye produces subsistence habitats as 'empty' landscapes, meaningful only in terms of a capitalist future and of their potential for producing a marketable surplus."[4] "Empty" landscapes had not been "improved" by human hands (the precise British meaning of which is discussed below), and so lay open to European possession and domination. However, the suggestion that these landscapes were meaningful "only" in terms of capitalist design is surely overstating the case. Plateau landscapes held far more complex meanings for British traders. Nevertheless, it is important to bear in mind that landscapes newly brought into the colonial ken were assessed primarily for their economic, and perhaps political, potential, and that such concerns profoundly shaped the European response to the land.

The Plateau was certainly an alien landscape—or more accurately, a series of landscapes—even for traders with experience in remote regions east of the Rockies. But traders' images were shaped by many factors, which often had little to do with the physical stature of the land. Most salient was the trader's very raison d'être: to collect furs for sale in world markets. From the perspective of "capitalist futures," desert or barrenness was contemptible as much for the absence it implied—the absence of fur-bearing animals—as for its assault on European aesthetics. It is no surprise that landscapes were often described according to their fur potential and other attributes affecting the accessibility of furs (navigability of rivers, accessibility of the terrain to horses, and the like). Even the "sterile" expanses of the central and southern Plateau were not entirely without merit on this account. The dry, thickly grassed reaches of Nez Percé and Cayuse country, for example, supported the horses so vital to Columbia operations. Most fur production, however, was in the back country on the fringes of the Plateau—the Salish Flathead and Kutenai regions, the Snake Country, and the Blue Mountains.

Although instrumental concerns might predominate in the writings of men who were here to trade furs, landscape, whatever one's purposes, is laden with symbolic and personal meanings. Perceptions of a given environment consist not only of more or less accurate renderings of technical and economic potentials, but of "value judgements . . . and phantasmic beliefs."[5] Cultural historian Simon Schama sees in landscape a process whereby we map the world physically, intellectually, and imaginatively. The process gives us insight into ourselves as we attempt to understand what lies beyond us.[6] Landscape is indeed a cultural image, comprised of layers of meaning particular to the society doing the seeing and the describing: the act of seeing is conditioned by what is already known. A pond is at its most prosaic a container of water, perhaps a haven for water fowl. An individual's perception of the pond depends on his or her interest in swimming, fishing, or birding, among other things, and on broader cultural attitudes toward these activities. Accretions of such personal and cultural meanings may transform the pond on a hot summer day into that most beautiful of places, the tranquil swimming hole.[7] Each society has its own ways of representing landscape; the fur traders' imaginings, and their ways of acting on the land, differed profoundly from those of the indigenous peoples of the region. The traders' ways are the subject of this chapter. In subsequent chapters, the focus will turn to their perceptions of Native American ways of inhabiting the land.

While commercial considerations guided traders' thoughts, their images of the Plateau were colored, however unconsciously, by their cultural knowledge and prior experience of landscape. The foundations for notions of beauty and utility in the land were laid, for most of the gentlemen of the North West and Hudson's Bay Companies, during their early years in Britain. Thus, their responses to Plateau landscapes were ambiguous from the start. They sought lands rich in fur-bearing animals, but such places were rather distant from the landscapes of their homes. In much of Scotland, wilderness was a stretch of heathland or a peak, a patch surrounded by settlement. The wilderness of the Highlands was more akin to Dr. Johnson's: here was "a wide extent of hopeless sterility," a land "dismissed by nature from her care and disinherited of her favours." But this Highland barrenness was relieved by the appearance of an occasional grainfield, or the knowledge that a gentleman's estate was nearby. As Johnson observed, what were these "spots of wilderness to the desarts [sic] of America?"[8] In the Plateau, wilderness was boundless. Indian settlement offered no respite; indeed, it was cast as part of the wilds. The enormity of nature was foreign, at once exhilarating and disorienting.

David Thompson was moved by the "stupendous and solitary Wilds" of Howse Pass in the northern Rocky Mountains. When he was not lamenting his loneliness, Alexander Ross was known to delight in the freedom of this vast, unknown place.[9] For the most part, however, traders were more at ease with the familiar than the stupendous. When necessary, they might invent it. Accordingly, Ross found in the Snake Country an "enchanting vale," a range of gentle hills traversed by "descending riverlets whose limits were line[d] with rows of bushes, as if set off by the hand of man."[10] The familiar was reproduced most ingeniously at the trade posts. Spokane House became a particular haven of civility, what with its ballroom, race course, garden, and liberal supplies of "Eatables Drinkables and other *Domestic Comforts.*"[11] Here wilderness was domesticated and tamed. This was progress, but it contained a threat. Traders were well aware by the early nineteenth century that the days of the fur trade were numbered. By uncovering the potential of the land (measured in European terms), they were contributing to the settlement impulse that

would seal the fate of their business. This chapter explores the
ways in which such varied, and often contending, forces shaped
traders' images of Plateau landscapes.

"A Country Well Stocked with Animals"

"A Country well stocked with animals" was how George Simpson,
overseas governor of the Hudson's Bay Company, at first described some areas of the Plateau. His words reflect the principal
interest of North West and HBC traders in assessing the land.
Those who explored new areas were expected to report, first and
foremost, on the products of the country—or, as the head of the
North West Company once put it, on its "riches and treasures."
Until these riches were disclosed, the country was essentially an
"unknown waste."[12] Descriptive passages frequently read as little
more than lists of commodities potentially "useful" in European
or Chinese markets or as food and other supplies for use in the
local prosecution of the business.

The central plain of the Columbia did not fare well by those
standards. Passing into this country of "no woods but a chance
tree," Thompson remarked, "Of course there can be no beaver,
they [Native people] have bears and rats [muskrats] with a few
sheep and black tailed deer." At least the land could support
horses, and the local Salish people had many.[13] Alexander Henry
the younger began his account of the more promising Kutenai
country as he began most such passages, with a catalogue of
animals "in which their country abounds . . . red and fallow deer,
moose, gray sheep, and white goats, while of the fur kinds beaver,
bear, otter, and other valuable skins abound." Ross Cox judged
the place in similar terms: there were "plenty of beavers, deer,
mountain sheep, and, at times, buffaloes." The land of the Salish
Flathead, meanwhile, was "well stocked with deer, mountain
sheep, bears, wild fowl, and fish." The Snake Country was simply
"a Country rich in Beaver."[14] Simon Fraser waxed eloquent on
the horrors of the river that would bear his name; beyond that,

his descriptions were to the point: the Shuswap region "consists of plains, well stocked with animals"; the Chilcotin River "runs through a fine country abounding with plenty of animals."[15]

By the time of his second visit to the Columbia in 1828–29, Governor Simpson was more measured in his estimations of the potential of the land. Nevertheless, his accounts were similarly focused. By now some areas were all but trapped out, or had turned out to be less "well stocked" than previously thought. The governor described the country around Thompson's River Post (the Shuswap region) as "poor in Beaver and small Furs." Chief Trader Archibald McDonald concurred. Production had reached its height in 1822, and now beaver were "on the verge of extermination." A person could walk "for days together without seeing the smallest quadrupeds, the little brown squirrel excepted": small comfort from the squirrel, whose pelts were not "adapted for" the market. Farther south, the few skins produced in the neighborhood of Fort Okanogan were "not worth naming," and the country around Fort Nez Percés was "not rich." The Snake Country "has never been rich for its extent," but produced well in absolute terms, and had an important strategic purpose.[16]

Trees, Timber, and "Vegetable Productions"

Furs were not the only asset of the Columbia of interest to the traders. Trees had great significance, and perhaps more so here, where large stretches of country were remarkable precisely for their treelessness, than in many other regions of fur-trade country. Robert Stuart was awed by "high Hills entirely destitute of Timber"; like other traders, he was driven to comment on that absence. Gabriel Franchère and David Thompson were struck by the dependence of Native people on scattered bits of driftwood.[17] Most traders were more concerned about their own dependence. The building of Fort Nez Percés was a challenge, for "the ground is not blessed with a single stick of any kind of wood," and wood had to be carried in by water a distance of about a hundred miles.

Simpson reported wood so scarce in the plain that passing
brigades often resorted to burning the palisades that surrounded
Native graves (a practice he considered "a most unwarrantable
liberty").[18]

Wood scarcity was by now something to which the British were
accustomed. During the eighteenth century enclosure of common
lands and burgeoning industrial development had radically
altered the English countryside, and much of the Scottish landscape as well. Hardwood reserves were disastrously depleted at
home, and the loss of the American colonies had been a serious,
if temporary, setback for timber supplies, which were much
sought after for naval use in this era of colonial expansion and
European wars. Such practical concerns explain the reaction of
Thompson on seeing the forests of northwestern Montana: "Along
the [Kootenay] river, in places are very fine woods of Larch, Red
Fir, Alder, Plane and other woods. . . . I could not help thinking
what fine Timber for the Navy [is found] in these forests."[19] He
regretted that the trees were in too remote an area to be
harvested for so noble a purpose. Simpson was always impressed
by stands of "fine Timber," and he particularly admired the
mixed forests of the lower Columbia, which he described as
"extensive and beautiful with sufficient Timber for use and
Ornament."[20]

Utilitarian, if not always commercial, considerations shaped
traders' views of northwestern forests. The frequency with which
trees were called "timber" is suggestive in itself. Yet beauty is
part of the discourse as well: "use and ornament," the instrumental and the aesthetic, are bound together. As one historian of
the English landscape has demonstrated, the historical conjunction during the period between 1750 and 1830 of escalating
material demands on forest and countryside, and growing appreciation of landscape as a cultural and aesthetic object, was no
mere coincidence. Precisely at the moment when large stretches
of rural landscape were being drastically marked by historical
change, came the "dramatic aesthetic and cultural discovery of

the countryside on the part of the middle class." Painters, poets, guidebook writers, politicians, gardeners, and others offered up nature, embodied in an idealized English countryside, in all manner of forms.[21] Political ends were served, as the English oak was once more figured as an icon of national identity.[22] This social response to the loss of forest and recognizable rural space evokes a familiar pattern of "imaginative recovery," the process by which the lost is reproduced in the imagination. British traders in the Northwest went through their own processes of imaginative recovery, as will be seen later in the chapter.

For the moment, according to the instrumental line of reasoning, trees were "timber." Apart from their value as building materials, they could also be indicators of beaver country. In the eastern Shuswap region, Ross noted the presence of poplars and other soft wood, "and wherever that timber and water were plenty there were beaver." The banks of the Grand Ronde River near Cayuse territory were "covered in particular Spots with dwarf Cottonwood, and the residue in a large and thick growth of Willows which afford an inexhaustible stock of Food for the incredible multitudes of the Furred race who reside in their bosoms."[23]

Densely wooded country, on the other hand, was judged as scarce in animals as was the treeless plain. Ross found little of redeeming value in the "impervious" forests of the Cascade foothills. Here the forest was enemy. In the area west of the Methow River, where Ross and a Native guide became lost, the earth appeared undisturbed; fallen timber and decayed vegetation lay thick on the ground. It did not look to Ross as though "the fire ever passed in this place."[24] This would appear to be a reference to the indigenous practice of controlled burning to remove undergrowth. This method kept areas where people regularly travelled or hunted open and "parklike," in the European estimation, and provided browse for wildlife (see chapter 6). Ross and his guide seem to have been wandering in country seldom used by the people of the region.

Trees and grasses also indicated the state of the soil. The agricultural potential of the countryside—the essence of "improvability"—was a recurring theme in traders' writings. Thompson was so struck by the extensive meadows lining the present-day Tobacco River in northern Idaho that he called it the "Fine Meadow River," and he planted garden seeds there.[25] After a month of travels in the vicinity of Salish House and the Flathead River (map 1), "the impression of my mind is, from the formation of the country and it's [sic] climate, it's extensive Meadows and fine Forests . . . that it will become the abode of civilized Man, whether Natives or other people; part of it will bear rich crops of grain, the greater part will be pastoral, as it is admirably adapted to the rearing of Cattle and Sheep."[26] Clearly, in Thompson's mind agricultural and pastoral use was the higher purpose for which the land was intended. Contemporary Native uses—gathering, fishing, hunting—failed to exploit its potential (although note that Thompson finds the people improvable as well). Landscapes untouched by European hands were defined by their potential.

Thompson's most extensive observations on agricultural potential are found in his published Narrative (written about 1840), so that it might be said he was merely commenting on developments already under way, or tailoring his observations to his audience. But he did fairly frequently note such prospects in his daily journals, no doubt reflecting the problems with food supply that had plagued him on his early travels. The entry in his notebook for June 18, 1811, as he travelled up the Colville valley toward Kettle Falls, is as explicit as that in the Narrative: "[t]he ground of the day seems very fit for cultivation, black deep mould and the higher Ground a kind of black gray greasy Earth."[27]

When he reached the Columbia District for the first time in the autumn of 1824, Governor Simpson's first priority was "oeconomy." Convinced that the district had from the day of its founding been "neglected, shamefully mismanaged and a scene of the most wasteful extravagance," he swiftly set about a program of rationalization.[28] A key element of the governor's plan was to develop agriculture at the posts in order to eliminate the need for expensive imported provisions. Given this preoccupation, Simpson was as likely to perceive the countryside in terms of its agricultural as its fur potential. Kettle Falls, for example, presented itself as a place where "as much Grain and potatoes may be raised as would feed all the Natives of the Columbia and a sufficient number of Cattle and Hogs to supply his Majestys [sic] Navy with Beef and Pork." On his second visit, after reporting on the "immediate business" of the fur trade at Fort Colville, which was set on a terrace above Kettle Falls, Simpson reported that while the place was hardly feeding the navy, its gardens were supplying grain for the whole Interior. On Simpson's final visit in 1841, the sight of Fort Colvile inspired pride: there was "a regular farm, with barn stalls etc., and several fine fields of corn which were under the hands of the reapers, there were others of Indian corn, potatoes &c &c, and fine herds of cattle grazing in various directions."[29]

District reports from HBC posts reveal the central importance of "the Nature of the Country Soil and Vegetable productions." This section of the report preceded even the category "Animals Fur Bearing." The landscape near Thompson's River was described as mountainous, and "[w]here the country happens to present of a more uniform appearance very little can be said in favour of the Soil." Gardens might be made where streams had deposited richer soil, but in general, "the intense heat and constant drough [sic] of the Summer are much against cultivation in the interior of the Columbia." The country around Walla Walla was described as "a Barren Waste covered in a kind of rough short Heath Grass Shrubbery etc.," where the soil was a rough sand mixed with clay and appeared "scorched by summer heat, drought." In fact, the drought perhaps more than the soil was the cause of the "unfitness for Agriculture."[30]

"Dread of Starvation"

Nature's provision of food was always a major concern for fur traders. It is not surprising that this was so in the early days of the trade in the Interior, before supply routes were worked out and gardens and farms were developed to supplement country produce.[31] The preoccupation with food is especially clear in Thompson's early journals. During his first season west of the Rockies in Kutenai territory, he and his party "tried several Methods to procure Food, but all had failed us." Living on berries and too weak to travel in the hilly country, Thompson was forced to "lay aside all Thoughts of Discovery for the present and bend my whole aim to an establishment for Trade &c."[32]

Thompson was quite exceptional among fur traders in that under the most trying circumstances he remained a keen observer of the landscape. Others embellished their original field notes and journals for publication, playing to the contemporary taste of British readers for landscape tours. There are passages in Thompson's original journals that rival the best of the published accounts. In the midst of "anxious thoughts" about whether he had found the Columbia (he had), how to find food, and whether the skins of mountain goats and lynx might prove lucrative on the European market, Thompson penned a long description of the valley of the Upper Columbia. West of Howse Pass, "Beaver seem to be plenty and the River, Islands and Valley seem expressly made for them. Of the Animals there are a few Bears and others, a few Red Deer and a small sort of Chevreuil [white-tail deer], one of whom 10 Men will very well eat at a Meal."[33] On the south, as Thompson approached Columbia Lake (source of the river), the woods opened out to reveal small meadows. The terrain

> soon becomes open clear Ground for Horses, bearing plenty of good Grass . . . the Spot that any Person is in, is a fine Meadow of Hill and valley and Gullies, with Hemlock planted upon it as

it were for Shelter against the Heat and bad weather, all the rest of the Country to the Spectator appears a thick Forest, but as he advances, he constantly finds the same open Meadows, which become more and more Spacious, as one proceeds to the southward, and the Red Deer and small Chevreuil becomes more and more plenty.[34]

It was in this setting that Thompson built Kootenay House (map 1). Availability of food was clearly a factor, but for many other reasons the place invited habitation. However, Thompson's experiences during the first winter at Kootenay House did not conform to his expectations. Nor did they fit with the view, apparently widely held east of the mountains, that on crossing the Continental Divide, one would find "a warm climate, and a fine country where all his troubles are at an end."[35] Even in as favorable a setting as the "fine Meadow" around Kootenay House, a subtle anxiety underlay traders' writings—an anxiety about their ability to survive in the alien landscape.

Food was a preoccupation for Cox and his colleagues in Salish Flathead country in 1812. It was in short supply during several days' travel through dense woods. As he emerged into the Bitterroot valley, Cox's description of the scene was colored by thoughts of the next meal: here were "undulating meadows, thinly wooded, in which our hunters killed some deer." Farther north, on the Thompson River, Finan McDonald could find solace in the "Cursed" place in the fact that the river was "alived [sic] with Salmon." Several years later at Spokane House, however, McDonald had had enough of the country west of the mountains. The problem, as phrased in his broad Scots brogue, was that the place was "gateing short for Pravesion [provisions]."[36]

Food remained a principal concern in the later years of the NWC's tenure on the Columbia. The only thing resembling a description of the country, in a letter written by Ross at the time of the founding of Fort Nez Percés (1818–19), is his remark that the area is "renowned for its number of Horses," the staple food of traders there. Ross would soon learn that horses were, in fact, in short supply. The demands of the local Native people were so great that few were available to traders, who were "often at a nonplus to find a supper for our people."[37]

Shortages of horses for the growing transport needs of Interior posts and trapping expeditions continued throughout the HBC years, and on Governor Simpson's orders, Walla Walla turned to salmon as its staple. This did not sit well with the traders. Chief Trader Samuel Black in the mid-1820s found himself in "dread of starvation" for lack of a reliable supply. The Columbia could certainly provide plenty. Black's problems arose from the reluctance of the local people to provision the post, and his own failure to equip his men to trade for salmon at The Dalles.[38]

Traders were impressed with the abundance of salmon in the Columbia and the Fraser and some of the smaller rivers. The Columbia provided Native groups with "abundant provision at little trouble for a great part of the year." During a good salmon run on the Fraser, a Native "hand expert" could pull in two to three hundred fish in a night. Runs were not so bountiful every year, however. In the case of a restricted run, like the early Fraser runs of 1843, a trader like Donald Manson might grow desperate: "we know not what to do, our sole dependence is on the Fraser."[39] At the best of times Columbia traders were not fond of a salmon diet. "God help him that passes many years on such poor stuff," one would moan; another described it as "horrid" food and conducive of dire "Medicinal" effects.[40] (This perception is discussed further in chapter 5.) Like it or not, they consumed huge quantities. At Fort Okanogan in 1826 three officers, twelve men, their Native families, and a number of local people ate 18,411 dried salmon and over 700 fresh ones. The men at Kamloops were always "hammering about after salmon," making several trips a year to the Fraser for the 12,000 fish required annually by the post, because they got very little from local Native groups. The dependence of Walla Walla on salmon is reflected in Black's description of the changing of the seasons: summer arrived around the beginning of May, "when the Salmon comes up here";

autumn began about the start of September, "when Salmon is bad coming back down the river (almost dead)." This marking of the seasons appears also to be informed by indigenous customs. Black noted elsewhere that among the local peoples spring was marked as the time when roots sprout and summer was "when the Salmon come."[41]

"The Perils of Uncertain Navigation"

Every trader in the Columbia District had his tale of the horrors of travel in the region. With the hyperbole one comes to expect in his published narratives, Alexander Ross declared that "every day's duty is as full of adventure, and hardships, as it could be on a voyage of discovery even were it to the north pole."[42] The landscapes of the region impressed the traders—and in some cases were intended to impress their readers—as much for the difficulties they posed for travel as for anything else.

Of course, traders' responses to their circumstances in fur-trade country were not of a piece. This will become especially clear in the chapters to follow. In descriptions of landscape, however, their responses show a certain uniformity. The pragmatic predominated, although it did not entirely prevail. With the exception of explorers like Thompson and Fraser, most traders were guided first and foremost by their interest in collecting furs—and even these two men were more concerned with what their forebear Alexander Mackenzie called "commercial views" than with landscape views.[43] Other factors, like isolation, fear, and the desire to retrieve the landscapes of home, impinged and were expressed to varying extents. Governor Simpson seldom betrayed such sentiments, while Ross Cox openly pined for Ireland. The purposes of their texts are undoubtedly relevant here. Simpson was generally writing for the London authorities, and even in a work like his 1842 *Narrative*, ghostwritten for publication, he was not one to betray his own vulnerability. The only work we have by Cox is his *Columbia River.* It was written expressly for the

British travel-literature audience or, as he put it, "[t]hose who love
to read of 'battle, murder, and sudden death'"—and somewhat
incongruously, for "such as are fond of nature."[44]

"Battle, murder, and sudden death" were central themes in the
travel writing of the late-eighteenth and nineteenth centuries. A
publisher could scarcely afford to produce a book that ignored
the prevailing landscape aesthetics of the day and the associated
narrative conventions of the picturesque and the sublime. (For
use of similar devices in contemporary painting, see fig. 1).[45]
Traders hoping to publish their work responded to such demands
with zeal. The conventions served their own needs as well. Using
the categories of the picturesque and the sublime, they could
translate alien landscapes into a familiar idiom, or at the very
least, describe them by contrast with the familiar. It is not so
important that narratives like Cox's at times strain credulity.
What is interesting is what Cox imagined he saw, and how that
related to what he had learned to see in landscape, and what he
believed his readers wished to see.

The classic accounts of "the perils of uncertain navigation"[46] in
the Plateau are tales of river travel. Simon Fraser's account of a
passage of the Fraser River north of present-day Lillooet is rich
in the sublime. All hands embarked,

> a corp perdu [à corps perdu, recklessly] upon the mercy of this
> Stygian tide. Once engaged the die was cast, and the great
> difficulty consisted in keeping the canoes in the medium . . .
> that is to say, clear of the precipice on one side, and of the
> gulphs formed by the waves on the other. However, thus
> skimming along like lightning, the crews cool and determined,
> followed each other in awful silence. And [when] we arrived at
> the end we stood gazing on our narrow escape from perdition.[47]

Some fifteen years later, in 1824, Simpson conveniently forgot
the more harrowing aspects of this ordeal, and recalled merely
that Fraser's party "went down and returned safe." Simpson's
grand plan was to reorient the Columbia and New Caledonia

Fig. 1. *Fort Okanogan*, by John Mix Stanley. Credit: Washington State Historical Society.

Districts to the central artery of the Fraser, and to that end he
convinced himself that it was "a fine large deep navigable
River."[48] His view altered dramatically when he travelled down
the river himself in 1828. Entering the Fraser Canyon, the aspect
changed:

> The banks now erected themselves, into perpendicular Moun-
> tains of Rock from the Waters edge . . . the descent of the
> Stream very rapid, the reaches short, and at the close of many
> of them, the Rocks . . . overhanging the foaming Waters, pent
> up, to from 20 to 30 yds. wide, running with immense velocity
> and momentarily threatening to sweep us to destruction.[49]

These mountains of rock were home to "scores of Naked
Wretches," who housed themselves in "Caverns and chasms"
that seemed hardly habitable for humans: here Native people
appear as a prop, enlivening a savage landscape. This was,
Simpson concluded, no place for traders. He estimated that the
passage down would be "certain Death, in nine attempts out of
Ten," and promised to speak no more of the navigability of the
river.[50] This would have been a difficult admission for Simpson to
make. He was a fiercely competitive man and revelled in a
challenge, be it from other men or from nature. On his first trip
up the Columbia, for example, Simpson boasted of the "hard
marching" of the canoes under his supervision, and he remarked
that despite the weakened state of the crews, their pace "beats
any thing of the kind hitherto known in the Columbia."[51]

The tensions that mark Simpson's account of the Fraser River—
awe and respect for the power of nature versus frustration at its
ability to thwart human plans, and pride in human efforts to
confront that power—mark the writings of other traders as well.
Thompson, for example, was awed by the "wild scenery" of the
Columbia in the vicinity of the Wenatchee River, but he did not
trust the river. Indeed, he sensed something sinister in the rivers
west of the Rockies. On the east side, one had audible warning
when approaching falls. On the west side, "the Dalles [rapids] of

the Rivers . . . make no noise, the narrow channel between their steep walls has a treacherous smoothness which lulls suspicion until the swift current hurries the Canoe on the fatal whirlpool, and eddies from which there is no retreat."[52]

Travel overland in the Plateau could be as taxing as travel by river. Wherever possible, traders followed well-worn Native trails. But trails did not ensure an easy journey. The footpaths on the cliffs above the Fraser Canyon took Fraser and his men through places "where no human being should venture":

> Yet in those places there is a regular footpath impressed. . . .
> And besides this, steps which are formed like a ladder, or the
> shrouds of a ship, by poles hanging to one another and crossed
> at certain distances with twigs and withes, suspended from the
> top to the foot of precipices, and fastened at both ends to stones
> and trees, furnished a safe and convenient passage to the
> Natives—but we, who had not the advantages of their exper-
> ience, were often in imminent danger.[53]

Jules Quesnel, a clerk in Fraser's party, concurred that travel à pied along the Fraser entailed "Les Montagnes les Plus affreuse, et que nous n'aurions jamais pus passer si les Natifs . . . ne nous eurent aider." Robert Stuart believed the hills lining the Columbia at The Dalles "in a civilized soil would be thought nearly impassable." Even these were dwarfed by Mount Hood, which loomed above them "as a Steeple overlooking the lowest Houses of a City."[54] Here again, the landscape is made comprehensible through the idiom of the familiar, that which is manageable, tolerable. The comparison of mountain peak and urban monument is particularly intriguing. Discussing the writings of travellers to Australia in the same period, art historian Bernard Smith notes that their attempts to follow picturesque conventions were constrained by the absence of "ancient monuments [and] places hallowed by historical associations"—always key sources of romantic sentiment.[55] In Stuart's description the missing reference points are supplied by the imagination.

The perils of travel in this alien landscape multiplied when there were no obvious trails. Ross was disoriented in the country west of the Methow River, which to him was a "pathless desert." He was skeptical of his guide's insistence that they were following the trade route used by Red Fox, an Okanagan leader, to travel to the coast. Ross kept hoping for the appearance of "some sort of a road or path," and his insecurity only increased in the Cascade mountain forests, where his compass was rendered useless by the constant clambering and changing of course.[56] Ross had no control here. Without even the vague comfort offered by the needle of a compass, he was at the whim of nature and of a Native guide, and distinctly uncomfortable in that position. The deep forests on the northeastern fringe of the Plateau inspired similar sentiments in Thompson. This was wilderness in the extreme, beyond the capacity of humans to control or even to use it. In such forests, in Thompson's words, "we were pigmies [sic]; in such forests what could we do with Axes of two pounds weight." Such musings aside, there is no doubt that traders like Thompson and Ross took a certain manly pride in having travelled in such places and survived.

The Snake Country was notoriously difficult for travel. Peter Skene Ogden, leader of the Snake expeditions from 1824 to 1830, considered it "a more wretched country [than] Christian—Indian or Brute ever travell'd over or probably ever will," a country that "no other inducement but filthy Lucre can induce an honest man to visit." His depiction of the life of a Snake Country trapper is evocative:

> the life of a Trapper . . . is certainly a most laborious one and one [which] in four years makes a young man look almost as if he had reached the advanced age of sixty. . . . [T]he cold water which more or less they are wading in two thirds of the day aded [sic] to the cold and sleeping often without fire and wet to the skin conduces to ruin their constitutions[. W]ell do they earn their 10 Shillings per Beaver[. A] convict in Botany Bay is a Gent living at his ease compared to them.[57]

Chief Factor McLoughlin, too, had compassion for the Snake Country trappers, and he believed that to lead such a group— "freemen in the plains with their families starving about them"— was "the most difficult, harrassing [sic] and dangerous charge in the whole Business."[58]

Added to the Snake Country landscape of rough travel, harsh weather, and scarce food were Native people hostile to the traders. In 1829 Ogden remarked that "it is almost incredible the numbers that have fallen in it [the Snake Country]." Of the men who had joined the original North West Company expedition a decade earlier, only one remained alive; of those who died, two had died natural deaths, while the rest had been killed by "Snakes" and Blackfoot.[59] On his first expedition John Work, successor to Ogden, found himself surrounded by "great rascals"— a reference to the Snakes' propensity to pilfer the traders' horses, traps, pelts, and other possessions. Work's assessment became more severe when one of his party was killed; now he was in the midst of "very treacherous barbarous Indians." The greatest danger was in the eastern reaches of Snake Country, where traders were likely to encounter raiding parties of Blackfoot. They were always on the lookout for "marks of Blackfeet"— tracks left in the snow or dirt by these people, who had gained a reputation for taking parties of traders by surprise. "Thus are people wandering through this country in quest of beaver continually in danger of falling into the hands of these ruthless savages and certainly of losing their lives in the most barbarous manner, independent of the privations and hardships of every other kind they subject themselves to."[60]

While landscape descriptions tended to be "empty" of human traces, in cases like these Indians became part of the setting. They figured centrally in traders' perceptions of the land around Walla Walla. Ross's first impression of the area was very favorable. The Walla Walla itself was "a beautiful little river," and on the plain near its mouth were gathered about fifteen hundred Nez Percé, Cayuse, and Wallawalla, who danced and sang for the

traders "in the usual symbol of peace and friendship." The year
was 1811. In 1813, Pacific Fur Company (Astorian) traders travelling
upriver were troubled by an "unusual movement and stir" among
the groups gathered at Walla Walla. They assigned the agitation
to the hanging of a Palus man by an Astorian the previous
summer. Far from a pastoral setting, Walla Walla was now a scene
of "wild commotion." The traders fled.[61]

Later that year, on their final brigade to the Interior, the
Astorians again found Walla Walla a menacing place. There was
a "dark cloud of dust" rising near the forks. People were assembling
from a great distance, and the formerly friendly Wallawalla
leader Tummatapam warned the traders that these Indians were
"as numerous as the grains of sand" and had "bad hearts" toward
the traders.[62] Relations between the traders and the Sahaptian
peoples remained strained throughout the tenure of the North
West Company and during the HBC years. The forks became
known as "the most hostile spot on the whole communication."
HBC traders were careful not to offend these "powerful and
Warlike" groups, on whom they were utterly dependent for
horses and for safe passage to the Interior and the Snake Country.[63]
Recounting the building of Fort Nez Percés (also known as Walla
Walla), Ross described the landscape as bold and impressive.
Again, Native people were part of it: they "cover the earth in
swarms," "crowds of moving bodies enliven and diversify" the
scene.[64] Such shifting perceptions reveal the extent to which
traders' responses to landscape were contingent on their circumstances. When they were among peoples they considered hostile,
the landscape too took a hostile turn.

Landscapes of Home

The landscapes that brought most pleasure to the traders were
those most reminiscent of home. These were landscapes with a
gentle face, picturesque patchworks of "hill and dale, wood and

plains."[65] For Simpson, the site of Fort Vancouver was the essence of beauty. Here was a fine plain, watered by "two very pretty small Lakes and studed [sic] as if artificially by clumps of Fine Timber. . . . [I]ndeed I have rarely seen a Gentleman's Seat in England possessing so many natural advantages and where ornament and use are so agreeably combined."[66] Use was never far from Simpson's mind. For others, ornament had charms of its own, quite apart from utility. Places like the valley Ross described in the Snake Country, which appeared "as if set off by the hand of man," were not gardens, of course. But they were perhaps not so far from the purposely "wild" landscapes that were the rage in Britain in the late eighteenth and nineteenth centuries.[67]

Stuart found such a place in the Grand Ronde valley, where he came upon "beautifull Hills, chequered with delightful pasture ground, which when added to the Rivulets murmuring over their gravely [gravelly?] serpentine beds toward the glade below, afford a scene truly romantic and such as is seldom to be met with in these regions."[68] Plateau landscapes several times induced Cox to fall to dreaming about Ireland. On the banks of a little river north of the Palouse, he found "a delightful wilderness of crimson haw, honeysuckles, wild roses, and currants. Its resemblance to a friend's summer-house . . . brought back home with all its endearing recollections." Such comforts in an alien landscape were ephemeral. Cox awoke from his reverie to find himself alone and lost. What had been delightful was now "wild, uninhabited." Here again, the dynamic nature of landscape is exposed. Cox would not return to his friend's summer house on that trip, but he did revive his reverie while passing a season in the comfort of Spokane House. He counted this as his most pleasant time in the Columbia: "Hunting, fishing, fowling, horse-racing, and fruit gathering, occupied the day; while reading, music, backgammon, &c., formed the evening pleasures of our small but friendly mess."[69] Cox yearned not just for the countryside, but for the pleasures of the country gentleman.

Landscaping Comfort and Control: The Posts

The gardens made by traders in the Plateau had important symbolic functions, in addition to the obvious practical purposes. Gardens were an expression of human control over nature, or at least over a patch of it. Agriculture was an art of "Civilized men."[70] The practice of this higher art was a key element distinguishing these white, British men from the "rude" hunter-gatherers in whose midst they dwelt. The marking of such boundaries between themselves and the "wilderness," including its inhabitants, was an important device of self-definition in a setting which threatened the traders' identities and, at times, their survival. Boundaries were most tangible at company posts. However, it was here that the ambiguity of the search for boundaries was most clearly revealed. Traders would retreat behind the walls, hoping to leave drought-stricken plains, perilous rivers, and unfriendly Indians behind. But the refuge they sought to construct was rooted in a cultural and political setting shot through with the antagonisms of ethnicity, class, and gender.[71] And there was a profound ambivalence at the heart of the project. As noted earlier, virtually every officer in the Columbia, and most servants, had Native or métis wives and families. They shared the space inside the post walls with these families, and to varying extents, with others of the Native people on whom their livelihoods depended.

Company posts were always enclosed within protective walls. According to Ross, the usual NWC post was surrounded by walls some three to five meters in height. At Walla Walla, the North Westers took precautions that Ross believed to be more characteristic of the HBC.[72] A formidable structure was needed to protect traders and to achieve the intended result: the taming of the "many war-like tribes that infest the country." Fort Walla Walla was the only NWC post protected by a double wall; Native traders were admitted through the outer wall and had to conduct trade through a small aperture in the inner one, which shielded the company dwellings and storehouse. The whole was surrounded by six-meter palisades and fortified towers, and was defended with cannons and muskets. Ross's enthusiasm at the building of Fort Walla Walla exposes the symbolic function of such a structure (for the traders, at least).[73] Dubbed "the Gibraltar of the Columbia," it kept "savagery" at bay: "as if by enchantment, the savage disposition of the Indians was either soothed or awed, a stronghold had arisen in the desert, while the British banner floating over it proudly proclaimed the mistress of a vast territory; it was an example of British energy and enterprise, of civilization over barbarism."[74]

The imperial message is loud and clear—and surely tailored to Ross's intended Victorian readership. Britannia prevails, and does so over a race that may be martial and powerful but is at base savage; the remark that the Indians are perhaps "soothed" by this assertion of British power even hints that they are aware of their own inferiority. A distinctly masculine discourse is embedded in and inseparable from the imperial. The warlike tribes are subdued by the appearance of this hulking fortress, and British traders have proved their worth, both as traders and as men. They have prevailed over the threat from these potential enemies, exhibiting their manliness in the very act of erecting the fort. It stands as a symbol of their "energy and enterprise," ultimate masculine virtues in the idioms of early-nineteenth-century capitalism and the fur trade alike. The passage is a superb—and superbly self-conscious—example of how the traders went about landscaping control.

As it turned out, such control over these groups was elusive. Ross soon resumed complaining about the "insolence" of the people around Walla Walla. His successors had similar difficulties. Simon McGillivray, chief trader at Walla Walla in 1831–32, found those before him had set the precedent of allowing "principal men" into the gentlemen's house. McGillivray, an irascible and embittered character, was determined to put an end to such uninvited guests. Apparently he never did effect the change. Several years later, Chief Trader Pierre Pambrun, who got along with the local people rather better than McGillivray did, was still entertaining them in company quarters.[75] Such gestures of goodwill were essential to the smooth operation of the trade, as will be demonstrated in later chapters. The presence of Native people at the posts was also inevitable in light of the traders' reliance on their labor for odd jobs, and for longer-term occupations such as horse tending. For a variety of reasons the ideal of separating the predominantly white from the Native sphere by means of a six-meter-high wall was never realized.

Most traders did not wish such a separation. Myriad sources reveal the importance familial attachments had for the traders, for economic and diplomatic purposes, and not least for the "many tender ties" that helped to soften life at the fur-trade posts.[76] Family life provided respite from the monotony and trials of fur-trade country. As George Barnston, a long-time Columbia trader observed, as long as there was love "within doors . . . many a bitter blast may be born from without." Archibald McDonald wrote warmly of the "delightful confusion" of his houseful of children, and John Work called his little ones "almost the only pleasure I have."[77]

Officers in the Columbia generally made some effort to acculturate their families to British ways, perhaps mainly because they hoped eventually to take them out to Red River, Canada, or even to Britain. Two years after the union of the companies, the Council of the Northern Department introduced regulations to facilitate the process of "civilization and moral improvement" of families attached to the posts. Every man, woman, and child was to be required to attend Sunday divine service, along with any Native people on hand or "whom it may be proper to invite." During the week women and children were to be given appropriate "useful occupation . . . best calculated to suppress vicious and promote virtuous habits." Fathers were ordered to speak to their families in English or French rather than Indian languages, and to spend part of their leisure time teaching their children.[78]

The posts were to be places of proper British morality and industry.

It is impossible to tell from the available records to what extent these moral "improvements" were effected in the Interior. Physical arrangements are more accessible. Not only racial but also class hierarchies were encoded in the arrangement of social space in fur-trade country. Provisions to accommodate the gentlemen, and to distinguish them from the servant class, were highly formalized. The new post built at Okanogan in 1816 was a typical smaller Columbia post. Despite its modest size, it was designed as something of a sanctuary—if not exactly a haven of civility, at least a retreat. Within the "strong palisades fifteen feet high" was a house for the gentleman and his family, comprising four rooms and a spacious dining hall. (There was generally only one gentleman at Okanogan, often a clerk, although officers from passing brigades and their families would come to stay.) There were two smaller houses for the servants, one of which may have been shared by married servants and their families, and the other by bachelors. Finally, there was a storehouse for furs and trade goods, and a trading shop.[79]

Research from other regions of the fur trade indicates that the early nineteenth century was a period of hardening social distinctions in housing at Hudson's Bay Company establishments as elsewhere. Whereas in the eighteenth century tradesmen (the "labor aristocracy" of the fur trade) and laborers had generally lived together in barracks-style accommodations, where the laborers even shared beds, by the early 1800s there was a movement toward smaller, more stratified dwellings for all classes. At least at larger establishments, tradesmen and laborers came to be housed in separate buildings. Similarly, married and unmarried men of the different occupational classes were housed separately. And whereas senior and junior officers had often shared a single officers' bastion, senior officers now enjoyed detached residences. Married tradesmen and laborers, by contrast, were forced to keep their families in cabins on the periphery of the establishment.[80]

The advent of private family dwellings for the elite of the fur trade echoed developments in middle-class housing in Britain at the time. As Leonore Davidoff and Catherine Hall have shown, acquisition of a comfortable private home was the "utmost ambition" of middle-class families by the turn of the nineteenth century. Not only was the home a symbol of status, proof that one had arrived; it was a sanctuary from external pressures. The home constituted one of the most powerful "shields" available to the prosperous, a shield that took a practical as well as a symbolic form in the house and garden "and in the organization of the immediate environment through behaviour, speech and dress."[81] Housing, dress, and social behavior functioned in parallel ways at fur-trade posts, where the alien environment and peoples were perceived as threats to the civilized white order and added to the class and gender pressures of daily working life.

Officers set themselves apart in dress by ordering goods tailor-made from Britain or local post tailors. Until early in the nineteenth century, the special-occasion dress of company officers in fur-trade country echoed the flamboyant formal dress of British men of business, running to lace collars and cuffs, silk waistcoats, and long coats. By then officers' dress was undergoing a dramatic change in line with the shift in British middle- and professional-class dress, to reflect a growing concern with industry and occupation rather than conspicuous virility.[82] Francis Heron's 1834 order for Petersham cloth captures the nature of the change in fur-trade country. The cloth, a thick-ribbed silk or cotton, was to be "bottle green," a shade a tad loud for contemporary business sensibilities. But he would have it made into a fashionable frock coat with "two rows of ball buttons," trousers, and a vest, in place of the breeches and ruffled long coat of former days.[83] Tradesmen and laborers, meanwhile, received their basic items (cotton shirts and a few yards of common cloth) as part of their salary. This in itself became a social statement: the year after union, the Council of the Northern Department declared that the NWC practice of issuing clothing to officers was to be discontinued, as it was "derogatory to the dignity of the Chief Factors and Chief Traders" to be treated like servants in this way.[84]

Dining arrangements, too, offered an ideal opportunity for the display of social rank. It was customary for gentlemen and servants to dine separately. Ross considered the rituals of the dining hall a peculiarity of the class-conscious North Westers. At Columbia headquarters, "strict rules of subordination" applied, such that in the dining hall, "you take your seat, as a Chinese Mandarine [sic] would take his dress, according to your rank." Even the common beverage was class specific: there were three grades of China leaf tea, and as many of sugar. Gender segregation was also ritualized, the women and children eating on their own, after the men.[85] Whether this latter was a reflection of traditions in Native households, or of the quasi-military arrangement of the posts, is unclear. In any case, such practices were far more widespread than Ross intimated. As should be apparent by now, the HBC had its own provisions for social sorting and took the matter very seriously. In the same statement in which it denounced the issuing of clothing to officers, the Council decreed that in order to "draw a line of distinction" between servants and gentlemen, a prohibition had been issued on guides and interpreters dining with the officers. These men were in the upper ranks of the servant class, but they tended to be French Canadian or Native. Their occasional presence in the gentlemen's hall had apparently become a threat. Women and children continued to eat separately as well, although this practice gradually disappeared at many posts.[86]

Not only did the gentlemen "mess" separately, they messed more graciously than servants. Governor Simpson was astounded at the level of luxury achieved at Spokane House, where five or six boatloads of "Eatables Drinkables and other *Domestic Comforts*" were consumed annually. A similar situation prevailed at other Interior posts, such that thirty-five to forty men were employed in transporting goods from the coast in order to "accommodate Gentlemen in this manner."[87]

Simpson's "oeconomy" agenda put an end to the import of many luxury goods. But sufficient vestiges of civility remained to ensure a measure of comfort for HBC officers. It was taken as a matter of course that fresh meat, unless plentiful, was reserved for the gentlemen and their families. Thus John Tod's oblivion to the irony in his journal entry from Kamloops, recording that some Native hunters brought in fresh venison and an "old lame horse" was killed "as beef for the men." Consumption figures for Fort Okanogan in 1826 indicate the general pattern. The three gentlemen at the post and their families (three women and two children) consumed 799 pounds of venison, compared with just 344 pounds for twelve servants (their families were listed separately).[88]

While the HBC records provide few details on the lifestyles of the gentlemen, orders for Delft pottery, wine glasses, silver teaspoons, chocolate, and silk handkerchiefs provide some insight.[89] So does American visitor Thomas Jefferson Farnham's 1839 description of the dining hall at Fort Vancouver:

> At the end of a table twenty feet in length stands Governor McLaughlin [Chief Factor John McLoughlin], directing guests and gentlemen from neighbouring posts to their places, at distances from the Governor according to their rank in the service. . . . Roast beef and port, boiled mutton, baked salmon, boiled ham; beets, carrots, turnips, cabbage and potatoes, and wheaten bread, are tastefully distributed over the table among a dinner-set of elegant queen's ware, burnished with glittering glasses and decanters of various colored Italian wines.[90]

As historian Tina Loo points out, such ritual display accomplished more than the marking of social boundaries. The strict hierarchy of post society was central to the regulation of the fur-trade labor force. At the same time as such ritual reinforced the authority of the officers, it provided constant reminders to the laboring men of their appropriate station in the social structure. McLoughlin's place at the head of the table reiterated his place at the helm of the company in the Columbia, and his paternal role in relation to his men. The rituals of everyday life, as much as any other aspect of corporate structure, "went a fair distance to ordering [company] workers," even before they were subjected to the corporal punishment to which officers often resorted.[91]

Landscaping the Wilds: Wild Animals

At the newly fortified Fort Okanogan in 1816, Cox perceived no threat from the local people, whom he described as "an honest, quiet tribe," if "slothful." It was the rattlesnakes that concerned Cox. His map of the area reflects his preoccupation. The peninsula on which the fort stands is labelled "Oakinagan Point / All Prairie ground and / no Rattlesnakes." There is a small diagram of the fort, but the only other features marked, besides the rivers and a row of hills, are the "Plains/Rattlesnakes."[92] For Cox, it seems, Fort Okanogan functioned principally as a refuge from rattlesnakes.

Cox found snakes under every rock. In the back country between the Snake River and Spokane House, "as far as the eye extended, nothing was visible but immense plains covered with parched brown grass, swarming with rattlesnakes." He endowed the snakes with an aggressive, vindictive nature. In a typical encounter, he was about to lie down for the night when "a rattlesnake coiled, with the head erect, and the forked tongue extended in a state of frightful oscillation." As he always did, Cox destroyed the snake with a stick, but not before discovering several dozen more under the rocks. Visions of these creatures, together with "the howling of wolves and the growling of bears," plagued his disturbed imagination.[93]

For Ross wolves were the great menace. They serve in his narrative the function of rattlesnakes in Cox's: cruel and cunning, they were for Ross the corporeal manifestation of the cruelty of the place. They could wreak havoc on a herd of horses, particularly in crusty snow, which trapped the horses and left them vulnerable to attack. By Ross's account, wolves were the bane of both Indians and whites at Okanogan. He was skeptical when an

Okanagan chief warned him that a "great band of strange wolves" was approaching the area, that these wolves had already slaughtered thousands of horses, and that "none can escape them." He assured the chief that the traders' guns would take care of the vermin.[94] Ross clearly revelled in the power of firearms in the wilds. Guns allowed the traders physical dominance over the wolves (within limits), and a symbolic dominance over the Indians, who, according to Ross, were awed by this technology. After killing a wolf at a distance that he claimed to be equal to five arrow shots, the trader enthused that "nothing but [the Indians'] wonder could exceed their admiration of this effect of firearms."[95]

Ye-whell-come-tetsa, a prominent Okanagan leader, appears in Ross's narrative thanking him for his assistance and proclaiming "we have nothing to fear. . . . I shall always love the whites."[96] Here the trader triumphs over the Indians. In trader discourse, the manly power of the Indians was always constrained by the assertion that they lacked certain attributes that only the traders could supply. Nature was cruel, and the wolf cruelest, but in British technology lay the seeds of control.

In fact, control over the wolf proved elusive. Guns were no match for stealth. The wolves attacked at night, killing five of the company's horses. Ross turned to steel traps, and was horrified at the result. One trap held only a large foot, gnawed off by its owner. Another trap had disappeared, and a third held a wolf by the foreleg. Ross had never seen a more "ferocious" animal. It did not try to flee, but "on the contrary, now and then it sprang forward to get at us with its mouth wide open, teeth all broken, and its head covered with blood." Two shots finished off the huge animal. Ross then set off after the wolf that had escaped with a trap. He pursued it for more than six hours, and finally with his "faithful and trusty rifle arrested his career."[97]

Ross's description of the wolf's mode of attack conveys the evil he ascribed to these animals. The pack leaders approached the prey:

in the most playful and caressing manner . . . until the too
credulous and unsuspecting victim is completely off his guard
by curiosity and familiarity. During this time the gang squatted
on their hindquarters, looking on at a distance. After some time
spent in this way, the two assailants separate; when one
approaches the horse's head, the other his tail, with a slyness
and cunning peculiar to themselves . . . the hind one never lets
go till the horse is completely disabled. . . . The sinews are cut,
and in half the time I have been telling it, the horse is on his
side, his struggles are fruitless, the victory is won. . . . The
wolves, however, do not always kill to eat; wasteful hunters,
they often kill for the pleasure of killing.

Ross was oblivious to the irony of his later remark that traders,
too, hunted wolves, foxes, and other "wild animals" for "leisure."[98]

Wherever they were present in the fur-trade domain, wolves
were viewed as a menace to be destroyed.[99] Figures for the North
West Company era are not available, but fur returns for the HBC
years reveal a steady increase in wolf kills from 1827 onward. In
that year five wolf pelts were traded, and no doubt some larger
number were destroyed as vermin. In 1831, when the Interior
network of posts was well established, nearly five hundred wolf
pelts were traded. The number continued to climb, to a high of
some sixteen hundred pelts in 1847. Hunting of wolves achieved
the dual purpose of controlling a pest destructive to the interests
of the concern and providing limited returns in the marketplace.
The coyote, on the other hand, was merely reviled as a pest. As
Cox noted, traders did not "waste much powder and ball" in
hunting coyotes. These were the quintessential vermin of the
Columbia. They were numerous and destructive, on occasion
killing horses, but their pelts were worthless. Neither the traders
nor, according to Cox, Native hunters were willing to waste
ammunition "on objects that bring no remunerating value."[100]

Every group has its own "classificatory map" of the animals
among which it exists—which ones are commodities, which
vermin, which wild, domestic, or pets.[101] The traders' map was

complex and shifting. "Wild" animals could provoke unyielding hostility, as wolves and coyotes did, but that might be leavened with a measure of respect. Wild creatures were routinely designated for treatment the traders were loath to inflict on domesticated ones. At the outset, few gentlemen of the trade would willingly eat horse. Horses were a privileged species in British society, with a place rather closer to humans than many other domestic animals. It was simply uncivilized to contemplate consuming them. Donald McKenzie, the first British trader to travel deep into the Nez Percé and Snake countries, was scorned by his colleagues at headquarters as a man "only fit to eat horse flesh and shoot at a mark."[102]

In time, however, necessity made horse the staple food of traders in these regions. Cox confessed that he and those in his party initially found the idea of feasting on "so useful and noble an animal" repugnant. Hunger soon overcame these "little qualms of civilization." It is an intriguing irony that tame horses were preferred to wild:

> The flesh of those which are tame, well-fed, and occasionally worked, is tender and firm, and the fat hard and white. It is far superior to the wild horse, the flesh of which is loose and stringy. . . . We generally killed the former for our own table; and I can assure my readers, that if they sat down to a fat rib, or a rump-steak off a well-fed four-year-old, without knowing the animal, they would imagine themselves regaling on a piece of prime ox beef.[103]

Ross, too, was fully prepared to eat horse when there was no alternative. But he could not account for those who, offered buffalo meat, fowl, fish, or venison, actually chose horse. Still more incomprehensible was the habit of the French Canadians to "leave their rations of good venison and eat dogs' flesh!" The only explanation was that such people were "habituated" to the country and lived "almost as Indians," eating whatever came to hand. At times all the traders lived so, but there is a clear social distinction implicit in Ross's remark that "some [do so] from choice, others from necessity."[104] Necessity apparently absolved gentlemen traders of the guilt to which they might otherwise be subject.

So if eating horse was immoral, eating dog was far worse. Here again, a complex mix of sentiments came into play. Cox was appalled when he learned that several traders had breakfasted on Ponto, Robert Stuart's pet English spaniel. Among the officers who partook was Stuart himself. Cox could not account for it, "seeing there was no necessity to justify the murder of a *civilized* dog, while several of those which had been purchased at Oakinagan still remained untouched."[105] Indian dogs, pets or not, were fair game: "their keen eyes, sharp noses, and pointed upright ear, proclaim their wolfish origin, and fail to enlist our sympathies in their behalf." The killing of a "civilized" dog, by contrast, was murder. A dog's status mirrored that of its owner in this discourse. The owner in this instance rationalized the deed as a consequence of necessity: provisions were short. Cox was not convinced, given the availability of other dog meat. Perhaps the intimation was that Stuart had degenerated, had crossed the bounds of civility and was using need, an acceptable motive in the context of life in the wilderness, to justify an unacceptable act. Clearly, Stuart's dog had moved from one classificatory map to another, from pet to provision. Dog was never the chosen fare of gentlemen, but in time of need the traders swallowed their distaste and joined the Canadians in the repast. The bounds of acceptability in all this were indistinct. Even for Cox, things were not clear-cut. Tame horses were fine, but breakfasting on a pet spaniel was beyond the pale.[106]

Clever Beavers and Concluding Remarks

Many traders professed a deep respect for the beaver, the animal whose slaughter provided their livelihood. After describing methods of hunting the animal, and the flavor of its flesh,

Thompson turned to its "sagacity." Beaver dams were so cleverly constructed that no amount of water could damage them, whereas those erected "by the art of Man"—apparently a lesser art—were frequently washed away. Cox saw little need to comment on the beavers' "dexterity in cutting down trees, their skill in constructing their houses, and their foresight in collecting and storing provisions"; these things were well known to lovers of natural history. He was moved to comment on their social organization of labor, however: nothing could be more "wonderful," he suggested, than the skill and patience shown by parties of twenty or thirty beaver coming together to build their winter lodges. A few of the older animals superintended the felling of trees and processing of logs, "and it is no unusual sight to see them beating those who exhibit any symptoms of laziness. Should, however, any fellow be incorrigible . . . he is driven unanimously by the whole tribe to seek shelter and provisions elsewhere." Such outcasts Native people called "lazy beaver," according to Cox. They were condemned to a winter of hunger, and as a result their fur was not half as valuable as that of those whose "persevering industry and *prévoyance*" assured them of protection from the elements.[107]

The specifics of this anthropomorphization are intriguing. The traits celebrated in the beaver, industry and providence, are the very ones traders considered to be lacking in the indigenous peoples of the region; this is the main theme of the next chapter. The central paradox is that the traders' admiration for the beaver coexisted with—one might even say masked—the most predatory intentions. The paradox is emblematic of the contradictions that characterized traders' responses to the land.

CHAPTER FOUR

Traders and Fishers

Tales of the State of Nature

British fur traders arrived in the "unhallowed wilderness" of the Plateau to find the peoples of the region living by fishing, gathering, and hunting—living, as one trader phrased it, in a "rude state of nature."[1] As the discussion in this and subsequent chapters reveals, traders' ideas about what constituted this state turned on a complex interweaving of material and moral concerns. Even by the most mundane of material measures, all Plateau peoples were not created equal. Traders elaborated a ranking of relative wealth in which, in essence, those groups they called the "salmon tribes" were the poor and the "hunters" were the rich. And as they focused on the hard surfaces of life—methods of subsistence, food, clothing—the traders' "data collection" was mediated by a structure of ideas and values derived from their own society, mediated in turn by their rather extraordinary experiences in fur-trade country. Assessments of relative poverty and wealth, molded as they were by fur-trade concerns, were bound up with more nebulous notions of morality and vice, status and disrepute, proper manhood, and the like. The categories shifted, and were at times subtly redefined, as relations with the Native societies evolved, and as traders came and went, over the course of the Columbia fur trade.

British traders viewed Plateau societies across a frontier not only of culture, but of gender and class. Their privileging of men's activities—in particular hunting—had profound implications for their understanding of the roles of women, and as a result for their understanding of indigenous food-production systems as a whole. By underestimating women's contributions and disparaging the foods the women produced, traders disparaged the entire Native economy. Believing the societies they encountered to be largely dependent on fish and game, they were blind to the diversity and flexibility of Plateau economies. Such biases persist in many scholarly interpretations of Native American systems of production, down to the present day. In this chapter I explore traders' representations of the fishing way of life in the Plateau, exploring how these texts were shaped by culture, gender, and to a lesser extent, class—and how the representations were, at times, reformed by the encounter.

"To Indulge Their Sloth"

Indolence was the defining feature of the rude state of nature in which the fishing peoples of the Plateau were said to dwell. Traders used the term with abandon in their depictions of these groups. The concept was freighted with cultural meaning. Yet while it was often framed in terms of inherited ideas about the moral propriety of hard work, the principal subtext in trader discourse was "too indolent to hunt." Catching and preserving salmon were no heroic endeavors in the traders' eyes. They might be impressed by the skills fishermen displayed, or the novelty of their methods, but in general they expressed little admiration for those who made their living in this way.

Indolence had not always been the favored explanation for the failure of Interior peoples to hunt. In the early days of European exploration and trade in the region, David Thompson was convinced that these fisher-gatherers were "not willingly confined to the banks of the River"; they would hunt if they had the wherewithal.[2] Thompson's view was undoubtedly influenced by his sojourn among Woodland and buffalo-hunting peoples east of the mountains, for whom meat was a major resource. Such experience fostered and reinforced what became a common perception following the encounter of Europeans and Native peoples on the plains: "real" Indians rode on horseback and hunted big game. This theme is explored at length in chapter 7.

Thompson's belief that indigenous people did not willingly rely on fish as a staple was widely shared. The example of the "Snare Indians," the North Thompson Secwepemc, was held up as evidence that Natives would become hunters if supplied with material means and encouragement. These Secwepemc, Thompson reported, had been driven by the Blackfoot from their accustomed hunting grounds in the Rocky Mountain parklands to an area of the northern Plateau where "they contrive to snare chance animals in the narrow confines of the mountains"; by the traders' reckoning, only necessity made fish their staple. The Wallawalla provided further evidence. They were mostly fishermen, but there were hunters among them, "i.e. those rich enough to have Horses Guns and Ammunition." The peoples around Spokane were said to live chiefly on fish for the reason that large mammals were too scarce in the area to form "any material part of [their] food."[3] Traders' initial explanations for the failure of Columbia peoples to rely more heavily on the chase tended to focus on such environmental and technological factors. As time went on and they faced the reality that many groups in the region took little interest in the offerings of the fur trade, continuing instead to favor fishing and other accustomed pursuits, an alternative explanation was invoked. Fishing Indians were indolent.

The equation of hunting with exertion and fishing with sloth is very clear in traders' accounts from the Interior. Alexander Ross captured the contrast in his portrayal of the "War-are-reekas," the salmon-fishing Northern Shoshone of the Snake Country. In contrast to the "real" Shoshone, who "live in the plains hunting the buffalo" and were bold, rich, and attractive, the fishing peoples were "corpulent, slovenly, and indolent." Authentic Indians, apparently, hunted big game. It was believed that the Sanpoil lived in less bountiful country than that of the

Northern Shoshone and therefore they could not aspire to corpulence. Yet they were certainly judged to be lazy, living by fishing and "addicted" to gambling, which got in the way of work. The Okanagan shared the "addiction" and were "slothful." Their principal occupations were the catching and curing of salmon; only occasionally did they hunt deer and trap beaver. At Fort Colville in 1830, Francis Heron found that Native people with a good supply of dried salmon were given to "lounging about the premises" in winter, feasting and smoking tobacco. Quiet and untroublesome as they were, "still, as they are not in the way of hunting furs . . . the sight of them is nowise agreeable." Nevertheless, Heron could sympathize with the rationale: they "prefer remaining quiet and feeding well to hunting for animals with empty bellies."[4]

On his first visit to the region, Governor Simpson, ever the uncompromising businessman, dismissed all the peoples living along the Columbia as "indolent and lazy to an extreme." The source of the vice was clear to him: the river and root grounds provided such abundant food supplies that these groups had no need to hunt, whether for their own provision or for the fur trade. What was more, they had shown little interest in European goods, and only occasionally trapped a few beaver—an activity which, he sardonically noted, they considered "a wonderful exertion"— in order to get tobacco, guns, ammunition, and beads. The governor concluded that if these groups would "but apply themselves to Hunting" in the back country during the winter, the Columbia trade would be greatly improved. Simpson's 1829 visit confirmed his low opinion of the Interior groups. Those in the Thompson River district were "exceedingly indolent," depending on the river and roots for their livelihood. Those around Fort Nez Percés were "a bold Warlike race [who] do little else than rove about in search of Scalps, plunder and amusement"; the post brought in a limited supply of furs, and those mostly from the Cayuse.[5]

At the same time as traders censured "sedentary" fishing communities for their indolence, they would admit that settlement and an end to the "roving" lifestyle was a prerequisite to "civilization" of the Indian.[6] Traders, of course, were not particularly concerned about civilizing anyone. While sedentary Indians presented a more fertile field of opportunity for missionaries, roving hunters (although not those as independent as the Nez Percé) better answered fur traders' needs.

Simpson's dismissal of so many of the Interior peoples reflected his frustration at the limited fur returns of the region. The entire Columbia Department, which included all the territories west of the Rockies, accounted for an average of just 8 percent of total HBC fur exports from North America between 1825 and 1849. Granted, the department's share of the total increased markedly during that period, but the increase was in large part a result of the expansion of trade on the Northwest Coast, in combination with the steady contraction of returns from east of the mountains.[7] Taken together, the districts of the Columbia Interior—Fort Colville, Thompson River, and Fort Nez Percés (along with the Snake Country)—provided an average of one-third of Columbia Department fur production between 1825 and 1849. This was a significant contribution, but by far the largest share of it came from a single district, Colville, with its outposts among the productive Salish Flathead and Upper Kutenai hunters. Colville produced an average of 52 percent of all furs collected in the Columbia Interior over this period (about 18 percent of the total for the larger department). The Thompson River District came next, providing one-quarter of Interior returns (7.6 percent for the department). Fort Nez Percés contributed approximately one-eighth of Interior yields (4.2 percent for the department), while the Snake expeditions brought in marginally less.[8]

For many traders The Dalles symbolized all that was wrong with the fishing way of life. The abundance of the fishery there ensured that thousands of people—"all the gamblers, horsestealers, and other outcasts . . . for hundreds of miles round"— could live well at the height of the season with little effort. By Ross's reckoning, three thousand people would gather, "not for the purpose of catching salmon, but chiefly for gambling and speculation." He complained that the traders could get no fish there, as it seemed to be "devoured on the spot"; the Indians appeared unconcerned about laying in a winter supply. According to Robert Stuart, members of Sahaptian groups who travelled to The Dalles for their fish did so precisely to "indulge [their] sloth." The resources of their own lands, which he listed as roots and a few deer, required more exertion than he believed them willing to make.[9]

Ross and Stuart were right about the abundance of The Dalles. Owing largely to geological attributes, the ten-mile stretch between Celilo Falls and The Dalles was the most productive salmon fishery on the whole Columbia River. It was also the most significant trade center and a key social center, a fact these traders appear to have missed. (Also missing from their assessments is a sense of the importance of more diverse food sources to Plateau diets, a point taken up later in the chapter.) Archaeological evidence demonstrates that as long ago as nine thousand years, The Dalles and other smaller centers were key gathering places for trade in regional products. Centuries before Europeans arrived in the region, The Dalles had become the nucleus of the Northwest Coast–Plateau trade system. It has been argued that in terms of the variety of goods traded there, the diversity of cultures represented, and the sheer intensity and volume of trade, the place was preeminent among Native American trade rendezvous in North America.[10] From the Great Plains came buffalo robes and other buffalo products, feather headdresses, parfleches, and catlinite (pipestone); from the coast, whale and seal bone and oils and ornamental shells, including the prized *haiqua* (dentalium); from the Great Basin, obsidian and other stone tools; from the Plateau, basketwork, canoes, hemp and other plant materials, pelts and hides; and from the Plateau, Great Basin, and California, food plants like bitterroot, camas, and wapatoo. Goods traded at The Dalles have been traced to archaeological sites from Alaska to California, and a thousand miles to the east.[11]

To return to traders' impressions of fishing, it was denigrated because not only was it equated with failure to hunt but also the activity itself seemed to require minimal application. Fishing did not always assure the easy living traders witnessed at The Dalles. Even at such a favored site, where those who were careful and willing to exert themselves during the season could live in the midst of plenty the year-round, many were reduced to "the greatest distress" come winter. The fate of those at less-favored sites was bleaker still. Traders were convinced that improvidence was to blame.[12] Whatever the resources available, fishing suited what the traders saw as the Indians' natural aversion to labor.

The notion of a "natural aversion" to labor among the poor had wide currency in Britain at the time. The writings of that influential figure of the late Enlightenment, Thomas Malthus, helped popularize the idea that "torpor and corruption" were the original state of humans. The poor had not learned the civilized (i.e., middle-class) habits of industry; lacking such moral checks, they remained sunk in their poverty and contributed to their own misfortune. David Thompson made reference in his *Narrative* to this "axiom of the civilised world, that Poverty begets Poverty."[13] In extending that axiom to the fishers and gatherers of the Northwest, Thompson echoed the sentiments of generations of European travellers to native worlds. As he observed during his earlier encounters with Subarctic hunter-gatherers, they showed the weakness so frequently ascribed by Europeans to the natives of the colonies: they could not bear hard labor.[14]

The general view of the river dwellers of the Plateau was that if they failed to provide an adequate living for themselves from the abundant salmon resources of the region, their plight was of their own making. Many accounts disparaged the sedentary "Salmon tribes," who, as John McLeod wrote of the Northern Okanagan, were "such an indolent and improvident Set, that altho' their country in summer abound with Trout and Salmon, yet are starving for most part of winter and Spring, living on no other food in the spring of the year than roots and a kind of

Moss." Many expressed bewilderment at the failure of Columbia groups to capitalize on what appeared to them to be a resource going to waste. Indolence was the favored explanation. Dugald McTavish was blunt about it. The Indians of the Columbia were the most miserable he had ever seen, "all owing to their laziness"; instead of dedicating themselves to fishing salmon during the season, they passed their time "sleeping and gaming," with the result that before spring they were "dying like rotten sheep."[15] There is no evidence to support this extravagant claim, and few traders would have put it so baldly. Nevertheless, food shortage and hunger were widely seen as the outcome of the fishing way of life. Reasons for that perception are explored in the next chapter.

In an intriguing analysis of the semantics of "indolence" and "starvation" in the fur-trade lexicon, anthropologist Mary Black-Rogers argues that concepts like indolence were used almost exclusively to mean not hunting for furs. The cases she considers involve traders' writings on Subarctic hunting peoples, where she finds "ample evidence that ["lazy"] did *not* depict Indians sitting around doing nothing."[16] In the case of the fishing peoples of the Plateau, however, "lazy" often meant precisely that. These were people whose habits might drive fur traders to distraction. They were accustomed to living from the fruits of the rivers, which, as Simpson put it, afforded "abundant provision at little trouble." Consequently, they had little need to hunt. (Actually, many of these groups did a good deal of hunting, not to mention gathering of wild vegetables and fruits; the contours of their varied subsistence rounds are considered later in this and subsequent chapters.) Nor were they inclined to become hunters, as they could get what few European goods they sought by trading a trifle of furs now and then. Such people were, for a good part of the year, "independent" of the traders. Independence in the context of the fur trade meant having little involvement in the trade; it seldom implied a virtue.[17]

Improvidence was closely related to indolence in the discourse on fishing peoples. As punishment for their lack of foresight they were likely to be "reduced to wretchedness" by late winter. Then they might become dependent on the trade posts. Thus, the Wallawalla in the winter of 1831–32 became "beggars" about the fort, a fact the petulant Simon McGillivray linked directly to their improvidence.[18] Other possible interpretations of their behavior are considered below.

Gender and Indolence

There was a distinct gender dimension to the perception that the fishing peoples of the Columbia were indolent. While the men were portrayed as layabouts, the women—when they drew comment at all—were frequently cast as overburdened workhorses. Embedded in this image was perhaps the most damning critique of Indian men: their failure to adequately fulfil that basic responsibility of British manhood, providing for the family. In a number of ways this discourse might be seen as feminizing of Indian men. While I have not found any explicit statement of feminization in the Plateau record, the markers are there. These men were said to be so averse to labor that by spring their families were reduced to severe want. In Thompson's view the men could not bear hard labor. Worst of all, their women were saddled with tasks that in the "natural" order of things would be defined as manly duties. Feminized or not, the fishermen of the Plateau fell far short of the expectations of "civilized" manhood.

Plateau women challenged imported gender categories at least as profoundly as the men. The women's labor burden confirmed the failure of men to perform their proper roles, and went some way toward explaining the "inferiority" of Plateau economies more generally.[19] The "squaw drudge" is one of the most prominent and persistent images in travellers' commentaries on Native women throughout North America. (Its antithesis, the Indian princess, is discussed in a chapter 7.)[20] A classic version of the drudge image was penned in the 1770s by Samuel Hearne, travelling in the barren land en route to the Arctic Ocean.

Ostensibly quoting his Chipewyan guide Matonabbee, Hearne
wrote that:

> Women . . . were made for labor; one of them can carry, or
> haul, as much as two men can do. They also pitch our tents,
> make and mend our clothing, keep us warm at night; and, in
> fact, there is no such thing as travelling any considerable
> distance, or for any length of time, in this country, without their
> assistance . . . though they do every thing, [they] are main-
> tained at a trifling expence; for as they always stand cook, the
> very licking of their fingers in scarce times, is sufficient for their
> subsistence.[21]

If this was indeed Matonabbee's view, he was more accepting
of the arduous burdens of women than most European traders
were. Beast-of-burden rhetoric pervades these travellers' accounts.
More than a century earlier and far to the east, Pierre-Esprit
Radisson had written of women "laden like unto so many mules."
Among the Assiniboine, Henry Kelsey found women to be "like
a Slead dog or Bitch." James Isham spoke for many when he
observed that the "Robust nature and Strong Constitution" of
Native women "is Very surprizing."[22] The surprise lay in the extent
to which these women challenged European male, middle-class
expectations for appropriate gendered behavior. Not only was
the women's physical prowess at odds with the delicate female
form increasingly revered in bourgeois circles (a theme taken up
in chapter 7); at base, they performed a man's work. The intrusion of women into the realm of manual labor was a frontal
assault on masculine middle-class sensibilities.

A significant ethnographic gesture to take note of in these
descriptions is the way the writers homogenize women into a collective "they" and hone the essentializing further to create an
iconic "she" (Native woman). Woman's essential identity in the
narratives was that of victim, downtrodden by the lazy, thought-
less men in whose midst she found herself. However, the discur-
sive feat was not quite so readily achieved. While supposedly a
debased beast of burden, the Indian woman might at the same

time be robust and vigorous.[23] As will shortly be shown, a further aspect of her strength lay in her ability to dominate men. The woman of the Plateau eluded neat categorization.

The clear implication of many trader accounts was that the men made the women work in order to indulge their own leisure. As Ross Cox put it, women in Plateau societies were "great slaves" to their husbands.[24] The contrast was starkly drawn in John Work's account of the gender division of labor in the Colville region. The men, he observed, spent a small portion of their time making and repairing their tools, canoes, and so on, "but the far greater part is employed gambling . . . or loitered away in idlings." As for the women: "Besides their culinary and household duties, of dressing the victuals, fetching water, wood &c the dressing the skins of animals making them into clothing for themselves and family and ornamenting the clothing, cutting up and drying meat and fish, and the laborious business of digging up roots, fall to their lot."[25]

This seemingly skewed division of labor was remarked many times. Even Alexander Ross, who over time proved willing to admit that Native men could be industrious in their own right, nevertheless found women to serve in the "double capacity of wife and slave." Their time was spent in the endless toil of gathering roots and firewood, preserving fish, drying meat, dressing leather, and their other "domestic and family affairs."[26] (The impact of the intensification of buffalo hunting and trapping on women's lives is considered in chapter 6.) It is interesting that traders' minds were not troubled that many women in British and colonial society at the time were similarly tied to lives of toil.

It struck these British men as entirely unnatural that Native men should be enjoying their leisure while the women did the work of supporting the family. Samuel Black was most categorical about it. In the Sahaptian country of the southern Plateau, the men lived as "independent Gentlemen," gambling, horse racing, smoking, and so on, while the women were employed "digging Roots and geathering [sic] Berries to make all the family live."[27]

Black's observation is remarkable in that he was virtually alone among traders in acknowledging the importance of gathered vegetable foods to Plateau sustenance (see chapters 5 and 6). His impression that vegetable foods were staples in the region is confirmed by more recent studies. Botanist and anthropologist Eugene Hunn has calculated that among Sahaptian groups on the middle Columbia fully 60 percent of calories consumed came from plant foods. Independent studies by Angelo Anastasio and Verne Ray came up with figures of one-third to one-half as averages for Plateau societies generally.[28]

While Black recognized foods produced by women as staples, his observations were marked by a central contradiction, one that symbolizes the extent to which traders' interpretations of indigenous economies, and women's place in those economies, were hemmed in by both culture and gender: like his colleagues, Black classified indigenous peoples according to the activities of the men. Thus the Wallawalla were not gatherers but "fishermen," the Cayuse and the Nez Percé were at times "fishermen" and "hunters." Aside from their concerns about what they saw as the excessive labor of women, traders' reflections on the economic contributions of women were tangential to the main discussion. That discussion was about the activities (or inactivity) of men.

The formal questionnaire on "Natural History" that the London Committee of the Hudson's Bay Company began circulating to the posts in the mid-1820s speaks volumes about how gender structured contemporary British middle-class understandings of economy. The series of questions dealing with the "usual occupations" of the Indians began with the query "What are the usual occupations, besides hunting or fishing of the father and sons, in the family of an Indian?" "Occupations," it seems, were seen to be the domain of men. Next came queries about the age at which people married; how many children women bore, and over how many years; how difficult labor was; and whether women were well or ill treated by their husbands. Finally came the question "Are they [women] employed solely in household and culinary work or do they engage in hunting and fishing with the rest of their family or what are the usual occupations of the females?"[29] The assumptions are clear: women were viewed principally as reproducers (in the biological sense); food production and the support of the family were the appropriate responsibilities of men. Given the weight of such entrenched ideology, it seems all the more noteworthy that an individual like Samuel Black would recognize gathered foods as staples—and less surprising that in the next breath he would label the peoples of the southern Plateau "fishermen" and "hunters."[30]

Family and the Kinship Web

Black's remark that women "make all the family live" provides the opening for a brief examination of social organization in the Plateau, as seen through traders' texts. As in most other gathering-hunting societies, "family" encompassed a larger, more extended entity than the nuclear family. Ross, describing arrangements among Okanagan-Colville groups, explained that from one to six related families might occupy a single winter lodge, each having its own hearth. Although they had that level of autonomy from one another, the winter provisions of this extended kin unit were "considered as one common stock . . . served out in winter by each family in turn until the whole is consumed."[31]

Kinship was of the type that anthropologists identify as a bilateral kindred, apparently without any formal lineage or clan organizations.[32] That ties of kinship were traced through both mother and father and that marriages were exogamous (outside the local kin group) meant that kinship relations cast a wide net. Residential groupings, even during the settled winter season, were very fluid. Individuals could put down at any number of villages or camps where they had kin, for the purpose of food gathering, seeking a spouse, or visiting. The fluid and extended nature of kin groups goes some way to explaining the constant headaches traders had trying to sort out family relationships.

The entire Plateau has been characterized as a "vast kinship web."[33] The prevalence of the levirate and sororate (marriage of a man to his deceased brother's wife or to his deceased wife's sister, respectively) is evidence of the central concern with maintaining the ties established between families upon marriage. Polygyny was widely practiced, although as traders noted, the right to multiple wives tended to be the prerogative of "chiefs and other great men." Traders were appalled by the custom, which some saw as "the greatest source of evil" in the Columbia. According to Ross co-wives, unless they were sisters, lived separately with their own kin groups, a measure that was necessary to keep a lid on their animosity. The practice of a man taking sisters as co-wives, another reflection of the concern to protect the marriage bonds between families, was "still more revolting" to these British observers. More will be said about polygyny shortly.[34]

Extended families occupied permanent winter villages, but from spring through autumn they followed a complex seasonal round of gathering, fishing, and hunting. There were significant variations according to local resources: the Sxoielpi (Colville) and Lower Kutenai, for example, were more settled fishing-trading peoples, and the Salish Flathead and Upper Kutenai spent long periods in summer and winter in the buffalo hunting grounds. Ross's description of the seasonal movements of Okanagan-Colville groups is suggestive of the broader Plateau pattern. As soon as the snow melted in the spring, winter villages broke up and villagers dispersed into small parties along gender lines for gathering and hunting. In about mid-June they assembled again in "large bands" (kin groups and at times larger interethnic groupings) for the start of the salmon fishery. Fishing continued at intervals until October. At the height of a run all took part, the women preparing the fish caught by their male kin. During the root-gathering and berrying seasons, many of the women and girls would move to the favorite gathering grounds, and at intervals parties of men would join them to help with the transport and to hunt. At the close of the fishery, all the able-bodied members of the kin group set off on the autumn hunt in the mountains, before returning to the winter village when the cold weather returned.[35]

Marriage and Women's Freedom

Bride service was practised in these societies, which meant that grooms were expected to make ongoing gifts of the products of their labor to their in-laws, in particular their parents-in-law. Keeping up the flow of support was a principal means by which sons-in-law maintained the sympathy and goodwill of their wives' kin. Bride service was a central aspect of the continuing movement of goods and services through the social watershed of the kin group.[36]

Such societies have often been characterized as sexually egalitarian. The dominant line of such reasoning is the "different but equal" proposition: women and men were autonomous individuals with their own duties and rights, and access to positions which, though different, offered equal value and prestige. There was no significant gender asymmetry in "status," or so the argument goes, because women controlled access to their own resources, the conditions of their work, and the distribution of their products.[37]

While most scholars might agree that Native women enjoyed more authority and respect in their communities than their counterparts in Europe, the "different but equal" thesis is marked by a number of weaknesses. The purpose of the following discussion is simply to illuminate some of the pitfalls of generalizing analyses of "women's status," before returning to traders' representations of women. The purpose is not to seek a definitive statement on the role and "status" of women in Plateau societies: such a reconstruction would be impossible, given that the materials for this era are documents written postcontact by white men.

The "different but equal" proposition emerged in response to weighty questions being posed by anthropologists and feminist scholars in the 1970s: Was the position of women always and everywhere inferior and subordinate to that of men? If so, what were the "universal determinants" of this subordination? If not, what were the key variables behind cross-cultural differences in women's status? How did colonization and the rise of a capitalist world economy impact on the lives of women in colonial societies?[38]

More recently, under the influence of broadly poststructuralist critiques, many scholars have stepped back from such sweeping questions to probe the validity of the essentialist formulations of "womanhood," "manhood," "status," and "power" that the questions imply. As historian Nancy Shoemaker has written, power and status are not "tangible, measurable, immediately observable and knowable"; rather, their varied manifestations must be historically situated and contextualized in order to be understood. Shoemaker points out that in Native American societies, for example, generation and kinship are essential determinants, alongside gender, of an individual's place in the community.[39]

Both ethnographic and theoretical concerns increasingly point to the need for careful consideration of the role of cultural valuations and ideologies in the assessment of relative power and status. The issue is not just what women and men do relative to one another, and what practical or social rewards each receives, but what people *think* about what they do. For example, conventional anthropological accounts of the practice of sequestering young women at the onset of menstruation held that these women were viewed as potentially "polluting" to their communities and a threat to the activities of men. This may well have been the dominant male perspective. Yet women's views could differ sharply. Elder Athapaskan and Tlingit women of the southern Yukon viewed with great respect those whose seclusion was lengthy, apparently because such women gained very powerful ritual and practical knowledge—knowledge explicitly unavailable to men. Was such seclusion an expression of the subordination of women, or a means by which they gained power and autonomy in their own setting? From the perspective of the female elders, at least, the answer would seem to be the latter.[40]

By the same logic, the assertion that in Sahaptian societies women "make the family live," as Black put it, cannot be taken as simple proof of their elevated position: it tells us little about how the contributions and status of women were perceived, by women and men, in those societies. In line with the growing interest in the cultural construction and symbolic nature of gender, many would argue that while gender ideologies may originate in the context of particular social and economic relations, they "rarely accurately reflect male-female relations, men's and women's activities, and men's and women's contributions."[41]

Short of defining "status"—which I am not prepared to do, given its multidimensionality and historical and cultural specificity—I would offer a final caution. Evaluation of the relative status of individuals in any community requires judgments about what is good, desirable, and valuable. The criteria chosen by the observer—whether an early-nineteenth-century British trader or a more self-reflective late-twentieth-century scholar—may not be particularly meaningful to the women or men of the community in question. By reading against the grain of the historical documents and bringing to our work an informed scholarly perspective, we may well be able to offer insights into the workings of gender, power, and privilege in societies of the past. We will certainly raise intriguing questions. But throughout, it is useful to bear in mind that the cultural valuations and ideologies of scholars, perhaps as much as those of the historical informants, are very much at play in the representations being raised.

Marriage is a significant vehicle for the expression of gender ideologies. Traders found Plateau marriage practices at once fascinating and disturbing. They reported marriage to be a much-sought-after achievement for men in Plateau societies, but they provide considerable evidence that it was less coveted by young women. Marriage signalled the transition of the man to the status of responsible adult. As Alexander Ross said of Okanagan society, a man without a wife "is neither chief nor great man, according to their ideas of greatness, and is looked upon with contempt."[42] That "contempt" may have related to the threat that a bachelor posed to the marriages of other men. Nonetheless, it seems that for men marriage was a touchstone of adult and public stature.[43] To judge by traders' accounts, it provided no such benefit for women; indeed, it would appear that marriage may have curbed their autonomy, at least during the childbearing years. However, this point should not be taken too far.

Next to the division of labor, marriage was the aspect of Plateau gender relations about which traders had most to say. Their commentaries on marital relations seem paradoxical, given their views on women's labor burdens. Cox characterized women in the Spokane-Colville region as "most submissive to marital authority," but he was alone in doing so. Far more common were depictions of Plateau women ruling the men. Work went so far as to say that around Spokane, "favorite" wives exercised "complete ascendency" over their husbands. Ross observed that among Okanagan-Colville groups the family was "ruled by the joint authority of the husband and wife, but more particularly by the latter." Black intimated that in the region of Fort Nez Percés men were at pains not to offend their wives, and they treated them with great respect.[44] Once again the specter of the feminized Indian male is raised, although at the same time these women were judged to be overburdened with the duties of providing for their families and running the household. In trader discourse the Native woman is at once victim and aggressor. Paradox is central to her image.[45]

Governor Simpson took up the theme of women dominating their husbands in his discussion of the need for economy in the operations of the Columbia Interior. He saw the influence of Native wives over company men as a major obstacle to his program of economic rationalization. So powerful were these "petticoat politicians" that the men neglected the interests of the business "merely to administer to their comforts and guard against certain innocent indiscretions which these frail brown ones are so apt to indulge in." Simpson viewed the scene from a distinct perspective, concerned as he was to reduce the expenses of family maintenance in the fur trade. As always, the cultural blinkers and strategic interests of the commentator must be kept in mind. However, Simpson's portrayal of Native women as influential and independent-minded broadly concurs with those of other traders in the region.[46]

An aspect of women's autonomy that drew frequent comment from the traders was the women's control over their marital destiny. Ross was surprised to learn that in Okanagan communities a young woman could reject her prospective groom even after a period of bride service. Her parents would then "also change their sentiments, and the young woman marries, not the person she was betrothed to, but another." Cox found Salish Flathead women and their families to be very particular in their choice of mates. Although many tried, only one North Wester succeeded in winning a Flathead woman's hand during Cox's time in the country. The "happy man" was Pierre Michel, a métis engagé who had hunted on the plains with the Flathead and "won the affections of the whole tribe." Michel's proposal was contested by a young Flathead who believed he had a prior claim. According to Cox, Michel won out because the young woman preferred him. Perhaps it was relevant as well that her father was a "chieftain" and may have sought a firmer alliance with the company through the marriage, although the refusal of Flatheads to enter into marriages with other traders casts doubt on that explanation.[47]

Work found the bride's family to be the obstacle to marriage in eastern groups, where young men were often stymied in their attempts to marry by their inability to meet the bride-service demands of their prospective in-laws. In the same passage Work commented on the "complete ascendency" that favorite wives exercised over their husbands in polygynous marriages. Unfortunately, he said nothing about the less-favored wives.[48] For women who ended up in unhappy unions, there appears to have been one final recourse: they could run away. There are several reports of women leaving their husbands. Some took up with other men, while others seem to have disappeared.[49]

It has already been noted that traders reviled the practice of polygyny. It was viewed as an aspect of what many called the "trade" in women. Ross, who lived several years among the Southern Okanagan and married an Okanagan woman he called Sally, saw what others took to be "payment" for brides as part of the series of exchanges that traditionally took place between the families of the bride and groom, and the groom and his in-laws. He understood well that these exchanges cemented the "marriage alliance" between the families.[50]

Ross drew the line at polygyny. Like his colleagues, he had no difficulty grasping the benefits for men: they gained social status and the productive and reproductive power of additional women, not to mention their companionship and sexual favors.[51] The fur trade was an era of intensified demand for furs and hides, and demands for female labor to process these and other country produce increased apace. Whether Native men came to view multiple wives as a means to, as well as a symbol of, wealth, or as partners who contributed to and shared in that wealth, is difficult to ascertain. Such questions are explored further in chapter 6.

If they could readily see benefits for men in the practice of polygyny, traders saw no such boon for women. It seems curious that the same men who bemoaned the heavy burden of labor of Plateau women failed to consider that polygyny had the potential to alleviate that burden. The very practice they found most offensive, sororal polygyny, was perhaps most likely to benefit the wives. It has been demonstrated in other contexts that the presence of co-wives who were sisters could help to ease the transition to married life. Good relations among co-wives could provide the context for sharing of labor and other household responsibilities. For example, while one wife took over child care and cooking, another could devote her energies to tasks such as dressing skins, preparing food for storage, or making household items or fishnets. It has also been suggested that sororal polygyny enhanced the status of women by improving their ability to stand up to their husbands.[52]

Relations among co-wives were not always rosy. Ross was convinced that unrelated wives could never live under one roof, as they were so prone to "brawls and squabbles." Whether his observation reflects experience or Ross's assumptions about female nature is unclear. As for what women thought of polygyny, traders provide little insight. However, linguistic conventions may provide a clue. In the Nez Percé language co-wives who were sisters were called by an inclusive term used to refer to a woman's sisters and female friends. Unrelated co-wives were called "enemies."[53]

This discussion has taken us some distance from the initial assertion that Native women were widely viewed as beasts of burden and victims of marital oppression. There is suggestive evidence, even in the male-biased writings of nineteenth-century fur traders, that this was not the case. A glimpse at the actual experiences of Plateau women in this era reveals that they had considerable power in their own right. In the cultural realm that was their domain, they were able to forge roles that demonstrated and affirmed their value in society. And as will later be demonstrated, some were able to carve out roles for themselves in other, traditionally "male" arenas. The complexity of their roles is reflected in the complexity of traders' responses to women and to gender relations in the region. Beasts of burden, domineering wives (and, yet to come, erotic princesses): the great range of imagery of Plateau women speaks to the many ways in which they challenged British manly identities.

Gambling and "Idlings"

When John Work reported from the Colville region that Native men spent most of their time gambling or engaged in other "idlings," he struck a familiar chord. Gambling was widely seen as both symptom and cause of the indolence of Plateau men. Most agreed with Governor Simpson that the love of gambling was "deeply seated and most inveterate in all Indians on this side the Mountains." Some, however, saw it as a particular vice of the fishing groups. Archibald McDonald explained it as "an evil attendant on their sedentary life."[54] The "addiction" of the Sanpoil and Okanagan to gambling was noted above. The Spokane shared the vice, and in the view of at least one trader, were guiltier than their neighbors. Ross Cox described Spokane lands as pleasing and varied, offering an abundance of vegetal foods, game, and fish. Despite these "natural advantages," and though they were skilled hunters, such was the Spokane's improvidence and fondness for gambling that they were often reduced to starvation.[55]

Cox's view of Spokane country was apparently too sanguine. Alexander Kennedy, who had charge of the district in the early years of HBC tenure, reported that in fact the Spokane relied principally on fish, the area being "a wretched situation for procuring Food" (meaning food of the animal variety). They and the other peoples who frequented the post in winter—among them "hunters" like the Kalispel, Coeur d'Alene, and parties of Nez Percé—were an irritant to local traders. Reluctant to "tent off" in search of beaver, they chose instead to "los[e] their time here where they do nothing but dance and gamble their property a way [sic] a propensity to which they are much addicted."[56]

Work gave a somewhat more nuanced accounting of the activities of groups in the Spokane-Colville region, noting, as we saw earlier, that the men spent a portion of their spare time making and repairing fishing and hunting implements, canoes, and so forth. However, the "far greater part" of their leisure was spent gambling, an activity in which both sexes and all ages took part, and which "often absorbs every other consideration." The peoples of the district, he wrote, "seldom think of tomorrow," and when not gambling, "much time is loitered away in idlings." Among such "idlings" he included the young men's predilection for decorating themselves, time spent trading with neighbors, and "visiting, dancing, and singing, mostly of a religious nature." On a horse-trading trip deep into Nez Percé country in 1825, Work found "gambling, horse-racing and foot racing" to be favorite summer pastimes, and unquestionably detrimental to the horse trade. Similar complaints were levelled by traders at Fort Nez Percés, where the Native men were "independent Gentlemen," who spent much of their time gambling and horse racing, and when they had the means, "dressing lounging smoking chat[t]ing &c." Clearly, gambling and these other pursuits were perceived as competition for the fur trade. Gambling in particular was construed as "losing time" or "doing very little"—that is, very little of use to the traders.[57]

A careful reading of the fur-trade sources indicates that gambling may have been rather more to Plateau societies than an opportunity for "losing time." It was a central activity whenever large numbers gathered, as they did, for example, at root grounds in spring. Alexander Ross witnessed such a gathering in the spring of 1814. Entering the valley of the Yakima River along its northern reach, Ross and his companions came upon a massed camp:

> [W]e could see its beginning but not the end! This mammoth camp could not have contained less than 3,000 men, exclusive of women and children, and treble that number of horses. It was a grand and imposing sight in the wilderness, covering more than six miles in every direction. Councils, root-gathering, hunting, horse-racing, foot-racing, gambling, singing, dancing, drumming, yelling, and a thousand other things which I cannot mention were going on.[58]

This camp was quite likely at the site of what was known among the Yakama as "the big time." Informants of anthropologist

Gerald Desmond identified it as traditionally the major gambling forum of the year in their region.[59] The gathering took place in the vicinity of two villages in Kittitas (Northern Yakama) territory. Yakama from across their expansive territories in modern-day central Washington, as well as Wanapam from the middle Columbia, Wenatchi, and other Interior Salishan groups, came together early in June to dig roots at the abundant grounds here. The women were occupied much of the time in gathering and preparing the roots for storage, while the men did some hunting and took part in the councils and gambling activities recorded by Ross. Women joined in as time allowed. Gambling was a by-product rather than the cause of the gathering, but it had important social functions.

Desmond's informants reported that "people had a good time" gambling, and that "some people got rich that way." He found that accumulation of wealth was not admitted as a goal in itself, however. Rather, generosity was the ideal of social behavior. One who had material wealth was assured of no special status; one who had wealth and dispensed it liberally attained prestige. Traders were fascinated by this, marvelling, for example, at how even the smallest parcel of tobacco would be shared among all present. Goods continually flowed from one individual to another through established social networks. Generosity was key to the acquisition of authority as well as prestige in Plateau communities. As John Work noted, chiefs "were elected, or rather admitted to be such by degrees . . . as much as anything else [by] their generosity in relieving the wants of the indigent." Ross elaborated on their role: chiefs exercised "merely a nominal superiority. . . . [The] general maxim is that Indians were born to be free, and that no man has a natural right to the obedience of another, except he be rich in horses and has many wives." Such wealth permitted the requisite generosity. Gambling, it appears, was a means of acquiring disposable wealth.[60]

Gambling and Exchange

By its very ubiquity, it would seem that gambling was an important method of exchange and circulation of goods in the Plateau. Anthropologist David Chance has gone so far as to claim that gambling, rather than barter trade, was "the principal mode of exchange" at Kettle Falls. There is little historical evidence on which to base so confident a claim, although it seems reasonable to assume that it was a significant—not to say "the principal"—mode. Chance cites three pieces of evidence to support his theory: (1) he did not find any mention of actual trade transactions among Native people in documents from the region; (2) trader John Work's statement that gambling (in Chance's words) "absorbed every other consideration" of the Colville people; and (3) Alexander Ross's claim that (again in Chance's words) "all trading at The Dalles was accomplished through gambling."[61]

In fact, documents from Fort Colville do mention trade among the local groups. In a passage dealing with the district fur trade in his 1829 report, for example, Work noted that among the "neighbouring tribes" of the area, "a barter is carried on with articles as are wanted by the one and can be spared by the other." Other reports and journals note trade in salmon and local products. On the question of the prevalence of gambling—which he did indeed find troubling—Work wrote that it "*often* absorbs every other consideration" (emphasis added), not, as Chance's rendering would seem to suggest, that it *always* did so.[62] Finally, the relevant passage in Ross's published account is somewhat less definitive than Chance implies: the many goods exchanged at The Dalles, Ross wrote, "generally change hands through gambling."[63] Given the traders' disdain for gambling, which Ross certainly shared, his statement may not be the most reliable. His disdain for the people who gathered at The Dalles also gives the reader pause.

Ross was well aware of the importance of The Dalles as a trading center, calling it the "great emporium" of the Columbia, the key place where the Interior met the Coast. Yet at the same time as he acknowledged its significance as a fishing site and trade mart, Ross denounced the place as a rendezvous for "[a]ll the gamblers, horse-stealers, and other outcasts throughout the country, for hundreds of miles round." It was gambling, in particular, which "draws so many vagabonds together at this place, because they are always sure to live well here." People came to The Dalles to indulge their laziness and their love of gambling; the two went hand in hand. Ross's impatience with the "indolence" of gambling Indians is palpable: "For every fisherman there are fifty idlers, and all the fish caught are generally devoured on the spot, so that the natives of the place can seldom lay up their winter stock until the gambling season is over, and their troublesome visitors gone." Not only did these "idlers" fall prey to the perceived moral failings discussed earlier in this chapter: they stood in the way of trade. Ross and his colleagues saw huge quantities of salmon at The Dalles, "but what were they among so many? We could scarcely get a score of salmon to buy."[64]

The Dalles was notorious from the early days of the trade as a place where business was difficult, and the peoples who gathered there were at best indifferent, at worst violently hostile, to fur traders. Ross's account of the extent of gambling at this place must be read in the context of these views. Shot through with a fur trader's biases against gambling and The Dalles, the account nevertheless points to gambling as an important activity, not only socially, but economically.

Pity, Begging, and the Gift

A common thread running through traders' narratives on the "rude state of nature" in which Plateau fishing peoples dwelt was the want of "articles of British Manufacture."[65] Time and time again, testimony from Native people themselves appeared to confirm what traders already believed: that without guns, iron tools, and the other trappings of "civilization," they were doomed to a rude existence. Traders' translations of ceremonial speeches and individual appeals alike are laden with terms like "pitiful," "poor," and "helpless." Depending on the context (and the trader), such speeches generally were interpreted either as evidence of real need, or as a manipulative or "beggarly" attempt to get goods. The desire for goods was undoubtedly part of the message. However, the notion of "pity" in these societies has been shown to be far more complex. The place to begin is with the meaning of the gift.

Gift-giving was an essential element of trader-Native relations. As a chief trader at Fort Nez Percés explained it, gifts—mainly of clothing and tobacco for chiefs and "principal men," tobacco for the rest—enabled traders to "make friends" with the Indians. If there was no gift, there was no such relationship; without a social relationship, there could be no trade.[66]

Gift-giving has often been construed as a European device to bribe Native people to trade. Mary Louise Pratt offers a slightly more nuanced account, illustrating how rituals of reciprocity have long been a central act in the encounter between Europeans and indigenous peoples. I use the word "act" because in Pratt's estimation, gestures at reciprocity are part of a European-directed performance to ensure, in the first instance, personal safety in alien territory. The motivations are at base expansionist and commercial, but these are cloaked in a "drama of reciprocity."[67] Here Pratt draws on the work of Peter Hulme (by way of Karl Marx and Marcel Mauss), who shows that "however loudly its presence is trumpeted," under the social relations of capitalism reciprocity disappears. Reciprocity remains a tale that capitalism tells about itself, while the actual forces that bring people together are selfishness, gain, and private interest.[69]

Fur traders' stories are full of gestures of reciprocity, tales of "making friends" with Indians as a prelude to profit-driven trade. And while these agents of British commercial firms were certainly interested, first and foremost, in profit and personal gain, it seems there was more than chicanery to their gestures. Traders played at reciprocity because it was their only option. If they were to make trade in Indian worlds, they had to accommodate to the rituals and rigors of those worlds.

In recent years some students of colonial encounters have located the roots of gift-giving rituals not in the myths of capitalism, but in the power of the gift in indigenous cultures.[69] Writing of the Plateau in particular, anthropologist Eugene Hunn has described these societies as woven of two strands, "a warp of kinship and a weft of exchange." The basic unit of production and distribution was the family. As has been seen, it is more aptly described as the kin group, since the flow of goods and services extended to include distant cousins, uncles and aunts, and grandparents. Marriage constantly reinforced and extended the network. Kin terms for siblings-in-law reveal the central concern with maintaining the ties established between families upon marriage. Whereas English systems denote brother-in-law and sister-in-law, Sahaptin terms, for example, have a special category for in-laws of opposite sex: it translates as something like "potential spouse." The prevalence of people marrying their deceased spouses' sisters or brothers was noted earlier.[70]

Exchange among kin was of the nature of generalized reciprocity, that is, sharing what one had without expectation of return (or at least without obvious expectation). As has been noted, individuals did not tend to accumulate material wealth. Generosity rather than wealth accumulation was the social ideal. Goods might rest with an individual for a time, but were ultimately passed on through established social networks, the most immediate of these being the kin group. Gift-giving affirmed relationships among kin; gifts, in simplest terms, embodied messages about what each partner expected from the relationship. Decades before traders made it west of the Rockies, a Bay man gained insight into this aspect of social life:

> We find them kind, courteous, and benevolent to each other, relieving the wants and necessities of their distressed brethren

with the greatest good-nature, either by counsel, food or cloathing. The good effects of this excellent disposition are frequently experienced by themselves; for, as in their mode of life no one knows how soon it may be his own fate to be reduced to the verge of extremity, he secures for himself a return of kindness, should he experience that vicissitude.[71]

Relations within the kin group were the blueprint for wider social relations. Whenever one wished to establish or affirm a relationship with another party, one gave a gift. When Nlaka'pamux and Secwepemc communities came together near the Kamloops post for winter dance festivities in 1826, there was an extensive exchange of gifts. Both sides received sought-after items (horses, beaver robes, guns), but the interaction was framed as gift-giving, not trade.[72] However, the gifts were not given simply out of a sense of largesse. They were fundamental to the establishment of a social space in which peaceful relations could take place. The maintenance of this social space required ongoing exchanges of gifts, just as the maintenance of goodwill between a groom and his in-laws required ongoing gifts of his labor in bride service. To fail to give a gift was to threaten harmonious relations.[73]

The practice of gift exchange became integrated into the idiom of trade and diplomacy very early in the encounter with Native peoples in North America. If British traders in the Plateau were to establish good relations with Native groups, they too had to accommodate to the fundamental ethic of gift-giving—to mimic, in a sense, kin relationships. This was the only way of demonstrating that they could be trusted, and of determining whether they could in turn trust their prospective trading partners. In the process of establishing and maintaining peaceful trade relationships, they established figurative, and on many occasions real, kin relationships within these communities.[74]

The concept of "pity" was, and is, central to gift-giving in these societies. In an analysis of the meaning of the concept in Ojibwa idiom, linguists have determined that to "pity" means, in essence, to give a gift without thought of immediate return. The essential gift is a mother's milk, given freely to her child with no thought of return. There is a return, however, in the child's loyalty and love. In Ojibwa idiom, the mother "pities" her child with the gift of milk. The child, in receiving assistance from one more power-ful, is "pitied." To pity another, then, is to adopt or care for her or him as a parent or grandparent would a child; to be pitied is to receive aid from one more fortunate or powerful.[75] Similar meanings have been demonstrated for the Nlaka'pamux of the Interior Plateau. Dorothy Ursaki, an elderly Nlaka'pamux woman, explains that in her language to pity means "to give help, or give something they [the recipients] need." To seek pity is to declare oneself humble before the prospective donor: "humbling your-self, that's pity." The term "comes up in all ways" when one is asking for something. For instance, a request for food translates as "have pity on me for some food"; for tobacco, "have pity on me for some tobacco." According to Mrs. Ursaki, to seek pity is the "polite" way of asking.[76]

The quintessential pitying relationship in Plateau societies was the one between the individual and her or his guardian spirit. The child in quest of this "spirit helper" or "power" made herself pitiable in a number of ways. Under direction of an elder, most often a grandparent or shaman, she or he went alone to a remote and sacred place to fast while awaiting a vision of the spirit. She wore little clothing, even in winter. The child had learned the lesson of modesty toward all things in nature, and especially toward the guardian spirit. In this position of humility, she waited for her spirit to come and bestow its blessings—to "pity" her. The gifts of the spirit were the skills needed to lead a successful life, and protection in time of need. If she was visited by the spirit of the camas root, for example, she might develop special skills in harvesting roots. It is important to note that the quest was not for immediate gifts, but was principally a move to establish a rela-tionship, for *future* considerations.[77]

It is not surprising that fur traders, with their vast array of trade goods and their ample supply of gifts, "ranked with the bestowers of blessings."[78] This is not to argue, following Hunn, that early travellers like Thompson were necessarily viewed as supernatural beings. Hunn contends that Thompson was constantly asked for pity, and on occasion beseeched for mercy, because he represented the unfolding of people's apocalyptic expectations.[79] The issue of prophetic foretellings of the coming of the traders (and of catastrophic disease) was considered in chapter 2. Some were undoubtedly responding to the message of these prophecies when they greeted early traders with dancing, singing, and "speechifying." But the "speechifying" and the requests for blessings and pity were not reserved for pioneer traders, nor were they always accompanied by the other aspects of prophetic practice. Requests for pity on many occasions appear to have signified not fear or awe, but the desire to forge a relationship.

The address made by Wallawalla Chief Yellepit to Thompson at the mouth of the Walla Walla River in July 1811 stands as an archetype of the formal request for pity, or what might be called the pleading speech. Yellepit spoke long and passionately,

> pointing out to us their helpless state, and that under their present circumstances they could never hope to be better, "for we must continue in the state of our fathers, and our children will be the same, unless you white men will bring us Arms, Arrow shods of iron, axes, knives and many other things which you have and which we very much want."[80]

Thompson heard many such speeches. The Salish Flathead and Spokane "rejoiced" at the arrival of the traders, for now they could exchange their "rude lances and flint headed Arrows" for guns and iron arrowheads. In nearby Kalispel country, "the poor people informed me there were plenty of Beaver about them and the country, but they had nothing but pointed Sticks to work them, not an axe among them." The Sanpoil were in a similar position, having "only their hands to procure food and clothing." For his part, Thompson would assure them that his brigade was headed to the sea "to obtain all the Articles they were so much in need of, and [to] return to them, for which they must be industrious hunters." Ross and his Astorian colleagues heard similar appeals. Group after group celebrated the coming of the brigade with smoking, dancing, singing, and "speechifying," which to Ross signified that "they were happy now. The whites had visited their land; poverty and misery would no longer be known amongst them."[81]

Traders like Thompson, who had experience in other regions of the trade, would not have raised an eyebrow at such appeals. The pleading speech was a standard element of the dialogue and ritual that preceded formal trade. Andrew Graham, longtime trader and chief at the Hudson Bay posts in the mid-1700s, described the typical trading captain's "harangue" as including protestations of hard times and pleas to "take pity on us . . . I say."[82]

The response of most traders to such speeches reveals that they interpreted them purely as requests for material goods. There is no indication that Thompson or Ross questioned the need in the cases cited above, though on some occasions such appeals were greeted with skepticism. It is impossible to recover the cues that might cause one appeal to be judged legitimate and another a lie or exaggeration. Suffice it to say that "Indian report," in general, was regarded with some suspicion.

Starvation or food shortage was most often an aspect of "poverty and misery," both in the Natives' formulations and in traders' interpretations. Food shortage figured in Chief Yellepit's speech to Thompson. As the chief explained it, the Wallawalla were obliged to be very industrious during the fishing season, since their only way of hunting was the surround method, which seldom supplied sufficient meat for them all. The Sanpoil appeared to Thompson "slightly made" for want of proper nourishment (by which he meant meat). Cox found them pitiful indeed. Apologizing for stealing some company horses, a Sanpoil man told the trader that his people were "poor, and cold, and hungry . . . our wives and children starving." Wolves had destroyed many of their own horses, and their supply of dried salmon was spent. The man appealed for clemency, pleading that if the traders took their remaining horses, "we shall all die of hunger." Cox responded with a mixture of sympathy and skepticism: these people did appear to be in dire straits, but surely this was a manipulative way of securing goods.[83]

Such "beggarly" conduct was widely viewed with contempt. In these descriptions Native people (usually men) appear as indigents, incapable of meeting their most basic needs. Contempt is the defining feature of these passages: contempt for the failure of these men to fulfil their most fundamental manly duties; contempt for their impotence in the face of natural obstacles. While a man like Thompson might show some compassion for people in need, he was convinced that Plateau groups were powerless without "Arms [and] Arrow shods of iron." His belief that hunters were rendered more manly by the possession of such European manufactures is probed in chapter 7. Note the paradox in this view: if the gun was a marker of manhood, it was also a symbol of Native dependence on the traders. Manly as gun-toting hunter-warriors might be, their manliness was constrained, in trader discourse, by the assertion that they lacked certain attributes that only the traders could supply.

"Begging" may well be the most frequently occurring verb in post journals. In simplest terms, traders considered as begging any request for goods beyond those supplied through trade or ritual gift ceremonies. If an individual "came in with nothing" and asked for something, he or she was begging. The manner of asking also figured in the designation. Begging for traders' possessions or goods from the stores was especially annoying. At Fort Nez Percés in the early 1830s, Simon McGillivray was fixated on the habits of the "beggarly sett" who frequented the fort. By his account Cayuse, Wallawalla, Nez Percé, and others would come in at any hour of the day, begging food or tobacco, and a refusal was "almost tantamount to a battle." The term was not restricted to requests from those who had nothing to trade, since even hunters had the habit of "begging upon every Beaver"; neither was it restricted to the pedestrian usage of asking "humbly, earnestly, or supplicatingly." What were these people doing when they "begged"? How might this have differed from the traders' conception of their acts as beggarly requests for a handout? This question was considered in some measure in the discussion of the meaning of pity, and I will return to it shortly.[84]

Tobacco was the most frequent object of "begging" in the Plateau. The use of alcohol as a gift or form of credit for Native traders was strictly circumscribed from the earliest days of the trade west of the Rockies. Although liquor was widely used in these capacities elsewhere in fur-trade country, most extensively where the North West and Hudson's Bay Companies came into head-on competition prior to their amalgamation, the prohibition was quite effective in the Columbia Interior.[85] This was largely because the companies were not competing for the loyalty of indigenous suppliers of furs in most of the region. There are occasional references to chiefs being "treated to a dram," and liquor was used to some extent during competition with American traders on the southeastern frontier of the Plateau in the 1830s. However, in general traders not only abided by, but supported, the prohibition. Most would have agreed with John McLeod's sentiment that it was a "blessing" that liquor and "that ruinous plan of giving the natives debts" were not in use in the Interior—a blessing not only for Native people, but for everyone involved in the trade.[86]

Most traders accepted the constant demand for gifts of tobacco as a necessary evil. As McLeod put it in his Kamloops journal, he would not "in the least begrudge them a little tobacco now and then providing they all deserved it, but we are under the necessity of giving a Smoke to the undeserved as to the Deserved." Begging was an annoyance, but the begging of the "undeserved"—those who provided nothing for trade—was truly irksome.[87]

Traders understood well that "the regular smoking match" was essential to the maintenance of smooth relations. The mutual smoking of the pipe, a form of gift exchange, was basic to relations within and between Native societies, and as such, it became basic to trader-Native relations. Tobacco was always included in the "gratuities" given to chiefs and other "principal men." Instructions from Chief Factor McLoughlin to a trader in the Umpqua region of Oregon capture the purpose of these gratuities. The trader was directed to tell the local chief that in exchange for a gift of a suit of clothing—a gift made in the name of McLoughlin as chief of the traders—"I expect he will encourage his young men to work [i.e., trap for furs], and behave themselves well, and that he will endeavour to induce as many strange Indians to trade at the Fort as he can." The use of gratuities to ensure such cooperation from chiefs and leaders of trading parties is discussed further in chapter 5.[88]

The Okanagan Chief Nkwala provided some insight into the more spiritual role of tobacco. In a discussion with Archibald McDonald in 1827, Nkwala refused to admit that the love of the stuff "proceeds from a mere wish to gratify their desire of smoking," which apparently was McDonald's belief. Rather,

> [Nkwala] very ingeniously maintains that he and those of any good sense among them, smoak [sic] Tobacco from a *much different* and better motive—that which moves the white people to look in the Great Fathers Book: for the moment *he* takes his Pipe, he cannot help thinking of the Great Creation of the world and the number of good things done for their benefit the Indians cannot understand. I never saw a Savage that seems more consumed in the power of a Supreme being. He is convinced the Indians bring much of their present misery upon themselves by a total neglect of the great good conferred upon them and especially in showing too much levity in the very act of smoaking![89]

For a variety of reasons, then, tobacco became indispensable to trade.

Appeals for pity remained a persistent feature of trader-Native relations throughout the fur-trade era. When the HBC decided in the mid-1820s to shift its eastern district headquarters from Spokane House to a more favorable position at Kettle Falls, the

Spokane protested vigorously, declaring that "they will be pitiful when the Whites leave them." (Their protests were heeded. The new headquarters was established, but Spokane House was maintained.) When John Tod arrived at Kamloops in August 1841, he heard a similar story. Lolo St. Paul, an Iroquois employee of the company, had tended the post during the absence of the traders. He reported that he and his family "had suffered much from hunger, and that the Natives around in consequence of the want of ammunition had experienced much privation that way also." When Governor Simpson met a Kutenai hunter bearing a gift of fresh meat during the summer of 1841, he heard the familiar refrain. Asked how much of the meat he could spare, the hunter told Simpson, "my children are starving, but take as much as you please."[90]

To Simpson this may have looked like selfless, even careless, generosity. He was convinced, after all, that Indians seldom thought of tomorrow. Perhaps he took the hunter's words to be a veiled request for a handout, in which case he read the situation much as any of his colleagues would. The motivation for such assertions of helplessness, hunger, and poverty was not in question. In characteristic florid style, Samuel Black asserted that among Indians, "the Demon of Avarice reignes, Hectoring Domaneering pillaging Thieving and all kinds of Tricks [are used] to draw property from the Whites." Seeking pity—in the English idiom—was merely another of those tricks.[91]

It is intriguing to note how the tricks were all perpetrated by the Indians. Indian beggary, Indian pilfering, Indian scheming threatened the "friendship" cemented through gift-giving and other procedures. Only occasionally was a thought given to the traders' own infractions—to their greed for profits, or their weary and frustrated attempts to circumvent the rituals of engagement. The traders' design was to keep profits at a respectable level (a level monitored by headquarters).[92] Imbued as they were with this ethos, traders tended to extrapolate the motive to Indians as well.

One does not have to scratch far below the surface of trader accounts to find alternative readings of Native behavior. In a close reading of French accounts, historian Bruce White has come up with a subtle and complex analysis of Ojibwa and Dakota responses to European traders in their lands. White argues that while it appears in much of the documentary record that these people viewed the French as supernatural beings, the evidence indicates that the French were called "spirits" (esprit in the documents) because their merchandise was believed to possess special power. The term arose from Native peoples' appreciation for the goods the French offered, items that had many and varied applications to daily life.[93] In White's view, it was desire for goods that motivated requests for pity and incidents that the traders styled as begging and thieving. However, the aim was not personal accumulation, but access to the powers—spiritual and worldly—embodied in French guns, iron, and trade goods. Many of the actions of Native people in response to traders were guided by the desire to obtain a reliable and ongoing supply of items that offered many uses in their lives.[94]

Absent from all these interpretations is a still more elusive motivation, the desire to forge or reaffirm a relationship. To propose this explanation is not to deny the importance of more immediate material concerns. Yellepit was explicit about his people's desire for "Arms, Arrow shods of iron, axes, knives and many other things"; he was asking for European goods. However, the desire for merchandise is not sufficient to explain why he and others spoke so often of helplessness, starvation, and the need for pity. A clue is contained in the words of the Nlaka'pamux woman, Dorothy Ursaki: "humbling yourself, that's pity." To be humble was the appropriate way of asking. As indicated in the earlier discussion of guardian spirits and kin relations, the one seeking to establish a relationship would adopt a humble or pitiable stance. Modesty was not just recommended in these societies, it was required. An appeal couched in terms of helplessness or starvation was not necessarily—nor solely—a request for immediate goods or gifts. It may have been a move to establish a relationship, with an eye to future considerations.

This analysis sheds some light on the puzzling behavior of Simpson's Kutenai hunter. If his children were starving, was his most immediate concern likely to be "articles of British Manufacture"? Indeed, if he was sharing meat so freely, were his children starving at all? Perhaps the hunter's words simply embodied Kutenai speaking conventions, and the accepted way of initiating relations—that is, by appearing humble. By the same token, the hunter's gift demonstrated his interest in good relations with Simpson's party. The reference to his starving children becomes comprehensible against this background. The practice of what traders called begging, which often involved adopting a pitiable or powerless stance, may be understood in a similar light. Claims of starving and being "pitiful," "helpless," or "poor" appear to have functioned, in many instances, almost as a greeting, one that affirmed metaphorically the speaker's current relationship with the trader. While the ultimate aim may have been to receive the material benefits that would flow from the relationship (and in many cases, the ensuing social or political benefits), such tangible returns were not necessarily the immediate aim.[95]

This consciously self-humbling approach stood in sharp contrast to that followed by the British. Among traders it was considered virtually a sine qua non to assume a powerful stance in relations with Indians.[96] This is not to suggest that they believed they could proceed by coercion. In the interests of business, it was essential to be on good terms. As Chief Factor McLoughlin emphasized, Native people were "not such poltroons as to suffer themselves to be ill treated," especially in view of their superior numbers. The ideal of proper "management" was to treat them with "apparent openness and confidence," all the while maintaining their respect. Hence the juxtaposition of gift ceremonies and open hospitality at the posts, with fortifications, well-armed brigades, and the perpetual readiness to use force.[97] The customary Native manner must have seemed alien indeed.

"They Demand It as a Right"

Gift-giving was fundamental to the maintenance of good relations between traders and Native people. When the visitors failed to meet the requirements of the relationship so established, trouble often ensued. A trader at Spokane House articulated the change in the tone of relations that might occur on such occasions. In the winter of 1822–23, Alexander Kennedy found the sixty families who had their winter village near the post to be a great nuisance. They were "always begging" for tobacco, provisions, and ammunition. What was more, Kennedy found that "if we are slow in complying with their requests, they demand it as a right." This shift from what he viewed as "begging" to demanding "as a right" is telling. Traders often complained bitterly about what appeared to them to be a lopsided "reciprocal" relationship. In order to keep on good terms with local people, they were obliged to ply them with goods "for nothing." The Spokane, for example, were a "lazy indolent tribe who do not bring us one hundred Skins in the course of the Year," yet they expected "open House" at the post, as well as frequent gifts of "gratis tobacco" to smoke in their lodges.[98]

There is substantial evidence in Kennedy's own account to indicate that in the eyes of the Spokane the gifts were far from "gratis." The trader acknowledged that people from villages near the post "think us much beholden to them for allowing us to remain on their lands." Similarly, the three local chiefs who received annual clothings from the traders viewed the gifts as "a tribute which they look upon as their right for allowing us to remain on their lands." People from villages some distance away were likewise disposed to visit the post with regular requests for tobacco, ammunition, and medicine, which they regarded as their due. Governor Simpson's 1841 journal sheds further light on Native perceptions of their arrangements with the traders. At Kettle Falls, Simpson was visited by an "aged Chief," who on the governor's first visit in 1824 had made a "formal cession" of the land on which Fort Colville was to be built. It is impossible to be certain of the chief's understanding of the nature of this "cession" (the word is Simpson's), but it appears that he viewed the arrangement much as the Spokane had. Far from a cession in the English sense of a termination of rights, it was an agreement for ongoing reciprocal benefits. Even at this late date, the chief commanded these benefits. He had the ear of the governor for half an hour, and on his departure was given a capote (the standard-issue hooded coat), a shirt, a knife, ammunition, and tobacco.[99] Here was a tangible reaffirmation of the relationship long ago established between himself and the governor, between his people and the company.

Seven decades later, a group of Secwepemc, Okanagan, and Nlaka'pamux leaders spelled out the Native American view of this relationship more definitively. In an address to Canadian Prime Minister Sir Wilfrid Laurier in 1910, the chiefs explained that when the fur traders came to their territory, they became guests on the "ranches" of Native people. The chiefs used the "ranch" or "house" metaphor throughout their statement to explain their tenure on the land: "With us when a person enters our house he becomes our guest, and we must treat him hospitably as long as he shows no hostile intentions. At the same time we expect him to return to us equal treatment for what he receives."[100]

In the fur-trade era, at Fort Nez Percés, too, there is ample evidence that demands that a trader like Simon McGillivray might view as "extortions," motivated entirely by greed for goods, were seen in a rather different light by the people who made the demands. That the Natives viewed the goods they received as their due is indicated by several preconditions of trade: Native refusal of anything was "almost tantamount to a battle"; trade never got under way until the Native people "have had all from us" in the way of gratuities; and in general, "Indians in this quarter, will help themselves to any thing belonging to the Whites, without restitution."[101] McGillivray offered no explicit explanation for such conduct, apart from acknowledging that gifts were the customary way to "make friends." Yet it is abundantly clear from the historical record that the peoples in the vicinity of the Fort Nez Percés firmly believed they had legitimate claims on the company for the goods received—claims arising from their occasional intermarriages with traders, their accommodation of the traders on their lands, their granting regular safe passage up and down the river, and their provision through trade of some 250 horses each year, as well as furs.[102]

In fact, this position had been demonstrated to the North Westers nearly two decades before McGillivray's arrival. In autumn 1814 an NWC brigade, attempting to get down the Columbia as quickly as possible, tried to sneak past a large camp of Cayuse and Nez Percé at the forks of the Columbia and Snake Rivers. Men on horseback dashed into the river, forcibly hauled up the boats, and held them until the assembled people had "smoked themselves drunk." Only then were the North Westers allowed to resume their journey, and then with an admonition "never to attempt passing their camp again without first putting on shore and giving them a smoke." When the traders tried the trick the following summer, a violent struggle resulted and two Native men were shot dead. Ross, whose account is relied on here, believed that if the traders had simply observed the custom of sharing a smoke—the most basic of gifts—the incident would never have happened. Ross blamed the traders for the deterioration of relations in the vicinity of the forks over the next few years.[103]

McGillivray was not one to see such things. He resided at Fort Nez Percés for little more than a year (1831–32) and was an uncommonly petulant trader. His ill-humor may have arisen from his disappointment at the decrepit state of the post when he arrived, and from the company's refusal to grant him furlough. But his relationship with the local people was also a thorn. The misdeeds of his predecessor contributed to his difficulties, but McGillivray was quite capable of making waves on his own account. One wonders, for example, about the effect of his strong desire to be "White" on his relations with Native people. McGillivray was the métis son of a senior NWC partner and his Plains Cree wife. Raised and schooled as a Scottish Canadian, like many métis sons of the trade he cultivated that identity. Reflecting on the anticipated response of Native people to a rumor that Americans had caused the malaria outbreak on the lower Columbia in this period, McGillivray fretted that he and his colleagues would earn their wrath as well, for "We are Whites equally."[104]

McGillivray was not popular in the region. When local communities gathered near the fort for their winter dance in 1831, the chief trader was not among the invited, although it was customary to entertain the head of the post on the final day. His failure to understand and honor the requirements of the relationship long established between traders and Natives is very likely the key to his unpopularity. This is not to imply that he had no cause for complaint. Quite possibly people were more demanding of him than they had been of other chief traders, and there were certainly troublesome individuals about. On several occasions, McGillivray was accused of not treating people in the same "liberal manner" as his predecessor had done. He considered the charges bargaining ploys. They may well have been ploys, at least in part, but they carried a message about what was expected of the trader. Those expectations were based on the long-accepted terms of the relationship between traders and Native people, an arrangement whereby the partners indicated their mutual desire to remain on good terms through the vehicle of gift-giving.[105]

Concluding Remarks

This chapter has explored traders' representations of the fishing societies of the Plateau. While the approach has been to treat them as constructions, attempts have been made to speculatively "reconstruct"—to offer alternative readings by handling the accounts critically, placing each account in the context of the others and of other forms of evidence. In this way it has been possible to unpack the notion of indolence, for traders the defining feature of fishing peoples, and to provide suggestive alternative readings for practices that traders derided as gambling, begging, pleading, and demanding "as a right." A good deal of the chapter has been about cultural misunderstanding—the misapprehension, struggle, and dissension that inhere in the liminal space between distinct cultures. The extent to which traders' understandings of the workings of Plateau economies were bounded at once by culture, gender, and class was clearly revealed in the discussion of their perceptions of the economic contributions of women. The women of the Plateau performed tasks and "dominated" their men in ways that challenged the masculine middle-class sensibilities of these British observers. But the challenge was not so profound that it overturned inherited notions of the "natural" order of things. Even a man like Samuel Black, who stood apart from his colleagues in recognizing the central importance of women's gathered foods, nevertheless characterized Plateau societies as male-dominated "fishing" or "hunting tribes." The persistence of the notion that such societies relied largely on seasonal and fluctuating supplies of fish and game, and so lived a very precarious life, was highlighted: the view persists to a disturbing degree in present-day scholarly studies, many of which look to traders' writings for their evidence. Further examples will be examined in the chapters that follow.

This chapter has also been about the traders' efforts to step beyond the bounds of culture, to bridge—for reasons of expedience—the cultural gap. The desire of the British for furs and of Native peoples for trade goods forced an accommodation, the establishment of a social space in which trade relations could take place. The most significant ritual of that space was gift exchange. Through gift exchange, the space of Plateau kin groups was extended metaphorically to encompass the outsiders.

Traders willingly adopted the ritual, long since standard practice throughout fur-trade country, because it worked: gifts enabled traders to "make friends" with the Indians. The accommodation was not based, on either side, on any deep understanding of the other's motives. The conflicts and misunderstandings that arose when the accommodation faltered, as it so often did, make this abundantly clear. The accommodation worked out between traders and Native peoples in the Plateau was a pragmatic one, enacted in a fragile social space.

   The alleged indolence of the fishing peoples of the Plateau was, of course, linked to the fact that they were little interested in trapping furs for trade. However, there was far more to indolence than failure to trap. The Dalles epitomized the rude state of nature in which these peoples were said to dwell: here people gathered in the thousands to indulge, in the traders' view, their moral failings by gambling, thieving, and living off the riches of the river. The very reliance of Plateau peoples on the bounty of the Columbia and Fraser systems was seen as testimony to their indolence—or at least that of the men. The extent to which men relied on the labors of women was, in the eyes of these British observers, not only unnatural, but unmanly. The other predictable outcome of reliance on the rivers was winter food shortages or starvation. These are themes of the next chapter.

CHAPTER FIVE

The Want of Meat

Cultural Meanings of Hunger and Plenty

In the eyes of fur traders, the fishing peoples of the Plateau were the poor of the region. The ultimate manifestation of their poverty was starvation. Cases of "starving," "half starving," and the like were reported with startling frequency throughout the era of trade in the Interior. This chapter explores the complex meanings of such terms, beginning with an analysis of specific fur-trade connotations. The cultural roots of traders' conceptions of what constituted "good food" will then be considered, touching on the contrasts between their notions and indigenous Plateau notions. Salmon did not rank high on the traders' list, for a combination of historically specific and broader cultural reasons. Traders' misunderstandings of basic salmon biology, the seasonality and cyclical nature of the several species available in the Plateau, and the particular cultural uses to which the fish was put, contributed to the perception that subsistence on a diet heavy in fish was precarious.

For all the talk of starvation in traders' writings from the Plateau, the only record of deaths due to food scarcity is in a letter from Kamloops in the winter of 1829. Writing to a fur-trade colleague in March of that year, Francis Ermatinger reported that "the misery we have had is unprecedented. The natives all around us are actually in such a state of starvation, that it is impossible they can survive, some are already dead." Company employees, too, faced severe shortages, and seven men were sent down to Fort Vancouver to ease the burden on the post! The

Kamloops case is examined in detail in the latter part of this chapter, and consideration is given to the ways in which the fur trade may have affected indigenous subsistence strategies in that locale.

"Technical" Starvation

Reports of starvation in the documentary record of the fur trade are frequently taken at face value, leading to potentially serious misunderstandings of Native American subsistence patterns. As anthropologist Mary Black-Rogers has demonstrated in her study of traders' perceptions of Algonquian and Athapaskan cultures, "starving" came in many varieties and often had little to do with shortage of food.[2] Close analysis of the traders' uses of the term, and, as we have seen, of related concepts like "indolent" and "pitiful," reveals much about their perceptions of indigenous subsistence methods, and about the interfaces between those views and their business interests.

David Thompson made explicit the perceived link between a fishing way of life and deprivation when he wrote of the Lower Kutenai that they were "living on Fish . . . their Poverty owing to a War broke out between them and the Peagans [Piegan]." Cox found these people the most wretched of any he encountered, as they had "no horses, are poor hunters, go nearly naked, and subsist principally on fish." The image of the famished, impoverished fishing Indian was persistent. In 1822, a dozen years after Thompson, Alexander Kennedy would write from Spokane House that the Lower Kutenai still had no regular intercourse with the traders, and so remained fishermen, living "half starved and half naked."[3]

These are examples of what Black-Rogers has classified as the "technical" usage of starving and related concepts—terminology that was technical in the sense that it had very definite fur-trade connotations. This usage did not necessarily imply literal starvation, that is, "dying of hunger, or suffering from lack of food."[4]

It often did mean that people were not eating what the traders considered proper or adequate food. The principal message was that the people in question were in the position of having to direct primary attention to their own food needs, leaving little time for other activities—the activity of most concern to the traders, of course, being the trapping of furs. This goes a long way toward explaining the exasperation of Simon McGillivray during his posting at Fort Nez Percés in 1831–32. His journal is spiced with references to the people around the post "starving," "getting desperate for salmon," and "begging something to eat." By mid-March there was still no beaver trade, leading McGillivray to grumble that "the tribes of the Columbia, *do nothing in winter*, but procure a livelihood, and the latter with a great deal of trouble."[5] There may well have been food shortage involved, but McGillivray's central concern was clearly something other than the hunger of the local people.

Supplies of fresh food were indeed limited in winter in the Plateau, and stored foods were essential to survival. Nevertheless, context is crucial to understanding the condition of the people the traders were describing. Descriptions like McGillivray's, of Native people "starving" or "getting desperate," often meant that they were looking for food and as a result not "adding to our beaver," rather than that they were literally going without food. Governor Simpson's description of the Colville (Sxoielpi), whom he encountered at Kettle Falls on his first visit to the Columbia, is instructive. He noted that they were "more wretched than any I had seen on the East side the Mountains," a phrase suggestive of severe suffering. Then he elaborated: these people appeared to be living on "rotten" salmon and did not have "a single article of British Manufacture in their possession but a Gun and Beaver Trap." The Colville were on this occasion doubly wretched: by virtue of the pressure of their need to procure food, and their want of means to procure furs.[6]

Archibald McDonald's reflections on the state of the groups who frequented the post at Kamloops further illustrate this technical usage of "starving." In the post journal for 1826–27, he remarked that the people of the vicinity were "Starving four months in the year." Obviously they were not literally starving for that long, or there would have been reports of mortality. There is no mention of deaths from starvation or unknown causes in the journal. The district report for 1827 sheds some light on the puzzle.

In this report McDonald noted that beaver returns at Kamloops had been falling off for about four years and that the animal was "on the verge of extermination." He said the local people felt the loss, and "the rapid disappearance of wood animals also." Martens provided an alternative for trade, but circumstances were such that even the groups he cited as formerly the most productive fur hunters of the district—the Northern Okanagan, Similkameen, and North Thompson Secwepemc—were becoming dependent on salmon fishing for their living, and were often "reduced to roots." Again, the need to procure food was getting in the way of fur trapping, and was contributing to the traders' depiction of the Natives as "starving." The repercussions of the depletion of fur bearers and other animals in this region are discussed below in the section on the Kamloops case study. Later accounts from Kamloops indicate that factors other than food needs could interfere with fur collection. In the winter of 1843 large numbers of local people congregated around the post "for no other purpose than to see and hear the [newly arrived Catholic] priest." Such as might have been hunting were frittering away their time waiting to see the visitor, and—perhaps by extension—they were "starving of hunger."[7]

Native people were also judged to be in need when they were unable or unwilling to supply the traders with food, and especially meat. Simon Fraser, travelling among the Lower Nlaka'pamux in 1808, noted their generosity and helpfulness; however, although they provided Fraser's party with the best they had, including dried salmon, "that best was commonly wretched if not disgusting." David Thompson's ranking of fish and meat provides a clue to Fraser's complaint. In Thompson's words, "fish however plenty can never compensate the want of Deer, Sheep, and Goats," both for food and clothing.[8] Later in this chapter, I consider how such views bore on the image of those the traders called fishermen.

Rotten Fish and Salmon "Failure"

Although there is scant evidence of Native people starving to death in the Columbia Interior in the period under study, there is rather more evidence of people "suffering from lack of food," most often in late winter. In fur-trade idiom the notion of suffering, like starving, came in many shades.

Traders' writings from upstream locales like the Kootenays, Spokane, Colville, and Kamloops are larded with references to people collecting "dead and dying," "putrid," or "rotten" salmon. Fish collected on the lower and middle Columbia in autumn were described in similar terms. The eating of such fish was often equated with starvation, and the people collecting these specimens viewed as desperate "salmon eaters" indeed. Thus, a party Governor Simpson encountered on Lower Arrow Lake in October 1824 appeared "more wretched than any on the east side the Mountains." They were collecting "putrid salmon," which with "a few roots" would be their food for winter.[9]

Such observations must be viewed in the context of the time of year at which they were recorded, and the relevant phase of the salmon season. In most cases they were recorded in autumn, after the principal salmon runs. Most of the salmon described as "putrid"—and this state, too, came in varying degrees—would have been spawned-out or exhausted chinook or sockeye. Salmon generally do not feed during the migration to their natal streams and lakes, and the demands on their energy reserves for migration, maturation of gonads, spawning, and nest defence are great. Pre-migration fat reserves of sockeye, for example, are depleted by about 90 percent by the time of death at the spawning grounds, and protein reserves by one-third to two-thirds. Yet one's trash is another's treasure: lean fish are very suitable for preserving by the method of air drying. While fat chinook and sockeye were delectable and sought after by Native people to eat fresh, their high water and oil contents meant that extra care was required in drying, as they were prone to rancidity and bacterial infection. Lean fish were preferable for preservation.[10]

John Work gained insight into the movements and use of salmon on his first visit to the Kootenay region in 1823. He learned from Kutenai informants that the salmon came out of the sea in huge numbers and were "remarkably fine" when they first entered the Columbia. As they moved upstream, they grew leaner, "and finally get so emaciated that they die, they continue still struggling against the stream while they have life." The Kutenai Work encountered were busily collecting such fish for winter provisions.[11] Earlier in the season, higher-quality chinook would have been available from stocks that spawned near the headwaters of the Columbia. But at the best of times, regions this far inland had nothing like the quantity or quality of salmon available at such favored sites as The Dalles and Kettle Falls. Such differences in resource distributions were fundamental to Plateau social relations. These conditions made it essential to gather, fish, and hunt in other groups' territories. The multi-ethnic gatherings at Kettle Falls each summer, and the great assembly of people at "the big time" in Yakama territory, are examples of such cooperative utilization of favored harvest sites.

There is ample evidence of "fine" salmon being caught far upriver earlier in the season. At Spokane House in 1822–23, Alexander Kennedy saw both fine and "bad" salmon being collected, and noted their complementary roles in the local diet:

> In the month of Time [June] when the Salmon begin to come about in this part of the Country, the Natives generally resort to certain parts of the different Rivers, which fall into the Columbia, where they form villages and employ themselves in catching and drying Salmon for winter use. . . . In the fall of the

Year [the salmon] are seen striving against the Stream, when they have almost lost all their fins and tails with large spots on their bodies. In this state however they are never rejected by the Natives, even after they die and have lain two or three weeks in the water, they are eagerly sought after and hung up in their natural state, to be used when necessity requires.[12]

The least-desirable and half-rotten fish were taken for times of need as a hedge against possible shortages in winter. While it was not the principal food source, the inclusion of such fish in the diet suggests that, as one commentator has put it, "the margin of safety for winter survival was not overly generous."[13]

Salmon "failures" were cited as a cause of winter hunger from time to time, and the belief that salmon runs might inexplicably fail reinforced the notion that the fishing life was a precarious one. The year 1825 appears to have been a poor one for salmon on the Columbia, due to unusually low water. In October, Work expressed concern that people around Spokane were getting no "bad salmon," normally collected in abundance at this season, and he warned that "this will likely be a starving winter with the Indians." Three months earlier, John Dease had reported to Governor Simpson that the salmon fishery at Walla Walla "failed," that stocks of dried fish at the post were low, and that "the Indians all about are starving now." Things could not have been too urgent, for Dease made only passing mention of the problem in the midst of a discussion of the prospects for trade that year. He made no mention at all of steps to ameliorate the situation, raising the question of whether there was, in fact, a situation to ameliorate.[14]

Further reports of a possible salmon "failure" came the following July. Samuel Black noted in the post journal that "the is Ky ouse [Cayuse] and Walla Wallas are now almost all off the Ground (for this year there is no Salmon) to go to make their Harvest Roots." It is not clear what "no Salmon" meant: perhaps fewer than the trader had reason to expect? It is also possible that he recorded the observation between salmon runs. At any rate, it is instructive to note the evolution in Black's understanding of the economic strategies of local groups. The year 1826 was Black's first at Walla Walla. He was aware of the movement of people from the river to the root and berry grounds, and took this to be a consequence of the failure of the salmon run. By 1829, his fourth year in the district, Black had determined that "the great support of the Natives in this District is their Nutritive Roots . . . and a great Cause of their movements and residences at certain Seasons." Presumably, he would no longer interpret movement to the root grounds as a sign of the failure of salmon runs.[15]

Biological evidence indicates that salmon runs in these rivers never entirely "fail," except in a very rare instance such as the Fraser River landslide of 1913. The perceived "failure" of Columbia salmon runs in 1825 may have been a case of unusually low returns of the economically important chinook or steelhead species due to very low water. Runs are subject to dramatic fluctuation in the normal course of things. Floods, drought, landslides, and variation in other natural conditions all affect the size of runs. Sockeye exhibit a very marked four- or five-year cycle, an aspect of their life history that never ceased to baffle traders (see the Kamloops case study below). The biological properties of salmon and the other fauna of the Plateau continue to baffle many historians and anthropologists. Ignorance of basic natural history can result in seriously flawed conclusions. An example is found in anthropologist Peter Carstens's 1991 book on the Okanagan. Carstens uses a trader's account of food shortage among the Lil'wat in May 1846 as evidence that "the salmon run on the Fraser River failed in 1846." This is in turn used as evidence of periodic starvation among the Lil'wat, a state of affairs which Carstens argues was exacerbated by the fur trade. He appears unaware that there is not one, but many salmon runs every year on the Fraser, and that the first big runs generally do not reach the Lillooet area until late June.[16]

To return to the Columbia, the salmon run of most importance to the indigenous population was the early autumn chinook run (late August–early September). The bulk of winter stores came from this run. Columbia dwellers also exploited a smaller spring chinook run (late April–May); summer runs of sockeye, chinook, and steelhead (late June–July); an early autumn pink run (odd years only, and only on the lower river); and an October chum run (even years only). Figures for commercial yields on the Columbia (ca. 1880–1940) indicate that quantities available to Native American populations would have been far in excess of their needs.[17]

In addition to salmon, sought-after species in the rivers and lakes of the Plateau included trout, whitefish, suckers, eels, and other local types. Huge sturgeon were caught on the lower and middle Fraser River and the lower Columbia River. Where and when they were available, these species could be significant supplements to salmon in Native diets. Whitefish and suckers were the main fish resources available to the Salish Flathead in the far eastern Plateau, for example. Salmon was very important in the diet of most of the peoples of the region, but, as was shown in chapter 4, its role has often been overemphasized. Fur traders were as guilty of this as many later students have been; indeed, traders' accounts inform many subsequent interpretations. A careful reading of the fur-trade record points to the diversity of indigenous subsistence strategies and spreading of activities over several ecological zones to draw on a range of vegetable and animal foods. This argument is taken up further in chapter 6.

Winter Shortage and the Want of Meat

To argue that the various subsistence strategies used generally provided amply, begs the question of what happened when they did not. Recurrent food shortages—and the worst-case episode of deaths from starvation at Kamloops—demonstrate that the best safety mechanisms could fail. The possible impact of the fur trade on such mechanisms is considered in the Kamloops case study.

Winter scarcity was a recurrent reality in the Plateau. Fresh foods were very few; in many areas they were limited to lake fish taken through the ice and perhaps some tuberous perennials. Stored foods were essential to survival. To say that scarcity was recurrent is not to suggest that it was inevitable, nor that references to starvation in winter can be accepted uncritically. Examples from Work's reports from Colville in 1829 and 1830 make this very clear.[18] In his first report Work noted simply that the people of the district "suffer severely sometimes from famine." In the following year he elaborated, observing that the fishing groups of the district, and the Kettle Falls people (Sxoielpi) in particular, were "frequently reduced to the utmost degree of wretchedness in the winter season, and the small quantity and bad quality of what they often subsist on is almost incredible."[19] This is a surprising assertion, given that the Colville lived at the site of the main fishery of the upper Columbia. It becomes more meaningful in the context of the remainder of the report.

Work's comments on the plight of these fishing groups came on the heels of a description of the hunters of the district. The Salish Flathead, Kalispel, and Upper Kutenai were said to "seldom know the want of provisions." This raises the suspicion that the suffering of the fishing groups was defined by contrast to the experience of the hunters. Another trader, Alexander Henry, made just such a comparison some years earlier. In describing the "vast shoals of salmon" that passed up the Kootenay River in summer and fall, he noted that while some of the fish were large and fine, most were lean, and "such poor eating that the worst meat is far preferable." One wonders whether the contrasts being drawn here had more to do with eating meat versus not eating meat than with actual abundance and scarcity. David Thompson made the contrast explicit in his statement that fish "can never compensate the want of Deer, Sheep, and Goats."[20]

It was not that Thompson, Work, and their colleagues found anything intrinsically offensive about fish. Traders were appreciative of a fresh or well-cured salmon. They acknowledged that at particularly good fishing sites, fish provided an easy living; as Governor Simpson put it, salmon offered "abundant provision at little trouble." The abundance of the Dalles-Celilo fishery on the lower Columbia was legendary. Other major sites in the Plateau included Priest Rapids and Kettle Falls on the Columbia and the Fountain on the Fraser. At the height of a run at Kettle Falls, a single communal basket net could capture one thousand salmon in a day. During an excellent run on the Thompson River, a trader might see a spear expert take two to three hundred salmon in a night. Traders were impressed by these feats.[21] Nevertheless, such abundance was viewed as a highly localized and fleeting phenomenon. The more predictable outcome of reliance on salmon, they believed, was deprivation and winter starvation. And however plentiful fish might be, a diet heavy in fish—good salmon or otherwise—was seen as lamentable.

The Want of Meat: European Resonances

The flesh of animals has long occupied the paramount position in the hierarchy of foods in Western cultures, and in many other traditions. Here I can merely suggest some of the reasons for this. In material terms, the status of meat derives from its relative scarcity, unpredictability, and difficulty of capture, as well as the cost-efficiency of the hunting of large mammals (the high return per unit effort). The prestige, ritual, and myth that have grown up around hunting animals in many cultures relate in part, no doubt, to these issues of costliness and unpredictability. A recent study of the cultural meanings of meat in Western traditions locates its potency more narrowly in its symbolic expression of human control over nature. The act of consuming the muscle flesh of other highly evolved animals, writes social anthropologist Nick Fiddes, is the ultimate demonstration of human control of, and superiority over, the natural world.[22] Whatever the basis of this cultural affinity for meat, it is clear that it is deep-seated and symbolically charged, and far more than a question of economic and technical costs and benefits. What is considered good to eat is also, to borrow an evocative phrase, a matter of "value judgements . . . and phantasmic beliefs."[23]

In Western cultures the luxury value of meat has long defined it as a kind of "social cement," a measure of position in the social hierarchy and a means of reproducing that position. An illustration of this was found in chapter 3 where fur-trade officers were seen reserving scarce fresh game for themselves, leaving servants to eat dried fish and horse.[24] Historian Stephen Mennell has explored the workings of this social cement in England and France from the Middle Ages to the present. Meat has been a marker of social position throughout. The prodigious consumption of meat by the ecclesiastical and secular upper ranks during the long centuries of the Middle Ages is a familiar image. In stark contrast, the diet of the medieval peasantry was, for the most part, very heavy on cereals and very light on meat.[25] It was a self-perpetuating tendency. The relative scarcity of meat and its association with wealth made it all the more coveted: the social value of meat underlay, and reinforced, its economic value.

By the end of the eighteenth century, although the tastes of the upper classes in Britain had evolved in significant ways, and middle-class people of means had begun to emulate the carnivorous habits of the aristocracy, class differences in meat consumption were as pronounced as they had been in the Middle Ages.[26] If anything, consumption of meat by rural working people had declined as a consequence of progressive restrictions on hunting by the lower orders. Any meat consumed by working people had to be purchased from butchers, or poached—often at risk to life and limb—from the estates and other preserves of landed wealth. The basic diet of the working family still consisted of masses of bread, porridge, or potatoes. Meat, in the form of poorer cuts or offal, was purchased from the butcher perhaps once a week. These are sweeping generalizations; naturally, there were great variations among categories of working people, and from region to region.[27]

By the turn of the nineteenth century growing numbers of well-paid artisans, professionals, and others at the upper end of the middle class could afford to buy meat, poultry, and fish on a regular basis. Those who could were sure to do so. As E. P. Thompson has demonstrated, meat was "one of the first items upon which any increase in real wages will have been spent." Clearly, it was a powerful marker of social standing. Prosperous middle-class families, emulating the time-honored traditions of wealthy Britons, often made meals of several types of meat, fowl, and fish. If they ate bread at all at mealtimes, it was certain to be white bread. Bread, like meat, had social connotations; dark bread, like offal, connoted coarseness.[28]

The Want of Meat in the Fur Trade

A look at traders' perceptions of their own diets in fur-trade country will help to illuminate their impressions of indigenous diets. The record from the Columbia Interior is full of complaints about the "horrid stuff" on which traders were expected to subsist. Their grumbling must be considered in light of evidence on contemporary diet in the home territories. This is not to diminish the hardships traders faced in fur-trade country from time to time. But to measure those hardships against the standard of the late twentieth century, as more than one historian has done, is a meaningless exercise.[29]

Many in the servant class in the Columbia were recruited from the Highlands and islands of Scotland, and from Lower Canada. According to one seasoned fur-trade observer, those recruited from the Scottish isles had "Seldom, if Ever, Eat Any thing better than Pease or Barley Bread with Salt Sellocks [fish] and Kale."[30] The staples in the Orkneys and Hebrides were indeed oatmeal porridge, barley bread, and cabbages. Fish were widely eaten in coastal communities, and small farmers could keep a few household chickens or geese and perhaps a pig for feast times. Shetlanders ate potatoes in place of oatmeal and barley and had more access to lamb, but they, too, would have eaten far more fish than meat. One Shetland crofter in 1804 described his daily routine as coalfish for breakfast, coalfish and cabbage for the midday meal, and coalfish for dinner.[31]

In Lower Canada most fur-trade recruitment took place in the so-called voyageur parishes along the St. Lawrence River, and in the city of Montreal. The diet of working people in Montreal appears to have been broadly similar to that of working people in Britain at the time—heavy in bread and dried pulses, with limited supplements of butcher's meat. Things may have been somewhat better in the parishes, where people relied on subsistence agriculture. Estimates of wheat consumption at over two pounds per person per day, however, indicate that flour was by far the dominant staple. This makes company rations of a pound of flour per employee per day seem less extraordinary.[32]

Complaints about fur-trade food in the Interior, particularly from servants, were endless. Chief Trader John Tod sympathized with the men who walked off the job at Kamloops in the early 1840s to protest the "privations" of a steady diet of dried salmon. He noted that he had never heard of such an action in his thirty-six years in the fur trade, giving further credence to their grievances. Tod can be excused for not being aware that servants at Prince of Wales Fort had taken similar action in the 1750s, and for the same reason: too much dried fish on the menu.[33] While a steady diet of dried salmon sounds dreadful, it is hard to conceive of it as any worse than a steady diet of bread, oatmeal, or coalfish.[34] The issue of why a diet of salmon was considered so offensive is further considered below.

The eating habits of company men in the Columbia Interior went through several phases. Although detailed accounts are not available, it is clear that throughout the North West Company years and in the first years after the HBC merger, officers wanted for little in the way of familiar foods from home. A large assortment of imported provisions arrived annually on the supply ship from Britain. The goods were transported inland at great expense in brigade canoes and, where necessary, by horse brigade. Gardens were planted to try to reduce costs in the NWC years, but apart from some potatoes and turnips, few of the vegetables "came to perfection" in the Interior.[35] Among imported goods, the basics included flour and salt pork; the inventory ran to coffee, chocolate, a variety of sweets, preserves, and spices. The sheer volume of foods imported for the benefit of the gentlemen astounded the economy-minded Governor Simpson on his first visit in 1824.[36]

It is more difficult to ascertain what servants ate in the early years. They would have had regular rations of imported flour, and perhaps salt pork from time to time. On top of that, they undoubtedly supported themselves on rather fewer imported goods and rather more country produce. For most, that meant a great deal of dried salmon. Servants at Fort Nez Percés exercised a different option. Despite the post's position near one of the most productive fisheries on the Columbia River, they ate horse. The constant scarcity of horses for transport in the Interior was no deterrent. Some seven hundred of the animals were consumed at the post in the years 1823 to 1825 alone. Governor Simpson's crackdown on waste curtailed, but could not eliminate, the practice.[37]

Under Simpson's program of rationalization, company employees gradually settled into a hybrid dietary regime based largely on a mixture of fish, game, and gathered foods, locally raised crops, and domesticated animals.[38] Some importation, notably of flour, continued until the farm at Fort Colville was in full production. By 1830 the farm was "so productive as to render the place nearly independent of any other means of subsistence whatever." The local people were told to bring no more country produce but fat (partly as a means of encouraging them to trap more fur-bearers). Fort Colville was the granary of the Interior, including New Caledonia. Throughout the 1830s and 1840s it supplied between 75 and 90 percent of the grain demands of Interior posts. Gardening at Kamloops was confined to potatoes, which produced well. The small garden at Fort Nez Percés, meanwhile, apparently only provided vegetables enough for the chief factor's family.[39]

After 1825 the diet of a servant in the Columbia Interior was based on a daily ration of "one quart of Indian Corn or pease with two ounces Grease pr. Day," plus such fish, game, and other country produce as was available. This worked out to about eleven and one-half bushels of "corn" (wheat flour) per man per year. With the growing number of servants in the country—the number climbed from 184 in the year of merger to over 450 in 1835—demands for wheat swelled. Whereas 2,100 bushels were required in 1821, some 7,000 were needed in 1846.[40]

Dried salmon, of course, was the staple that rounded out the rations of flour, peas, and grease. Traders were not fond of it. This attitude was not confined to the Columbia, although it probably reached fullest expression there. East of the Rockies, service at so-called "fish posts" was widely viewed as a penance. At posts where meat was more plentiful, fish often found its way to the dogs.[41]

Employees in the Columbia consumed huge quantities of salmon. The example of Fort Okanogan in 1826 was discussed earlier: during a period just short of ten months, 18,411 dried salmon were eaten. All the fish came through trade with Native American fishers, the bulk of it from the Fraser River, since the Okanagan had little surplus for trade. This is a fine illustration of the extent to which fur traders were dependent on the services of Native people.[42]

Doing all this eating were three officers, each with a wife and two with a child; twelve men, their eight wives, and ten children; and an unspecified number of local Native people who came to the post for food from time to time when their supplies ran short (they ate only 670 fish). Each servant's daily ration was three fish, weighing an average of one pound each dried and boneless, plus two for his wife and one for each child. Three pounds of dried salmon may not sound like a herculean amount, but it is considerable. The company considered it the equivalent of ten pounds of fresh. The salmon ration alone in the Interior provided about 2,300 calories of food energy, the recommended daily intake for an adult male of small stature, and more than is required by a woman.[43]

Of course, humans have not only a physiological but a cultural need for variety in their diet. The diet of employees at Okanogan, as at other posts, was varied somewhat with seasonal inputs. These, too, were supplied in large part by the people of the region. Again, the officers fared rather better than the men. The distribution of country produce illustrates well the role of meat in reproducing the social hierarchy. In 1826 the three gentlemen, their wives, and two children at Okanogan ate 799 pounds of fresh venison, compared with just 344 pounds for the twelve servants. Wildfowl went entirely to the officers, as did small game (rabbits and badgers) and rare fresh bear meat. Proportionate to their numbers, the gentlemen also came in for a larger share of the fresh salmon (163 pounds to the men's 347 pounds), as well as berries and nuts. Additional items in the inventory included 284 pounds of horse meat and sixteen dogs, all eaten by the men, and some 48 gallons of roots, fairly evenly shared. While officers dined much better than their subordinates, it nevertheless appears that even for the servants, there was reasonable variation in the diet over the course of the year—perhaps more variety than many would have had access to in their home regions. It was the day-to-day monotony that was the source of many of the complaints.[44]

The Weakness of Fish

The dim view traders took of salmon is illustrative of another aspect of the food hierarchy in British cultural traditions. Non-red meats, fowl, and fish have long been construed as "weaker" than red meat, and are assigned to lower rungs in the hierarchy. Fowl was superior to fish in the traders' scheme because of its relative scarcity and, no doubt, because of the prestige it was accorded in Britain: by the eighteenth century the killing of game birds was largely reserved for the landed aristocracy. Weaker still in this long-standing hierarchy were secondary animal products like eggs and cheese, and at the bottom of the scale were vegetables and fruits.

As one student of the cultural meanings of meat has observed, in Western cultures "the status and meaning of meat is quintessentially found in red meat."[45] Red meat is, and long has been, perceived as strong food; the eating of it implies incorporation of some measure of the special powers of the animal consumed—the strength, aggression, sexuality, and other elements seen as the "animal nature" of humans. It comes as no surprise that the perceived strength of meat has long defined it as quintessentially masculine food. It has been seen as virile food, too much of it a threat to the more "delicate" constitutions of women, children, the old, and the infirm.

The power of such perceptions in the late-eighteenth and early-nineteenth centuries is manifest in contemporary prescriptions for good health. In Britain the most influential of health manuals for lay domestic use was William Buchan's *New Domestic Medicine.* "Dr. Buchan" went through myriad editions in Britain between 1769 and 1846, and was reprinted until 1913 in the United States. Significantly for present purposes, it was especially popular in Scotland, where by contemporary accounts there was "Scarcely a cottage but what contains on its shelf the Domestic Medicine."[46] The manual advised that animal flesh, being "wholesome" and "solid, with a sufficient degree of tenacity," was the best food for men. "Laborious" men, in particular, required sufficient red meat to fuel their bodies. In line with such prescriptions, training diets for soldiers and athletes called for enormous quantities. Dr. Buchan cautioned, however, that even for the laborious, there were limits: too much red meat was "too great a stimulus to the system." Those weaker in constitution, including women, children, the old, and the infirm, were advised to choose "lighter" foods—

chicken, fish, eggs, and the like. Red meat stood at the masculine pole of a highly gendered code of food.[47]

While none made reference to Dr. Buchan's prescriptions, it is clear that traders in the Plateau were influenced by such discourse on the inferior nutritional properties of fish. They were not expressing mere preference, or the bias of a jaded palate, when they denigrated fish as a staple. Jules Quesnel expounded on the bad effect several years of such "*mauvaise nouriture*" had on the constitution of his previously robust colleagues in New Caledonia, and Thomas Dears complained that he had grown so emaciated he was in danger of "slipping through my Breeks." John McLean remarked that until traders got used to it, a steady diet of salmon affected them like a dose of Glauber salts.[48]

Descriptions of the indigenous peoples believed to live on a diet of fish, or fish and roots, reflect these views. The Sanpoil, living on dried salmon and roots, were said to be "meagre wretches" whose features would be improved with better nourishment—that is, with meat. The banks of the Columbia south of Okanogan were lined during the fishing season with people judged to be of similar appearance. Simon McGillivray was quick to blame the illness of some Native people around Walla Walla in the spring of 1831 on their "bad fare during winter"; more likely, these people had contracted malaria, which at the time was raging on the lower Columbia (see chapter 2). When Ross encountered some Secwepemc living on fish, roots, and berries, they were in his view in "wretched condition," though paradoxically they seemed "comfortable and happy" enough.[49]

At a particularly good fishing site Native people might appear to better advantage. Simpson found the people at Kettle Falls, for example, to be "very good looking and generally stouter than the natives of the East side the Mountain." Thompson's assessment of the Wenatchi provides an instructive contrast. In comparison to many of the groups he had seen living on fish on the upper Columbia, the Wenatchi were "more full in form," owing to what he took to be the superior nourishment in the flesh of "Antelopes, Mountain Sheep [Big Horn], and Goats."[50]

"Reduced to Roots"

If fish made a poor staple, vegetable foods were worse. Many traders acknowledged the value of such foods as a nutritious supplement to fish or meat, and for variety. Even on a trader's plate, these strange roots, "mosses," and the like might serve as potatoes, or the "rough bread" of the country. But such foods had no place as a staple. The assumption was that living on vegetable foods was an act of desperation, an option of last resort. Thus Gabriel Franchre observed that even the Salish Flathead, noted buffalo hunters, could be "reduced" to living on roots when badly harassed by their enemies from the plains.[51] The importance of gathered foods to even these most productive hunters is considered in chapter 6.

If a diet of roots was seen as an unhappy fate, scantier still was subsistence on "moss" (black tree lichens). The eating of moss always signified hunger to traders. Baked in cakes, the foreigners found it tolerable—at best tasteless, at worst like soap. But it was "just nourishment [enough] to keep a person alive," and in Thompson's view this was all it was doing for a party of Kutenai he met in the harsh winter of 1808. Thompson wished he could find game enough to release his own party from a dreadful diet of "moss cakes" and dried suckers. Franchère found Sxoielpi who were subsisting on the cakes to be "thin and gaunt, scarcely able to move"; again, he observed that they were often "reduced" to this in winter and spring, when the hunting was poor and the salmon had not yet arrived.[52] The Sanpoil were believed to be in a particularly bad state, deriving, by Thompson's estimate, two-thirds of their diet from roots and berries. The result of this lack of manly meat was that they were "slightly made," and could not bear steady labor. They caught limited quantities of fish with a weir, but he saw no nets or seines in use.

He concluded that "their whole time is taken up in expedients for self preservation."[53]

Thompson's "two-thirds" estimate was astute, given the findings of recent studies, noted in chapter 4, which indicate that vegetable foods accounted for one-third to as much as 60 percent of the calories consumed by Plateau groups. The failure of most traders to recognize the importance of gathered foods in the Plateau diet reflects both their cultural biases in favor of meat and their tendency to undervalue the economic activities of women and the foods that women produced. Another aspect of their denigration of women's contributions was their belittling of the techniques involved in gathering. In the few cases where any effort was made to describe the methods of root gathering, it was figured as "crawling about" like a bear or simply turning the earth with a pointed stick.[54] Technologies for fishing and hunting captured the imaginations of traders, and they were known to describe in detail the formation of a hunting surround or the elasticity of a sinew bow. The technologies associated with gathering, by contrast, were scarcely acknowledged. As their language reveals ("crawling about," "turning up with pointed Stick"), most traders found little to distinguish root gathering from the activities of squirrels and bears.

These kinds of biases persist to a disturbing degree in much of the academic literature on hunting-gathering societies. The very label "hunter-gatherer" speaks to the problem. The precedence long given to hunting in studies of such societies reflects the way in which Western observers have systematically privileged the activities and concerns of men, a bias that in some instances has been affirmed and reinforced by indigenous male informants. For example, anthropologist Theodore Stern notes that the buffalo-hunting peoples of the southern Plateau referred to themselves as "Prairie Indians," in distinction to the river-dwelling fishing people. The defining feature of the Prairie Indian was the male occupation of hunting in the plains. The biases of the scholar must be kept in mind here: Stern speaks rather loosely of two categories of southern Plateau peoples, the "Prairie elite" and the "riverine conservatives and poor." His interpretation echoes that of other popular and scholarly works, which frequently cast the horseback-riding, buffalo-hunting Cayuse and Nez Percé as "imperial tribesmen" of the region.[55] Stern's key authorities for the early nineteenth century, of course, are fur traders and missionaries. It need hardly be repeated that their own perceptions colored their accounts.

However, there are intriguing indications that Native American informants may have played with similar imagery. Hunting ability was (and is) an important symbolic expression of manhood in many Plateau communities, including fishing-gathering communities. In the Sahaptian communities of the middle Columbia a boy's first kill on the hunt was a traditional rite of passage to manhood and a prerequisite for marriage. Eugene Hunn states that even in the fishing communities the first kill was "a minimal test of a man's capacity and willingness to contribute substantially to the task of feeding the next generation."[56] In such a context it would not be surprising if young men talked and boasted about their hunting exploits. At times the boasting might take on other connotations. Some Nez Percé hunters apparently told missionary Samuel Parker that the Wallawalla (who were principally fisher-gatherers) were descendants of their slaves. Another Euro-American reported that Cayuse men viewed it as degrading to marry Wallawalla women, and trader McGillivray noted in his journal that the Nez Percé would not "degrade themselves" to join the Wallawalla in a dance.[57] Whether such things were the product of a sense of real superiority on the part of hunters, or stock statements of the "we're better than them" mentality so common to ethnic discourse, is impossible to tell. The fur-trade record simply does not permit a close analysis of Plateau people's perceptions. However, the available evidence casts shadows on Stern's sharp distinction between "Prairie elites" and "riverine poor." His own genealogical reconstructions show that Cayuse men *did* marry into the middle-Columbia

fishing communities. In addition, the reluctant Nez Percé *did* join the Wallawalla dance. Fear of degradation may be McGillivray's spin on things: the more significant factor holding the Nez Percé back for a time may have been fear of contracting malaria.[58]
To return to scholarly labels, since the 1960s a growing body of research has indicated that for the majority of indigenous societies labels like "hunting societies" or "hunter-gatherers" are not very accurate (arctic societies excepted). Many argue that notations like "gatherer-hunter," "gatherer-fisher-hunter," or the awkward but apt "eclectic subsister" would more closely reflect the relative contributions of various methods of food production.[59] Scholarly interest in women's technologies of food production is recent and limited. In contrast to the notion—subscribed to by not only fur traders but also generations of anthropologists—that gathering plant foods was a simple task, several students of the Plateau have compiled evidence of active management of plant resources by Native American women. In Nez Percé territory, for example, families gathered their plant foods at sites where they had rights based on habitual use. Women were careful to keep to those areas, a practice that had the effect of limiting overuse of any one site. The harvesting was usually the job of women, but as traders' accounts reveal, whole families might pitch in on a large harvest, and certainly the job of transporting roots to storage points near the winter village called for family participation. A root-gathering group might consist of four or five related families. Although the women worked side by side and kept each other company, there was no pooling of the harvest. Each woman took home only what she, and perhaps her young helpers, had produced.[60]
The range of plant foods in use was very extensive. Experts among the Nlaka'pamux, most notably female herbalists, are said to have named at least 350 species of native plants, many of which were used in manufactures, and over a hundred of which were eaten.[61] Roots were the most important of the edible varieties, but traders also saw in use huge quantities of berries

and nuts, a variety of wild vegetables, lichens, fungi, and the cambium and resin of certain trees. In addition to the use of fire to manage these crops, there is evidence of regular culling of root beds and replanting of small roots for later harvest. The harvest itself demanded detailed knowledge of the land, and of plant associations and life cycles. Botanist Nancy Turner argues that indigenous management techniques ensured the continued productivity of even the most intensively used, long-term harvest sites, citing the example of Botanie Valley in Nlaka'pamux territory. There is ample evidence in the traders' journals of such favored sites being used year after year by huge gatherings of people.[62]

While traders were unequivocal in their own views of gathered foods, their writings provide little sense of the value Native people placed on these foods. The anthropological record provides clues. In thanksgiving or "first foods" ceremonies in the fishing-gathering communities of the middle Columbia, foods were traditionally presented in the following order: water, salmon, bitterroot, lomatium species, huckleberries. As Hunn points out, salmon was the first food on the list, but the gathered foods so honored were more numerous. When Hunn asked his Sahaptian collaborator James Selam to rank the major foods in order of importance, he repeatedly refused to do so, saying "all the foods are most important." Selam was unwilling to ascribe to food the kind of hierarchy which for British traders was beyond question.

Starving to Death: A Kamloops Case Study

As the only account of deaths due to starvation in the entire fur-trade record for the Columbia Interior, Francis Ermatinger's account of "unprecedented" suffering at Kamloops in the winter of 1829 calls for further investigation. Unfortunately, there is very little to go on; he said no more than that "the natives all around us are actually in such a state of starvation, that it is impossible they can survive, some are already dead."[63] No other records from the district survive for the year 1829. Archibald McDonald's report of two years earlier referred to people "Starving four months in the year," but his account bore the marks of the technical use of the term, and it lacked any sense of urgency. The most likely explanation for the suffering that Ermatinger witnessed is a coincidence of unfavorable factors, both ecological and fur-trade-related.

That Ermatinger called the suffering "unprecedented" underlines how unusual such a calamity was. He was well acquainted with the region, having spent several years at the Okanogan outpost before moving to Kamloops. While it is impossible to assess the accuracy of the vague statement "some are already dead," equally, there is no reason to doubt it. People starved to death in the winter of 1829, and in light of Ermatinger's comments and the absence of other such accounts for the period under study, it was a rare occurrence.[64] In the course of examining the factors that may have contributed to starvation, we have the opportunity to consider some impacts of the fur trade on the communities of the Thompson River District. Impacts on other areas of the Plateau are explored in chapter 6.

Ecological Factors

Salmon Cycles

A key point to consider in deciphering Ermatinger's account is the cyclic nature of salmon runs in the Fraser-Thompson system. North Wester Finan McDonald was the first trader to draw attention to this phenomenon. In mid-September 1815, McDonald wrote from Kamloops to headquarters that salmon returns were excellent in the region: "Sin 5 years ago there was not so many salmon here the river is alived with Salmon which Exspect plenty Salmon round about here without going to Frasure River."[65] The passage speaks volumes, albeit in singular style, about the nature of sockeye runs. It also highlights a key reason for the traders' concern about the salmon supply. Salmon was the staple at Fort Kamloops, and regular forays were necessary to the fishery and trade center at the Fountain area on the Fraser (in Lil'wat territory) to meet the post's needs.

By far the most important salmon run in the Thompson district is the renowned Adams River sockeye run, which generally passes the Thompson trunk and its south branch in late August. This run is extremely cyclic, with peaks occurring every four or five years. Peak years see several million sockeye migrate from the sea to their spawning grounds in the Adams River, some 230 miles upstream, in the space of about twelve days. The extraordinary return witnessed by McDonald, when the river was "ailved" with salmon, would have been such a run. Since records have been kept, the peak-year run has been up to 250 times the size of the smallest run in the cycle, and about 9 times the size of the sub-peak-year run. While the magnitude of the gap between peak and lesser runs may have differed in degree in the early nineteenth century, it was certainly very marked.[66]

Record keepers at Kamloops regularly interpreted the lesser runs as failures. Recording events at the post in 1843, John Tod wrote as though an unforeseen catastrophe were unfolding. Fearing for the welfare of his men as well as for the Native people, Tod noted that the Indians were "much alarmed" and "greatly disappointed" at the "unusual scarcity of salmon." The more usual situation, according to Tod, was as it had been the year before, when by late August the local people had an abundance of dried salmon and immense quantities were "still flowing in on them." The early arrival of "white" salmon (probably chinook, which normally follow sockeye here) led people to predict a general scarcity in 1843 and to "give up all hopes of securing anything here for winter subsistence." Such an occurrence may indeed have been a disappointment to the local people, but by no means would it have been unexpected. Tod, on the other hand, had been at the post just two years. To him, a low year looked like a disaster. That he did not understand the nature of sockeye runs is further revealed by his apprehension that the Fraser fishery, too, would "fail."[67]

Sockeye is only one of five species to ascend the Fraser system (six if steelhead is included), and the Adams River run is only one race of sockeye.[68] Successive sockeye runs ascend the Fraser between early July and September, all of them on a four- or five-year cycle, although the others are less extreme than the Adams River cycle. In addition, Native groups on the middle Fraser were generally able to exploit other salmon runs: three chinook runs (big runs in early July and late September–October, and a smaller run in August); a pink run in August-September (odd-numbered years only, and only on the lower river); a coho run in September-October; and a chum run in October (even-numbered years only). Chinook are far less abundant than the other species, but what they lack in number, they make up for in size. In combination, the catch from these numerous and varied runs provided an abundant and reliable food source on the Fraser.[69] Barring an event like the disastrous 1913 landslide in the Fraser Canyon, the Fraser would not fail to provide. The Secwepemc, living in a less-favored area for fishing, regularly travelled to the Fountain, in Fraser River Lil'wat territory, to trade for salmon. Traders were likely to interpret such movement as an act of desperation. For instance, when Secwepemc trading parties set out for the Fraser in the autumn of 1843, Tod saw it as an unusual move, a symbol of their distress at the "failure" of their own salmon fishery. In fact, his journal reveals that they had also made the trip the previous winter, following a highly successful salmon season.[70]

Wildlife Depletion

Like other indigenous groups in the Plateau, the Secwepemc and others who traded at Kamloops were not wholly dependent on the salmon fishery for their subsistence. Hunting and gathering of plant foods provided vital shares of their food supplies. Evidence from two years earlier suggests that by the time of Ermatinger's report, hunting conditions had deteriorated. In the post journal for 1827, Archibald McDonald wrote that "Beaver are on the verge of extermination, which the natives themselves observe, and not only deprecate this loss, but the rapid disappearance of the wood animals also." The decline of the beaver was dramatic. Fur returns from the region were always modest, peaking at just under three thousand pelts in 1822, the bulk of which were beaver.[71] By 1826, however, returns had fallen to one-third their peak level, and McDonald would note that "even the name of a Beaver is scarcely heard among the natives." Returns from the most productive and highly regarded hunters, the North Thompson Secwepemc, were "woefully falling off." The steel trap and commercial trade had taken their toll, and the population would not readily recover. Nevertheless, McDonald urged the local people to hunt such fur bearers as they could find, and in 1827 a record four hundred martens were procured. This marked the emergence of marten as the major fur export from the Thompson River District. Its pelts would never reach the volume of beaver in earlier years, but McDonald's hope that marten would prove to be "adapted for the China Market" was fulfilled, and the district contributed to the steady growth in marten exports until it became the largest single fur export from the Columbia in the 1840s.[72]

While beaver were clearly hit hard by the new demands of production for exchange, McDonald's account of the "rapid disappearance" of wood animals is more puzzling. As evidence of this decline, he suggested that groups like the Similkameen and Northern Okanagan, whom he identified as formerly good hunters, had been forced by the decline of animal resources to rely on fish for their livelihood. This may reveal more about

McDonald's views on the relative status of fishing and hunting as means of subsistence than about the dynamics of wildlife populations. Earlier traders had not found the Okanagan to be productive hunters; they were frequently disparaged as "indolent." McDonald's remarks on the "disappearance" of game appear to be rooted in his general impression of that part of the Thompson's River district that he had come to know since he had arrived a year before. He held out little hope for the productivity of the place: a person could walk "for days together without seeing the smallest quadrupeds, the little brown squirrel excepted." Perhaps because of the near extermination of the beaver, McDonald read scarcity as a sign of recent depletion.[73]

It is appropriate to recall at this point that the southern Secwepemc country around Kamloops lies in the bunchgrass–ponderosa pine zone of the Interior Plateau, the driest biogeoclimatic zone in British Columbia and an area not rich in wildlife. The landscape impressed traders and other early travellers as desert; vast stretches of bunchgrass and scrubby sagebrush ran to sparse pine cover on the hills. Indigenous subsistence hunting took place in the back country and hills, where the Douglas fir and subalpine spruce and hemlock sheltered richer quarries of wildlife. Much of this hunting was invisible to the traders except when snow drove the deer to the lowlands for browse. The whole region had the reputation of being, in Governor Simpson's words, a "very unprofitable" place, although one that with proper management might just pay its way. The Kamloops and Okanogan posts were kept up not "for the sake of the few Furs collected," but principally as way stations for brigades travelling between the Columbia and New Caledonia districts and, in the case of Kamloops, as a depot for horses used by Interior brigades.[74]

It is difficult to accept that deer, elk, and other large game disappeared as rapidly as McDonald intimated under the conditions of the Thompson River fur trade. There is no evidence that the trade created extraordinary pressures on fauna (as it did in some regions east of the Rockies), with the obvious exception of fur-bearers. Native hunters supplied fresh meat to the post from time to time, and occasionally they brought in hides to trade, but the quantities were much too small to have an impact on the faunal biomass of the region. In 1827, the only year for which there are figures, the post consumed just under 1,300 pounds of fresh venison—that is, the meat of about 15 deer or somewhat fewer elk or caribou. The quantities of other game consumed were insignificant: just over 200 fowl (mostly partridges and ducks), 64 badgers, 29 rabbits, and twenty-five pounds of fresh bear meat.[75] Journals from other years reveal that game was always a luxury at the post. It is also clear that traders were not permitted to do their own hunting or fishing in the region; there are no references to their people hunting (save the occasional shooting of fowl). As McDonald put it, the post was "entirely dependent" for its living on remote parts of the country, and especially on the salmon trade of the Fraser River.[76] That the traders came in for so little game suggests that there may have been limited disposable surplus among the Native people at the best of times.

It is certainly possible that the use of firearms for subsistence hunting created extraordinary pressures on local game populations. At the turn of the twentieth century, ethnographer James Teit collected oral traditions that indicated elk were scarce by the 1830s or 1840s and "practically extinct" by mid-century. Teit surmised that the widespread adoption of firearms led to the decline. Caribou also were said to have disappeared from the southern Shuswap district.[77] Such factors may well have contributed to the alarm that McDonald described in the winter of 1827. There is no evidence that deer were affected, however. If deer were scarce that winter, it was probably due to particularly poor climatic conditions—extreme cold, too little or too much snow for effective hunting, or high mortality of fawns in the previous season due to extreme conditions.[78]

Fur-Trade Factors

Dependence on Post Food

If there is any conclusion to be drawn from the above discussion, it is that ecological factors were not alone responsible for starvation in the winter of 1829. Specific historical factors relating to the fur trade must be taken into account. The whole question of the impact of the trade on Native societies is an enormously complex one, as the discussions here and in chapter 6 make clear. At the center of fur-trade scholarship for two decades have been the issues of the extent of Native American dependence on the trade, the role of Native people as active agents in the trade, and Native motivations. Few would now argue for either complete dependence or independence. The effects of the trade were, to borrow a phrase, "neither monolithic nor total."[79]

At issue here is the impact on Native subsistence in the Thompson River district. The available evidence suggests that in the realm of subsistence, the effects of the Thompson River trade were significant but limited. It is possible only to speculate on the impact the devastation of the beaver population may have had. Beaver were eaten locally, but were probably much less important for both food and clothing than were deer, elk, caribou, and in northern regions, moose.[80] Beaver were the original currency of the fur trade, however; and their loss may have created difficulties for people accustomed to getting their trade goods in this way.

In many fur-trade settings the attraction of the new trade goods led families to spend considerable time in the vicinity of the post. Reliance on the post for such goods could lead to reliance for food as well, at least in times of scarcity. A decision to collect furs

or other goods for trade with the company might lead people
away from their usual subsistence activities and from areas of
seasonal abundance. Such diversion of effort could cut into food
stores, thereby reducing the already slim margin of safety for the
lean winter months. The individuals and families affected might
then find themselves in need of handouts from the post. No description of this recurrent sequence of events is found in the
record from Kamloops, but entries like this one from Fort Colville
in 1831 capture it well: "Our best beaver hunters the Lake Indians
are forced to remain on the ground owing to the severity of the
season, and the want of food, they having cured no salmon last
summer, to these Indians on account of their worth and neces-
sities we are obliged to support almost entirely on potatoes."[81]
The implication seems to be that these people had neglected
their fishing the previous summer in order to trap beaver, and as
a result they had to rely on the post for food come winter. In a
less severe winter they would certainly have contributed to their
own support by hunting. Elsewhere in the same journal, Francis
Heron complained about the "homeguards" becoming "a torment"
in spring. "Homeguard" is the fur-trade term for Native people
who set up their winter quarters about the posts.[82] For most of
the season they lived off stored provisions and were very active
in supplying the posts with food, but in spring, before the first
roots were ready, they sometimes turned to the posts for
support.[83]

   Such dependency does not appear to have developed to any
extent in the Thompson River district. While there are frequent
accounts of food scarcity, and what the traders perceived to be
scarcity, during the winter months, there are very few references
to traders feeding the hungry. The only explicit statement is from
the winter of 1826–27, when McDonald was so concerned about
the decline of wildlife. It was during this period that 670 dried
salmon were supplied to "starving Indians" at the Okanogan post.
If one considers that it took three fish to feed a man for one day
(although a "starving Indian" may have made do with rather less),

this amount would not have gone far. Twelve servants at the post, by contrast, consumed almost 10,000 of the fish in the same period. There are frequent references to "starving" Okanagan who were too "indolent and improvident" to lay away sufficient stores of dried provisions and who posed a threat to the company's horses in the lean winter period. In general, however, even when large gatherings around the post were "a drain on the tobacco," they were not being fed. This was as true in the 1840s as in the 1820s. From the available evidence, it must be concluded that the Native people of the region were not trapping furs to the point of compromising their subsistence activities. If dependence on post food was a factor in the starvation of 1829, it was so only for a few. Judging by the evidence, the general hardship cannot be attributed to dependence on post provisions.[84]

The scarcity of reports of winter illness outbreaks at Kamloops may be further evidence that gatherings of large numbers of people around the post were not the norm here. Winter illnesses of various types broke out frequently at other Interior posts. The concentration of large numbers of Native people in the vicinity of the posts, where it did occur, created the conditions for the spread of viral infections (see chapter 2). The only account of winter illness in the scattered journals from Kamloops is a report of an outbreak of whooping cough in 1827. A "severe attack," it reportedly raised the alarm "among all the Indians in this quarter." There is no indication of the number affected, but children died in villages around Kamloops, on the lower Thompson, and on the Fraser.[85] The absence of other reports of winter illness in the district may well be due to spotty documentation, but may also indicate that the large winter gatherings of Native people near the post, so characteristic of many other areas and so conducive to the spread of disease, were not a feature at Kamloops.

Far from viewing the Thompson River peoples as dependent on the local trade post, traders often noted with dismay their lack of interest in trapping furs. There are many examples of subsistence activities taking priority over trapping. The local Secwepemc dropped everything when the sockeye arrived, and the descent of deer from the hills brought the same response. Although by 1827 a post had been in their midst for fifteen years, McDonald complained that the Secwepemc and other "salmon tribes" of the district remained too "indolent" to trap furs. McDonald was also annoyed that, although there was a rich local fishery, "we come in for very little of what is caught on these streams."[86] Instead, the company had to rely on four or five trading trips a year to the Fountain on the Fraser for a supply of dried fish. Right through the early 1840s local people took little interest in producing either fish or furs for trade, which suggests that their needs for trade goods remained very limited. Far from becoming dependent on the trade, the groups around Kamloops retained their essential economic autonomy from the company.

Interethnic Conflict

To their irritation, traders also found that political events could conspire against fur trapping. In November 1822 the death of the widely respected Okanagan leader Pelkamulox (known to traders as "Grand Picotte") at the hands of a group of Fraser River Lil'wat turned the attentions of the Okanagan, Secwepemc, and neighboring Nlaka'pamux to retaliation. John McLeod fervently wished they would drop the plan to attack the Lil'wat, which would prove "materially detrimental to the affairs of the post": not only would it interfere with trapping, it would create difficulties for the post's salmon trade with the Lil'wat as well.[87]

Ethnographers have recorded that parties of Secwepemc and Lil'wat traditionally made attacks on each other "for plunder, adventure, or revenge."[88] In this instance, McLeod had no doubt that the fur traders were implicated in the hostilities. By his account, the Lil'wat considered Pelkamulox to have been an envoy of the traders (for what purpose McLeod does not say), and they saw the company as being on the side of the Secwepemc,

Okanagan, and their allies. The Lil'wat very likely were jealous of the advantages—in particular, ready access to guns and ammunition—that these other groups received as a result of having a trade post in their territory. Far fewer guns were supplied to the Lil'wat than to the peoples around Kamloops. While guns, ammunition, steel traps, and kettles were the staples of trade at Kamloops, a typical outfit for the salmon trade with the Lil'wat comprised hatchets, blades, knives, rings, lengths of baize and calico, tobacco, and a limited quantity of traps and ammunition. The Fraser River Lil'wat requested a post in their own territory, but this was not to be.[89]

Conflict between Secwepemc and other groups in the region may have been exacerbated by the presence of fur traders; however, oral traditions recorded at the turn of the twentieth century held that the Secwepemc—the Kamloops, Fraser River, and Bonaparte divisions in particular—long had been known as "a warlike people." Teit was told of a history of extensive raiding in precontact times between these Secwepemc groups and various of the Okanagan, Nlaka'pamux, and Lil'wat, as well as the Chilcotin and others beyond the Plateau.[90] One secondary source points to animosity among Secwepemc communities themselves as a result of competition for fur-trapping territories.[91] If this was the case, it implies a very significant departure from aboriginal patterns of land use. Among the Secwepemc, as was the rule throughout the Plateau, "everyone had a right to all parts of the common country for any purpose."[92]

Traders had almost nothing to say on patterns of land tenure in the Plateau, but their descriptions of gatherings of varied ethnic groups at salmon, root, and other harvest sites bear witness to the pattern of communal access. There was no individual or family property in land. Of course, each village or cluster of villages had its accustomed hunting and gathering places, generally the most productive sites within reach of their settlements. Among the Secwepemc, for example, people of other Secwepemc villages or regions could freely hunt and gather at

such sites without being considered intruders. Others related by
blood to the Secwepemc also had full access to these grounds.
"Full access" did not extend, however, to the right to use deer
fences or salmon-fishing stations; these were considered the
property of those who built or maintained them.[93]

The impact on indigenous property relations of declining beaver
populations and of hugely increased demands on other fur-
bearers has been widely examined in the fur-trade literature. I
share the view that jealously guarded family hunting territories,
where they existed, were more likely a product of these fur-trade
pressures than of any aboriginal arrangement.[94] However, there
is nothing in the limited fur-trade record to indicate that such
jealously guarded territories emerged in the Secwepemc region
during this period.

Conflict with Fur Traders

Growing hostility to the fur traders themselves is an indication of
the kinds of tensions created by the fur trade. In 1840 the peoples
of the Thompson River district were said to be "at war among
themselves." It seems hostilities with the Fraser River Lil'wat
were still percolating. That these Lil'wat were involved is suggested by Chief Factor McLoughlin's concern that the conflict
would lead them to neglect their salmon fishing, on which the
post was completely dependent.[95] In 1841 Donald Manson reported
that Secwepemc groups between Kamloops and Alexandria (the
southernmost post of New Caledonia) had "repeatedly plundered,
grossly insulted and frequently nearly murdered several of our
People." The Okanagan, too, had "given great annoyance during
the past few years." By this time relations between the traders
and the population in the immediate vicinity of the Thompson
River post had deteriorated dangerously.[96]

Late in the autumn of 1841, Chief Trader Samuel Black was shot
to death inside the post. The culprit was identified as "a single
Indian belonging to the place." Apparently he was a young man

named Kikoskin, nephew of Kamloops Chief Tranquille. The killing betrayed deep tensions between the local Secwepemc and the company. Archibald McDonald, relating the events to Fort Vancouver, linked the incident to the recent death of Tranquille. By McDonald's account, the chief, who had long since fallen from favor at the post, had applied to Black several times for a gun and had been refused. On a trading trip to Lil'wat territory the previous month, Tranquille had taken ill and died. As McDonald explained it, "it was rumoured among the Indians, and insidiously propagated by the [Indian] Doctors . . . [that] his death must be ascribed to the bad medicine of the whites and revenged." Black, seeing that the traders were held responsible for the death, sent gifts and men to assist with the burial. The attempt at appeasement failed, and Black was killed in revenge.[97]

At the outset of the Kamloops trade, relations between traders and the Secwepemc and Okanagan had been good. David Stuart and Alexander Ross, working out of the Astorian post in 1811 and 1812, described both groups as "well-disposed" and anxious to trade. By the mid-1820s there were signs of minor trouble. During the NWC and early HBC years, traders customarily entrusted the post during their summer absence to the local chief, Court Apatte, and his son-in-law Tranquille. In 1826, dissatisfied with the way the chief and his followers had looked after the place, the traders instead turned over the keys to Chief Nkwala of the Okanagan. This act "gave some umbrage to the Shewhaps and the consequence as might be expected was not the entire Security of the Fort." McDonald found Court Apatte and Tranquille a nuisance, describing them as "hanging about the fort," generally "empty handed" or with "nothing to trade but a few salmon." In 1826 he curtailed the gratuities given to the "useless fellow," Court Apatte. Nkwala, meanwhile, was acknowledged as "a staunch partisan to the whites," and he remained so throughout the period under study. After the killing of Black, while the animosity of the Secwepemc was feared, Nkwala "and a few other good Staunch Indians" rallied to the support of the establishment.[98] From the little documentation available, it is clear that the traders' actions continually reinforced the tensions between themselves and the Secwepemc. As discussed in chapter 4, gifts to a chief had far more than material significance; an act like the curtailing of gratuities implied a serious rift in the relationship.

Changes in Leadership

Traders were always enlisting "Staunch Indians"—invariably men—to assist in the trade. The rewards they were offered for encouraging members of their families or bands to trap and hunt, and for other services rendered, enabled these men to establish and maintain positions of influence in their communities. In many cases the men so honored were bona fide village leaders; in others, they were not. The sanction of the traders became a new avenue of influence for young men who may have had no other claim to prominence. Such figures are known in the fur-trade literature as "trading chiefs" or "trading captains."

When a party arrived at a post to trade, the transaction was always preceded by a gift of tobacco and perhaps other small items. The ritual distribution of tobacco to his followers was a symbolic affirmation of the chief's special relationship with the traders, a relationship that enabled him to bring trade goods to his people. In this way, the gift validated his position. Traders often spoke of "paying" chiefs with tobacco and other "gratuities."

The most dramatic display of the traders' sanction was the annual chief's clothing. A full "rigging" echoed the dress costume of an eighteenth-century English gentleman: a coat of red or blue cloth, adorned with regimental cuffs and collar in brightly colored lace; waistcoat and breeches; a white or checked shirt; wool stockings; pumps; and a hat (beaver, no doubt) trimmed with feather plumes. Scaled-down versions were widely used in the Columbia. At Kamloops in the mid-1820s Nkwala and Court Apatte (until he was cut off) were getting outfits of a standard hooded cape, trousers, waistcoat, and shirt. At Fort Nez Percés in

1832 at least seven chiefs were being similarly clothed. There are few references to chiefs and trading captains actually wearing these outfits, the hats excepted. The fate of the rest of the finery was probably the same as with other gifts from the traders: the goods were distributed. More will be said about changing patterns of leadership in the era of the fur trade in the next chapter.

New Production Technologies

The effects of the Thompson River fur trade on local production technologies were hinted at above. Most obvious was the adoption of the gun and the steel trap. Whereas spears had previously been used for killing beaver, within ten years of the start of the Kamloops trade it was reported that steel traps were the only implement in use. Guns, ammunition, and traps were among the most sought-after trade items throughout the period. Trade goods for the post in 1827, for example, included guns, ammunition, traps, tobacco, blankets, brass kettles, and "small items" to the value of £200.[99] There are many references to Native people being reluctant to trade their furs when the goods of their choice were not available. They also complained loudly when quality was inferior. In a typical exchange, in December 1822, hunters brought in a large number of skins, "for which they demand guns and traps." The trader had none to give and had to work hard to persuade a Nlaka'pamux hunter to leave his pelts for anything other than a gun. Persuasion was not always successful, and when not satisfied with the goods offered, hunters might simply refuse to trade. This could be a powerful tool at a post like Kamloops, where returns were limited at the best of times. Another option was for hunters to resort to another post. The falloff of Fort Okanogan returns in the mid-1820s was attributed to the diversion of some furs to Fort Colville, where traders were permitted to pay above the standard Interior tariff in order to meet American competition. Fort Langley on the lower Fraser also received Thompson River furs from time to time.[100]

Traders believed Native people to have grown quickly dependent on the new technologies offered in trade, particularly guns.
When the Secwepemc chief Tranquille demanded a high price for
deer meat and hides in the autumn of 1827, McDonald considered
it a price well paid: "as their demand is generally in Ammunition,
we conceive it not such a mighty sin to accommodate them in
an article so essential for their support." Formerly, guns had been
given mainly in payment for beaver. As John Tod wrote in the
summer of 1841, the Indians suffered "much privation" when in
need of ammunition.[101] Such concern was not entirely humani-
tarian. Native people suffering "privation" naturally made poor
fur trappers. Traders also stood to benefit more directly from the
use of guns, obtaining coveted venison from time to time. Most
trade and many gift-giving transactions included ammunition.

The belief that firearms, once acquired, became indispensable
to Native people was a commonplace among fur traders. Such a
view reflects European biases about the requirements for successful hunting, of course. But guns did, indeed, become very important to many Native American societies, both for hunting and for
defence. Evidence that bows and arrows and other indigenous
tools were not displaced by firearms, but continued in use, will
be considered in chapter 6. Briefly, it is important to bear in mind
that guns were better suited to certain types of hunting, bows and
arrows to others. Here the effects of the fur trade may have been
significant. Trapping for trade was most efficiently carried out by
individuals and small groups. Separation into small groups would
have made the common method of hunting deer and elk by the
labor-intensive surround impossible. For individuals or small
parties, deer, elk and other large game were pursued more effectively with firearms. On the other hand, where larger numbers
of hunters came together in the chase, the method of the surround using bows and arrows would have been employed very
effectively. Bows and arrows had the obvious advantages of being
more readily available and maintained. Maintenance of firearms
was a constant problem, as revealed in the remark of a Kamloops

trader in 1822, that "scarcely a day passes without some of [the Indians] come in with either a broken Gun, or trap to be repaired."[102]

Disease at Thompson River and Beyond

A final effect of the fur trade and the European presence with potentially enormous consequences was introduced disease. The limitations of the archival material once again make the full story elusive, and nowhere is this more true than in the Kamloops district. The possible impacts of such disease were treated in chapter 2.

Concluding Remarks

To fur traders, the "salmon tribes" of the Plateau—the communities they judged to live principally on fish—were the poor of the region. Starvation was the ultimate manifestation of that poverty. But starvation came in many varieties in traders' writings, one of the most frequent usages of the term being the "technical" one: by that definition, "starving" meant that Native people were directing primary attention to their own needs rather than trapping furs.

Starvation was also the verdict when Native people were eating foods that traders deemed for some reason deficient. "Rotten" fish and "moss" are prime examples. We have seen how profoundly the traders' culturally and socially derived assumptions about what constituted proper food colored their perceptions of indigenous economies in the Plateau. Their biases against salmon were a product of not only cultural inheritance but historical circumstance: they were awash in salmon at Interior posts. Such biases combined with their inevitable ignorance of the natural history of the species to lead the traders to seriously flawed notions of indigenous subsistence strategies—notions that have been perpetuated or reproduced by more recent students of the region. Nevertheless, some traders did gain important insights. Witness Alexander Kennedy, who learned from the Spokane about the seasonal and complementary use of "good" and "bad" salmon, and Samuel Black, who came to understand that roots were a key food source in the southern Plateau, dictating people's movements in spring and summer.

The Thompson River case study illustrates well the complexity of traders' notions of starvation and poverty among fishing peoples. The Secwepemc and their neighbors were portrayed as starving and desperate when the salmon cycle was in a low year, when they were eating gathered foods, and when wildlife was said to have "disappeared." Close analysis of the fur-trade record from the district suggests, however, that the impact of the fur trade in the region was distinctly limited, and that starvation was in large part a construct of the traders. This is not to deny the recurrence of winter shortages, nor the real suffering that must have occurred in the winter of 1829; however, the sources indicate that, far from becoming dependent on the post for food, local Secwepemc, Okanagan, and Nlaka'pamux communities took only limited interest in producing goods for trade, preferring for the most part to attend to their own needs and concerns. Given the paucity of material, few hard conclusions can be drawn from the Thompson River study. As will become clear in the next chapter, many of the conclusions intimated by the study are reinforced by evidence from elsewhere in the Plateau.

CHAPTER SIX

Traders and Hunters I

Tales of Continuity and Change

The men were generally tall, raw-boned, and well-dressed, having all buffalo robes, deerskin leggings, very white, and most of them garnished with porcupine quills . . . altogether their appearance indicated wealth. Their voices were strong and masculine. . . . The women wore garments of well-dressed deerskin down to their heels, many of them richly garnished with beads, higuas, and other trinkets. . . . The Shaw Haptens and Cajouses, with part of the Walla Wallas, were armed with guns, and the others with bows and arrows. . . . On the whole, they differed widely in appearance from the piscatory tribes we had seen along the river.[1]

This passage from Alexander Ross's narrative of his early years on the Columbia speaks volumes about the contrasts in traders' views of the hunting and fishing peoples of the Plateau. In distinction to the "piscatory tribes," those labelled as hunters were depicted as wealthy, masculine, and brave. This imagery is the subject of the next two chapters.

If hunting was generally viewed as superior to fishing as a means of making a living, all forms of hunting were not equally esteemed. Every Plateau community included some hunting in its annual round, but the routine snaring of small mammals and the pursuit with bow and arrow of deer or bighorn sheep, skilful as these activities might be, came in for faint praise from fur traders. Their heroes were the buffalo hunters. The elevation of the buffalo-hunting peoples of the eastern Plateau to hero status was certainly aided by the fact that they happened, partly by virtue of geography, to be the most productive fur trappers in the Columbia Interior, as well as suppliers of essential leather goods and pemmican. Important as those considerations were, there was far more than instrumental logic to the veneration of these hunters. Symbolic associations—with contemporary notions of masculinity, with emerging notions of the "real" Indian—are explored in chapter 7. Before coming to that, it is necessary to consider the emergence of horse and buffalo culture itself.

Traders were aware that the Plateau horse and buffalo culture that they esteemed so highly was a recent phenomenon. The forces of change that accompanied the coming of the horse, the elaboration of the buffalo hunt, and the extension of the fur trade to the Plateau are worth considering at length because these forces have never been examined in a historical study. Also, fur traders were the first to record the changes, the consequences of which were embedded in their perceptions of the buffalo-hunting peoples in complex and important ways.

Material Concerns: "Remarkably Fine" Indians

On his first trade trip to the Flathead outpost in the summer of 1824, John Work expressed neatly the conceptual link in traders' minds between the hunting skills of a Native group and their merit as a people. Of the four groups trading at the post that season (Salish Flathead, Kutenai, Kalispel, and Piegan), Work reported, "it was from the two former tribes that our primary trade was procured, they are remarkably fine Indians."[2] Good fur producers were fine Indians—an unsurprising sentiment from a fur trader, and one that was expressed time and time again.

It was shown in the previous chapter how the North Thompson Shuswap, the most productive trappers in the Thompson River district, quickly established themselves as the most highly regarded of the groups frequenting the post at Kamloops. At Fort Nez Percés that distinction was reserved for the Cayuse. Although they were, in the words of Samuel Black, "domaneering [sic] and troublesome characters," they also "excel in bravery hunting and athletic exercise." Here Black turns to the symbolic significance of hunting, the complex link between hunting and masculinity. But the material logic lies not far below the surface: these manly Cayuse produced perhaps two-thirds of the furs traded at the post.[3]

Fur traders in the Plateau throughout the North West and Hudson's Bay Company eras reserved their greatest admiration for the Salish Flathead, even ahead of their buffalo-hunting .partners.[4] Once trade was established among them during the North West Company years, the Flathead became reliable and productive hunters of provisions and pelts. Naturally, this assured them of a favorable reputation among traders. But the Flathead had been distinguished from other groups from the time of their first encounter with Euro-Americans. In 1805 a member of the Lewis and Clark expedition described them as "the likelyest and honestst Savages we have ever yet Seen." David Thompson struck a similar note, depicting them as a "fine race of moral Indians," indeed, the finest he had seen. Many years later Alexander Ross, in charge of the Flathead House for the HBC in 1824–25, observed that "it is allowed by those who know them that they bear the highest character of any Indian tribe from the Rocky Mountains to the Pacific Ocean."[5] It is impossible to know to what extent cross-fertilization of ideas was at play here: for example, Thompson had almost certainly read the first published journal from the Lewis and Clark expedition.[6] But whether there was cross-fertilization or not, the Salish Flathead remained the favorites of the traders throughout the era of the fur trade. Their activities as trappers and provisioners contributed materially to that reputation, but as we shall see in the next chapter, there was much more to their perceived merit than furs.

The furs produced by Salish Flathead and Kutenai trappers were critical to the profits of the trading concerns on the Columbia.

During the Hudson's Bay Company era, the Colville district produced, on average, 52 percent of total returns from the Columbia Interior; Salish Flathead and Upper Kutenai hunters were responsible for the largest share of those returns. While precise figures are not available, accounts kept at Spokane and Colville during the 1820s indicate that the Flathead outpost produced an average of almost 40 percent of the district's beaver pelts, while the Kootenay outpost contributed just over 25 percent. Together, then, the two outposts brought in more than 65 percent of the returns of this most prosperous district. Flathead returns included those of Kalispel hunters, and occasionally others, but the Flathead share was by far the largest. In 1827, for example, Chief Trader John Dease noted that the Flathead alone brought in one-third of all of the beaver pelts collected in the Colville district.[7]

By the mid-1820s the lucrative Salish Flathead and Kutenai trades were being "materially injured" by the presence of American traders in the upper Missouri country and in the Rocky Mountains.[8] The concerted efforts made to secure those trades indicate the importance the HBC attached to them. Early in the 1830s the company began equipping small parties, comprised mostly of freemen trappers, to make trading excursions from the Flathead post onto the plains on both sides of the Rockies.[9] Members of the "Plains Expedition," as the excursions came to be known, relied on the protection of a Flathead escort during their hazardous travels in buffalo country. By 1835 the expedition was proceeding on "a most extensive scale." Despite a growing number of men, it remained entirely dependent on the Flathead and their hunting partners for protection from members of the Blackfoot alliance (Siksika, Piegan, and Blood). Even with that protection, the expedition was a dangerous undertaking. In 1837, for instance, three traders were killed by Blackfoot. The reasons for Blackfoot hostility are considered shortly.[10]

The buffalo hunts of the Salish Flathead and Upper Kutenai, with their Kalispel and other hunting partners, were also vital to

Columbia operations. The hunts were the only source in the Columbia Department of leather pack cords, portable hide lodges (tipis), and horse gear. The hunts also provided a quantity of fresh and dried meat for the local outposts and travel food; such provisions were especially important until about 1830, by which time the farm at Fort Colville was thriving. These hunters could never fully satisfy the demands of the trading companies for leather goods and meat, and the companies continued to import from posts east of the Rockies. The risks of violence and horse theft on the buffalo plains (discussed below) limited the number of packhorses that Plateau hunters could safely employ on the hunt, sharply curtailing the quantity of goods they could carry back to the Columbia district.[11]

The Rise of Horse and Buffalo Culture

Salish Flathead tradition holds that they acquired horses earlier than the Blackfoot; it is generally accepted by students of the Plateau that this important change occurred in the second or third decade of the eighteenth century. The animals passed from the Spanish settlements of the Southwest to the Plateau along well-worn Native American trade routes. The Shoshone Rendezvous in southwestern Wyoming became the principal source of horses for the Pacific Northwest. The rendezvous was central to indigenous trade throughout North America. Trading parties from over a wide area would meet at a prearranged time and place to trade goods from still more distant regions. Formal procedures existed for setting aside hostilities, where these prevailed, for the duration of the trade. Through the rendezvous Spanish, French, and British goods reached many indigenous peoples well ahead of their original purveyors.[12]

Eastern Plateau peoples—the Salish Flathead, Upper Kutenai, and bands of Kalispel and Nez Percé foremost among them—had been making regular mounted excursions to hunt buffalo on the Great Plains east of the Rockies, in the Rocky Mountain parklands, and in the upper Snake River region, for at least several decades by the turn of the nineteenth century. To what extent they, and possibly other Plateau peoples, engaged in buffalo hunting before acquiring the horse is unclear. The standard ethnographic accounts suggest buffalo hunting by Plateau peoples was a cultural adaptation that followed acquisition of the horse.[13] However, the ethnographer Teit contended that the Salish Flathead, as well as groups he identified as Salish Tuna'xe and Kutenai Tuna'xa, actually occupied territories on the eastern slopes of the Rockies in pre-horse times, where they hunted buffalo on foot. Interestingly, in the first decade of the nineteenth century David Thompson heard a similar account of Flathead and Upper Kutenai history. He, like Teit, believed that these peoples were driven by the Blackfoot from their western-plains homes to the refuge of Plateau valleys sometime around the mid-eighteenth century.[14]

The Kutenai presence east of the Rockies was more persistent. Both Thompson and Alexander Henry recorded that Kutenai had long inhabited lands in the eastern foothills of the Rockies before finally being driven west by the Piegan. North Westers based at Rocky Mountain House in the upper Saskatchewan country traded with bands of Kutenai at Kootenai Plain as late as the start of the nineteenth century. French, Native, and métis traders who formed the advance guard of the NWC approach to the Pacific Northwest followed the well-travelled Kutenai trail through the mountains.[15]

Until as late as the 1840s the range of the buffalo extended west of the Rockies into the Lemhi valley and upper Snake River plains of southern Idaho, in the so-called Snake Country (map 5).[16] Whatever the previous home territories of the buffalo-hunting peoples, it seems very likely that many had engaged in buffalo hunting on a small scale before acquiring the horse. The animal made the activity much more efficient and profitable. The swiftness and thoroughness with which many Plateau societies adapted to the horse is remarkable. In a matter of two or three generations the horse all but replaced foot and canoe as a means

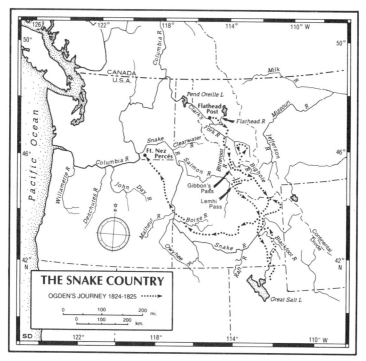

Map 5

of transportation for many of these communities. Some, most notably the Nez Percé, had learned to geld their stallions and to breed selectively. By the turn of the nineteenth century the majority of Plateau peoples had acquired at least some horses.[17]

An Era of Violence

The mid-eighteenth to mid-nineteenth century was a period of escalating violence on the eastern and southern frontiers of the Plateau. Skirmishes with the Blackfoot were a fact of life for Plateau buffalo hunters and for fur traders and trappers who ventured to the buffalo grounds. It was a time of often bloody confrontation as the Blackfoot, Piegan, Blood, Gros Ventre, Crow, Northern and Eastern Shoshone, and Plateau groups contended for territory in the mounting struggle for horses, firearms, hides, and furs. Pressure on the buffalo mounted as eastern Plains peoples moved westward, driven by the march of American settlement, and as Plateau and Great Basin hunters staked their claim on the herds from the west. The fine horse herds of the Salish Flathead, Kalispel, and Upper Kutenai became the target of Blackfoot horse-raiding parties whose power was often fortified by firearms. So central were horses to the hostilities that the Salish Flathead term for "going to war" is the same as that for "stealing horses."[18] Raid and counter-raid also came to mark relations between the Sahaptian groups of the southern Columbia and the "Snake" (Northern Paiute peoples known as the Bannock, and their mounted Shoshone allies).[19] Many young men in these Plateau groups made names for themselves on such exploits. Raiding for booty was not a novel phenomenon in the region, but it appears to have increased dramatically in scale and frequency with the introduction of horses.

In the century and more since the Hudson's Bay Company had established itself on Hudson Bay, firearms had found their way southward and westward through Cree and Assiniboine middlemen to the Canadian prairies and the upper Missouri. The Blackfoot and their allies on the western plains obtained their first guns well before the 1750s. Although guns, like horses, spread slowly from region to region, both had a dramatic effect on raiding and warfare as communities gained at different rates the advantages of firepower or mobility.[20] In the winter of 1786–87 an elderly Cree man named Saukamappee told David Thompson the fascinating story of the meeting of the horse and gun frontiers, probably in the early 1730s, in a battle between the Piegan and the Shoshone. The Piegan had attempted to establish new territory on the western reaches of the South Saskatchewan River, but found themselves challenged by the Shoshone. Horses had given the Shoshone the advantage in battle before Plains groups acquired guns. As Saukamappee explained to Thompson:

> [O]ur enemies the Snake Indians and their allies had Misstutim (Big Dogs, that is Horses) on which they rode, swift as the Deer, on which they dashed the Peegans, and with their stone Pukamoggan [axes] knocked them on the head, and they had thus lost several of their best men. . . . [This] alarmed us, for we had no idea of Horses and could not make out what they were.[21]

The Piegan sought help from their allies, the Cree and Assiniboine, who supplied many men, including about ten armed with muskets. Saukamappee told of the next big battle with the Shoshone. The guns were kept secret, and scattered along the Piegan line. When the Shoshone drew their bows, the muskets were fired. Their deadly effect caused panic along the Shoshone line. Many fled, and most of those who fought on were killed.[22] The battle was a harbinger of the decades of bloody violence to follow.

During the 1780s and 1790s members of the Blackfoot alliance achieved ascendancy on the western plains as provisioners to North West and Hudson's Bay Company traders pushing their way westward. With direct access to guns, liquor, and the other fruits of the British fur trade, they were no longer dependent on middlemen suppliers. The fur trade was a key, but not the only factor, in the rising fortunes of the Blackfoot: plainswide population migrations, depopulation due to disease, and cultural developments related to the horse and trade all played a role.[23] By 1800, David Thompson would report that Blackfoot lands extended from the northern edge of the plains to the Missouri River, and 300 miles east from the Rockies.[24]

At this time Blackfoot groups began raiding the eastern Plateau for horses. However, Blackfoot hegemony was soon threatened as their rivals themselves gained access to firearms, both through intertribal trade and through British and American fur traders.

The Salish Flathead, for example, gained a few guns through Indian trade networks as early as the 1790s. In the first decade of the nineteenth century a party of Flathead traders travelled with the Crow as far east as the Mandan trade fair, a key market for firearms.[25]

The Blackfoot violently resisted the extension of the fur trade to their Plateau rivals, earning for themselves the unremitting animosity of British traders in the Plateau. In the first decade of the nineteenth century North West Company traders finally succeeded in penetrating Blackfoot territory to the Continental Divide, and between 1807 and 1810 they established posts among the Salish Flathead, Kutenai, and their neighbors. The result of the first major Flathead assault on the Blackfoot in which the Flathead were equipped with firearms is described in chapter 7.[26]

The dangers inherent in travel in buffalo country led Plateau hunters to adopt the practice of moving together in large camps in order to "form but one against the common enemies of their country."[27] Traders reported parties ranging in size from several hundred to over two thousand, including women and children. The largest contingents were Salish Flathead and Upper Kutenai. It appears that the entire Flathead population took part, save the old and infirm, who in the era of the fur trade remained in a camp near the trade post "in security."[28] The Flathead and Kutenai were invariably accompanied by eastern Kalispel, and generally by parties of Nez Percé; others who frequently joined included Coeur d'Alene, Spokane, Columbia, Yakima, Wallawalla, Palus, and Cayuse. The party Ross traded with on its return from the plains in the autumn of 1824 was fairly typical: there were 800 people and 1,800 horses, comprising forty-two lodges of Flathead, thirty-six lodges of Kutenai, thirty-four of Kalispel, twelve of Nez Percé, and four of Spokane.[29]

Impacts of Firearms

The Salish Flathead and Upper Kutenai, being on the frontier between the Plateau and the Great Plains, bore the brunt of hostilities with the Blackfoot. The combined effects of devastating smallpox epidemics in the 1770s and 1800–1801 and ongoing battles with the Blackfoot appear to have taken a particularly heavy toll on the Flathead. In 1810, Thompson observed that they had forty lodges without men in a population of at most a thousand (five to eight people per lodge). Ross Cox noted in 1814 that the Flathead were "formerly much more numerous than they were at this period," and he was convinced that had they not gained firearms from the fur traders, they would have faced annihilation at the hands of the Blackfoot.[30]

The Salish Flathead were by far the best supplied with firearms during the fur-trade era. There were more guns than men in the Flathead camp that came in to trade at the Flathead outpost after the autumn hunt in 1824 (180 guns to 168 "men and lads"). Even the Kutenai, the next most productive hunters in the trade, had far fewer (62 guns among 114 males).[31] The discrepancy undoubt-edly illustrates the favored status traders bestowed on the Flat-head. A proportion of the guns would have been gifts supplied for good service.

Plateau hunters who ventured to the buffalo plains clearly benefited from access to firearms for martial use. The benefits of guns for hunting were less straightforward. As has already been noted, it was widely assumed by traders (and has long been assumed by many scholars) that the guns that traders supplied were indispensable to effective hunting. In the early years of the trade Thompson and others even explained the failure of Columbia peoples to rely more on the hunt as a function of lack of firearms. The general view was that Indians would hunt if they had the wherewithal.

The traders' confidence in European technology aside, there is ample evidence in their writings to indicate that even among the most productive hunters indigenous weapons remained very much in use during the fur-trade period. As late as 1827, Samuel Black reported from Fort Nez Percés that "Guns and Bows and arrows" were the tools of the hunt. Other evidence suggests that the continued use of bows and arrows was not simply a function of limited access to firearms. Work observed that at Fort Colville, whenever firearms or ammunition were in short supply or in need of repair—a not uncommon occurrence—bows and arrows were in use. They were often preferred to guns for buffalo hunting from horseback, as detailed in the next chapter.[32] In other fur-trade regions it has been shown that there was a generational transition from bows to firearms, repeated generation after generation: boys were trained to hunt with bows, and they continued to do so until they could afford their own guns. The practice, noted among the western Ojibwa, for example, suggests that acquisition of a gun may have come to be viewed as a significant mark of manhood.[33]

No less an advocate of European technology than David Thompson believed the bow and arrow to be superior to the gun for deer hunting, since the noise of the gun frightened the animals. However, he felt sure that iron-headed arrows, which "carry silent certain death," were a vast improvement over the indigenous flint-headed variety.[34] Alexander Henry was most expansive in praise of the bow. Henry described the bows of the eastern Plateau as the "handsomest" he had ever seen. Indeed, he reported, those made of horn or cedar overlaid with sinew were so exceptional that Piegan hunters had been known to trade a gun or a horse for one. This is remarkable, given the curtailments on access to guns that the Piegan would have been facing at the time (1811) as a result of hostilities with British traders. According to Henry, the eastern Plateau bows had an elastic quality and shot "an amazing distance." They were a fine tool with either long flint or iron-tipped arrows. Their only drawback, he noted, was that they required careful maintenance.[35]

Maintenance was equally a drawback of firearms. The standard trade gun at this time was the muzzle-loading flintlock musket. It had come to be known as the "North West Gun," although it was standard issue of the Hudson's Bay Company as well. The basic design of the musket limited its effectiveness, particularly for hunting on horseback. It was a single-shot weapon and cumbersome to reload; with its smoothbore barrel, it was not noted for its accuracy. Native men adopted the practice of carrying bullets in their mouths and dropping them into the powder without wadding, which speeded up the process of reloading and firing, though the lack of wadding reduced range and accuracy even more.[36] Poor weather conditions could compound problems of design. Rain made it difficult to keep the priming powder dry, and wind would often disperse the sparks before the powder ignited; in cold weather, the firing mechanism was subject to freezing. As for daily upkeep, the flintlock required a reliable supply of not only ammunition but also two kinds of powder, as well as flints.[37]

Shortage or late delivery of ammunition and other essential supplies rendered firearms useless, as the Salish Flathead learned early on, when they were forced to waste part of the buffalo cow season waiting for traders to arrive with replenishments. In general, company blacksmiths charged with the task of keeping the guns in repair found their services to be in great demand. Daily complaints about broken guns at Kamloops in 1822 are evidence of this.[38] In sum, the benefits of this particular European technology were questionable in the period under study. Nevertheless, most traders would have agreed with Thompson that the gun improved the ability of hunters to exert their authority over the forces of nature. This theme is explored in the next chapter.

Impacts of the Horse: Changes in the Land

Well before the first European traders reached the Plateau, many southern and eastern groups had amassed enormous numbers of horses, and northern peoples like the Upper Nlaka'pamux were also well supplied. In the east huge herds ran wild in Kutenai country, and traders admired the skill of the Kutenai at the "wild rough riding business" of catching and breaking the animals.[39]

In traders' accounts the most successful herders were the Nez Percé, Cayuse, Palus, and Yakama. Their territories harbored snow-free valleys rich in bunchgrasses, the abundance of which was encouraged by the extensive burning practices witnessed by traders. They derided this "careless" burning; their journals, particularly in late summer, often contained comments like "the country all around us is on fire." None understood how powerful a tool of land management and food production fire could be for Plateau peoples.

Writing of the Columbia plain west of Walla Walla, Governor Simpson noted that it was "clothed with a fine herbage" (fresh growth of bunchgrasses) in the spring and that the local people yearly set it on fire, but he did not connect the two observations. On the Kootenay River in western Montana, Simpson again overlooked the link between the landscape and fire. He found on the bank of the river a prairie that put him in mind of a park: "here and there were thick clumps of trees, yielding an inviting shade, in other places the trees stood wide and formed grand avenues, and all around was fine pasture." For Simpson the lay of the land was unrelated to the fires in the surrounding woods in previous weeks.[40]

Similarly, Cox described the prairie of the Palouse region as richly cloaked in mixed grasses and occasional patches of "chappallel" (chaparral, that is, sagebrush and rabbit brush). The "annual burning of the grass" he saw as a tool for driving deer in the hunt.[41] What neither Simpson nor Cox recognized was that this burning maintained the grasslands that supported the local herds of horses. Burning cleared the previous year's growth and destroyed excessive mulch, allowing the spring sun to warm the ground more quickly and encourage earlier regrowth and higher yields. This early food supply was vital to horses after the often-lean winter season.

After the coming of the horse, the use of controlled burning in this region was perhaps as important for grassland maintenance as it was for hunting and maintaining forest clearings. It might be expected that the use of burning, both for grassland rejuvenation and to clear the understory for ease of travel, would have increased with the expanding use of horses. However, fire chronology studies of the Salish Flathead and Kutenai region of western Montana, which record the incidence of fire as far back as the late seventeenth century, show no indication of increased burning after the early eighteenth century. What the studies do reveal is frequent and very extensive use of low-intensity fires over a long period.[42]

Cox was right about the use of fire to drive and surround game. Predictably, he contrasted the practice unfavorably with the "excellent sport" he and his colleagues enjoyed in hunting mule deer around Spokane. The Native practice of hunting with fire involved determining the direction in which the deer herd was headed and sending a party of hunters to cut them off; meanwhile, "those behind set fire to the long grass, the flames of which spread with great rapidity." The fleeing deer were intercepted by the advance guard, and "great numbers fall by the arrows of the Indians." The practice may not have been as "sporting" as the sport hunter's method of individual pursuit, but it was certainly more efficient.[43]

Fire also contributed to hunting by stimulating growth of herbs and shrubs on the forest edge. The browse created in this way is the preferred summer food for elk and whitetail deer, for instance. Controlled burning was used to enhance production of foods and medicinal plants for human use as well; notably, the coveted mountain huckleberry flourished in burn sites.[44] Intentional as the use of fire frequently was, the contemporary sources point to potentially deleterious environmental effects. In the Thompson River area fires at times burned out of control and destroyed large areas of woodland. It is not clear whether the spectacular fires described between 1841 and 1843 in the Kamloops journals were set for the Natives' purposes or touched off by lightening. They certainly reduced timber cover in this already arid landscape.[45]

Impacts of the Horse: The Meeting of Horse and Buffalo

The meeting of horse and buffalo in the western plains and mountain parklands made possible the elaboration of the Plateau buffalo hunt. The horse offered myriad new possibilities for travel, trade, and communication. Hunters could now travel farther in pursuit of the herds, carry more gear, and transport more produce of the hunt back to their village sites. Buffalo hunting became a possibility for the first time for Spokane, Columbia, Wallawalla, and other hunters who lived far from the buffalo plains. On horseback an individual could travel up to seventy miles in a day, so that even hunters from the westernmost Plateau could reach the plains within a month.[46] Only small numbers chose to do so, but the horse provided the option.

In more general terms, enhanced mobility meant that much larger quantities of food could be transported from harvest to village sites, and as a result more food could be produced for storage than in the days when goods were transported by people or dogs. Horses made it possible to transport berries, roots, fish, and meat in their bulkier fresh state, rather than having to dry them at the harvest site, a time-consuming task that could cut into harvest activities.[47]

It appears from traders' descriptions of the seasonal activities of the Salish Flathead and Upper Kutenai that even for these most active buffalo hunters the development of the mounted hunt brought about a shift in emphasis, rather than a wholesale change, in the seasonal round. For the most part, buffalo hunting took place in seasons during which other kinds of hunting had normally been carried out. There were usually two buffalo hunts each year, the first running roughly from July until September and the second from December until March or April. Some small parties would stay out for as long as two years. Bulls were the quarry early in the season, and by late summer the cows, whose meat and hides were preferred, could be hunted. The whole herd was in good condition in early winter. Summer hides were best suited for tipi covers, and the thicker winter coats made the best robes.[48]

Traders' accounts indicate that buffalo-hunting communities continued to exploit a wide range of resources according to a pattern that was probably broadly similar to that of pre-horse times. The timing of the hunt allowed the Flathead, for example, to "pass the Spring [on] the Root Plains."[49] They harvested bitterroot in early spring, wild carrots in late spring, and camas in early summer. Berries and other gathered foods, some fish (principally trout and suckers), and other game remained part of the round. Buffalo took priority over, but did not supplant, whitetail and mule deer, elk, antelope, bighorn sheep, and bear as the quarry of the hunter.[50]

Traders saw the adoption of the buffalo hunt as proof of what one called the Indians' "unconquerable" love of the chase (see chapter 7).[51] The more plausible explanation is that those who took up large-scale buffalo hunting did so because it introduced greater security and diversity to the sustenance round. Significantly, the groups for whom buffalo hunting became a major part of the seasonal round were those who were most remote from the salmon wealth of the Columbia and Fraser systems.

Important as the flesh of the buffalo was while the hunting parties remained on the plains, it appears that very little was imported back to Plateau villages. The limiting factor was the horse. Because enemy raiders were a constant risk to horses in buffalo country, only a limited number could be taken on the expedition. Traders' accounts indicate that three to four horses per hunter was the usual number.[52] Assuming that one was required to carry hunting and other equipment, and another to carry the hide tipi, at most two would be available to carry buffalo products home. Meat would have had a low priority in the list of goods to be transported. For the Salish Flathead there were other food resources to be relied on during the seasons spent in Plateau locales. For those like the Spokane, who lived in the midst of salmon bounty, carting buffalo meat home would have been like taking the proverbial coals to Newcastle.[53] Of far more interest were buffalo hides for robes and blankets, and other prestigious buffalo and Plains items for use in trade and marriage exchanges.

Given their relative scarcity and novelty in the Plateau, hide robes and the other products of the hunt became prized items in gift exchanges. The prestige they brought to those able to supply them reflected this scarcity. The risk factor must also have figured into the equation: the perception was universal that venturing onto the buffalo-hunting grounds was fraught with danger. As the Salish Flathead chief known to traders as Cartier expressed it, "when [we] go to hunt the bison, we also prepare for war."[54]

Impacts of the Horse: The Flash Flood of Trade

The coming of the horse, the elaboration of the buffalo hunt, and the extension of the fur trade to the Plateau quickened the pace of trade in materials and new ideas to what has aptly been described as a "flash flood."[55] However, it should be emphasized that trade had long been a pillar of Plateau economies, and incorporation of "exotic" goods into evolving Plateau uses was not a new phenomenon. As discussed in chapter 4, even before the coming of the horse in the eighteenth century, items associated with the buffalo hunt and Plains cultures had become available in the Plateau, albeit in limited quantities, through indigenous trade networks.

Beyond The Dalles and the smaller regional trade centers, Plateau traders had access to the riches on offer at the Shoshone Rendezvous and the trade centers of the middle Missouri. Before they had acquired horses, parties of Nez Percé men are known to have made extended excursions on foot to Hidatsa villages on the Missouri to trade dried salmon, hemp, and other Plateau products for leather clothing, parfleches, feather headdresses, and so forth. The frequency of such outings, and the quantity of goods exchanged, would have increased dramatically with the coming of the horse. The regular inclusion of women in the trading parties (for now they were needed to assist in the buffalo hunt) very likely resulted in new choices of trade goods, and new ideas being carried back to the Plateau. An example is the adoption of Crow, Ojibwa, and Cree styles of dress decoration with their trademark intricate beadwork. In 1807, Simon Fraser saw "cloathing such as the Cree women wear" as far west as the Upper Nlaka'pamux country.[56]

Another illustration of the readiness of Plateau groups to incorporate "exotic" materials comes from the Salish Flathead. With their increasing concentration on buffalo hunting, the Flathead began to use more portable hide bags of Plains design in place of their traditional woven baskets, and lodges covered in buffalo skin (like the Plains tipi) in place of mat-covered dwellings. By the time traders had arrived in the region, Flathead basketry appears to have been largely displaced by leatherwork. Portability was an important consideration; another must have been that Flathead women found themselves so busy with the preparation of meat and hides during the winter season, the time when the labor-intensive basketwork was traditionally done, that they no longer had time for basketry. However, this is not to suggest that women's craft skills disappeared. The creation of novel items—such as the attractive leather-and-quillwork headstalls fashioned for favorite horses—indicates a readiness to play with new styles and new materials.[57]

Many European trade goods were assigned indigenous meanings and adapted to existing uses in much the same way as goods acquired through Native trade. Examples abound. North West Company trade tokens initially intended as markers of the amount of credit a hunter could claim at a post soon appeared strung on necklaces. Cloth and the ubiquitous trade beads were used in place of some of the natural dyes, shells, quill, and puncture work that had long been favored decorations. The results of such incorporation could be amusing. On his journey down the Columbia in 1811, David Thompson was surprised to meet a Wanapam man with the handle of a teakettle "for an ornament about his head." Two decades later, Samuel Black remarked on the fondness of the Nez Percé for ornamentation, noting that they would work into their dress "anything polished sparkling or shining": in an exquisite illustration of the point, one man had plaited a brass candlestick into his braid.[58]

Traders frequently remarked on the taste of Native people for European clothing. As early as 1811, Thompson reported that groups in the eastern Plateau were abandoning their leather dress for sensible British woolens. Judging by later accounts, this was wishful thinking. In 1829, Work made the more limited claim that the people of the Colville region preferred European to indigenous clothing when they were able to get it. Yet it is clear from his own detailed description of local dress that even at this late date few European items had been adopted, even by those in "better circumstances." Four years earlier Ross had noted that the only European article in evidence in Flathead dress was the strips of red cloth that had become popular substitutes for dyes as color accents on leather. Samuel Black's account of dress in the Walla Walla region, also written in 1829, may shed some light on these seeming contradictions. Black explained that the people of the area "like [European clothes] as a change and a Badge of Riches, but return to their own dresses."[59]

In the same passage, Black described other methods of fashioning the "Badge of Riches," including face painting and decoration of clothing with a range of indigenous and traded items. Trade beads were in use, but the local people had very discriminating tastes. Black found that they preferred "the Green dark Green and only take the Blue transparent when they can get none else." Even dark green beads were no match for *haiqua*—these small white dentalium shells traded from the coast remained the most sought-after accessory. Wealthy people "have always a good supply of Haiquas about them in the garnishing way and in their Hair Ears &c."[60]

The two imported elements with the most profound impacts on Plateau societies in the era under study were the horse and epidemic disease. The horse, as has been shown, facilitated the elaboration of the buffalo hunt and greatly enhanced mobility and portability. Nevertheless, it appears from the record of the fur-trade era that it did not radically alter the plan of Plateau life so much as it accelerated preexistent patterns of mobility and seasonal resource specialization.[61] The impact of the animal on social relations is considered briefly below. As demonstrated in chapter 2, epidemic disease had disastrous effects, although in this early period of encounter it too was dealt with from within a framework of indigenous practices and beliefs.

From the mid-eighteenth to the mid-nineteenth century, European trade goods and increasing quantities of "foreign" Native goods provided the raw materials for a period of great cultural creativity during which indigenous features were richly embellished. This process, so much chronicled by students of the Northwest Coast, has seldom been remarked for the Plateau.[62] The results are less striking to the Western eye, expressed as they were in clothing, utensils, and prosaic items rather than in totem poles and the other spectacular artistic productions of settled coastal societies. However, the results are no less significant. As they had long done, Plateau peoples explored the flood tide of new materials and influences and adapted them to evolving indigenous uses.

Impacts of the Horse: Wealth and Leadership

Long before British traders reached the Plateau in 1807, horses had become not only an instrument but also a highly esteemed symbol of prosperity. Traders were amazed at the size of some personal herds. Among the largest was the herd owned by the Cayuse chief Five Ravens (Pakhat Qôqô, known to traders as "Five Crows"), which numbered more than a thousand head. Governor

Simpson in 1841 described Five Crows as "one of the richest men in the country."[63]

In Simpson's view, wealth qua wealth brought social status to Five Crows. As indicated in chapter 4, in Plateau societies it was not accumulation of personal wealth but *distribution* of that wealth that determined an individual's standing in the community. One who had wealth and hoarded it was assured of no special recognition; indeed, hoarding was viewed as intensely antisocial.[64] One who had wealth and dispensed it liberally attained prestige. Work put it well in his remark that chiefs were chosen "as much as anything else for their generosity in relieving the wants of the indigent."[65]

The horse provided a new vehicle of influence. Men with large herds were able to attract horse-poor followers, and loans or gifts of horses became an important means of acquiring influence and prestige. As Theodore Stern notes in his study of social relations in the Fort Nez Percés district, although the bounds of authority were circumscribed in these societies, some men were able to gain large followings—not least through their largesse with horses. Young men in particular, who relied on older men with herds for their first mounts, incurred a moral obligation of loyalty to these elders.[66]

Women certainly owned horses, and traders were impressed with their skills as riders (see fig. 2),[67] but the only woman mentioned in the fur-trade record as possessing a large herd was the Kutenai "chieftainess" from whom Simpson and his party purchased "a fine coyed mare and two year old colt" in 1841.[68] This certainly does not rule out the possibility that other women owned herds, but it does imply that they were rare.

Horses contributed to success in other spheres. Most obviously, those with a good supply increased their chances of distinguishing themselves as hunters. As Black said of the Wallawalla, most of the men were fishers, the only hunters being "those rich enough to have Horses Guns and Ammunition."[69] This leads to the next point, the link between horses and access to trade goods. A

Marie Quilaxp à la bataille contre Les Corbeaux (Août 1846).

Fig. 2. *Marie Quilax à la bataille contre Les Corbeaux (Août 1846)* ("Marie Quilax at war with the Crow [August 1846]"), by Nicholas Point. Credit: Jean De Smet Papers, Washington State University Libraries.

quarry of horses for trade at the post ensured the owner of a supply of guns and ammunition. Access to surplus horses, meat, and the other fruits of the hunt ensured access to a whole range of other trade goods that could be distributed through ritual offerings and gift exchange. It was a spiral effect, with horses at the origin. Those without horses depended on the liberality of those with many to get their own mounts. They would incur reciprocal obligations to their donors, and these obligations probably contributed to the growth of horse-raiding. Raiding was perhaps the easiest way for young men to acquire mounts for their own use and to meet their exchange obligations. The fur-trade sources reveal that raiding for horses from enemy groups, and stealing them from fur traders, became a regular activity for some young men—an activity that itself became a source of prestige.[70]

The importance people attached to their horses was made abundantly clear by their reluctance to part with them. The horse trade was always one of the biggest headaches of the Plateau fur trade. Traders at Fort Nez Percés, the main supply center for horses for the Interior, expended a good deal of mental energy trying to devise ways to control the trade and the prices demanded for horses. For the most part Native traders, especially the Nez Percé and Cayuse, who owned the major herds, retained the upper hand.[71] Samuel Black, who had charge of the post from 1825 to 1830, was as vexed as anyone by the difficulty of securing sufficient numbers of horses for Interior operations, but he was not indifferent to the reasons for the unwillingness to trade. In the spring of 1826, for instance, he warned the authorities at Fort Vancouver that herders in the area had lost many horses to the harsh winter and had "stretched a point" even in trading a few feeble animals to the company. They also faced competing demands from other Native groups in long-standing exchange and trade networks. That winter the Cayuse had traded horses to the Shoshone in exchange for buffalo robes, items they obviously found more attractive than anything the HBC could provide.

Some Nez Percé had exchanged their available horses with Sahaptian villagers on the river, in return for dried salmon.[72] Clearly, Native people with horses to spare had their own priorities, and these were not to be dictated by the demands of the Hudson's Bay Company.

These reflections on the horse and trade goods as vehicles of influence point to the conclusion that the fur trade in the Plateau reinforced a prior pattern whereby individuals, in particular men, could enhance their social standing through the generous distribution of wealth. Traders at Kamloops saw the process in action at a feast hosted by the Secwepemc chief Court Apatte during winter dance festivities in 1826. Archibald McDonald, who acknowledged that he did not understand the proceedings, was puzzled that the chief and other prominent men took charge of serving the three hundred assembled Secwepemc and Nlaka'pamux guests (again, all men). The feast appears to have been, at least in part, a display of the chiefs' liberality. Guests were expected to accept all that was offered. Many ate until they vomited, a result McDonald called "the most convincing proof of their being treated to their heart's content." During the celebration there was an exchange of lavish gifts in which members of the Nlaka'pamux delegation gave the Secwepemc horses and guns, and the Secwepemc returned the favor with guns, robes, beads, and beaver traps.[73]

Bewildered as he professed himself to be, McDonald hit the mark when he described the feast as an opportunity for these groups to "pledge friendship to one another." The distribution of goods was part of the system of ongoing exchange that secured peaceful relations between the Secwepemc and the Nlaka'pamux. Both sides framed the exchange in the idiom of gift-giving rather than trade. The account demonstrates how horses and the trade goods supplied at the post—guns, beaver traps, beads—fulfilled social functions that transcended their basic utilitarian value. In the eastern and southern Plateau, buffalo hides and other products of the hunt came to occupy primacy of place in gift exchanges; here in the northern Plateau, horses and European goods fulfilled that role. The social standing of Court Apatte and other leading figures would have been enhanced by their facility for generosity. Court Apatte's position as a "trading chief" in the Kamloops fur trade, while it lasted, gave him preferential access to these most prestigious items for giveaway.[74]

The issue of the changing nature of leadership among Plateau societies after acquisition of the horse is complex. It is widely accepted by anthropologists that political organization among the buffalo-hunting peoples of the eastern and southern Plateau became more centralized. Traders' accounts do point to the possible emergence of a paramount leader who was in charge for the duration of the buffalo expedition; however, they also indicate the continuance of a more limited and diffuse form of civil leadership during the remainder of the year. Among the Salish Flathead, according to Ross Cox:

> The principal chief of the tribe is hereditary; but from their constant wars, they have adopted the . . . custom of electing, as their leader in battle, that warrior in whom the greatest portion of wisdom, strength, and bravery are combined. . . . This "war-chief," as they term him, has no authority whatever when at home, and is as equally amenable as any of the tribe to the hereditary chief; but when the warriors set out on their hunting excursions to the buffalo plains, he assumes the supreme command, which he exercises with despotic sway until their return.[75]

Ross concurred with Cox that a Flathead "war chief" ruled the assembled party on the buffalo plains. Thompson, on the other hand, while acknowledging that the highly experienced Flathead generally led the expedition, contended that negotiation and consensus remained essential on questions of security and relations with the Blackfoot.[76] As for peacetime leadership back in the Plateau, only Cox spoke of a "principal chief." Others identified multiple chiefs in the Flathead community. Ross, for example, recognized six Flathead men as chiefs when he had charge of Flathead House in 1824–25. Some of them may have been "trading chiefs"; nevertheless, that Cox was alone in identifying a hereditary "principal chief" casts doubt on the existence of this figure.[77]

In other settings traders spoke of not only "war chiefs" but also "hunt chiefs" and "salmon chiefs." The picture that emerges is one of limited and highly diffused authority. Work, who remarked that generosity was the first duty of leaders, went on to add that "[t]he authority of the chiefs is very limited." Black made a similar observation of the groups around Fort Nez Percés, noting that "[t]here is little Government among the Indians," except when some matter of importance required the chiefs to take the lead in village councils. Chiefs enjoyed no special privileges "further than now and then helping themselves to a Fish or Commanding someone to go on some errand for them." Similarly, among Okanagan-Colville groups, Ross reported that chiefs exercised only a "nominal superiority." A man with a large herd of horses was in a good position to attain leadership. But a chief, no matter what his credentials, always sought the assistance of the village or band council on matters of importance. Here again, horses appear to have figured into the equation: to qualify for membership of the council, according to Ross, a man had to have proved his worth by some "praiseworthy deed," or by acquiring wealth in horses or in wives.[78]

The conclusion to be drawn is that while the horse opened important new avenues of influence for men, it does not appear to have fostered the kind of centralized authority that emerged in some Plains societies.[79] Authority remained highly diffuse. In addition, with the possible exception of the Salish Flathead and Upper Kutenai, the elaboration of the mounted buffalo hunt did not bring about the kind of dramatic change in productive processes that occurred in many Plains societies. Even those two Plateau peoples continued to mark a seasonal round that was broadly similar to that of pre-horse times, as the discussion in the next section indicates.

What, then, is to be made of the more usual view that the peoples of the southern and eastern Plateau became rapidly "acculturated" to a Plains way of life? The symbolism of Plains cultures is certainly powerful, as the quotation at the opening of this chapter reveals (and as the analysis in the next chapter illustrates). It appears, however, that the power of the symbolism continues to blind some scholars to the more subtle evidence below the surface. Anthropologist Stern, for example, accepts as evidence of acculturation and "transformation" in lifestyle the comments of Lewis and Clark, who reported the Umatilla to be much more impressive when accompanied by their horse herds than they were without. Stern clearly attaches Plains-style symbolism to the equestrian Nez Percé and Cayuse when he describes them as a "Prairie elite"—in contrast, not surprisingly, to the "poor" fishing tribes. His interpretation echoes that offered in the popular works of Robert Ruby and John Brown, who persistently cast Plateau societies as divided into two ranks, the more powerful and affluent being the horseback-riding, buffalo-hunting "imperial tribesmen" (Cayuse and Nez Percé).[80] For Stern's part, his authorities are Samuel Black, who is quoted on the "great influence" of the Cayuse; and various trader and missionary reports of Nez Percé and Cayuse reluctance to interact with river dwellers, and of the alleged poverty of the latter. To be sure, Stern also draws on the reports of Native informants; he admits, however, that these statements are far more ambiguous than those of nineteenth-century white commentators.[81]

A central proposition of this work, by contrast, is that the reader needs to be constantly attentive to the cultural lenses through which such commentators viewed (and view) indigenous societies. How did the material interests of the fur traders shape their perception of the hunters as rich and industrious, the fishers as poor and lazy? How might contemporary Western notions about such things as land use, food hierarchies, and appropriate gender roles have shaped these commentaries? What was the influence of contemporary notions of proper masculinity? Some of these issues have been addressed; others await the next chapter. In the meantime, suffice it to say, once again, that reports of Plains-style "imperial tribesmen" and "riverine poor" in the Plateau must be read with a critical eye. Likewise accounts of more general acculturation to Plains ways should be reconsidered. The evidence available in the fur-trade record—scattered and incomplete as it is—calls for caution in making such claims. Many symbols of Plains life were indeed adopted by Plateau societies in this era, but it does not appear that these societies underwent a wholesale change in terms of the values and practices associated with horse ownership, wealth, and leadership. Instead there is much in the Plateau record to suggest that horses, the buffalo hunt, and Plains materials were adopted into Plateau value systems, adapted to evolving Plateau ways.

Women and Horse and Buffalo Culture

If horses and the buffalo hunt opened new avenues of wealth and influence for men, what were the impacts on women? In chapter 4 the general opinion of British observers was revealed: women in Plateau societies worked far harder than was considered appropriate for the "sweet" sex.[82] Still more disturbing to these observers was the position of women in the "hunting" and "horse" tribes. The dominant image was of women as beasts of burden. As Work described it, women in buffalo-hunting groups added to an already heavy workload the following tasks:

> striking the lodges in the morning, tieing [sic] up the baggage ... loading the horses of burden and conducting them through the days march, and in the evening unloading them, pitching the lodge and arranging all the stuff.... Those who have no horses, in addition to the above duties ... when travelling overland carry their effects on their backs.[83]

Ross, too, was struck that women had charge of the packhorses. When parties of Salish Flathead came to the HBC outpost to trade, the men arrived with great fanfare, "mounted on horseback ... chanting the song of peace." The leading men were entertained in the gentlemen's cabin. After the festivities the women arrived, on horseback also, and leading the animals that were "loaded with furs and provisions."[84]

Such physical labor was considered entirely unnatural for women and was further evidence of the laziness and despotism of their men. Black, for example, was concerned that this heavy work was the cause of miscarriages. Elsewhere in the same report, however, he noted that childbirth seemed remarkably trouble-free, and that even around the time of the birth, women were "seldom confined from their usual occupations."[85] Coming from a society that viewed childbirth as "the time of women's greatest travail,"[86] fur traders frequently expressed surprise at the ease with which Native women gave birth. The ability of these women to rebound from childbirth "as if nothing had happened" underlines that so much of what is taken as "natural" about women's roles and behavior is actually a product of cultural attitudes and conditioning. As one commentator has put it, "physiology presents possibilities; it does not determine cultural elaboration."[87]

There is no question that the development of the large-scale buffalo hunt and trade in hides and pemmican intensified the already heavy demands on women's time and energy. Hide dressing and meat processing were labor-intensive activities. Consider the dressing of the hides: while an expert hunter could kill four or five animals in a single run at a herd (the work of as little as thirty minutes to an hour), it took an experienced woman with little else to do three days to dress one hide. Taking into account her other duties, including the time-consuming preparation of the meat, it was more likely to be the work of ten days.[88]

The initial skinning and rough butchering was performed by the hunter in the field, and the portions to be saved were carried back to the camp with the help of a party of his kin. The women then took over. Hides were stretched on wooden pegs, and any remaining flesh was scraped off with a chisel-like knife. Metal knives obtained through trade were a boon for this work. If it was to be soft-dressed, rather than left as rawhide, the hide was rubbed with an oily concoction of buffalo brains as a preservative. After soaking for a time in warm water, the hide was suspended again and rubbed with a stone until it reached the desired flexibility. This was the basic dressing process; the finishing work to make robes, lodges, packs, and the myriad other domestic essentials and trade goods involved yet more labor. A single hide tipi could consume as many as fifteen to twenty hides, and many person-hours of labor. Much of the finishing work was done after the hunting season.[89]

There have been no studies, as yet, of the impact of the mercantile buffalo economy on Plateau women. Studies of its impact on women in Plains societies generally argue for a substantial erosion of their power and autonomy. It is widely accepted that as the buffalo hunt shifted from a communal activity oriented to consumption and simple exchange to a form of surplus production, Plains societies became increasingly male-oriented.[90] Involvement in the fast-growing commercial trade led men to spend more and more time hunting, raiding for horses, and fighting over access to hunting grounds. Men owned the horses acquired in prestigious raiding; they owned the horses ridden on the buffalo hunt. There was little space left for women in these activities. Increasingly their efforts became focused on processing the products of their male kin's labor. While women were still said to own the products of the hunt, the various obligations and rights that accrued to the (male) hunters meant that, in reality, the benefits and meaning of that ownership were confined. Indeed, it has been argued that in communities involved in the commercial hide trade, women—as the processors of goods that were converted into wealth—themselves "became objects of wealth, status symbols for their husbands."[91] As Alan Klein has argued, women in such societies "became workers in a highly specialized production process over which men had ultimate control."[92] Increased polygyny, an increasing tendency toward residence with the man's kin (especially in areas where competition led to

frequent raiding or fighting), and the growth of the all-male institutions associated with a Plains-type "tribal complex" (warrior
societies, etc.) are said to have further limited women's latitude
and autonomy.

While Plains societies are not the main concern here, a caveat
does seem to be in order before proceeding to look at comparative Plateau material. The evidence from Plains societies is persuasive: women's autonomy and influence appears to have been
eroded under the conditions of the commercial hide trade. But
the warning of historian Nancy Shoemaker comes to mind.
Women's power and status are not "tangible, measurable, immediately observable and knowable"; nor can we safely generalize
from anthropological observations in one community or society
to "the Plains" as a whole. The decline in female status was not
uniform across Plains societies, nor was it absolute. Work by
numerous anthropologists and historians has shown that women
retained power in their own spheres.[93] A recent essay by Alice
Beck Kehoe on a Piegan community in Montana, for example,
underlines the importance of attending to the local realities of
women's lives and their roles and status in the spheres that
comprised "women's business." Kehoe shows how Piegan men
talked to anthropologists about their exploits in hunting, raiding,
war, and secret societies; women, meanwhile, talked about family
and kin relationships and the strains on the family of adjusting
to economic and political change. In the realm of "women's
business" women had authority and autonomy.[94] The structural
reality in the era of the commercial hunt may have been one of
eroding opportunities for women and increasing labor burdens—
and surely the implications of this context should not be downplayed—but neither should we merely accept the view, purveyed
first by fur traders, that women in these societies became slaves
to the men, helpless chattel in the clutches of commodity
capitalism.

The fur-trade record of the Plateau indicates a rather different
pattern of change than in the Plains region, although given the

limited nature of the historical evidence at hand, any conclusions must remain speculative. The first point, drawn from evidence on the Salish Flathead, reiterates an argument made above. Flathead productive activities during the era under study became concentrated on the buffalo hunt to a much more limited extent than in many Plains societies. As was demonstrated earlier, the Flathead continued to follow a complex annual round in which the gathering of plant foods by women remained a vital component. Traders frequently noted that "all" the Flathead were off to the root grounds—women, men, chiefs, entire communities—an indication that the movement and composition of residence groups continued to be determined by the activity at hand, whether it was an activity controlled by women or by men. The men often hunted while the women gathered, but their movements were, in the first instance, determined by availability of roots. Traders' accounts suggest that women retained autonomy in an area of subsistence production that remained vital to the reproduction of the society.[95]

Furthermore, it appears that for the most part Plateau women retained control of the products of their own labor. Evidence for this claim is that they regularly traded on their own account at company posts. There are scattered references in the journals to women trading grass mats, the pelts of small mammals, roots, berries, and a variety of other items they produced themselves, in exchange for knives, metal awls and needles, kettles, cloth, and so forth. Unfortunately, goods traded by women are all too rarely separated out from those traded by men in post accounts, making it impossible to construct a detailed picture of their trading activities.

As for goods that were produced by the combined labor of women and men—most notably for present purposes, leather items and pemmican—it is difficult to tell from traders' accounts who controlled their disposal. Women had control of the products for domestic use—the hides used for clothing and tipis, and the meat for immediate family use and winter storage. In the journal from the Flathead outpost, both women and men are seen trading dried meat and tallow, hides, and leather goods. The "staple articles" supplied by the company were guns, ammunition, kettles, knives, and tobacco.[96] The presence of kettles in this list would seem to suggest that women were very active in the trade. As usual, things are not quite so straightforward. Useful as they were as cooking vessels, kettles were not sought purely for domestic purposes. They were often broken apart for their copper, which found its way into tools, accessories, and other items. Given such varied uses, men may have traded for kettles as well. The evidence does not allow for any definitive statements, but it does seem likely that women controlled the distribution of some portion of the hides they produced, and used them to trade at the posts.

As was demonstrated in chapter 4, it is not enough to say that women controlled access to their own resources and the distribution of their own products and thus were in a position of equality with men. Cultural perceptions of the relative positions of women and men are not simple reflections of productive processes and relations. Once again, marriage provides clues to the elusive issue of how gender roles were construed.

Polygyny was widely practiced by Plateau groups. There is no indication, however, that the incidence of multiple marriages increased as a result of the hide trade as it did in many Plains societies. Much as they abhorred it, traders saw polygyny principally as a means by which a man attained prestige. As Ross put it, a man with no wife "is neither chief nor great man"; many had two wives, and occasionally three or four, "according to their means and influence." Ross said nothing about their labor needs.[97] In fact, there is nothing in the Plateau fur-trade record to indicate that during this era women were forced into polygynous relationships by men who needed their labor. On the contrary, as was shown earlier, traders remarked time and again that women exercised considerable control over their marital destiny. Interestingly, although the Flathead were among the most dedicated buffalo hunters, traders had little to say about polygyny among them at all. It was often remarked that Flathead men treated their wives well. Indeed, one of the traits Cox most admired in the Flathead was their respect for women, and he singled out one "war chief" who was so overcome by grief at the loss of his wife that he refused to take another even after her death. It would be rash to draw conclusions from such anecdotal evidence, but there is simply nothing in the record to suggest increased polygyny among the Flathead or others as a consequence of the buffalo hunt.[98] The available evidence indicates that the impacts of the commercial hide trade were a good deal more limited in the Plateau than among Plains groups, and the implications for women similarly so.

The Berdache Phenomenon and the Marking of Gender

A central paradox of traders' commentaries on the ability of women to act, speak out, and make decisions for themselves is that they come in the midst of depictions of these buffalo-hunting societies as eminently masculine. As will be seen in the chapter that follows, traders perceived the buffalo hunters as brave and martial, in every way fulfilling the role of manly hunter-warriors. The intriguing question that arises is, to what extent did people in these societies themselves mark virtue and gender in these ways? Not surprisingly, traders' writings provide few answers. However, their remarks on berdaches raise intriguing possibilities.

Berdache, a word that appears to have its origin in the French fur trade,[99] is the term used by students of Native North American cultures to refer to individuals of a transformed, dual, or third gender. Some scholars use "berdache" to refer only to men who adopted (or adopt) alternative gender roles, applying the parallel term *amazon* to women of transformed gender. Both terms are contrived: each Native American society has its own terms for these individuals, which often translate as "man-woman" or "half man–half woman."[100] Following the usage of fur traders and bearing in mind the artificiality of general labels for an institution that varied from culture to culture, I use "berdache" for both men and women of transformed or intermediate gender.[101]

The berdache phenomenon has been positively identified in an enormous range of indigenous cultures in North America.[102] In general, berdaches changed gender status by adopting the dress, and often the occupations and behavior, of the opposite sex. The shift was most often made in childhood or adolescence. The result for males was frequently a kind of intermediate status drawing on conventional social attributes of male and female. For females the new role appears more often to have been a conventional masculine gender role. Much of the ethnographic literature— which gives the lion's share of attention to male berdaches— points to the extraordinary achievements of these individuals. For example, a Zuni *lhmanas*, known as We'Wha, was renowned at once for his incredible physical strength and for his exquisite weaving and pottery. The Crow berdache Osh-Tisch, while adopting many of the attributes of a woman, nevertheless became a hero for his exploits as a warrior.[103] For present purposes, the berdache phenomenon is remarkable for what it may tell us about the way in which gender was marked in Native American communities, specifically those of the Plateau, in the early nineteenth century.

The earliest account of a berdache in the Columbia district is of the Kutenai woman known to traders as Ko-come-ne-peca; her Kutenai name was probably Kauxuma-nupika ("Gone to the Spirits"). As described in chapter 2, Kauxuma-nupika arrived at Fort Astoria on the lower Columbia in June 1811, dressed as a man and accompanied by her wife. She carried the bow and arrow of a hunter, and some at the post were convinced she was male; however, David Thompson recognized her as the former wife of a North West Company servant. Thompson described Kauxuma-nupika as a woman who had "set herself up for a prophetess, and gradually had gained, by her shrewdness, some influence among the Natives as a dreamer, and expounder of dreams." Ross depicted her as a woman who, during her time among the whites, had learned "all the arts of well instructed cheats."[104] The traders were less concerned with her gender than with her prophecies, which were examined in chapter 2. What is significant here is that Kauxuma-nupika as a berdache enjoyed considerable influence as she moved about the Interior. She and her partner travelled upriver just ahead of the Astorian brigade, prophesying both disease and a coming time of plenty. By Ross's account, these "adventurous Amazons" were the object of attention at every village along the way, and they so "astonished" local people with their stories that they gave them their most prized possessions, gifts of beaver robes, horses, leather, and *haiqua*.[105]

The next account comes from Ross Cox, who encountered a berdache in the position of chief of a small Spokane village in 1814. The individual was a man who dressed and wore the accessories and hairstyle of a woman. In spite of what Cox derided as "extraordinary" behavior, the chief was very highly respected by both men and women in the village, and Cox found him to be wise and dignified.[106] Perhaps owing to the sparseness of documentation, there are no further accounts until 1825, when during a winter spent at Flathead Post, John Work encountered a Kutenai woman known to traders by the name Berdache. Work described the woman as "a leading character" among her people. She "goes in mens cloths [*sic*] . . . assumes a masculine character"; although not herself a chief, she arrived at the post with the chief and other "principal men," at the head of a party of Kutenai hunters come to trade. Like the chief, she was given a gift of ammunition and beads after the trade was completed. Work was impressed with her skills at interpreting, noting that she spoke the Salish Flathead language very well. It seems highly unlikely that this woman was Kauxuma-nupika, since Work would almost certainly have been told about her by Ross or others.[107]

A final, more puzzling, case is the man known to traders at Fort Nez Percés as the Cayuse chief Old Berdache or The Berdache.

There is no reference to him changing gender, but given the meaning of his name in fur-trade idiom, he must at some point in his life have "assumed the character" of the opposite sex. What is clear is that he was an influential figure in the region during the fur-trade era. He appears regularly in Simon McGillivray's journal, and he accompanied John Work on various expeditions, including one to California in 1832–33.[108]

What these people had in common, in addition to being berdaches, was that all were "leading characters" of some sort. There is a good deal of historical documentation of gender transformation in Native North American societies, and of not merely the toleration but also the institutionalization of changes in gender status in these societies.[109] From the examples seen here, it is apparent that in at least some Plateau societies, women and men were at liberty to assume roles associated with the opposite sex. The traders' accounts tell us nothing about the process by which individuals became berdaches—whether by receiving supernatural validation through a vision quest in adolescence, as one anthropological explanation would have it; or by simply showing expertise in the accustomed roles of the other sex, as has been reported for some societies; or by some other route.[110]

What the traders' accounts do indicate is that in some Plateau societies individuals could alter or transcend their biological sex roles without stigma, and indeed they could achieve high status if they were successful in their new social roles. Thus the Kutenai woman known simply as Berdache was accepted among the "principal men" in a party of Kutenai hunters, and the Spokane man who styled himself as a woman could become a highly respected chief. Such evidence strongly suggests that prestige in these societies attached to success in one's social roles, regardless of one's biological identity. It suggests that in contrast to the kind of hardened gender boundaries that prevailed in the societies from which the traders hailed, gender boundaries in Plateau societies could be far more fluid. And it returns us to the trenchant observation, offered earlier, that physiology presents possibilities but does not determine cultural elaboration.

Concluding Remarks

This first, and explicitly tentative, effort to illuminate some of the key economic and social changes underway in Plateau societies as a result of horse and buffalo culture and the fur trade points to a number of conclusions. We have seen in earlier chapters that the scope of the Plateau fur trade was more limited than that of many other regions, partly as a consequence of the limited availability of fur-bearing animals, and partly as a result of the lack of interest of the peoples of the region in trapping furs for trade. In this chapter we have explored evidence that the impact of the trade on Plateau lifeways was similarly limited.

It is fundamental to the argument here that the effects of acquisition of things like the horse, firearms, and other European trade goods cannot be understood in isolation from the social and historical contexts in which they became embedded. David Thompson's initial confidence in the value of guns for hunting notwithstanding, access to firearms was a signal development in the southern and eastern Plateau not so much for what it meant for hunting, but for the security it offered the hunters while in the Plains region. Thompson's confidence in the superiority of British woolens aside, items of European clothing were sought more as a "Badge of Riches" than a convenience. The influence of European goods in these societies, be they horses or green glass beads, must be assessed with reference to evolving indigenous meanings and patterns of social relations.

The most profound repercussions of the European presence to be felt in the Plateau during this era were also the most indirect—epidemic disease and the horse. The effects of acquisition of the horse were registered in every facet of Plateau life: patterns of land use, trade, and travel; patterns of raiding and violence, leadership and gender relations. The argument here has been that while these effects were very significant, they were not transformative. Rather than radically altering the plan of Plateau life, the horse tended to accelerate preexisting patterns of seasonal resource specialization and mobility. The elaboration of the large-scale buffalo hunt was one of the most significant developments, but Plateau groups appear to have concentrated on the hunt to a much more limited extent than many Plains societies; Plateau peoples continued to follow a complex annual round, in which foods produced by women remained central. The hunt certainly increased demands on women's labor, though there is nothing in the fur-trade record to suggest that Plateau women suffered the kind of erosion of economic control and autonomy that has been indicated for their counterparts in many Plains societies.

Far from transforming patterns of social reward and leadership, the horse reinforced the process whereby individuals—and in particular, men—acquired social standing through the generous distribution of goods. Exotic Indian trade goods and the European goods supplied at the posts were similarly incorporated into preexisting systems of exchange and reward. Firearms are a good example. The guns given as gifts at the Secwepemc feast in 1826 fulfilled a social role at least as significant as their practical purpose. Guns, horses, and the buffalo products they enabled their owners to procure came to hold primacy of place among the goods that, in the giving, brought prestige and influence. In short, the new materials and ideas that reached the Plateau during the period from the mid-eighteenth to the mid-nineteenth century were adapted to indigenous uses, and they were assigned meanings that reflected evolving indigenous priorities and practices.

CHAPTER SEVEN

Traders and Hunters II

Images of Wealth and Manly Virtue

The previous chapter examined the emergence of horse and buffalo culture on the Plateau and the contributions of the buffalo-hunting groups to the fur trade of the region. At the outset the point was made that there was far more than instrumental logic to the traders' admiration of these hunters. The focus of this chapter is the rich symbolic associations that gave such power to the image of the buffalo hunter—associations with contemporary notions of masculinity and with emerging notions of the "real" Indian.[1]

Images of Buffalo Hunting: The Outline of the Hunt

The most detailed description of the communal buffalo hunt by Plateau hunters comes not from a fur trader, but from Father Nicolas Point, a Jesuit priest involved in the founding of the first Catholic missions west of the Rockies in the 1840s.[2] Point frequently accompanied hunting parties on their excursions to the buffalo plains, and his written accounts, together with his remarkable miniature paintings, provide a unique record of this aspect of Native American history in the eastern Plateau. Material from Point's accounts is presented here for its descriptive value.

Buffalo-hunting expeditions generally assembled in the Bitterroot valley in Salish Flathead territory. The trip to the buffalo grounds could be long and arduous. On the autumn hunt in 1842, on which Point was present, it took twenty-four days for the massed party to reach the herds across the Continental Divide. The distance that had to be travelled is indicative of the extent of depletion of far-western herds at this time.

By Point's reckoning, the most demanding role on the hunt was that of the women, who were in charge of the packhorses and baggage as well as making camp and preparing food. The next most important role was that of hunt chief. This "head chief," often called by traders the "war chief," led the expedition, choosing the route and campsites and setting an example by his "courage and vigilance." Arriving in promising country, the chief sent out scouts to spot herds and, equally important, enemy parties. On the scouts' return a smoking ceremony was held at which they reported their findings. The hunt chief "stands among the lodges and solemnly announces: 'My children, let us thank the Great Spirit, for game has been discovered. Prepare your arms and your best horses.' "[3]

Stalking the buffalo required great skill, since the animals startled easily. Point's depiction of the drive is vivid:

> After the hunters have knelt and recited their prayers, they mount and, taking advantage of the most favorable natural concealment, advance as noiselessly as possible.... When the hunters have arrived at a point where they have the wind in their faces, three things are sufficient for the Indians to reach their prey, namely, the formation of a straight line, the signal from their chief, and the full gallop of their horses.... The running hunt is an attack to the death. The animal belongs to the first one who hits him.... In an instant pell-mell ensues.... Columns of fleeing animals can be seen to detach themselves from the main herd, some pounding off in one direction, others in another.... For the skillful hunter this is the moment for making the choice of game. If the number of animals is large, everyone makes haste to do this. But the hunters are all respectful, one to another. One never finishes what another has begun. If an animal has been wounded but

not mortally, the horseman maneuvers [sic] until he can deal
the death blow most effectively. If the animal has been
wounded mortally, the hunter pursues it calmly, knowing that
it will soon fall. . . . There is nothing more majestic than the fall
of a bison. It seems that to redeem itself from the shame it has
suffered, it holds out to the bitter end without betraying any
sign of weakness. When the buffalo has finally fallen, the
hunter does not tarry to skin it, but goes immediately in hot
pursuit of a second, a third, and so on, just as long as the vigor
of his horse can respond to his own ardor.[4]

Significantly, Point reported that even at this late date bow
and arrow, rather than musket, was the chosen weapon for the
hunt.[5] The usual problems associated with the reloading of
muzzle-loaders were compounded when the hunter was
mounted on a galloping horse. When the horses were exhausted
or the herd dispersed, each hunter returned to collect his own
quarry and perform the initial butchering. Back at the camp the
women took over, carrying out the full butchering, drying the
meat, and dressing the hides. Most of the arduous finishing work
on the hides was done after the hunting season.[6]

Point noted that if buffalo were particularly plentiful and provisions in good supply, only the coveted tongues and humps, which
were excellent for drying, might be recovered. Generally, the
entire animal was put to use. While the party was in the field,
loins and other cuts not worth preserving were "daily bread";
tongues and humps were saved for "great occasions." The marrow,
a delicacy that Point compared to cheese, was used for travel
food, and the entrails and brains were also eaten. Hides furnished
robes, tipis, parfleches, shields, bridles, saddles, stirrups, and
rope, while horns were fashioned into spoons and bowls, powder
horns, bows, and sheaths. The tail provided whips and ornaments,
and the hair was woven into horse halters and cloth. The bladder
was useful for storing liquids, grease, and paint, and the bones
were fashioned into knives and gadgets for use in games. Finally,
the dung went to good use where firewood was scarce.[7]

Images of Hunters: The Hunt and the Food of Men

As Ross's comments cited at the opening of chapter 6 reveal, physique was, in the traders' estimation, the most visible distinguishing characteristic of hunters. Ross's language points to the way in which representation of the body was morally charged and defined by a particular masculine ideology: the men were "tall, raw-boned, well-dressed," their clothing white, their voices strong and manly, their women decorous. Concern with physical detail had long been generic to travel and other "ethnographic" writing, but the emphasis on the morality of the body was reflective of a broader contemporary trend. As historian Billie Melman has demonstrated, by the late eighteenth century there was a perceptible shift toward morally charged physical description in travel writing, anticipating the Victorian tradition of physiognomy (the assessment of human and social character from physical features of face and body).[8] In the words of Johann Kaspar Lavater, founder of the popular "science" of physiognomy, human physical expression was an index not only to the emotions and the intellect "but, most important, to the possibilities of moral life." Outward appearance was a manifestation of inner values, physical details an index to morals.[9]

The fine physique attributed to the hunters was ascribed first and foremost to their diet. If those judged to live on fish and roots were "slightly made," those identified as hunters were "tall, raw-boned," "fully formed," "well made for activity." It was noted in earlier chapters that traders believed meat to be the proper food of "laborious men." The assumption was that hunters ate a great deal of meat, and that this was the material source of their masculine vigor. A corollary of this was that hunters worked harder than fishers, and so needed this superior sustenance.

Traders' reflections on their own diet illuminate these assumptions. A steady diet of pemmican, the staple of the fur trade east of the Rockies, might be monotonous, but it was "wholesome" food, not to mention "well tasted." So potent was the dried meat that even the "gluttonous" French Canadian boatmen, accustomed to eating eight pounds of fresh meat a day, were content with a pound-and-a-half of pemmican. Men, and particularly men who engaged in strenuous physical activity, needed meat, it was believed, to deliver and sustain the physical demands of manhood. The assumption was extended to Native people, as in the traders' belief that meat was the Natives' chosen food when it was available—or at least the choice of brave hunting men. The dietary preferences of Native women were not discussed.[10] The point has been amply made that traders overstated the role of meat in the Plateau diet. Even the most productive buffalo hunters continued to rely on gathered foods and fish for a significant portion of their diet.

Images of Hunters: "Badges of Riches"

Clothing is, of course, another highly visible marker of wealth and moral character; it is a reflection of the symbolic weight of dress that for centuries the most common epithet for the British poor was "the ragged."[11] Next to physique, leather clothing was the outward symbol of wealth most frequently noted by traders in the Plateau. There were pragmatic considerations at issue: leather signified the ability to hunt successfully, and the commitment to such productive pursuits.[12] Beyond that, it provided durable and handsome clothing, in styles familiar to Europeans. As Governor Simpson described it, the dress of eastern Plateau hunters was "very classical and neat, consisting of a tunic reaching to the knees and leggings, of white dressed skins." Kutenai women wore a leather gown "not unlike that in which the character of Norma is represented on the English stage."[13]

Clothing served well in the traders' rough-and-ready index as a marker of the state of development of a society. Nakedness (referred to most often by euphemisms connected with nature) or simplicity of clothing intimated crudeness. Simpson put the point clearly when he noted of Lower Kutenai fishing bands that the dress of the men consisted of "a skin thrown over [the] shoulders," while the children had "no other dress than nature had provided for them."[14] Cox's summary sketches of the peoples of the Columbia highlight the contrast so often drawn between those who dressed in suits of leather and those who wore fur shawls or garments of bark, grasses, and hemp. Sahaptian groups were well clothed in clean leather shirts and leggings, and Okanagan-Colville groups were praised for their "decency in covering." The fishing groups who gathered in the summer on the Columbia above Priests Rapid, by contrast, were "wretchedly poor and nearly naked."[15] Nakedness, like starvation, was a relative concept. It seldom meant the entire absence of clothing, but referred to degrees of concealment that to British sensibilities appeared scanty.

The impropriety of women going about this way was a particularly common theme. Propriety, modesty, and chastity were paramount virtues in Enlightenment and bourgeois discourses on womanhood. Yet it is an irony often remarked that the same men who harbored these expectations viewed women principally as sexual objects. The tensions between the traders' expectations of propriety and their sexual desire speak to their social and sexual anxieties. These anxieties emerge in sharp relief in their descriptions of women's dress. If the extent to which women covered their bodies was the first thing noted, the endowments of those bodies was the next. Yet serious middle-class men could not be seen obsessing over the intricacies of the female form. Better to focus on the clothing and leave the rest to the imagination. Writing of the northern Secwepemc in 1827, Joseph McGillivray praised their deerskin robes, which in the case of the women were combined with "dressed Leather Petticoat[s]" to conceal the entire body. In the next breath he confided that Secwepemc women were "slenderly made—and some have a good figure."[16] In keeping with expectations for his own propriety, McGillivray offered more detail on dress than undress; but the intimations were there.

Modesty was not an advantage of the fur blankets and cedar skirts worn by the women of the "piscatory tribes" on the lower Columbia. Several traders commented that these women might as well have been nude, and Ross indulged in a little titillation, remarking that the skirt "does not screen nature from the prying eye." One wonders whose eye was prying.[17] Seasonality was apparently no part of traders' calculations in their assessments of female dress: summer or winter, full-length robes were the ideal.

"Handsome" leather clothing was thus a badge of the "best equipped indian tribes." The Okanagan, whom Ross judged to be hunters of moderate ability, had access to leather shirts and shifts that were attractive enough when new, white, and clean. However, they wore them until they were "rotten with grease and filth on their backs." It was a common observation that only people "of good circumstances" could afford to replace old suits with new. Writing of the southern groups, for example, Samuel Black remarked that "a Good hunter will change his dress three times or more in a year . . . [while] Necessity obliges the poor to own their dress until it wears off their backs." The implication was, of course, that those "of good circumstances" were hunters and their families.[18]

Cleanliness was an essential aspect of respectability in dress. Traders were quite obsessed with cleanliness. It had connotations beyond the absence of the "vermin" that so annoyed visitors in lodges on the lower Columbia. Moral criteria, much more than anxiety over physical health, shaped the concern with dirt and disorder. Some undoubtedly shared the contemporary view, purveyed with vigor by Dr. Buchan, that dirt was "infectious." Infection was meant not in the later biomedical sense, but in the eighteenth-century sense, in which it was synonymous with "miasma" and "contagion" and was believed to originate in stagnant air and putrescence.[19]

More important than such functional criteria was the symbolism of dirt: as dirt connoted sloth, so cleanliness signified industry. Thompson recalled in his *Narrative* that the peoples west of the mountains "pride themselves on their industry, and their skill in doing anything, and are as neat as their circumstances will allow." The specific circumstance he had in mind was the absence of soap. He was impressed by the ability of some of these groups to keep clean without this essential of "civilized" life. In the view of every trader who met them, the Salish Flathead won the prize for superiority in cleanliness. Their clothes were judged to be clean and well kept, and their lodges tidy and free of vermin. Cox ranked cleanliness on a par with bravery, honesty, industry, and compliance with authority as the supreme virtues of the Flathead.[20]

If traders admired the rich leather clothing of the hunters, they were more ambivalent about their penchant for decoration. Black hinted at the vanity of the "Badge of Riches" devised by Sahaptian men—the face painting, hairdressing, and lavish accessorizing.[21] Writing of the Colville region, Work was more categorical: "The young, and especially the males . . . occupy no inconsiderable portion of the morning decorating themselves; in point of time, and the degree of pains taken to ornament their hair, paint their faces &c they may compete with the more accomplished fops in the civilised world."[22]

The resonance with early-nineteenth-century middle-class notions of respectable manhood is striking. The alternative model against which such foppery was measured would seem to be one of serious manhood, modesty, self-restraint—or to quote Governor Simpson, the gentleman-trader ideal of "zeal, firmness, and restraint."

Symbolism and the Buffalo Hunt: The Stuff of Real Men

The fur traders' vision of the heroic buffalo hunt drew on a potent cultural repertoire of interrelated notions about manly virtues, sportsmanship, and man's mastery of nature. This language is used self-consciously: such notions were heavily gendered. In addition to cultural assumptions about manliness, the traders' imagery of the buffalo hunter drew on and gave force to what was by this time becoming a common assumption about Indianness: the notion that real Indians rode on horseback and hunted big game. These two clusters of cultural imagery—of real men and real Indians—are the focus of the remainder of this chapter.

The principal distinguishing feature of the buffalo hunt, as traders saw it, was the premium it placed on bravery. Bravery was a prerequisite because, as the Salish Flathead chief known as Cartier told Thompson, "when [we] go to hunt the Bison, we also prepare for war."[23] Hunting by Plateau groups in the parklands of the Rocky Mountains and the plains on the east brought them into pitched competition with their longstanding Plains foes, the members of the Blackfoot confederacy. Traders based in the Plateau favored local hunters in these confrontations, not least because the Blackfoot had so resolutely resisted traders' attempts to penetrate their territory on the route westward in the opening years of the century.

Traders endowed the buffalo hunting of Plateau groups with a lofty moral significance. In his ethnographic summary of Plateau peoples, Cox noted that those qualities that "ranked among the virtues" were most conspicuous among the buffalo hunters. He singled out the Salish Flathead and Upper Kutenai for special praise: "Their bravery is pre-eminent; a love of truth they think necessary to a warrior's character. They are too proud to be dishonest, too candid to be cunning. Their many avocations leave them no leisure for gambling; and their strict subordination, joined to the necessity of exerting all their energies against the common enemy, prevents them from quarrelling."[24]

Burdened as it is by Cox's taste for purple prose, the passage captures well the perceived nobility of these hunters. Here is the noble savage in all his glory: brave to a fault, proud, morally upright, diligent. The "warrior's character" was an essential aspect of the image. Buffalo hunters were fine warriors, their hunting having trained them in bravery and discipline for war.

Warrior imagery pervades traders' accounts. Plateau hunters' war exploits against the Blackfoot were rendered in gripping detail in a number of the narratives. Thompson's account of the activities of these hunters on the plains made very explicit the link between buffalo hunting and war. According to Thompson, by 1811, three years after their first trade of muskets from the North Westers, the Salish Flathead and Kutenai had regained much of the buffalo territory that they had long claimed as their own. An elderly Kalispel man told the trader of the fear his people had experienced when the Blackfoot first met them with firearms. The Kalispel were for a time badly harassed, their horses stolen, and their camps attacked. With guns, he told Thompson, "we no longer hide ourselves but have regained much of our country, hunt the Bisons for food and clothing, and have good leather tents."[25] Here was deliverance not only from "pitiful" defenselessness—a kind of enforced cowardliness, in Thompson's view—but from the clutches of poverty as well: now the Kalispel had meat, leather clothing, and lodges, all the trappings of Indian wealth.

Having reclaimed former territory, in the summer of 1812 a massed party of about 350 Salish Flathead, Kutenai, Kalispel, Spokane, and unnamed others set off on a war footing to extend their hunting territory into lands claimed by the Blackfoot. Thompson was impressed with the sentiments expressed in the council that preceded the battle. Much as they would prefer peace, since it could not be relied on in present circumstances, the Plateau hunters would go to war. He was especially impressed with Chief Cartier, who urged the people, in Thompson's rendition, to "show ourselves to be men, and make ourselves respected."[26]

At the appointed time in August, when the buffalo bulls were in condition, the Plateau party proceeded to the Plains:

> [T]he hunting was carried on with cautious boldness into the lands of their enemies, this insult brought on a battle . . . [after preparations on both sides, the Blackfoot] advanced singing and dancing, the Saleesh saw the time was come to bring their whole force into line . . . they also sung and danced their wild

war dance; the Peegans [sic] advanced to within about one hundred and fifty yards, the song and the dance ceased, the wild war yell was given, and the rush forward; it was gallantly met, several were slain on each side, and three times as many wounded, and with difficulty the Peegans carried off their dead and wounded and they accounted themselves defeated.[27]

In Thompson's eyes, the Flathead and their allies had indeed shown themselves to be men. What began as courageous hunting soon developed into its natural extension, war. Here two of the most enduring and powerful images of idealized masculinity in the Western tradition, that of the hunter and that of the warrior, form a potent combination.

Thompson's account also betrays the tensions and ambiguities in the valorizing of indigenous buffalo hunters. The traits that defined their exceptional masculinity were the very traits that marked them as Indian and therefore inferior to their British observers. The boundary between the heroic hunter-warrior culture and savage nature is a brittle one in trader discourse. What starts as a display of masculine bravery ends in an account of "primitive" nature—the "wild war dance" and the "wild war yell"—playing itself out in the enmity of two savage peoples. Thompson reveals just how close, in the trader's view, the noble savage was to his ignoble alter ego, how quickly the brave hunter could become the murderous brute. Governor Simpson slipped into similar essentialist assumptions. On one occasion he extolled the Kutenai as a fine set of hunters; on another, he scorned them as treacherous barbarians bent on plunder.[28] The buffalo hunter might be manly and noble, but he was still representative of a savage race. The tensions in this hunter-warrior imagery ran very deep.

Man over Nature

Quite apart from the warfare it entailed, the buffalo hunt was seen as requiring courage of another sort. Whereas the wolf epitomized savage nature in the central Plateau, the buffalo fulfilled that role in the eastern Plateau and on the plains. Buffalo travelled in enormous herds, presenting an awesome spectacle. Alexander Ross reported seeing one herd that numbered at least ten thousand. With his customary flourish, and with the Victorian adventure reader clearly in mind, he asserted that there was no animal more fierce than a buffalo bull in rutting season: "Neither the polar bear nor the Bengal tiger surpass that animal in ferocity."[29] Ross's preoccupation with heady adventure narrative and his allusion to other British colonial possessions place his work squarely in the tradition of imperial adventure tales, a tradition just coming into full flower at the time his narratives were published.

According to traders' accounts, when not mortally wounded the buffalo was known to turn on its hunter. It fairly defied man to kill it. So savage was this beast that, in Thompson's words, it was "never pitied." Ross recounted how a badly wounded animal propped itself on front legs and stared him down until he and his colleagues had pumped ten balls into its mass. Even then they kept their distance, "for such is their agility of body, their quickness of eye, and so hideous are the looks of the beast, that we dared not for some time approach him."[30]

In this instance Ross himself donned the mantle of heroic hunter. In doing so, he may well have been influenced by the model of manhood presented by the Indian hunters; given the traders' preoccupation with this imagery, it is clear that it was a potent one. Ross's depiction of his own hunting exploits brings to mind the observation by cultural theorist Homi Bhabha that representation of cultural others always involves an ambiguous process of projection and introjection, of condemnation and desire.[31] In casting himself in the role of manly buffalo hunter, pitted against the West's most savage foe, Ross is momentarily united with the Indian hunter of his imagination.

Again, this imagery is complex. In his big-game hunting exploits, Ross has another point of identification, one that lies closer to his own ethnic home. Generations of more privileged men in Britain had routinely sought to prove their manhood—and their social status—in the pursuit of this most excellent sport. By the early nineteenth century the hunting cult of the British upper classes had been extended to the colonies, and to men who in Britain might have had no claim to gentility. At mid-century, when Ross published his Plateau narratives, growing numbers of British traders, army officers, colonial administrators, and others were testing their masculine mettle against the big game of Africa, India, and to a lesser extent, North America. "Shooting madness" was an increasingly common affliction, one that Ross could be sure his readers would appreciate. The emerging class, national, and gender connotations of big-game hunting go some way toward explaining Ross's proud portrayal of his encounter with a buffalo, and his invoking of Bengal tigers and polar bears. His location in the midst of brave hunters, and his desire to publish his experiences in the adventure travel genre, sheds light on his subscription to a model of manhood not widely shared by men of the middle class.[32]

A central feature of Victorian hunting discourse was its preoccupation with the masculinity of *British* hunters. In pointing up the exceptional manliness of white sportsmen, Victorian hunting ideology, as discussed earlier, tended to emphasize the cowardliness and wastefulness of indigenous hunters. The pattern is clearly revealed in the narratives of British sport hunters in Africa and India in the mid- and late-nineteenth century.[33] Ross sought to cast his lot with these imperial hunters, but he stopped short of representing indigenous hunters in the reverse role. The explanation for this peculiarity of trader accounts may well be that they were operating in a very different political-economic context than later imperial hunters. Fur traders were in the advance guard of colonialism. Their needs and interests differed sharply from those of the settlers and colonial officials who would follow them. Traders were not in competition with indigenous people for land and resources; rather, they were dependent on them for access to those resources. Not until the fur trade gave way to the settlement frontier would material competition lead to a hardening of colonial discourse and a systematic refiguring of the Indian hunter as wasteful brute.

Given the dual challenge of Plains enemies and savage beasts, the buffalo hunt represented the supreme test of the courage and fortitude of manly Indian hunters. In facing such challenges, Plateau hunters distinguished themselves yet again through their successful application of the tools of European technology. And once again, the tensions implicit in making heroes of these hunters come to the surface. By Cox's account, Salish hunters had been brave even before they had acquired firearms from the traders. They had yearly marched to the buffalo plains with nothing to oppose the Blackfoot "but arrows and their own undaunted bravery." This bravery had the whisper of a fatal flaw. The Salish were frequently routed by their better-armed foes, but despite the losses appeared unable to restrain themselves. What was at the root of this destructive obsession? It was the love of the hunt, what Cox called their "unconquerable hereditary attachment" to the chase.[34] The Salish were brave—braver, perhaps, than Cox could ever hope to be—but that bravery was itself a mark of their Indianness. Their desire to hunt was "unconquerable"; there was an element of unreason to it. In Cox's Indian hunter, reason is subordinated to primitive nature. As is so often the case in such colonial discourses, in the midst of a passage praising the virtues of the Indian comes a forceful—perhaps an anxious—reminder of his difference.

Thompson differed with Cox on the question of the hunters' manliness in the absence of firearms. Thompson recalled the joy of Salish elders in 1810 at the "alacrity" with which the younger men went off to the plains with their new guns. A dogged proponent of European technology, Thompson reasoned that without guns the Salish would have been "pitiful," "defenceless," forced to operate in the plains "by stealth." Stealth, in his view, was the mode of cowards. Real men would "hunt boldly and try a battle."[35]

The image of these hunters as possessors of new, progressive power over the forces of nature and human foes is most pronounced in Thompson's writings. His devotion to the theme is not surprising, given his personal commitment to the technologies of the day. During most of his twenty-six years in fur-trade country Thompson's principal motivation was exploration of the Northwest using the techniques of scientific survey and observation. The product of his labors was a series of remarkably accurate maps of the whole vast area between Hudson Bay and the Pacific Ocean, south to the Columbia River. Thompson's activities are in many ways emblematic of his age, an age of increasing confidence in the capacity of humans to delve into and master the secrets of the natural world.

Thompson's views on the salutary effects of firearms were registered in his account of improvements in Salish and Kutenai hunting. He was convinced that guns allowed these hunters greater technical mastery of the hunt. Their flint-headed arrows "broke against the Shield of tough Bison hide . . . their only aim was the face; these [bows and arrows] they were now to exchange for Guns, Ammunition and Iron headed arrows," the better to face both beasts and men.[36] I have demonstrated elsewhere that Thompson's optimism about the superiority of firearms for buffalo hunting was overstated. His views might have moderated had he stayed in the Columbia beyond 1812 and seen that bows and arrows remained in wide use long after guns became available.

Implicit in all this discussion of bravery in the face of beastly foes and technology in the service of men is a whole set of Western ideas about the human capacity to dominate nature. Contemporary discourse on the subject, and on the relationship between a society and its physical environment, is too complex to rehearse here (see chapter 1).[37] By the measures of the day, Plateau peoples dwelt in the state of nature, the rudimentary "hunter" stage. It would require a rash leap of logic to suggest that British traders equated the killing of buffalo by Indian hunters with the perceived domination of nature by European culture. But a critical aspect of the presumed relationship between humans and their environment was its mutability. Progress out of the rude state of nature was possible, indeed many would say inevitable. In the minds of the traders, the first imperative of that progress was mastery of the tools of a superior technology. The native skills of the buffalo hunters enabled them to master those tools and extend their authority over nature.

The perception that buffalo hunters were rendered more manly, more powerful by the possession of firearms at once reinforced and checked their imagined masculinity. Many remarked that those they defined as hunters—in contrast to "fishermen"—were better equipped to cope with the demands of this new and powerful Western technology. Writing of the Salish and Kutenai, Thompson noted that their long practice at hunting deer from horseback made them adept with bow and arrow, and prepared them well for the change to muskets. Another trader made a similar observation about the Cayuse, remarking that their experience as hunters gave them a "singular dexterity." Interestingly, Thompson described the skill of the Plateau hunters as superior to that of their Plains foes.[38] This observation probably says more about traders' biases against the Blackfoot than it does about relative hunting abilities.

In an intriguing inversion of such reasoning, the gun also served as a marker of the native hunters' inferiority. Whether the hunters were heroic or "pitiful" before the gun, all were rendered dependent on the traders for its benefits. The narratives speak volumes about the confidence this advantage bestowed. In his first winter in the Plateau (1811), Ross found his musket to be of profound practical and symbolic benefit. Recall how it gave him a sense of security in the face of a wolf attack, an event which by his account had terrorized the Indians. The gun also afforded a symbolic dominance over the Indians, who, according to Ross, were awed by this technology. After killing a wolf at a great distance, the trader enthused that "nothing but [the Indians'] wonder could exceed their admiration of this effect of firearms."

Ye-whell-come-tetsa, a prominent Okanagan leader, appears in the narrative thanking Ross for his assistance and proclaiming "[W]e have nothing to fear. . . . I shall always love the whites."[39] Manly as the hunter-warriors might be, they were in the end representatives of a primitive race. Their manliness was always constrained, in trader discourse, by the assertion that they lacked certain attributes that only the British traders could supply. This rhetorical strategy had the added benefit of securing the traders' own masculinity. The "warrior" nature of Plateau hunters at times posed a great threat to the traders, who had to live safely among these people if they were to succeed in their venture—and if they were to retain their own manly identities. Recall Ross's enormously self-conscious assertion of imperial masculine hegemony in his recounting of the construction of Fort Walla Walla (chapter 3). A formidable structure was needed to "tame" the "war-like tribes" who occupied the country. Ross's enthusiasm at the building of the fort points to the symbolic function of the structure (for the traders, at least).[40] The fort became known as "the Gibraltar of the Columbia," supposedly soothing the savage disposition of the Indians.

The imperial discourse is loud and clear—and surely tailored to Ross's intended Victorian readership. Britannia prevails, and does so over a race that may be martial and powerful, but is at base savage; that Indians were perhaps "soothed" by this assertion of British power even hints that they were aware of their own inferiority. The masculine discourse is embedded in and inseparable from the imperial.[41] The warlike tribes are subdued by the appearance of this hulking fortress, and British traders have proven their worth, both as traders and as men. They have prevailed over the threat from these potential enemies and have exhibited their manliness in the very act of erecting the fort. It stands as a symbol of their "energy and enterprise," ultimate masculine virtues in the idioms of early nineteenth-century capitalism and the fur trade alike.

Now, such control over these groups was elusive. Ross soon resumed complaining about the "insolence" and "independence" of the people around Walla Walla, and his successors had similar difficulties.[42] The historical accuracy or inaccuracy of Ross's account is not the point. The gap between his initial, confident assumption of British male authority and his later accounts of continued challenges to that authority speaks to the gap that probably will always exist between imagined and lived masculine identities. Ross anxiously hoped that British traders would prevail over Indian hunters in this desert "wilderness." The reality, it seems, was continual challenges to British manhood, continual contests between variant expressions of masculine identity. Still, Ross's writings reveal a great deal about the gendered nature of traders' relationships with indigenous men, and the ways in which trader discourse was constituted through hierarchies of gender, race, and class.[43]

The Material Benefits of Bravery

As we have seen, Plateau buffalo hunters captured the imaginations of British traders in the region, and the idealization of the hunter was rich in symbolic content. But to explore these associations is not to deny the importance of more strategic concerns. Material considerations were very much at play: these hunters produced a significant proportion of the furs traded in the Columbia Interior, and essential stocks of food and other provisions.

The bravery of buffalo hunters had clear practical benefits for fur traders in the Plateau as well. The Snake Country expeditions and later plains expeditions depended on the escort of buffalo parties for their security. The Snake Country expedition was a regular feature of company operations on the southern and eastern frontiers of the Columbia district after 1818. The participants were mainly imported freemen trappers, most of whom were métis or eastern Native men, many of them discharged or retired from company service. Expedition leaders considered the escort of the buffalo hunters indispensable in this "Country of Wars and Murders."[44]

On his first excursion in 1824, expedition leader Peter Skene Ogden initially refused to venture near the upper Snake River (map 5), a place that was rich in beaver but happened also to be "the general rendezvouz [sic] of all the War Tribes." When a camp of Salish Flathead hunters arrived, Ogden no longer had the least hesitation, "[now that] we shall have the Flat Heads to protect us."[45] The assistance offered by the Flathead and their hunting partners was more active than mere boosting of numbers. Their highly detailed environmental knowledge enabled them to keep tabs on the movements of both human and beast. The Flathead chief known as La Breche, for example, impressed traders by "reading" tracks left by the Blackfoot, estimating their numbers and movements with remarkable accuracy. A war chief, La Breche was one of several of his people who regularly served as guides and couriers, leading expedition members to good beaver streams and hunting grounds, guiding laden parties safely back to the Flathead post, and delivering correspondence from the post to expedition leaders in the field.[46] Traders openly acknowledged the indispensable assistance they received from these hunters.

The Buffalo Hunter as the "Real" Indian

The image of the horseback-riding, buffalo-hunting Indian is an extraordinarily potent and enduring one. The responses of fur traders to the power of the image in many ways anticipated the responses of generations of North Americans and Europeans to come. So powerful was this iconography that by the late nineteenth century Plains Indians had all but displaced their eastern Woodlands cousins as *the* Indians of the Western imagination: Pocahontas, Pontiac, and their vaguely Algonquian kin were pushed aside by Sacajawea and Sitting Bull, clad in fine leather, perpetually on horseback, the stern old chief in feather headdress chasing down buffalo.[47]

Traders and explorers were the first to encounter the picturesque buffalo hunters of the Great Plains and Plateau. Before them Spanish, French, and British had travelled over portions of this vast region between the time of the arrival of Coronado in the 1540s and the Louisiana Purchase in 1803. These earliest inter-lopers produced no popular literature or paintings from their travels, and the peoples they met remained largely unknown on the eastern seaboard and in Europe. The British and American traders who travelled among these peoples in the late-eighteenth and early-nineteenth centuries for the most part did not publish their writings until the 1840s and 1850s, so that it was some time before the imagery became familiar to a wider audience.

Perhaps the most influential early portrait of a hunter-warrior of the Plains was Charles Bird King's canvas of Petalesharro, a young Pawnee chief who was part of a delegation of lower-Missouri peoples to Washington in 1821. James Fenimore Cooper found inspiration for his novel *The Prairie* in his meeting with this "fine physical and moral man."[48] Cooper later declared that among Plains chiefs was found a "loftiness of spirit, of noble bearing and of savage heroism . . . that it might embarrass the fertility of the richest imagination to equal."[49] Such figures richly fulfilled white expectations for the noble savage. As we have seen, British traders felt no such admiration for the peoples of the western plains; however, there are resounding echoes in Cooper's writings of their depictions of the Salish Flathead.[50]

As settler penetration of the plains proceeded, illustrated periodicals and books slowly began to disseminate images of the indigenous peoples. One soon to be clichéd was Peter Rindis-bacher's drawing, "Sioux Warrior Charging," published in an American sporting magazine in 1829. The Swiss-born Rindisbacher had considerable experience on the plains, having moved in 1821 with his parents to the HBC-sponsored settlement at the Red River of the North, where he had remained five years. Another Rindisbacher work, "Hunting the Buffaloe," became the frontis-piece of the first volume of McKenney and Hall's classic *History of the Indian Tribes of North America* (1836–44). Despite the wide distribution of Rindisbacher originals and lithographs in North America and Britain, the more familiar imagery of the eastern Woodland Indian continued to predominate at this time.[51]

The most influential purveyor of Plains imagery was the American artist George Catlin. Convinced that Plains peoples were doomed to extinction in the face of westering hordes of whites, Catlin set out to the upper Missouri and southern plains in 1832, intent on "becoming their historian."[52] A similar desire to capture Plains Indians on canvas before they disappeared motivated many of the artists of the day, and the belief that they were a vanishing race no doubt enhanced the power and romance of the image. Catlin's exhibition of his own works and Plains "curios" met with great enthusiasm in the cities of the East and in London and Paris in the early 1840s. His *Letters and Notes on the North American Indians* (London, 1841) went a long way toward fixing the image of the Plains buffalo hunter in the popular mind. A huge commercial success, the book made clear Catlin's affinity for these "wildest and most remote tribes." The Blackfoot and Crow, for instance, "enjoy[ed] life to the greatest perfection" as their efforts were all turned to the pursuit of "flying herds of buffaloes" and the colorful war parade: the characters are different, but again there are strong echoes of trader accounts from the Plateau.[53]

For the Canadian painter Paul Kane, Catlin's portrayal of "Nature's noblemen" was a revelation. Kane had been stymied in his first effort to paint Indian life on the shores of the Great Lakes: he found the people "despoiled" by their long exposure to white society. Catlin's work inspired Kane to hurry west, to seek the noble savage in "his original state" before "he" too disappeared. In 1846, Kane travelled under the auspices of the Hudson's Bay Company across the prairies to the Rockies, and down the Columbia to the sea. The products of his artistic labors were enthusiastically received in Toronto in 1848. People flocked to see his exhibit of 500 sketches, of which the majority were powerful images of hunters: buffalo hunters in feather headdress and hide robe, hunters on horseback chasing down their hulking prey. The one hundred canvases he completed in the 1850s formed a very popular collection, and his memoir, *Wanderings of an Artist* (1859), was a best-seller in English and went into several European editions.[54]

The works of painters like Rindisbacher, Catlin, and Kane did much to stimulate a popular craving for Plains imagery. Many others followed in their footsteps, among them Alfred Jacob Miller (fig. 3) and John Mix Stanley, whose travels took them to the Plateau. By the early 1850s the buffalo hunter of the plains had arrived in the popular imagination. By this time American school textbooks were beginning to carry images of the first peoples of the Northeast sporting feather headdresses, living in Plains-style tipis, and draped in buffalo robes. Amusingly, the first illustrated edition of Henry Wadsworth Longfellow's *Hiawatha*, published in 1855, pictured the Ojibwa of the shores of Gitchee-Gumee (Lake Superior) in the styles of the upper Missouri. Clearly, this was powerful iconography.[55]

While such artistic influences were very significant, it took the fighting resistance of the Plains peoples, and of Plateau peoples like the Nez Percé, to indelibly etch the image of the warrior-hunter on the imagination of the North American public. As historian Rayna Green has argued, the potency of the image owes much to the fact that these peoples were "the last and most resilient enemy of Americanization."[56] The persistence of the image is revealed in the acclaim accorded the Hollywood epic *Dances With Wolves*—where as always, the virtuous hunter-warrior stands close beside his murderous alter ego.

Whether "Nature's noblemen" or "civilisation's" arch foe, the buffalo hunter-warrior had by the latter half of the nineteenth century become the quintessential Indian. Had the earlier fur traders' writings reached a wider audience, they would be cited alongside the artists as originators of the image. Cox anticipated Cooper when he extolled the bravery, industry, and high moral

Fig. 3. *Hunting the Buffalo in Herds*, by Alfred Jacob Miller. Credit: National Archives of Canada, C-000429.

character of the Salish Flathead and Upper Kutenai. Ross anticipated many when he wrote, of the Shoshone, that the "real" ones rode on horseback and hunted buffalo.[57]

A Glance at Colonial Comparisons

In casting Plateau buffalo hunters as manly, virtuous, and industrious, traders' narratives appear to depart from what is often taken to be a basic theme of the colonial encounter—the theme of indigenous hunters as wasteful, lazy, the farthest thing from manly. By the second half of the eighteenth century the hunting way of life was associated with a backward social state: witness its position as the rudimentary hunter phase in Adam Smith's four-stages theory of social development. In settler commentaries from the eastern woodlands of North America at this time, hunters were frequently condemned as indolent and improvident. Even in fur-trader narratives from farther west, there was scant tradition of laudatory discourse on Indian hunters. David Thompson expressed a general view in his 1785 account of Subarctic hunter-gatherers. In the regions south and west of Hudson Bay a relatively mild climate and the abundance of game assured the hunters of a "manly appearance," Thompson wrote. But while they were tall and of fine physique, they bore the weakness so frequently ascribed by Europeans to the natives of the colonies: they could not tolerate hard work. The hunters' very choice of activity was proof of their degeneracy. These lazy people would rather rove six hours over rough terrain "than work one hour with pick axe and spade." Thompson capped the observation by noting that "naturally [the Indians] are not industrious." The similarities to Plateau trader narratives of fishing peoples are striking.

Similar commentaries may be found in many other colonial settings in the late-eighteenth and nineteenth centuries. These sorts of images dominated in the Victorian era, and they have been the subject of much analysis by scholars interested in ecological change and conservation ideology in the colonial era.[58] With all this attention to the colonial image of indigenous peoples as despoilers of nature, scholars run the risk of overlooking earlier, contrary notions. The travellers' impressions early in the colonial encounter could be far less condemning of native hunting. The most harshly critical accounts of indigenous hunters really gained ascendancy only as colonizer and colonized came into intense competition for access to wildlife, other resources, and land. For example, early British reports from India and southern Africa on occasion parallel the enthusiastic accounts from the Plateau. Attitudes swiftly hardened as competition for resources mounted. A similar hardening would take place in the Plateau when the fur-trade frontier gave way to permanent settlement.

British perceptions of the wildlife encountered in India initially were shaped by the anxiety to eliminate "ferocious" carnivores, and by the quest for trophies. Hunting by Indians offered little impediment to these aims. On the contrary, Indian hunters were integral to the task of controlling the countryside. From at least 1820 onward, rewards were offered to indigenous hunters to kill tigers, lions, cheetahs, and other perceived enemies of humans.[59] However, to argue that Indian hunters were useful in the early years of the colonial project is not to suggest that they were idealized in the way Plateau buffalo hunters were. Ideas about the abilities of the native hunters in India were ambiguous in the nineteenth century. There were those who doubted whether Indians, whatever their caste, were made of the stuff to kill large game. On the other hand were those like Daniel Johnson, an officer in the East India Company, who in the 1830s regularly hired low-caste hunters to supply his table and protect his home. Johnson was highly impressed with their skills, and he thought their devices for release of poisoned arrows to be just as effective as British-made spring guns.[60]

Much like the traders in the Plateau, Johnson reserved his greatest admiration for the massed communal hunts. His description of the royal hunt of a northern ruler, the king of Oudh, rings true with contemporary accounts of the buffalo hunt. The enormous camp, comprising nobles on elephants and hundreds of beaters, including men, women, and children, made an impressive sight: "[T]he cavalcade . . . present[ed] the appearance of a large army going to a field of battle, rather than that of a hunting party . . . [a war] not against men, but against the destroyers of men."[61] Here is the familiar link between the demands of the large-scale hunt and war, in the familiar idiom of the supremacy of man over nature.

It was only later in the nineteenth century, as British authorities moved to protect their own access to Indian wildlife and other resources, that hunting by Indians came to be defined systematically as inferior to the European version. By the 1870s officials in various parts of British India were expressing concern about the depletion of game. The Forest Act of 1878 was in part a response to those concerns. That act hugely increased the land area controlled by the colonial state, and it granted the colonial government ownership of all game products in reserved areas. The aim was not simply to protect the quarry of British sport, although this was certainly part of it. The Victorian hunting craze in its Indian incarnation was much more than a form of amusement. It served to affirm the position of the British as a racially distinct and exclusive elite. It comes as no surprise that an essential aspect of the emerging British sporting code was the perception of Indian hunters as poachers—weak and ineffectual or, more often, cruel and wasteful.[62]

Colonial hunting ideology appears to have gone through a broadly similar shift in southern Africa. In the early period of white exploration in the interior (in the late-eighteenth and early-nineteenth centuries) game constituted an essential expansionist resource: it kept body and soul together, was a means of paying labor, and became an object of trade with which to subsidize other activities, such as missionizing. The parties of Dutch traders who began heading out from Cape Colony to the eastern Cape in search of ivory in the early eighteenth century styled themselves hunters, but probably obtained most of their ivory from African hunters. Later British travellers and colonists in the Cape interior relied equally heavily on local hunters, the Khoikhoi in particular, for their subsistence. Such dependence led to at least a grudging acknowledgment of their skills, and at best measured admiration.[63] The ambiguities were close to the surface. "Indolence" and "idleness" were the terms most frequently called upon to describe the Khoikhoi way of life. As one student of African colonial literatures has put it, the mobile hunting and mixed subsistence patterns of these Africans were read as a rejection of British ethics of discipline and labor, in favor of a lifestyle "in which the fruits of the earth are enjoyed as they drop into the hand, [and] work is avoided as an evil."[64]

From the earliest days of the colonial encounter, it was thus a subtext of much colonial discourse that indigenous hunters were indolent. Harsher condemnations came with heightened British interest in colonial riches. In Cape Colony the shift occurred early in the nineteenth century. As the British presence brought the region into the international marketplace, local animal resources began to be studied for science and hunted for sport. By the 1820s the increasing tendency to view the Cape as a hunting estate had led to a hardening of discourse about indigenous hunters. In that decade British officials recognized that game was fast being destroyed, and they introduced the first game legislation. The shift in the tenor of the discourse on indigenous hunting was immediate and perceptible. Now these hunters were likely to be portrayed as wanton, cruel, or cowardly as well as indolent.[65]

The views articulated by William Cornwallis Harris are emblematic of the shift. An army officer in the East India Company, Harris professed himself afflicted with "shooting madness." He had cut his hunting teeth in India before being invalided to the Cape Colony in 1836,[66] where he got his long-awaited opportunity to kill elephants. What is most striking about Harris's views on indigenous hunting is his ability to invert causation. Like so many of his peers, Harris was unquestionably a profligate hunter;

like so many, he blamed Africans for the precipitate destruction of game. While he and his hunting comrades were sportsmen, the Ndebele were "expert[s] in the destruction of the elephant." The compound of their king, Mzilikazi, was "strewed with the bones of wild animals."[67] As William Beinart and others have so convincingly demonstrated, the perception that Africans were cruel to animals and ravaged nature, while the British were kind to animals and managed nature, was an important subtext of colonial ideology.[68] But it is important to note that it became so only when colonists and indigenous peoples came into competition for resources. In the early period of colonial penetration, the period of trade and exploration during which European travellers often relied on African hunting expertise for their survival, the discourse could be rather more generous.

Caution is required in pointing up what at first looks like a sharp contrast between British fur traders' perceptions of Plateau buffalo hunting and the views of indigenous hunting purveyed by colonial agents in other parts of the British empire. Fur traders were in the advance guard of colonialism. Their needs and interests were very different from those of the settlers who would follow them. Perhaps their perceptions were not so different from those of early colonial explorers, hunters, and traders in India and southern Africa, whose views of indigenous hunting were similarly shaped by their need for assistance from local hunters and had not yet hardened as a result of competition with those hunters. The fur traders were far less condemning than later writers, who would depict indigenous peoples as despoilers of nature; however, it seems one would be hard pressed to find in the writings of even the earliest travellers in India and Africa the type of idealized accounts that fur traders produced about the buffalo hunters of the Plateau.

Concluding Remarks

The elevation of Plateau buffalo-hunting peoples to a kind of hero status was certainly aided by the fact that they happened to be the most productive fur trappers in the Columbia Interior. They also provided an array of buffalo products, from pemmican to pack cords, and rendered essential services to traders in the field. Their activities no doubt seemed all the more praiseworthy in a region where most groups, derided as "salmon eaters," took limited interest in the fur trade or hunting and were judged lazy and beggarly. Important as such considerations were, it is clear from the traders' writings that there was far more than instrumental logic to the image of the buffalo hunters. The idealization of these hunters was critically bound up with contemporary notions of masculinity and the domination of man over nature, and with emerging notions of the "real" Indian. The massed, mounted expeditions to the buffalo plains captured traders' imaginations, as they would fuel the Indian fantasies of white North Americans and Europeans for generations to come.

CHAPTER EIGHT

Concluding Remarks

If George Simpson was unimpressed with the "indolent and lazy" fishing people he encountered on the middle Columbia in the 1820s, his colleagues were more favorably disposed toward the brave and industrious buffalo hunters to the east. The contrast traders drew between the "fishing tribes" and the "hunting tribes" reads as if painted in black and white—though one need not look far below the surface to find the shades of grey. Fishers were lazy, feckless, frequently "starving." Yet they supplied the posts with enormous quantities of staple salmon. And there is ample evidence in trader accounts to indicate that they followed a complex seasonal round that took them well beyond the river, tracking game into the mountains in autumn, digging vast stores of edible roots and vegetables in other seasons, trading with their neighbors throughout the year. If the salmon tribes were poor, the hunters—and particularly those supreme buffalo hunters, the Salish Flathead and Upper Kutenai—were handsome, brave, and hard-working. Yet, while handsome, they tended to "foppery"; while brave, their virtue was marked by savagery. The buffalo hunter might be manly and noble, but he was, at base, representative of a savage race. The tensions in this imagery ran very deep.

In the preceding chapters I have probed the content of British fur traders' representations of Indian hunters and fishermen in the Plateau. The focus has been on the ways in which race, gender, and class articulated with and at times contradicted one another in the construction of this particular strain of colonial discourse. The point was made at the outset that traders' writings were informed by a cultural logic that was white, male, British, and middle-class. My primary aim has been to identify the influences of that logic, to isolate the strands of inherited meaning woven into trader discourse on the Plateau and its peoples. However, fur traders were not "typical" British men (as if there were any such thing), straight off the boat and spouting unreformed metropolitan rhetoric. A large part of the project has been to assess how these men's cultural knowledge of "the Indian" was produced, reproduced, and at times reordered in the context of the Plateau fur trade. Enmeshed in a cultural encounter of profound dimensions, British traders saw their most basic cultural meanings challenged and jarred.

Yet those basic meanings provided a ground from which trader narratives proceeded. Consider their reflections on their status as the "gentlemen" of fur-trade society. That identity was shaped through their manipulations, conscious and otherwise, of space and time—the rituals they followed to mark off the spaces of housing, dining, and trading; their daily rhythms of work and leisure. Traders' actions were grounded in a vision of manhood that was clearly British middle-class. When John Work remarked that young hunters mimicked the "fops" of the civilized world in their overweening attention to appearances, his referent was the model of serious manhood, modesty, and self-restraint that defined the British man of enterprise in this era. Yet, at the same time, traders were not unmoved by the alternative models of manhood presented on the Plateau stage. George Simpson took great pride in his own manly sporting pursuits, and Alexander Ross donned the mantle of a heroic hunter, perhaps inspired by the images he saw before him on the buffalo plains. However, Plateau hunters were not Ross's only point of reference. The emerging tradition of big-game hunting in the colonies by men possessed of "shooting madness" also informed Ross's adventure tale. He drew on a range of associations, some of them grounded in a colonial reality some distance from his intellectual home.

If my first aim in *Traders' Tales* has been to unpack traders' narratives, to unsettle the images and expose the roots of their notions of poverty, indolence, wealth, and manly virtue, my second purpose has been to uncover alternative readings of their writings. There is an uneasy tension between these dual objectives. The tension is introduced in the attempt to find alternatives, to provide other readings, in a study so convinced of the constructedness of representations of the other. I have stressed throughout that these alternative readings are offered not as definitive statements of Plateau "reality," but as speculations on the nature of shifting realities. The fur-trade record is one of the richest archives of the early encounter between indigenous peoples and Europeans. Clear images do begin to emerge when documents are subjected to disciplined analysis, when they are set in the larger context of the fur-trade record and of archaeological, anthropological, biological, and other evidence (partial and constructed as all these forms are).

In fact, the first aim of *Traders' Tales* has led quite naturally to the second. We have seen how traders' assertions about Plateau peoples can contain the seeds of their own rebuttal. In 1812, Alexander Henry declared the Lower Kutenai to be starving. In the same breath he reported that "vast shoals" of salmon passed up the Kootenay River in summer and fall. The puzzling contradiction was resolved in his contention that "the worst meat" was preferable to the kind of fish available in the region. Statements like Henry's provide the fodder for a close analysis of specific social and historical connotations of hunger and plenty. Such assertions demonstrate how the traders' pragmatic purposes constantly interacted with their inherited assumptions and beliefs in the production of their cultural knowledge about Plateau societies. The need for this kind of close analysis is driven home in that scholars and other commentators continue to look to traders' writings for clues to the past—and continue to use them very uncritically.

Cultural knowledge is a potent mix, yet its content is open to inventive refashioning. Perhaps the most explicit illustration of this process in the course of the Columbia trade is Samuel Black's reassessment of southern Plateau subsistence strategies. Black initially interpreted the movement of Sahaptian fishermen from the river to the root grounds much as his colleagues would have done, as an act of desperation. Over time he came to appreciate that roots were one of the most important staple foods of the region, and that Sahaptian women therefore played a key role in food production. This represents a very significant reappraisal of Native American subsistence strategies. In another telling example, Archibald McDonald declared himself at a loss to explain a lavish gift exchange between Secwepemc and Nlaka'pamux, where horses, guns, and other coveted goods were freely given away; he ultimately came to the conclusion that it was an opportunity for these communities to "pledge friendship to one another."

Such insights, and the pragmatic accommodations to Native ways that traders showed themselves willing to make, do not appear to reflect any fundamental reworking of dominant cultural assumptions. The power and persistence of images like that of the lazy fisherman and the manly hunter are manifest in traders' writings at every turn. The desire of the traders for furs and of Native peoples for trade goods forced an accommodation, the establishment of a social space in which peaceful trade relations could take place. As it was for the Secwepemc and Nlaka'pamux, gift exchange was the most significant ritual of that space. Through gift exchange the social space of Plateau kin groups was extended metaphorically to encompass the traders. But the accommodation was not based, on either side, on any deep understanding of the other's motives. The misunderstanding and conflict that arose when the accommodation faltered, as it so often did, underlines this point. The accommodation worked out between traders and Native peoples in the Plateau was a pragmatic one, enacted in a fragile social space.

The importance of gift-exchange ceremonies points to another basic tenet of *Traders' Tales*, the contention that the contours of the encounter between Europeans and indigenous peoples depended in part on local cultural mediation—on indigenous orchestration. Even the most cataclysmic consequence of the encounter, smallpox epidemics, was dealt with from within a framework of indigenous beliefs and practices. The introduction of the powerful technology of the firearm is another example. Notwithstanding the fur traders' confidence in the superiority of firearms for hunting and other uses, there is much in their own writings to suggest that indigenous technologies remained very much in use throughout the first half of the nineteenth century. Access to the gun was indeed a signal development in these societies, but in the eastern Plateau, for example, it appears that it was so more for its impact on shifting power relations between Plateau groups and their Plains adversaries than for its practical effects on hunting. Clearly, the influences of the early white presence cannot be abstracted from the social and historical contexts in which they became embedded.

The danger of this kind of analysis is that it may seem to suggest an unbending "traditionalism," or simply to argue for cultural persistence as against cultural absorption. This has not been my approach in this study. While a key argument has been that the arrival of the fur traders (or of their influences, prior to their physical arrival) did not bring about a sharp break in Plateau history, I have emphasized equally that Plateau cultures were dynamic, inventive, and themselves a product of history. Their history did not begin, or end, with the arrival of British fur traders.

The response of Plateau societies to the coming of the horse provides one of the best examples of the dynamism of these cultures. The effects of acquisition of the horse were registered in every facet of Plateau life: in patterns of land use and trade, leadership and gender relations, raids and other violence. And yet, the evidence of the fur-trade record indicates that, rather than radically altering the plan of Plateau life, the horse tended to accelerate preexistent patterns of seasonal resource specialization and mobility. For example, early traders learned that Salish Flathead and Kutenai communities had occupied territories on the eastern slopes of the Rockies before the coming of the horse, and from there they had hunted buffalo on foot on a small scale. The horse facilitated the elaboration of the hunt to the large-scale communal enterprise that it had become by the late eighteenth century. Later traders learned that even these most productive and dedicated hunters continued to follow a complex seasonal round that was probably very similar in outline to that of pre-horse times.

I have argued that far from transforming patterns of social reward and leadership, the horse reinforced the process whereby individuals, particularly men, acquired social standing through the generous distribution of goods. There is much in the fur-trade record to suggest that the horse, the goods that became available as a result of ownership of horses (e.g., hides and other products of the buffalo hunt), and many European trade goods were incorporated for indigenous purposes that transcended their basic "utilitarian" values. Those who possessed large numbers of horses, for example, attracted horse-poor followers; their loans and gifts became an important means of achieving prestige. Buffalo products, horses, and trade goods acquired at the posts also came to play key roles in the networks of exchange that maintained the safe social space so necessary to peaceful relations among distant communities. Women's access to the kinds of social networks that enabled a person to amass large numbers of horses was more restricted than that of men, but women's autonomy and influence continued to be exercised in other spheres.

To emphasize the social and political uses of such goods is not to deny their instrumental value: horses, firearms, copper kettles, iron, and beaver traps were eminently useful objects, and they

set in train significant changes in Plateau societies. But to emphasize the ways in which their function was bent to indigenous
purposes is to underline that European goods did not suddenly
wash in upon communities hermetically shielded from outside
influences. "Exotic" materials and ideas had long been available
to Plateau communities through kin networks that spanned the
Plateau, and through indigenous trade networks that spanned
half the continent. The late-eighteenth to mid-nineteenth centuries saw a flood of new imported goods, but where there was
now a flood there had long been a steady stream. In the era of
the fur trade, Plateau peoples explored the materials and influences that accompanied the Europeans, and adapted many of
them to evolving indigenous uses.

It has been argued that the involvement of most Plateau
peoples in the fur trade was distinctly limited, in part as a result
of the scarcity of fur-bearing animals in much of the region, and
in part because the subsistence strategies of most of these groups
were based more on fishing and gathering than hunting and
trapping. Given that these strategies generally provided amply,
most took limited interest in trapping furs for trade. Even the
very productive and highly regarded Salish Flathead and Upper
Kutenai do not appear to have departed dramatically from their
usual seasonal occupations to take part in the trade. The largest
proportion of their returns came in the form of hides and buffalo
meat rather than small furs, and the furs were mostly trapped en
route to and from the buffalo grounds. However, the political
situation of the eastern Plateau-Plains frontier demanded that
these groups take an active role in the trade in order to secure
a steady supply of firearms. Apart from this local dependence on
firearms, there is little evidence in the record of the Columbia
Interior to indicate that the peoples of the region became dependent on the posts for trade goods or food. Accounts of winter
illnesses preventing people from decamping and moving off to
hunt point to a disturbing trend repeated in other fur-trade
regions; however, it does not appear from the scattered accounts

available that this became an annual problem in the Interior. The material presented in chapter 2, partial and speculative as it is, suggests that the most consequential impact of the early white presence was the smallpox epidemics that swept the entire region some years before the first traders arrived.

With the coming of permanent white settlers to the region in the 1840s (somewhat later in the northern Plateau), the pragmatic accommodation that characterized the fur trade soon gave way to conflict. Conflict turned on land. Notions implicit in traders' narratives—notions about the supposedly primitive and wasteful ways in which Native Americans inhabited the land— hardened as colonizer and Native came into increasingly intense competition for its resources. Nor did those ideas die with the early settlers. The persistence of such Eurocentric discourse is revealed daily, in British Columbia at least, in the fear-mongering rhetoric of those who oppose "concessions" to Native communities in current B.C. treaty and land negotiations.[1]

The persistence of such discourse is revealed with disturbing force in *Delgamuukw v. British Columbia*, the court case mounted by the hereditary chiefs of the Gitksan and Wet'suwet'en peoples of northwestern British Columbia that was mentioned in the introduction. For over one hundred years the province had refused to negotiate land-title settlements with Native peoples, and when it reiterated that refusal in the late 1970s, despite a federal government decision calling for negotiation, the Gitksan and Wet'suwet'en turned to the courts. The details of the case, which remained before presiding Chief Justice Allan McEachern from 1987 to 1990, are discussed elsewhere.[2] What is of interest here is the imprint of very specific cultural assumptions on Chief Justice McEachern's decision to reject the Gitksan and Wet'suwet'en assertion of continuing Native title to their territories.

The fundamental assumption informing McEachern's decision is that societies like the aboriginal Gitksan and Wet'suwet'en stood lower on a social evolutionary ladder than the "advanced" civilizations of the West. Calling life in the precontact period "nasty, brutish, and short," the chief justice dismisses as "romantic" much of the evidence to the contrary, which had been provided in thousands of hours of testimony by community leaders and elders and a battery of academics. Much of the Native testimony, in particular, is described in the court's decision as "not literally true."[3] McEachern frequently draws a contrast between "cultural belief" and "fact." At one point he notes that nearly every word of testimony had both cultural and factual content. That his application of this rule of thumb is less than rigorous is demonstrated in his failure to acknowledge the cultural content of his own views. But it is most clearly demonstrated in his treatment of fur traders' writings.

For McEachern the content of those writings is indisputable fact. The traders were, after all, "actually on the scene dealing with these problems." His privileging of written evidence over oral and other forms is summed up in his statement that certain of the written documents "largely spoke for themselves."[4] Veteran Columbia trader Peter Skene Ogden is quoted on the "primitive condition" of the people of the region in the 1830s. McEachern's favorite authority, however, is Chief Trader William Brown. Referring to Brown's 1820s writings from Fort Kilmaurs, the judge asserts that he has "no hesitation accepting the information contained in them." Among notable "facts" offered by Brown and uncritically echoed by McEachern are the contention that the people of the region suffered from "addiction to gambling," that warfare was "constant," and that they were "hardly amenable to obedience to anything but the most rudimentary form of custom." Reflecting on such evidence, McEachern comes to a very familiar conclusion about the root cause of the plight of Native peoples like the Gitksan and Wet'suwet'en: they were indolent. He cloaks the message in a mantle of cultural relativism, commenting that Indians were "not as industrious in the new economic climate as was thought to be necessary by the newcomers in the Colony." The effect is the same. Native peoples were conquered not by force, nor by disease or economic and political exclusion. They were defeated by the "relentless energy" of the colonizers.[5]

As fur traders' narratives so often do, McEachern's judgment contains the seeds of its own rebuttal. Responding to the common view that Native people "did not do as much for themselves as they might have done," he offers in their defence that they "probably did not understand what was happening to them."[6] The record of Native American political activity since the earliest years of the fur trade strongly suggests otherwise.

Notes

1. Introduction

1. HBCA D.3/1, fols. 61–62; George Simpson, *Journal 1824–25*, 94–95. All file numbers listed hereafter are HBCA (Hudson's Bay Company Archives) unless otherwise indicated.

2. Henry, *Journal*, 707.

3. For discussions of the complexity and ambivalence of European attitudes toward the indigenous peoples of the Americas, see Hugh Honour, *New Golden Land*; Tzvetan Todorov, *Conquest of America*; Mary Louise Pratt, *Imperial Eyes*; Robert Berkhofer, *White Man's Indian*; Anthony Pagden, *Fall of Natural Man*; Fredi Chiapelli, ed., *First Images of America*; P. J. Marshall and Glyndwr Williams, *Great Map of Mankind*; Antonello Gerbi, *Dispute of the New World*.

4. The phrase is from Clifford Geertz, *Interpretation of Cultures*, 5. Geertz's influence has been profound in fields described variously as the new cultural history, the new historicism (in anthropology and literature), and cultural materialism.

5. For some introductions, see Lynn Hunt, ed., *New Cultural History*; Nicholas Dirks, Geoff Eley, and Sherry Ortner, eds., *Culture/Power/History*. A suggestive recent work dealing with the Pacific Northwest is Tina Loo's *Making Law, Order, and Authority in British Columbia*.

6. The discussion in this section draws on Jennifer S. H. Brown and Elizabeth Vibert, "Introduction," *Reading Beyond Words*.

7. This apt phrase is from Clifford, *Predicament of Culture*.

8. The notion of the "ideological work" of language comes from Mary Poovey, *Uneven Developments*, and was spurred by my reading of Loo, *Making Law*, "Introduction."

9. Chief Justice Allan McEachern, *Delgamuukw v. British Columbia*, "Reasons for Judgement," 13, 52.

10. James Clifford, *Predicament of Culture*, 15. See also Virginia Dominguez, "Invoking Culture."

11. Homi Bhabha, *Location of Culture*, 162 and passim.

12. Aletta Biersack, "Local Knowledge, Local History," 83.

13. Historical studies of the North American fur trade are legion. For accessible overviews, see Glyndwr Williams, "Hudson's Bay Company and the Fur Trade"; E. E. Rich, *Fur Trade and the Northwest to 1857*. Harold Innis's classic *Fur Trade in Canada* must also be recommended. For more detail on the western and American trades, see Theodore Karamanski, *Fur Trade and Exploration*. For an international perspective, see Eric Wolf, *Europe and the People Without History*, chap. 6.

14. For formulations of the older view, see, e.g., Rich, *Fur Trade and the Northwest*, quotation on 102; Eleanor Leacock, "Montagnais 'Hunting Territory,'" 24; Leacock, "Relations of Production in Band Society," 160. For a recent restatement, see Peter Carstens, *Queen's People*, chap. 2.

15. For an intriguing analysis of such narrative devices in the writing of environmental and Native American history, see William Cronon, "A Place for Stories."

16. Daniel Francis and Toby Morantz, *Partners in Furs*. Other influential works demonstrating the same position, all dealing with the Subarctic or Northeast, include A. J. Ray, *Indians in the Fur Trade*; Arthur J. Ray and Donald Freeman, *"Give Us Good Measure"*; Bruce Trigger, *Natives and Newcomers*. Other useful works in the genre are too numerous to mention here, but will be referenced where appropriate in the following chapters. A handy guide to the literature is found in Shepard Krech, *Native Canadian Anthropology and History*.

17. Robin Fisher pays more attention than others to the Interior fur trade in his influential work *Contact and Conflict*. Yet his coverage is cursory and amounts to only a few pages, most of those about New Caledonia, the region north of the Columbia Interior. A 1993 study of trade relationships at Fort Nez Percés does an admirable job of bringing attention to the southern Plateau. See Theodore Stern, *Chiefs and Chief Traders*. However, Stern draws little on the insights of the new fur-trade scholarship.

18. Innis, *Fur Trade in Canada*, 16–18; Washburn, "Symbol, Utility, and Aesthetics in the Indian Fur Trade," 50 and passim; Cornelius Jaenen, "Amerindian Views of French Culture," 265–67.

19. Trigger, *Children of Aataentsic*, 360, 429–31; "Early Native North American Responses," 1195–96.

20. George Hamell, "Strawberries, Floating Islands, and Rabbit Captains"; Christopher Miller and George Hamell, "New Perspective on Indian-White Contact."

21. White, "Encounters with Spirits," 369–76, 393–96.

22. The list of admirable studies that have focused on the derivative content of notions of noble and ignoble savagery is long, and growing. Among early ones is Robert Berkhofer, *White Man's Indian*; more recent is Daniel Francis, *Imaginary Indian*. See also sources listed in n. 3, above.

23. Lewis Saum, *Fur Trader and the Indian*. Several suggestive studies of individual traders' writings have been published more recently, notable among them Jennifer Brown and Robert Brightman, *"Orders of the Dreamed."*

24. Prakash, "Introduction: After Colonialism," 3.

25. Clifford, *Predicament of Culture*, 9, 50–51, 344 and passim. See also Bhabha, *Location of Culture*, 70–75. Both authors are clearly indebted to Foucault's conceptualization of power as multifocal and dispersed, rather than located in symmetrical or dialectical relations of colonizer to colonized, master to slave. For examples of postcolonialist writing in this tradition, see the essays in Gyan Prakash, ed., *After Colonialism*; Ranajit Guha, ed., *Selected Subaltern Studies*; Gayatri Chakravorty Spivak, *In Other Worlds*.

26. "Fiction" here is as in the Latin *fictio*, "something made"; ethnographies are fictionalized in the sense that they are something made or constructed.

27. For Bourdieu on habitus, see especially his *Outline of a Theory of Practice*, 1, 72–73, 95. For a helpful example of the process at work, see 159–97. For a good analysis of Bourdieu's position in relation to other poststructuralist theorists, see Biersack, "Local Knowledge, Local History."

28. Alexander Ross, *Adventures of the First Settlers*, 308–68.

29. B.146/a/1, B.146/a/2. That McGillivray was himself the métis son of a Scottish trader and his Cree wife raises intriguing questions. Was he trying to submerge his Indian ancestry? Sylvia Van Kirk considers such

attempts by other métis sons in "*Many Tender Ties*" and in "'What if Mama Is an Indian?'"

30. Richard Grove, *Green Imperialism*, chap. 4; Ludmilla Jordanova, *Sexual Visions*, 23–25. Jordanova explores the gendered notions of, e.g., the Baconian promise to reveal how a feminine Nature could be enslaved to a masculine Science. Grove points out that Western views of nature were never monolithically "imperialist." On the latter theme, see also Simon Schama, *Landscape and Memory*.

31. Grove, *Green Expansion*, chap. 4; Jordanova, "Earth Science and Environmental Medicine," 119–21.

32. Mrs. Thrale is quoted in Marshall and Williams, *Great Map of Mankind*, 282; PP 1828-1, Queries Connected with the Natural History.

33. Adam Smith, *Lectures on Jurisprudence*, 107, 260–69; R. L. Meek, *Social Science and the Ignoble Savage*, 32, 68, 116–17. Smith and Turgot worked independently of one another.

34. Jean-Jacques Rousseau, *A Discourse on Inequality*, 115–16.

35. See Meek, *Social Science*, 176, chap. 6.

36. See, e.g., the map of native subsistence in R. Cole Harris, ed., *Historical Atlas of Canada*, 1:plate 18, which shows Plateau subsistence to be based on deer and fish. Readers might consult almost any historical account of Native peoples in the Pacific Northwest and find similar emphasis on meat and fish.

37. D.3/1, fols. 61–62. On this manuscript Frederick Merk based his *Fur Trade and Empire: George Simpson's Journal . . . 1824–25*; see 94–95.

38. A. L. Kroeber, *Cultural and Natural Areas of Native North America*, 2. The culture-area concept continues to serve as the organizing principle for many studies, and has generated important comparative work: witness the Smithsonian Institution's authoritative *Handbook of North American Indians*, of which most of the volumes are defined by culture area. Most unfortunately, the *Plateau* volume had not been published at the time of writing *Traders' Tales*.

39. Kutenai is a language isolate, and Cayuse is of a separate stock (Waiilatpuan).

40. "Tribe" is another profoundly contested concept, with origins in Western administrative requirements rather than any essential "tribal" quality; nevertheless, it has become a strategic focus of identity for many indigenous peoples. "Tribe" tends to be used to refer to a "politically or socially coherent and autonomous group . . . claiming a particular

territory" (Yvonne Hajda, "Regional Social Organization in the Greater Lower Columbia," 8). In Canada such a group is more likely to call itself a "First Nation."

41. Ross, *Adventures*, 311–16. Traders' conceptions of Plateau political organization are discussed further in chapters 4, 5, and 6.

42. Ross, Adventures, 312; Hajda, "Regional Social Organization," quoting Mrs. Luscier (1942), 9–10.

43. See further discussion of social organization in chapter 4.

44. Eugene Hunn, *Nch'i-Wana, The Big River*, 212.

45. Métis is used here with small-case "m" and without italics to highlight inclusiveness and widespread usage. It refers to all people of mixed Native-European ancestry. The political term Métis tends to refer to the offspring of Cree and French who evolved a distinct political identity in the Prairie West. See Jacqueline Peterson and Jennifer S. H. Brown, eds., *New Peoples*, "Introduction."

46. Jennifer S. H. Brown, "Blind Men and the Elephant," 16.

47. See the instructive theoretical piece by Roger Chartier, "Texts, Printing, Readings."

48. PP 1828-1, Queries Connected with the Natural History.

49. On the growing influence of the scientific community, see especially Grove, *Green Expansion*, introduction and chap. 4; and his "Origins of Western Environmentalism."

50. For a very suggestive treatment, see I. S. MacLaren, "Exploration/Travel Literature."

51. W. Kaye Lamb, ed., *Journals and Letters of Sir Alexander Mackenzie*, 57; also quoted in MacLaren, "Exploration/Travel Literature," 43.

52. Gabriel Franchère's account of his journey across the Plateau, which is referred to from time to time in later chapters, was published in 1820 in French, but not until 1840 in English.

53. Ross Cox, *Columbia River*, xxxi.

54. Cox, *Columbia*, 128–29.

55. See MacLaren, "Exploration/Travel Literature," 46–47.

56. MacLaren, "Exploration/Travel Literature," 45–55. MacLaren also draws examples from published editions of Samuel Hearne's and Paul Kane's journals, and while they reveal a heavy editor's imprint, they are not nearly as extreme as Douglas' editions of Cook. For other suggestive interpretations of Cook's encounters, cf. Marshall Sahlins, *Islands of*

History; Gananath Obeyesekere, *Apotheosis of Captain Cook*; Daniel Clayton, "Captain Cook and the Spaces of Contact at 'Nootka Sound.'"
57. Ross, "Journal . . . Snake Country Expedition, 1824," 377–78.
58. Ross, *Fur Hunters of the Far West*, 235. For the full account, see 222–35.
59. D.3/2, fol. 88.
60. Simpson, *Narrative of a Journey*, 130.
61. The best comparative studies of the institutional structures of the companies are found in Brown, *Strangers in Blood*, chaps. 1 and 2; and Van Kirk, "*Many Tender Ties*," chap. 1.
62. David Thompson is a special case, having been with the HBC for thirteen years before joining the NWC in 1797. A total of thirty-five traders are cited in this work, a few of them only in a single letter or a secondhand quotation.
63. The Orkneys and the Hebrides were popular recruiting grounds for "stout" and "serious" young men with few economic alternatives. They were never figured as Scots by their superiors, although they were less "other" than French Canadian, métis, Native, or Hawaiian men.
64. Trudy Nicks, "Iroquois and the Fur Trade in Western Canada"; James Gibson, *Farming the Frontier*, 20; Galbraith, *Hudson's Bay Company as an Imperial Factor*, 21.
65. Brown, *Strangers in Blood*, 120.
66. Public Archives of Canada (PAC), Ermatinger Papers, 53 (trancript in University of British Columbia [UBC] Special Collections [UBC Sp. Coll. hereafter]).
67. B.45/e/2, fol. 5.
68. Leonore Davidoff and Catherine Hall, *Family Fortunes*, 108–18.
69. Sylvia Van Kirk, "Donald McKenzie," *Dictionary of Canadian Biography (DCB)*, 8:557.
70. J. V. Smith, "Manners, Morals and Mentalities," 25–28. I am very grateful to Orkney historian James A. Troup for his assistance, in conversations and in correspondence, with my questions about Scottish education.
71. James Scotland, *History of Scottish Education*, 66, chaps. 7 and 8. See also H. M. Knox, *Two Hundred and Fifty Years of Scottish Education*.
72. On the contrast between Scottish parish schools and English charity schools, and the dangers of drawing too sharp a contrast, see Christopher Martin, *A Short History of English Schools*, 9–10; Asa Briggs,

Age of Improvement, 71; Smith, "Manners, Morals and Mentalities,"
25–28. For Thompson, see John Nicks, "David Thompson," *DCB*, 8:878.

73. Quoted in Brown, *Strangers in Blood*, 49.

74. G. P. de T. Glazebrook, ed., *Hargrave Correspondence*, 18, 19, 62,
70–71, 112; UBC Sp. Coll., Ermatinger Papers, 75.

75. Madge Wolfenden, "John Tod," *DCB*, 11:882. The library was probably the legacy of trader Daniel Harmon.

76. Michael Payne and Gregory Thomas, "Literacy, Literature and
Libraries," 44–53.

77. Payne and Thomas, "Literacy, Literature, and Libraries," 47.

78. See, inter alia, Rich, *Fur Trade and the Northwest*, chaps. 13 and
14; D. W. Meinig, *Great Columbia Plain*; Gibson, *Farming the Frontier*;
Williams, "Hudson's Bay Company and the Fur Trade," chap. 8.

79. For Simpson's view, see Simpson, *Journal 1824–25*.

80. UBC Sp. Coll., Ermatinger Papers, 83: John Tod to Edward
Ermatinger, Thompson's River Post, March 1844.

81. See especially Richard Mackie, "Hudson's Bay Company on the
Pacific"; Gibson, *Farming the Frontier*; Rich, *Fur Trade of the Northwest*,
279 and chap. 14.

2. "The Natives Were Strong to Live":
Plague, Prophecy, and the Prelude to the Encounter

1. An earlier version of this chapter was published in *Ethnohistory*
(1995).

2. Archaeologist Sarah Campbell makes a case for a Western
Hemisphere–wide epidemic having reached the Plateau in the early
sixteenth century. The evidence she has compiled points to a rebuilding
of the population after that period until the last quarter of the eighteenth
century, followed by a sharp decline, which Campbell relates to disease.
There is no indication in the archaeological record of population
recovery in the nineteenth century (Campbell, *PostColumbian Culture
History*). On the other hand, Daniel T. Reff's work on northern Mexico
and the southwestern United States provides persuasive evidence to
counter claims of a sixteenth-century epidemic in the northern
cordillera. Reff, *Disease, Depopulation, and Culture Change*.

3. Boyd, "Introduction of Infectious Diseases"; "Demographic History, 1774–1784." For a crash course in current theories, readers are
directed to the following collections: David H. Thomas, ed., *Columbian*

Consequences; John W. Verano and Douglas H. Ubelaker, eds., *Disease and Demography in the Americas*; and to William Denevan, "Native American Populations in 1492"; and Henry Dobyns, "Disease Transfer at Contact." Such theorists meet one local critic in Robin Fisher, who assails "an intellectual climate where the prevailing assumption is that epidemics caused major depopulation" (*Contact and Conflict*, xvi).

4. Harris, "Voices of Disaster," 618.

5. The World Health Organization recognizes two smallpox viruses, *Variola major* and *Variola minor*. *V. major*, the classic form of the disease, comprises numerous strains. *V. minor* was not recognized until late in the nineteenth century. Populations are referred to as "virgin" when they (1) have had no experience of the disease within the lifetime of present members or (2) have never had any experience of the disease. Since there is evidence of a sixteenth-century epidemic on the Plateau, it would seem that the eighteenth-century Native populations are best described as type one. The 30 percent fatality rate derives from both general epidemiological data and a conservative extrapolation from Alfred Crosby's 1976 analysis of twenty outbreaks in the Americas ("Virgin Soil Epidemics in the Aboriginal Depopulation of America"). Data on the 1770s epidemic in North America indicate much higher mortality in many other regions than in the Plateau. In addition to sources in note 2, see George Guilmet et al., "Legacy of Introduced Disease"; Russell Thornton, *American Indian Holocaust and Survival*; Ann Ramenofsky, *Vectors of Death*. It is instructive to inject here Crosby's recent caution that close regional analyses must be carried out, lest we assume that epidemics "rain[ed] down uniformly" on the peoples of this hemisphere ("Summary on Population Size," 278).

6. Boyd, "Introduction of Infectious Diseases"; Guilmet et al., "Legacy of Introduced Disease," 2; Thornton, *American Indian Holocaust*, 46–47; David Stannard, "Consequences of Contact," 519–40.

7. William H. McNeill, "Historical Patterns of Migration," 96; Ramenofsky, *Vectors of Death*, chap. 5; Stannard, "Consequences of Contact," 524.

8. Ann Ramenofsky, "Loss of Innocence," 41–43.

9. Boyd, "Introduction of Infectious Diseases," 52; Guilmet et al., "Legacy of Introduced Disease"; Campbell, *PostColumbian Culture History*, 176–77; Stannard, "Consequences of Contact."

10. Boyd, "Introduction of Infectious Diseases," chap. 2; Henry Dobyns, "Estimating Aboriginal American Populations."

11. Harris, "Voices of Disaster," 604–5.

12. Cox, *Columbia*, 169.

13. B.45/e/2, fol. 2.

14. Asa Smith, in Clifford H. Drury, ed., *Diaries and Letters of Henry H. Spaulding*, 136–37.

15. Gregory Mengarini, *Recollections of the Flathead Mission*, 193–94; H. H. Turney-High, *Ethnography of the Kutenai*, 132.

16. Angelo Anastasio, "Southern Plateau"; Nancy Turner, Randy Bouchard, and Dorothy Kennedy, *Ethnobotany of the Okanagan-Colville Indians*; David H. Chance, *Influences of the Hudson's Bay Company*.

17. Teit, "Salishan Tribes," 211–12, 315.

18. See, for example, the work of Julie Cruikshank, especially "Oral Tradition and Oral History."

19. The first account from the Kamloops area is David Stuart's of 1812, reported secondhand in Ross, *Adventures of the First Settlers*, 163–63; the earliest extant post journal is from 1822–23 (B.97/a/1).

20. As pointed out in note 2, the emerging archaeological record also supports this proposition.

21. Fraser, *Journal*, 94; Teit, "Salishan Tribes," 211; Teit, "Thompson Indians," 175–77.

22. Harris contends that there was no 1800–1801 epidemic in the Strait–Puget Sound region and what Fraser saw was marks of the outbreak of ca. 1780 ("Voices of Disaster," 606).

23. Boyd, "Introduction of Infectious Diseases," 105–9.

24. Fraser, *Journal*, 119; T. C. Elliott, ed., "David Thompson's Narrative of the Expedition to the Kootenae," 45.

25. B.45/a/1, fol. 27.

26. B.45/a/1, fols. 26–27.

27. Re malaria, see Boyd, "Introduction of Infectious Diseases," chaps. 3 and 7.

28. The phrase is from Eugene Hunn, *Nch'i-Wana*, 241.

29. Leslie Spier, *Prophet Dance of the Northwest and Its Derivatives*, 5.

30. Raymond DeMallie has made a similar argument in "Lakota Ghost Dance," 385–405. My approach draws on his interpretation of the 1890 movement as "part of the integral, ongoing whole of Lakota culture," and his admonition to scholars to "consider seriously the symbolic

content of Indian cultures" (388). For similar perspectives, see Alice Beck Kehoe, *Ghost Dance*, and Benjamin Kracht, "Kiowa Ghost Dance."

31. Walter Cline, "Religion and World View," 172–76; Christopher Miller, *Prophetic Worlds*; Hunn, *Nch'i-Wana*.

32. DeMallie, "Lakota Ghost Dance," 388.

33. Spier, *Prophet Dance*, 11.

34. For illustrative narratives told by a Plateau oral historian, see Harry Robinson, *Write It on Your Heart*.

35. See, inter alia, Clifford, *Predicament of Culture*; David W. Cohen, "Undefining of Oral Tradition"; Julie Cruikshank, "Discovering Gold on the Klondike."

36. The 1870 and the better-known 1890 Ghost Dance originated among the Paviotso (Northern Paiute) of western Nevada. The 1890 movement spread to the plains, culminating in the massacre of as many as 370 Sioux at Wounded Knee, South Dakota. Inspired by the visions of the prophet Wovoka, who foretold the return of the dead and a better world after the destruction of the whites, the Sioux followers confronted the Seventh U.S. Cavalry. The literature on the Ghost Dance is vast. See, inter alia, James Mooney, *Ghost-Dance Religion*; Cora Du Bois, "1870 Ghost Dance"; Kehoe, *Ghost Dance*; DeMallie, "Lakota Ghost Dance"; Russell Thornton, *We Shall Live Again*; Kracht, "Kiowa Ghost Dance."

37. Lanternari, *Religions of the Oppressed*, 134.

38. Ralph Linton, "Nativistic Movements"; Wallace, "Revitalization Movements." For further development of Wallace's argument, see his *Death and Rebirth of the Seneca*.

39. Aberle, "Prophet Dance and Reactions to White Contact."

40. Walker, "New Light on the Prophet Dance Controversy," 250 and passim.

41. Miller, *Prophetic Worlds*, chaps. 2 and 3.

42. See, for instance, William Swagerty, "Indian Trade in the Trans-Mississippi West," and his "Protohistoric Trade in Western North America"; Jacqueline Peterson, "Prophetic Worlds" (review).

43. Lanternari, "Revolution and/or Integration in African Socio-Religious Movements." For a useful review of Africanist literature, see Terence O. Ranger, "Religious Movements and Politics in Sub-Saharan Africa."

44. Suttles's original essay, "The Plateau Prophet Dance Among the Coast Salish," downplayed the level of indirect white influence in the late

eighteenth century, but in a later reissue, he quietly admits "more and earlier white influence" (*Coast Salish Essays*, 198). See also Robin Ridington, *Swan People*, and his *Trail to Heaven*.

45. Ridington, *Swan People*, passim.

46. John M. Janzen, "Tradition of Renewal in Kongo Religion," 75–76.

47. Miller, *Prophetic Worlds*, 41.

48. Peires, *Dead Will Arise*, x, 124, passim.

49. Walker, "New Light on the Prophet Dance Controversy," 250; Peires, *Dead Will Arise*, 124.

50. Cline, "Religion and World View," 172–75.

51. David Thompson, *Narrative*, 475–95.

52. Thompson, *Narrative*, 479.

53. Thompson, *Narrative*, 479.

54. Hunn, *Nch'i-Wana*, 247.

55. Spier, *Prophet Dance*, 55, 58; Cline, "Religion and World View," 172; Teit, "Salishan Tribes," 291–92.

56. Quoted in Spier, *Prophet Dance*, 57–58.

57. Hunn, *Nch'i-Wana*, 250–51.

58. Thompson, *Narrative*, 492–93.

59. Spier, *Prophet Dance*, 17.

60. Quoted in Hunn, *Nch'i-Wana*, 249–50.

61. The most detailed account of Kauxuma-nupika's life was published by Claude Schaeffer in 1965 ("The Kutenai Female Berdache"). Further discussion of Kauxuma-nupika and the berdache tradition follows in chapter 6.

62. Thompson, *Narrative*, 437, 512–13; see also Gabriel Franchère, *Journal*, 85, 88; Ross, *Adventures*, 92, 111.

63. Thompson, *Narrative*, 513; see also T. C. Elliott, ed., "Thompson's Journal: Voyage to the Mouth of the Columbia," 111. Quotation marks are added to this passage for clarity.

64. Thompson, *Narrative*, 513.

65. Ross, *Adventures*, 156–58.

66. Schaeffer, "Kutenai Female Berdache," 211–12.

67. For brief discussions of the "cargo cult" mentality as it may have related to the Plateau, see Walker, "New Light on the Prophet Dance Controversy," 251–52; and Hunn, *Nch'i-Wana*, 250–51.

68. Ross, *Adventures*, 311.

69. A similar argument has been made by Russell Thornton in his studies of prophetic movements among the nineteenth-century Cherokee and the 1870 and 1890 Ghost Dances. Thornton, "Boundary Dissolution and Revitalization Movements"; and Thornton, *We Shall Live Again*.

70. Hunn, *Nch'i-Wana*, 242; Ridington, *Swan People* and *Trail to Heaven*.

71. Quoted in Hunn, *Nch'i-Wana*, 243–46.

72. Miller, *Prophetic Worlds*, chap. 1; Robinson, *Write It on Your Heart*; Hunn, *Nch'i-Wana*, 241–42; Deward Walker, "Nez Perce Sorcery," 67–72; Verne Ray, *Cultural Relations in the Plateau*, 95–99.

73. Hunn, *Nch'i-Wana*, 193, 198, 241; Robinson, *Write It on Your Heart*; Ray, *Cultural Relations in the Plateau*, 95–102.

74. B.146/a/2, fols. 5, 6; Ross, *Adventures*, 327.

75. Boyd, "Introduction of Infectious Diseases," 54–56; Russell Thornton, Jonathan Warren, and Tim Miller, "Depopulation in the Southeast After 1492," 191–92; Ramenofsky, *Vectors of Death*.

76. W. H. McNeill looks at inoculation in India, Arabia, and southern Africa in his *Plagues and Peoples*; see especially discussion on 233. Terence Ranger provides examples of the development in African societies of control mechanisms like personification of the disease and inoculation in "Plagues of Beasts and Men," 248–49.

3. Landscaping the Wilds: Traders Imagine the Plateau

1. Ross, *Adventures of the First Settlers*, 147, 158. He makes similar observations on 131, 149, 217, 227 and in his *Fur Hunters*, 31, 54.

2. The Columbia Plain covers the south-central Plateau. The plain's treeless, scrubby landscape defined the entire Interior for many traders. For the geography, see Meinig, *Great Columbia Plain*, chap. 1. For the melancholy inspired in British observers by Australian plains and deserts, see Bernard Smith, *European Vision and the South Pacific*, especially 224–33.

3. Thompson, *Narrative*, 518, 520; Simpson, *Journal 1824–25*, 126; D.3/1, fol. 89; Ross, *Fur Hunters*, 104. The whole of fur-trade country was sometimes referred to as a desert: Columbia Chief Trader James Douglas wrote of the arrival of white women in the country, "to pine and languish in the desert"; see Glazebrook, *Hargrave Correspondence*, 310.

4. Pratt, *Imperial Eyes*, 61.

5. The phrase is from Maurice Godelier, *Mental and the Material*, 35.

6. This notion is developed throughout Schama's *Landscape and Memory.*

7. Jonathan Smith, "Slightly Different Thing That Is Said," 82; Stephen Daniels and Denis Cosgrove, "Introduction: Iconography and Landscape," 1.

8. Samuel Johnson, *A Journey to the Western Islands of Scotland*, 39, 41, and passim. For similar reflections, see Daniel Defoe, *A Tour Thro' the Whole Island of Great Britain*, 2:819–22.

9. T. C. Elliott, ed., "Thompson's Narrative of the Expedition to the Kootenae," 29; Ross, *Fur Hunters*, 82.

10. Ross, *Fur Hunters*, 275.

11. D.3/1, fol. 28; Simpson, *Journal 1824–25*, 47 (emphasis in original).

12. Philip A. Rollins, ed., "Robert Stuart's Narratives," 277; F.3/2, fol. 115; Ross, *Fur Hunters*, 98, 103.

13. T. C. Elliott, ed., "Thompson's Journal: Voyage to the Mouth," 48–49.

14. Henry, *Journal*, 708; Cox, *Columbia*, 109, 135; F.3/2, fols. 208–9. Neither red nor fallow deer are native; Henry would have seen whitetail deer (quite "red" in summer) and mule deer. "Gray sheep" were Rocky Mountain bighorns. See Ian Cowan and Charles Guiguet, *Mammals of British Columbia*, and Stephen Whitney, ed., *Western Forests*.

15. Lamb, ed., *Letters and Journals of Simon Fraser*, 65, 73.

16. E. E. Rich, ed., *Simpson's Dispatch 1829*, 30, 50, 52; B.97/e/1, fols. 2–4.

17. Rollins, ed., "Robert Stuart's Narratives," 61; Franchère, *Journal*, 149; Thompson, *Narrative*, 491, 495.

18. F.3/2, fols. 208–9; Ross, *Fur Hunters*, 120; Simpson, *Journal 1824–25*, 53. The predominant vegetation was a stunted form of sagebrush.

19. Thompson, *Narrative*, 387. "Red Fir" is not native to the region; this was likely Grand Fir. "Plane" was a deciduous tree, probably maple. See Whitney, *Western Forests*, 361, 393.

20. D.3/1, fols. 25–26; Simpson, *Journal 1824–25*, 44; Rich, ed., *Simpson's Dispatch 1829*, 168.

21. Ann Bermingham, *Landscape and Ideology*, 9–10.

22. Schama, *Landscape and Memory*; Stephen Daniels, "Political Iconography of Woodland."

23. Ross, *Fur Hunters*, 101; Rollins, ed., "Robert Stuart's Narratives," 78.

24. Ross, *Fur Hunters*, 38.

25. M. Catherine White, ed., *David Thompson's Journals Relating to Montana*, 15, 17, 35.

26. Thompson, *Narrative*, 422. He commented elsewhere that the Native peoples west of the mountains, unlike those to the east, "pride themselves on their industry" and one day they would be civilized, i.e., adopt agriculture (414–15).

27. T. C. Elliott, ed., "Thompson's Journeys in the Spokane Country," 14; cf. Thompson, *Narrative*, 466.

28. D.3/1, fol. 24.

29. Simpson, *Journal 1824–25*, 139; Rich, ed *Simpson's Dispatch 1829*, 47–49; D.3/2, fol. 100d (cited in Glyndwr Williams, ed., *London Correspondence Inward from Sir George Simpson*, 54n.1).

30. B.97/e/1, fol. 2; B.146/e/1; B.146/e/2, fol. 3.

31. Country produce west of the mountains did not include a convenient staple like the pemmican available to the east. The staple here, until Simpson's retrenchment plan, was horse flesh.

32. Elliott, ed., "Thompson's Narrative of Expedition to the Kootenae," 40, 35–36; see also White, *Thompson's Journals Relating to Montana*, 18–20, 26, 36–38, 62–63.

33. The French word *chevreuil* was used for deer.

34. Elliott, ed., "Thompson's Narrative of Expedition to Kootenae," 35–40.

35. Alexander Henry made these remarks in a letter to Duncan Cameron, Fort Vermilion, 1 October 1809: PAC, Selkirk Papers, vol. 29, fols. 8835–39 (transcript in BCARS). Simpson made similar remarks on first crossing the Rockies (D.3/1, fols. 19–20).

36. Cox, *Columbia*, 111; F.3/2, fols. 125–26, 202.

37. F.3/2, fols. 208–9.

38. B.146/e/1, fol. 2; B.223/b/2, fol. 16.

39. D.3/1, fol. 61; B.97/a/1, fol. 4; BCARS, Thompson's River Post Journal, 1841–43, entry for 30 August 1843.

40. James McMillan, quoted in B.97/a/1, fol. 5; UBC Sp. Coll., Edward Ermatinger Papers, 288–90.

41. Figures for Okanagan salmon consumption are cited in Gibson, *Farming the Frontier*, 24; B.97/e/1, fol. 3; B.146/e/1, fol. 2; B.146/e/2, fols. 3, 9.

42. Ross, *Fur Hunters*, 98.

43. Lamb, ed., *Letters and Journals of Sir Alexander Mackenzie*, 57. I. S. MacLaren provides a very interesting perspective in "Alexander Mackenzie and Landscapes of Commerce."

44. Cox, *Columbia*, 5.

45. Briefly stated, the aesthetic of the Picturesque celebrated "the accord between man and nature, and the contentment of English rural life"; the Sublime, on the other hand, celebrated the awesome, i.e., absence of the familiar, absence of comforts, danger, isolation. MacLaren, "Mackenzie and Landscapes," 149 and passim; MacLaren, "Aesthetic Mapping of Nature," 40–41; Bermingham, *Landscape and Ideology*.

46. The quote is from Ross, *Adventures*, 306.

47. Fraser, *Journal*, 76.

48. D.3/1, fol. 46.

49. Rich, ed., *Simpson's Dispatch 1829*, 37–38.

50. Rich, ed., *Simpson's Dispatch 1829*, 37–39.

51. Simpson, *Journal 1824–25*, 140; D.3/1, fol. 102.

52. Thompson, *Narrative*, 471, 481.

53. Fraser, *Journal*, 96.

54. Jules Quesnel to J. M. Lamothe, May 1809, in Lamb, ed., *Letters and Journals of Simon Fraser*, 262; Rollins, ed., "Robert Stuart's Narratives," 59–60.

55. Smith, *European Vision and the South Pacific*, 295.

56. Ross, *Fur Hunters*, 36–39.

57. E. E. Rich, ed., *Peter Skene Ogden's Snake Country Journals*, 171; K. G. Davies, ed., *Peter Skene Ogden's Snake Country Journal*, 26, 94.

58. E. E. Rich, ed., *Letters of John McLoughlin*, 1:50.

59. Williams, ed., *Peter Skene Ogden's Snake Country Journals*, 120. Traders often used the label "Snake" indiscriminately to refer to the peoples living in the mountains and plains of northern Nevada, southern Idaho, southeast Oregon, and western Wyoming, known collectively to anthropologists as Northern, Eastern, and Western Shoshone and Northern Paiute.

60. BCARS, John Work, Journal 8, fols. 10, 16, 58, passim; Work, Journal 11, fols. 10, 13.

61. Ross, *Adventures*, 136, 229–31, 242–43; cf. Cox, *Columbia*, 118, 128. This plain, where within six miles both the Snake and the Walla Walla River join the Columbia, was commonly called Walla Walla or "the forks."

62. Ross, *Adventures*, 267–68. See also discussion of these events in Stern, *Chiefs and Chief Traders*, 3–5.

63. See Ross, *Fur Hunters*, 42–46, 119–21; D.3/1, fol. 33. For troubled relations, see Ross, *Fur Hunters*; John Stuart to Ross Cox, 25 April 1815, in Cox, *Columbia*, 217, 195–205; B.223/b/2, fols. 9, 21, 42.

64. Ross, *Fur Hunters*, 54.

65. Ross, *Fur Hunters*, 40; Fraser uses similar language (Fraser, *Journal*, 63), as does Simpson (D.3/1, fol. 24).

66. Simpson, *Journal 1824–25*, 124; D.3/1, fols. 87–88.

67. Ross, *Fur Hunters*, 275, quoted above. Keith Thomas charts the evolution of the taste for the "wild," epitomized by the gardens of Lancelot "Capability" Brown, in *Man and the Natural World*, especially chap. 5. See also Bermingham, *Landscape and Ideology*.

68. Rollins, ed., "Robert Stuart's Narratives," 77.

69. Cox, *Columbia*, 93–94, 215.

70. The quote is from UBC Sp. Coll., Ermatinger Papers, 237–38, McLoughlin to Ermatinger, 1 Feb. 1836; the theme is pervasive in traders' writings.

71. These themes are developed to a greater extent and in a distinct analytical framework in my article "Real Men Hunt Buffalo."

72. It was the original intention of HBC authorities in London to have fortresslike posts; during the eighteenth century, as forts became more permanent homes and military preparedness appeared less relevant, the posts came to be seen more as places of business and residence, and less as forts. See Brown, *Strangers in Blood*, 16–18.

73. Alexander Ross's enthusiasm apparently got the better of him. Archaeological evidence indicates that the fort was rather smaller than Ross recalled. See Stern, *Chiefs and Chief Traders*, chap. 1.

74. Ross, *Fur Hunters*, 119–20, 144–46.

75. Ross, *Fur Hunters*, 154–55; B.146/a/1, 2, passim; B.223/b/11, fol. 49. On McGillivray, see Stern, *Chiefs and Chief Traders*, chap. 6.

76. By the nineteenth century unions *à la façon du pays* were sanctioned by "immemorial custom" as proper marriages (B.223/b/21, fols. 4–12).

77. Glazebrook, ed., *Hargrave Correspondence*, 381; UBC Sp. Coll., Ermatinger Papers, McDonald to Ermatinger, 30 Mar. 1842; Van Kirk, *Many Tender Ties*, 136–37. The roles of native women in the Columbia trade are discussed below in chapters 4 and 5. The best analyses of the

roles of women in the trade are Van Kirk, *Many Tender Ties*, and Brown, *Strangers in Blood*.

78. The rules were codified in 1828 in the "Standing Rules and Regulations," D.4/92, fol. 90d.

79. Cox, *Columbia*, 230.

80. See Michael Payne, "Daily Life on Western Hudson Bay, 389–90.

81. Leonore Davidoff and Catherine Hall, *Family Fortunes*, 17, 357, and chap. 8 passim.

82. Davidoff and Hall, *Family Fortunes*, 410–15.

83. Glazebrook, ed., *Hargrave Correspondence*, 138.

84. R. Harvey Fleming, ed., *Minutes of Council, Northern Department*, 26.

85. Ross, *Fur Hunters*, 19–20, 7–10; Cox, *Columbia*, 360.

86. Fleming, ed., *Minutes of Council*, 25–26; see, e.g., B.223/b/4, fol. 31. For further discussion, see Van Kirk, *Many Tender Ties*, 123–26.

87. Simpson, *Journal 1824–25*, 48; D.3/1, fol. 28.

88. B.97/e/1, fol. 3.

89. See especially Fort Vancouver Correspondence Books (B.223/b/1–31): e.g., B.223/b/2, fol. 45; B.223/b/3, fol. 3; B.223/b/4, fol. 31; B.223/b/10, fol. 25.

90. Quoted in Loo, *Making Law, Order, and Authority*, 29.

91. Loo, *Making Law, Order, and Authority*, chap. 1.

92. Cox, *Columbia*, 229–33.

93. Cox, *Columbia*, 92, 94–97, 100, 238.

94. Ross, *Fur Hunters*, 48–52.

95. Ross, *Fur Hunters*, 114.

96. Ross, *Fur Hunters*, 48–52 (quotation on p. 48).

97. Ross, *Fur Hunters*, 48–50.

98. Ross, *Fur Hunters*, 51–52, 114.

99. For example, in the 1820s and 1830s, the Committee issued directives re the control of wolves on the plains and at Red River Colony.

100. E. E. Rich, ed., *Letters of John McLoughlin*, 2:164; Lorne Hammond, "'Any Ordinary Degree of System,'" 50–51; Cox, *Columbia*, 239. Cox called these animals wolves, but since they were smaller and the Native people believed their skins worthless, they must have been coyotes. Ross said the white wolf skin was "an article of royalty" among the Okanagan (*Fur Hunters*, 50).

101. This useful notion is from William Beinart's review article, "Empire, Hunting, and Ecological Change," 175. Donald Worster explores the idea in some depth in *Nature's Economy*, especially in chap. 13. For a valuable discussion of the way in which maps in general are embedded in social values, see J. B. Harley, "Deconstructing the Map."

102. Ross, *Fur Hunters*, 71. For the development of such prohibitions, see Thomas, *Man and the Natural World*, 100–120.

103. Cox, *Columbia*, 84, 114. The traders' packhorses were often too emaciated to be eaten.

104. Ross, *Fur Hunters*, 180.

105. Cox, *Columbia*, 208 (emphasis in original). He no doubt anticipated his readers' sensibilities would be offended.

106. Cox, *Columbia*, 208. Cox later learned that the demise of Ponto was a joke.

107. Thompson, *Narrative*, 199–206; Cox, *Columbia*, 141–42; also Ross, *Fur Hunters*, 100–101.

4. Traders and Fishers: Tales of the State of Nature

1. Henry, *Journal*, 707. The "unhallowed wilderness" phrase is from Ross, *Adventures*, 158.

2. Thompson, *Narrative*, 475.

3. B.208/e/1, fols. 2, 3; B.146/e/2, fol. 4; Rich, *Simpson's Dispatch 1829*, 31.

4. Ross, *Fur Hunters*, 166, 178; Cox, *Columbia*, 233–34; B.208/e/1, fol. 3; B.45/a/1, fol. 26.

5. D.3/1, fols. 61–62; Simpson, *Journal 1824–25*, 94–95; Rich, ed., *Simpson's Dispatch 1829*, 31, 49–51.

6. See, e.g., D.5/1, fol. 174; D.5/2, fol. 125; Simpson, *Journal*, 106, 333–36.

7. Figures are based on numbers of pelts. The Columbia Department provided just under 5 percent of North American returns from 1825 through 1830, and fully 15 percent by 1840–46. The key document for calculation of Columbia Department returns is BCARS, Fur Trade Returns for Columbia and New Caledonia, 1825–57 (A/B/20/V3). A useful analysis of the figures is found in Hammond, "'Any Ordinary Degree of System.'"

8. BCARS, Fur Trade Returns—Columbia; Hammond, "'Any Ordinary Degree of System,'" 64.

9. Ross, *Adventures*, 127–28; Rollins, ed., "Robert Stuart's Narratives," 62.

10. Swagerty, "Indian Trade," 353; W. R. Wood, "Plains Trade in Prehistoric and Protohistoric Intertribal Relations."

11. Swagerty, "Indian Trade," 353.

12. The quotes are from D.3/1, fols. 61–62, the original manuscript on which Simpson, *Journal 1824–25* is based.

13. Thompson, *Narrative*, 417. If Malthus softened the message of his original *Essay on the Principle of Population* (1798) in the revised edition (1803), it was the original that remained most influential. See Gertrude Himmelfarb, *Idea of Poverty*, chap. 4; Roy Porter, "Mixed Feelings," 16.

14. Thompson, *Narrative*, 80.

15. B.208/e/1, fol. 7, also B.97/e/1, fol. 4; PAC, John McLeod Papers, fol. 53 (microfilm in BCARS, A1656); Glazebrook, ed., *Hargrave Correspondence*, 308.

16. I acknowledge my debt to Black-Rogers's study, published as "Varieties of 'Starving'" (1986). Emphasis in original.

17. D.3/1, fols. 61–62; Simpson, *Journal 1824–25*, 94–95.

18. B.45/e/3; B.146/a/2, entry for 14 Dec. 1831.

19. The same point is well made in Kathleen M. Brown's recent study of English images of coastal Algonquian gender relations in the early seventeenth century. See her "Anglo-Algonquian Gender Frontier."

20. See Katherine Weist, "Beasts of Burden and Menial Slaves"; David Smits, "'Squaw Drudge'"; Van Kirk, *Many Tender Ties*, 17–19.

21. Quoted in Germaine Warkentin, ed., *Canadian Exploration Literature*, 113.

22. Extracts from the writings of Radisson, Kelsey, Isham, and many other traders are presented in the very useful collection edited by Germaine Warkentin, ed., *Canadian Exploration Literature*. These quotations are from pp. 17, 35, and 63.

23. For reflections from other colonial settings, see Pratt, *Imperial Eyes*, 63–64 and chap. 3; Melman, *Women's Orients*, 61.

24. Cox, *Columbia*, 261; Ross, *Fur Hunters*, 195.

25. HBCA, PP 1828-1, Queries Connected with Natural History, fol. 1; B.45/e/2, fol. 5.

26. Ross, *Adventures*, 317–18; see also D.3/2, fol. 97; Cox, *Columbia*, 261–62.

27. B.146/e/2, fols. 5, 6.

28. Such estimates are notoriously difficult to calculate. See Angelo Anastasio, "Southern Plateau: An Ecological Analysis"; Verne Ray, *Cultural Relations in the Plateau*; Eugene Hunn, "Mobility as a Factor Limiting Resource Use." Following convention, the term "root" is used here as a shorthand for true roots and any other edible underground parts (corms, bulbs, rhizomes, tubers).

29. HBCA, PP 1828-1, Queries Connected with Natural History, fol. 1, queries 41–44.

30. The context in which Black came to understand economic strategies in the region is important. He had been posted to Walla Walla in 1825 by Governor Simpson, in the throes of the governor's economic retrenchment program. Black was under strict orders to reduce the dependence of the post on horse meat and imported foods. Accordingly, he developed a trade with local producers in salmon and other fish, small mammals, roots, and berries. The pursuit of this trade no doubt improved his insight into the seasonal rounds and eating habits of local communities. I thank Theodore Stern for emphasizing the significance of this context.

31. Ross, *Adventures*, 337–38.

32. For contradictory evidence see Brian Hayden, ed., *A Complex Culture of the British Columbia Plateau*. Hayden's volume concerns the Stl'atl'imx (Lil'wat), who figure to only a limited extent in the present study.

33. Anastasio, "Southern Plateau," 174.

34. The comments on polygyny are in Ross, *Adventures*, 318.

35. Ross, *Adventures*, 337–40.

36. On bride service, see especially Jane Collier and Michelle Rosaldo, "Politics and Gender in Simple Societies."

37. The most influential proponent of this position has been Eleanor Leacock. See especially Leacock, "Women's Status in Egalitarian Society"; Mona Etienne and Eleanor Leacock, eds., *Women and Colonization*. For a useful review of this position and its critiques, see Henrietta Moore, *Feminism and Anthropology*, especially 30–34; Nancy Shoemaker, *Negotiators of Change*, "Introduction." On the Plateau, see Hunn et al., *Nch'i-Wana*, 208; Lillian Ackerman, "Sexual Equality on the Colville Indian Reservation."

38. The questions are assessed in Carol Mukhopadhyay and Patricia Higgins, "Anthropological Studies of Women's Status Revisited"; and in Shoemaker, "Introduction."

39. Shoemaker, "Introduction," 13, 5.

40. See Angela Sidney's account and Cruikshank, "Introduction," in *Julie Cruikshank* et al., *Life Lived Like a Story*, 98–101, 10–11. For a discussion of men's fears of women's power among the Ojibwa, see Laura Peers, *Ojibwa of Western Canada*, 84–85.

41. The quotation is from Sherry Ortner and Harriet Whitehead, eds., *Sexual Meanings*, 10; Collier and Rosaldo, "Politics and Gender in Simple Societies," 275–82. See also discussion in Moore, *Feminism and Anthropology*, chap. 2.

42. Ross, *Adventures*, 318.

43. See discussion in Collier and Rosaldo, "Politics and Gender," 280–85.

44. B.45/e/2, fol. 5; Ross, *Adventures*, 318; B.146/e/2, fol. 6. See also BCARS, Thompson's River Post Journal, 1841–43, entries for 14 Feb., 1–3 April, 1843; B.146/a/1, fol. 7, Work, Journal No. 12, fols. 8–14.

45. For further discussion, see Melman, *Women's Orients*, chap. 2. Homi Bhabha explains how the stereotype depends for its effectiveness on paradox or ambivalence: the fissures and gaps contained within the stereotype as a result of its indeterminacy and ambivalence ensure its malleability and repeatability, and inform its strategies of individuation and marginalization. See Bhabha, "Other Question."

46. D.3/1, fol. 94; Simpson, *Journal 1824–25*, 58, 104–5, 131–32, 150–51.

47. Ross, *Adventures*, 324–25; Cox, *Columbia*, 136–37, 142–43.

48. B.45/e/2, fol. 5.

49. See, e.g., BCARS, Thompson's River Post Journal, 1841–43, entry for 3 Apr. 1843; B.223/b/17, fol. 35; Work, Journal No. 11, fol. 11; Work, Journal No. 12, fols. 8, 14, 40–48.

50. Ross, *Adventures*, 322–25.

51. Cf. Ross, *Adventures*, 318; B.45/e/2, fol. 5; B.146/e/2, fol. 4.

52. Weist, "Beasts of Burden," 43–44; Megan Vaughan, *Story of an African Famine*, especially chap. 5.

53. Ross, *Adventures*, 318; Hunn et al., *Nch'i-Wana*, 205.

54. D.3/2, fol. 91; B.97/e/1, fol. 4.

55. Cox, *Columbia*, 261.

56. B.208/e/1, fols. 2, 3; B.208/a/1, fols. 2, 5.

57. B.45/e/2, fol. 5; B.146/e/2, fol. 6; Work, Journal No. 4, fols. 28, 21; F.3/2, fols. 234–35. Work's district report (B.45/e/2) and Samuel Black's

1829 report from Fort Nez Percés (B.146/e/2) are especially enlightening when read in conjunction with HBCA, PP 1828-1, Queries Connected with Natural History.

58. Ross, *Fur Hunters*, 22–23.

59. In 1944, Desmond collected the accounts of elders (born between 1862 and 1871) for his classic monograph "Gambling Among the Yakima." I am grateful to Eugene Hunn for bringing this monograph to my attention.

60. Desmond, "Gambling Among the Yakima," 50; B.45/e/2, fol. 10; Ross, *Adventures*, 315. The power and influence of chiefs in Plateau communities is discussed later in this and subsequent chapters.

61. David Chance, *Influences of the Hudson's Bay Company*, 23.

62. B.45/e/2, fol. 12; B.45/e/3, fol. 5. Re trade, see also B.45/e/2, fol. 14; B.208/a/1, fol. 9.

63. Ross, *Adventures*, 128.

64. Ross, *Adventures*, 127–28.

65. D.3/1, fol. 22.

66. B.146/a/2, entry for 15 Dec. 1831.

67. Pratt, *Imperial Eyes*, 80–84.

68. Peter Hulme, *Colonial Encounters*, 147; Pratt, *Imperial Eyes*, 84–85; Karl Marx, *Capital*, 1:455. Anthropologist Marcel Mauss was perhaps first to explore the meaning of gift exchange in noncapitalist societies. In such societies reciprocity, he argued, was the basis of social interaction. See Mauss, *Gift*.

69. In addition to Mauss, *Gift*, see Marshall Sahlins's notion of "generalized reciprocity" in his *Stone Age Economics*. On Native North Americans, see, e.g., Bruce White, "Give Us a Little Milk" and "Encounters with Spirits"; Black-Rogers, "Varieties of 'Starving,'" 365–70; Laura Peers, "Rich Man, Poor Man, Beggarman, Chief."

70. Hunn et al., *Nch'i-Wana*, 203–4, 217.

71. Edward Umfreville, *Present State of Hudson's Bay*, 19.

72. B.97/a/2, fols. 13, 14.

73. See especially White, "Give Us a Little Milk," 185–86; George Dalton, "Impact of Colonization on Aboriginal Economies"; Hunn et al., *Nch'i-Wana*, 217.

74. On traders' marriages into Native societies, see Brown, *Strangers in Blood* and Van Kirk, *Many Tender Ties*.

75. See Black-Rogers, "Varieties of Starving," 367–69.

76. Dorothy Ursaki, personal communication, 4 May 1992. I am also grateful to Wendy Wickwire for informative discussions of this issue.

77. The spirit quest differed in certain details from group to group. Among many, for instance, the spirit vision was "forgotten" until maturity, when expertise in some field made clear the identity of the guardian; among others, it was reported right away. See Verne Ray, *Sanpoil and Nespelem*; Ray, *Cultural Relations*; Christopher Miller, *Prophetic Worlds*; Deward Walker, *Conflict and Schism in Nez Percé Acculturation*; Hunn et al., *Nch'i-Wana*.

78. Black-Rogers, "Varieties of Starving," 368.

79. Hunn et al., *Nch'i-Wana*, 241–51.

80. Quotation marks added for clarity. Thompson, *Narrative*, 490–91.

81. Thompson, *Narrative*, 411, 413, 474–76, 487; Ross, *Adventures*, 150–54.

82. Williams, ed., *Graham's Observations*, 85–86.

83. Thompson, *Narrative*, 474–76; Cox, *Columbia*, 251.

84. McGillivray's comments are in B.146/a/1 and a/2, passim. The definition of "beg" is from *A New English Dictionary on Historical Principles*, J. A. H. Murray, ed. (Oxford, 1888).

85. It should be emphasized that it was prohibited only to distribute liquor to Native people; there was plenty for company officers and, on special occasions, for the men.

86. B.97/a/1, fol. 8 and also fol. 13; B.223/b/5, fol. 22; B.223/b/17, fols. 3, 4; B.223/c/1, fols. 59a, 206; D.5/1, fol. 174; Simpson, *Journal 1824–25*, 109, 321, 333; Fleming, ed., *Minutes of Council, Northern Department*, 56; Rich, ed., *Letters of John McLoughlin*, 1:232.

87. B.97/a/1, fol. 8.

88. B.223/b/17, fol. 36. Re gratuities see also B.146/a/2, entry for 4 Dec. 1831; B.208/e/1, fols. 3–4; Work, Journal No. 4, fol. 20.

89. B.97/a/2, fol. 11. Nkwala's Okanagan name was Hwistesmetxe'qEn; Nkwala comes from the name traders gave him, Nicholas or Nicola.

90. Work, Journal No. 4, fol. 220; BCARS, Thompson's River Post Journals, 1841–43, entry for 3 Aug. 1841; D.3/2, fols. 91, 94.

91. B.146/e/2, fol. 9.

92. For an excellent discussion of the contours of HBC commercial policy, see Arthur J. Ray and Donald Freeman, *"Give Us Good Measure,"* especially chapters 6 and 7; and Arthur J. Ray, *Indians in the Fur Trade*, chaps. 3 and 4.

93. Bruce White, "Encounters with Spirits," 369–76. White acknowledges that in the *early* period of encounter, there is evidence that the French themselves were viewed as supernatural—but this did not last long.

94. White, "Encounters with Spirits," 393–96.

95. This discussion is informed by Black-Rogers, "Varieties of Starving," especially 365–70, and Hunn et al., *Nch'i-Wana*, chap. 6.

96. For a useful discussion of HBC policy for punishment and control of its own employees, see Loo, *Making Law, Order, and Authority*, chap. 1.

97. These are persistent themes in fur-trade records. The "poltroon" passage is from B.223/b/30, fol. 49, John McLoughlin to the Governor and Committee, 15 Nov. 1843 [encl.]; see also Rich, ed., *Letters of John McLoughlin*, 1:48; D.5/6, fols. 173–74.

98. B.208/e/1, fols. 3–4.

99. B.208/e/1, fols. 3–4; D.3/2, fol. 102.

100. BCARS, Memorial to Sir Wilfrid Laurier, Premier of the Dominion of Canada from the Chiefs of the Shuswap, Okanagan and Couteau Tribes of British Columbia, Kamloops, 25 August, 1910, fol. 2. James Teit assisted in translation of the address. I thank Wendy Wickwire for bringing this document to my attention.

101. B.146/a/1 and B.146/a/2, passim.

102. Stern discusses at length the various tensions between traders and the home guard (those who lived most of the year in the vicinity of the post) and other Indians of the region. Among other stresses were the behavior of individual employees and Indians, sexual jealousies, disputes over traders' expectations for Indian labor, and McGillivray's constant readiness to use corporal punishment against both his men and local Indians. Stern, *Chiefs and Chief Traders*, chaps. 7 and 8.

103. Ross, *Fur Hunters*, 43–46.

104. Information on McGillivray's history is drawn from Stern, *Chiefs and Chief Traders*, 91–95.

105. B.146/a/1 and B.146/a/2, passim.

5. The Want of Meat:
Cultural Meanings of Hunger and Plenty

1. PAC, John McLeod Papers, 1823–49, fols. 236–38: F. Ermatinger to J. McLeod, 8 Mar. 1829.

2. Black-Rogers, "Varieties of 'Starving.'"
3. White, ed., *Thompson's Journals Relating to Montana*, 97.
4. *Oxford English Dictionary.*
5. Emphasis added. B.146/a/2, entries for 20 Feb. and 17 Mar. 1832.
6. D.4/122, fol. 21; Simpson, *Journal 1824-25*, 40.
7. B.97/a/2, especially entry for 16 Jan. 1827; B.97/e/1, fols. 3, 4; BCARS, Thompson's River Post Journal, 1841-43, entry for 2 Mar. 1843.
8. Fraser, *Journal*, 93; Thompson, *Narrative*, 487.
9. D.3/1, fols. 22-23. For other examples of collection of "rotten" fish, see D.3/2, fol. 91; F.3/2, fol. 8; Thompson, *Narrative*, 540; Henry, *Journal*, 708; Work, Journal No. 1, fols. 40, 43; Work, Journal No. 4, fol. 113; BCARS, Thompson's River Post Journal, 1841-43, entry for 6 Sept. 1843.
10. Robert Burgner, "Life History of Sockeye Salmon," 15; Steven Romanoff, "Fraser Lillooet Salmon Fishing," 119-34.
11. Work, Journal No. 1, fols. 40-41.
12. B.208/e/1, fol. 2. See also BCARS, Thompson's River Post Journal, 1841-43, entries for 12-27 Aug. 1841.
13. Hunn et al., *Nch'i-Wana*, 132-34.
14. Work, Journal No. 4, fol. 113; D.4/119, fol. 16.
15. B.223/b/2, fol. 41; B.146/e/2.
16. Carstens, *Queen's People*, 35. The details of salmon cycles will have altered somewhat since the onset of commercial fishing in the late 1800s, but general patterns are believed to be persistent.
17. Eugene Hunn has made the calculations (*Nch'i-Wana*, 148-49); Hunn et al., "Mobility as a Factor," 31-32; James Baker, "Archaeological Research Concerning the Okanagan," 42; Teit, "Thompson Indians of British Columbia," 252-53.
18. Anthropologist David Chance, whose 1973 study *Influences of the Hudson's Bay Company on the Native Cultures of the Colvile District* has been very influential, accepted such reports of starvation and salmon failure rather uncritically. See especially pp. 21-22.
19. B.45/e/2, fol. 3; B.45/e/3, fols. 2-5.
20. Henry, *Journal*, 708; Thompson, *Narrative*, 487.
21. Simpson, *Journal 1824-25*, 94; Work, Journal No. 5, fol. 32; D.3/2, fol. 101; B.97/a/1, fol. 4.
22. Nick Fiddes, *Meat: A Natural Symbol*, 2 and passim.

23. I am grateful to Krys Sieciechowicz for her comments on the issues associated with meat in the hierarchy of foods. The "phantasmic beliefs" quotation is from Maurice Godelier, *Mental and the Material*, 35. See also Mary Douglas, *Implicit Meanings: Essays in Anthropology* and her *Natural Symbols*; Marshall Sahlins, *Culture and Practical Reason*, chap. 4. For a critique of "idealist" treatments, see Marvin Harris, *Sacred Cow and the Abominable Pig*.

24. For a fascinating exploration of the social meanings of meat in Scotland, see A. Gibson and T. C. Smout, "Food and Hierarchy in Scotland, 1550-1650."

25. Stephen Mennell, *All Manners of Food*, chap. 3. The long period of low population after the Black Death, approximately 1350-1550, was exceptional as a period of greatly increased production and per capita consumption of meat, but even then, the pattern of "class" feeding largely prevailed (45-46).

26. Mennell, *All Manners of Food*, 62, 303, chap. 8 passim.

27. For changes in the diet of working people, e.g., from coarser grains to wheat in England by the late 1700s, and from bread or oatmeal increasingly to potatoes, cf. E. P. Thompson, *Making of the English Working Class*, chap. 10. See also Margaret Visser, *Much Depends on Dinner*. Among the important regional variations is the fact that people in the north of England had more access to dairy products.

28. Thompson, *English Working Class*, 348-49; Mennell, *All Manners of Food*, 303, 310-15; John Burnett, *A History of the Cost of Living*, 167-68; Payne, "Daily Life," 477-78.

29. See, e.g., influential popular historian Peter C. Newman's *Company of Adventurers*, 8, where he contends that traders were forced to exist "near the limits of human endurance."

30. Chief Trader Ferdinand Jacobs, quoted in Payne, "Daily Life," 475. Sellocks are fish fry.

31. Payne, "Daily Life," 479.

32. Dale Miquelon, *New France, 1701-1744*, 223-24; Payne, "Daily Life," 471; Allan Greer, *Fur Trade Labor*, 197-214.

33. D.5/19, fol. 299; Payne, "Daily Life," 440.

34. Michael Payne has argued persuasively that for most servants, fur-trade food was an improvement over food back home, both in terms of quantities of meat, fish, and fowl consumed, and in terms of variety.

Columbia servants did not do as well as those in other regions on the meat index. Payne, "Daily Life," chap. 8.

35. Cox, *Columbia*, 254.

36. Simpson, *Journal 1824–25*, 48.

37. Simpson, *Journal 1824–25*, 128–29.

38. For developments in agriculture at the posts, see Gibson, *Farming the Frontier*, chap. 2.

39. Rich, ed., *Simpson's Dispatch 1829*, 49; B.45/e/3, fol. 10; BCARS, Thompson's River Post Journal, 1841–43, fol. 39; Gibson, *Farming the Frontier*, 47–48, 52–55.

40. Rich, ed., *Letters of John McLoughlin* 1:235; Simpson, *Journal 1824–25*, 86; Gibson, *Farming the Frontier*, 18–20. Gibson's figures for numbers of servants include only employees on salaries, not freemen trappers. The figures are for both the Columbia and the more northerly New Caledonia district.

41. F.3/2, fols. 125–26; B.97/a/1, fol. 5; UBC Sp. Coll., Ermatinger Papers, 288–90. Re fish posts, see Payne, "Daily Life," 439.

42. B.97/e/1, fol. 3.

43. The flour ration provided up to 1,600 calories, for a total with salmon of almost 4,000. The *Canada Food Guide* recommends 2,700 to 3,000 kcal. for a larger man, and rather more for one engaged in strenuous exercise. On food values of dried salmon, see Eugene Hunn and David French, "Lomatium: A Key Resource"; Hunn et al., *Nch'i-Wana*, 150; Payne, "Daily Life," 457.

44. B.97/e/1, fol. 3.

45. Julia Twigg, "Vegetarianism and the Meanings of Meat," 22.

46. A. Jeffrey, 1836, quoted in C. J. Lawrence, "William Buchan: Medicine Laid Open," 32. The edition used here is Buchan, *New Domestic Medicine* (London, 1827).

47. Buchan, *Domestic Medicine*, 19, 57, 65, 594, and passim. See also Sahlins, *Culture and Practical Reason*, 171; Twigg, "Vegetarianism," passim. For a fascinating account of the long and varied tradition of "delicacy" and abstinence in women's diet, see Joan Jacobs Brumberg, *Fasting Girls*.

48. Quesnel to J. M. Lamothe, May 1809, in Fraser, *Journal*, 262; UBC Sp. Coll., Ermatinger Papers, 288–90; John McLean, *Notes of a Twenty-Five Years' Service*, 186.

49. Cox, *Columbia*, 251, 260; Edward Ermatinger, "York Factory Express Journal . . . 1827–28," 115; Work, Journal No. 7, fol. 10; B.146/a/1, entry for 7 April 1831; Ross, *Fur Hunters*, 100.

50. D.3/1, fol. 24; Thompson, *Narrative*, 476, 483–84, 487. Thompson often referred to deer as antelopes. His sheep and goats were Rocky Mountain bighorns.

51. Franchère, *Journal*, 155.

52. Thompson, *Narrative*, 388–89, 461; Fraser, *Journal*, 86; Franchère, *Journal*, 155; Ross, *Adventures*, 342.

53. Thompson, *Narrative*, 392, 474, 476–77, 484.

54. Work, Journal No. 5, fol. 61; Simpson, *Journal*, 58; Thompson, *Narrative*, 413.

55. See especially Ruby and Brown, *Cayuse Indians*, 3–4, 8, and passim. For a fuller discussion of this issue, see chap. 6.

56. Hunn et al., *Nch'i-Wana*, 138–39.

57. Stern, *Chiefs and Chief Traders*, 58; B.146/a/1, entry for 28 Oct. 1831.

58. Stern, *Chiefs and Chief Traders*, 55, 58; B.146/a/1, entry for 30 Oct. 1831. For a view of river dwellers in sharp contrast to Stern's, see Hunn et al., *Nch'i-Wana*.

59. See Richard Lee, "What Hunters Do for a Living," and "Discussions, Part II," in *Man the Hunter*, ed. Richard Lee and Irven De Vore; Frances Dahlberg, *Woman the Gatherer*; Eleanor Leacock and Richard Lee, *Politics and History in Band Societies*, "Introduction"; Hunn et al., *Nch'i-Wana*, 206–11; citations in Mukhopadhyay and Higgins, "Anthropological Studies of Women's Status."

60. See, e.g., Nancy Turner et al., *Thompson Ethnobotany*; Alan Marshall, "Nez Percé Subsistence," 13; Gary Palmer, "Cultural Ecology in the Canadian Plateau," 223; Teit, "Shuswap"; Ray, *Sanpoil and Nespelem*, 98.

61. Turner, Bouchard, and Kennedy, *Ethnobotany of the Okanagan-Colville Indians*.

62. Turner et al., *Thompson Ethnobotany*, 13, 28; Marshall, "Nez Percé Subsistence." For traders' accounts of root-ground gatherings, see, e.g., White, ed., *Thompson's Journals Relating to Montana*, 102; Ross, *Fur Hunters*, 22–23; B.208/a/1, fol. 3; B.45/e/2, fol. 3.

63. PAC, John McLeod Papers, fols. 236–38.

64. PAC, John McLeod Papers, fols. 236–38; BCARS, Thompson's River Post Journal, 1841–43, entries for 12 Aug.–13 Nov. 1843.

65. F.3/2, fols. 125–26.

66. Burgner, "Sockeye Salmon," 14–15, 94–96.

67. BCARS, Thompson's River Post Journals, 1841–43, entries for Aug., Sept. 1843.

68. The species are *Oncorhynchus nerka* (sockeye, or sometimes blueback in the U.S.); *O. tshawytscha* (chinook); *O. kisutch* (coho or silver); *O. gorbuscha* (pink or humpback); and *O. keta* (chum or dog). Steelhead "trout" have recently been included within the genus *Oncorhynchus*.

69. Information on salmon runs is compiled from Groot and Margolis, *Pacific Salmon Life Histories*. See also Michael Kew, "Salmon Availability, Technology, and Cultural Adaptation."

70. BCARS, Thompson's River Post Journal, 1841–43, entries for 12 Aug.–25 Sept. 1843, 22 Jan. 1843.

71. See B.97/a/1, fol. 3; B.208/e/1, fols. 6ff.

72. B.97/a/2, fols. 3, 7, 33; B.97/e/1, fols. 2–4; Hammond, "'Any Ordinary Degree of System,'" 43–45.

73. B.97/e/1, passim.

74. Rich, ed., *Simpson's Dispatch 1829*, 30–31; B.97/e/1, fols. 2, 3. On the brigade routes, see Bob Harris, Hatfield, and Tassie, *Okanagan Brigade Trail in the South Okanagan*; and Holt, Jahnke, and Tassie, *Okanagan Brigade Trail*.

75. B.97/e/1, passim.

76. B.97/a/2, fol. 2.

77. Teit, "Shuswap," 513.

78. I am grateful to Dick Cannings for guidance on the question of how deer were affected.

79. Toby Morantz, "Fur Trade and the Cree of James Bay," 39.

80. See, e.g., B.208/e/1, passim.

81. B.45/a/1, fol. 29.

82. See Stern, *Chiefs and Chief Traders*, chap. 8, for a discussion of Wallawalla and other homeguard at Fort Nez Percés.

83. B.45/a/1, fol. 24.

84. See B.97/e/1, fol. 3; B.97/a/1, B.97/a/2 passim; B.208/e/1, fol. 7; BCARS, Thompson's River Post Journal, 1841–43, passim.

85. B.97/a/2, fol. 18.

86. Archibald McDonald called all the groups of the region "salmon tribes," except the Shuswap of the North Thompson, and the Northern Okanagan and Similkameen. B.97/e/1, passim.

87. B.97/a/1, fols. 9–11 and passim.

88. See, for instance, Teit, "Thompson Indians," 268–69; Teit, "Shuswap," 540, 555; Ray, *Cultural Relations*, 37–39.

89. B.97/a/2, fol. 5 and passim. For other explanations of the conflict between Pelkamulox and the Lil'wat, cf. Marie Brent, "Indian Lore: My Life," 107. Carstens contends that Pelkamulox was killed because he "threatened Lillooet control of the salmon fishing industry on their section of the Fraser River" (Carstens, *Queen's People*, 20). Because he offers no evidence for the claim, and none has been found, it is rejected here.

90. Teit, "Shuswap," 540–63; Teit, "Salishan Tribes of the Western Plateaus," 214–17.

91. John Coffey et al., *Shuswap History*, 14.

92. The fullest discussion of aboriginal land tenure, and the quote cited here, is found in Teit, "Thompson Indians," 293–94.

93. Teit, "Shuswap," 540–63; Teit, "Thompson Indians," 293–94; see also Chance, *Influences of the HBC*, 14; Anastasio, "Southern Plateau," especially 146–59.

94. See, e.g., essays in Shepard Krech, ed., *Subarctic Fur Trade*, especially Charles Bishop, "First Century," and Toby Morantz, "Economic and Social Accommodations of the James Bay Inlanders"; also Morantz, "Probability of Family Hunting Territories."

95. B.97/a/1, fol. 16; B.97/e/1, fol. 2; D.5/7, fols. 346–48.

96. D.5/7, fols. 346–48.

97. B.97/e/1, fol. 2; B.223/b/27, fols. 37, 77–79.

98. Ross, *Adventures*, 163–64, 215; B.97/a/2, fols. 3, 11, passim; B.223/b/27, fol. 79.

99. B.97/a/1, fol. 7; B.97/a/2, fol. 2.

100. B.97/a/1, fols. 9,12; B.97/e/1, fol. 4; B.97/a/2, fol. 4; BCARS, Thompson's River Post Journal, 1841–43, entry for 3 Feb. 1842.

101. B.97/a/2, fol. 5; BCARS, Thompson's River Post Journal, 1841–43, entry for 3 Aug. 1841.

102. B.97/a/1, fol. 9.

6. Traders and Hunters I: Tales of Continuity and Change

1. Ross, *Adventures*, 137, the account of his first meeting, in 1811, with the Sahaptian groups of the Walla Walla region. His "Shaw Haptens" are Nez Percés.

2. Work, Journal No. 1, fol. 79.

3. B.146/e/2, fol. 4; B.223/b/2, fols. 4, 41. The two-thirds figure is Peter Skene Ogden's: see Williams, ed., *Ogden's Snake Country Journals*, 31.

4. The name "Flathead" is used here because traders knew them as the Flathead and it remains in general use. The people themselves now use Salish, but this usage would be confusing in this study.

5. Joseph Whitehouse, "Journal," 150; Thompson, *Narrative*, 422; B.69/e/1, fol. 1; Work, Journal No. 8, fol. 38.

6. Patrick Gass's journal of the expedition was published in 1807. Re Thompson's access, see T. C. Elliott, "Fur Trade in the Columbia River Basin Prior to 1811," 246; White, ed., *Thompson's Journals Relating to Montana*, 206 n. 94. Cox, too, may have consulted the Lewis and Clark journals before publishing his work; his comparison of interior women to Chinookan women on the coast bears a close resemblance to theirs. For other glowing accounts of the Salish Flathead see, e.g., Cox, *Columbia*, 111, 134–43, 264; Henry, *Journal*, 710.

7. B.45/e/3, fols. 5–7; B.45/e/1; BCARS, Fur Trade Returns—Columbia.

8. B.45/e/3, fol. 6.

9. An additional aim of the Plains expedition was to establish a supply trade with independent American trappers, who had no ready source of supply in the region. D.5/4, fol. 35.

10. Sources on the Plains expedition are few and scattered. See B.223/b/8, fol. 46; B.223/b/10, fol. 46; B.223/b/11, fol. 49; D.5/4, fol. 37; Glazebrook, ed., *Hargrave Correspondence*, 236; B.223/b/9, fol. 24; B.223/b/17, fol. 30; B.223/b/18, fol. 28; Rich, ed., *Ogden's Snake Country Journals*, 138.

11. BCARS, Fur Trade Returns—Columbia; Rich, ed., *Letters of John McLoughlin*, 1:59–60; Work, Journal No. 5, fol. 58; B.45/e/3, fol. 6; Meinig, *Great Columbia Plain*, 89.

12. The classic source on the coming of the horse remains Francis Haines, "Northward Spread of Horses," 435–36. See also Swagerty, "Indian Trade in the Trans-Mississippi West to 1870," 353; John Ewers, *Indian Life on the Upper Missouri*, 17–18; Teit, "Salishan Tribes," 351.

13. See, e.g., Teit, "Salishan Tribes"; H. H. Turney-High, "Flathead Indians of Montana." See also Samuel Lang, "Cultural Ecology and the Horse." Cox said the Flathead had been hunting buffalo for "several generations" when fur traders arrived (Cox, *Columbia*, 135).

14. Teit, "Salishan Tribes," 316–22; Thompson, *Narrative*, 327–28. Cf. Turney-High, "Flathead Indians," 11–12. More recently, historian Anthony McGinnis follows Thompson's account and has the Flathead and Kutenai driven from the western plains, along with the Shoshone, in the late 1700s. McGinnis, *Counting Coup*, 9–10, 25.

15. Henry, *Journal*, 703–5; T. C. Elliott, "In the Land of the Kootenai," 280–84.

16. See, e.g., Cox, *Columbia*, 135. The term "buffalo plains" or "plains" in this text refers to this extended range; "plains" (lowercase *p*) refers to the Great Plains east of the Continental Divide. On the buffalo range, see Robert Murphy and Yolanda Murphy, "Northern Shoshone and Bannock," 285; George Arthur, "Introduction to the Ecology of Early Historic Communal Bison Hunting," 56–57.

17. Teit, "Thompson Indians," 257, gives the later date of about 1830 for acquisition of the horse by the most northerly Plateau group, the Shuswap.

18. Peterson, *Sacred Encounters*, 49. The verb is *tcinés-geílci*.

19. See, e.g., Thompson, *Narrative*, 551; Ross, *Fur Hunters*, 121–24, 263–66; F.3/2, fol. 15.

20. On these developments see McGinnis, *Counting Coup*, chap. 1.

21. Thompson, *Narrative*, 330.

22. Thompson, *Narrative*, 328–32.

23. For more detailed discussion of the influence of tribal migrations, horses, disease, and trade on the rise of the Blackfoot in the region, see McGinnis, *Counting Coup*, chap. 1.

24. Thompson, *Narrative*, 345.

25. Henry, *Journal*, 399; Laura Peers, "Trade and Change on the Plateau," 3. On guns, see Ewers, *Indian Life*, chap. 3. On the Mandan horse and gun trade, see Peers, *Ojibwa of Western Canada*, 46–47, 78–79.

26. On Blackfoot resistance, see also Henry, *Journal*, chapters 19–21, 703–5; Thompson, *Narrative*, 389, 411, 423–24, 463; Cox, *Columbia*, 135; Elliott, ed., "Ross's Snake Country Journal." The extension of the fur trade to the Plateau, and the roughly coincident arrival of Americans intending to trap on their own account in Blackfoot lands, left the Blackfoot surrounded by those who would challenge their control of the trade of the western plains. Until 1831 no trader, British or American, was safe in Blackfoot territory. In that year the Blackfoot agreed to allow

the American Fur Company to build a post on their lands. For more detail and Blackfoot motivations, see Loretta Fowler, *Shared Symbols, Contested Meanings*, 24–27; McGinnis, *Counting Coup*, 31–34; Swagerty, "Indian Trade," 360–64.

27. B.69/e/1, fol. 1.

28. Thompson, *Narrative*, 422.

29. B.69/a/1, fol. 3. According to Ross, there were six to eight people per lodge. See also Anastasio, "Southern Plateau," 130–36.

30. Thompson, *Narrative*, 548–49; Cox, *Columbia*, 133–34, 169; Swagerty, "Indian Trade," 363.

31. B.69/a/1, fol. 3.

32. Thompson, *Narrative*, 533; B.45/e/2, fol. 7; B.146/e/2, fols. 7–8; B.97/a/1, fol. 9.

33. Peers, *Ojibwa of Western Canada*, 11–12.

34. Thompson, *Narrative*, 476.

35. Henry, *Journal*, 713–14.

36. Ewers, *Indian Life*, chap. 3. Breechloading repeating rifles were not in widespread use until the 1870s.

37. An excellent study is Joan Townsend, "Firearms Against Native Arms."

38. Thompson, *Narrative*, 533; B.97/a/1, fol. 9.

39. Henry, *Journal*, 708.

40. D.3/2, fols. 86, 87, 108.

41. Cox, *Columbia*, 258.

42. Stephen Barrett and Stephen Arno, "Indian Fires as an Ecological Influence," 647–50. Re grassland maintenance and other uses of burning, see Richard White, *Roots of Dependency*, 184–85; and more generally Stephen Pyne, *Fire in America*.

43. Cox, *Columbia*, 214.

44. D.3/2, fol. 108; Cox, *Columbia*, 95, 258. Re extensiveness of burning, see B.208/a/1, fol. 10; D.3/2, fol. 86; BCARS, Thompson's River Post Journal, 1841–43, entries for 18 Aug. 1841, 2 May and 19 Aug. 1842.

45. BCARS, Thompson's River Post Journal, 1841–43, e.g., entries for 18 Aug. 1841; 2 May, 18 Aug. 1842.

46. Anastasio, "Southern Plateau," 128.

47. Nancy Turner, personal communication, 25 Nov. 1991; Stuart Chalfant, "Ethnological Field Investigation," 186–87; Teit, "Salishan Tribes," 151–52.

48. B.69/a/1; Anastasio, "Southern Plateau," 130; Arthur, "Ecology of Early Bison Hunting," 99–101; Lang, "Cultural Ecology," 69.

49. White, ed., *Thompson's Journals Relating to Montana*, 102.

50. White, ed., *Thompson's Journals Relating to Montana*, 36–39, 46, 58, 94, 102, 204, 213; B.69/a/1, fols. 3, 6, 7; B.45/e/2, fol. 4; Work, Journal No. 8, fols. 33, 38; Work, Journal No. 10, Pt. II, fol. 73; Nicolas Point, "Journals," 120–28, 163–66.

51. Cox, *Columbia*, 134. On Plains buffalo hunters, cf. Richard White, *"It's Your Misfortune and None of My Own,"* 19–24.

52. B.69/a/1, fol. 3; B.45/e/2, fols. 3, 4.

53. Anastasio, "Southern Plateau," 132; Hunn et al., *Nch'i-Wana*, 22–25.

54. Thompson, *Narrative*, 533.

55. Peers, "Trade and Change," 1.

56. See especially Swagerty, "Indian Trade"; Erna Gunther, "Westward Movement of Some Plains Traits"; Peers, "Trade and Change," 1; Fraser, *Journal*, 86–87.

57. B.69/a/1; Teit, "Salishan Tribes," 342, 352–55; Lang, "Cultural Ecology," 68. For fine examples of craft work, see Peterson, *Sacred Encounters*, 52–63.

58. Elliott, ed., "Thompson's Journal: Voyage to the Mouth," 55; B.146/e/2, fol. 7.

59. Thompson, *Narrative*, 421–22; B.45/e/2, fol. 6; B.69/e/1, fol. 1; B.146/e/2, fol. 7.

60. B.223/b/2, fol. 43, Black to John McLoughlin, 25 July 1826; B.146/e/2, fol. 7; Ross, *Adventures*, 319.

61. Here I differ with Theodore Stern, who ascribes to the horse a "revolution in perspective" among the Cayuse and Nez Percé (*Chiefs and Chief Traders*, 42). As should be clear from discussion in chapters 4 and 7, I also differ with Stern on the interpretation of traders' reports of wealth and poverty among southern Plateau societies.

62. For an excellent study of the process on the coast, see Victoria Wyatt, *Shapes of Their Thoughts*, and her essay "Art and Exploration."

63. D.3/2, fol. 109.

64. See, e.g., discussion in Hunn et al., *Nch'i-Wana*, 220–25.

65. B.45/e/2, fol. 10.

66. Stern, *Chiefs and Chief Traders*, 62.

67. Jesuit Father Nicolas Point, too, was impressed with the riding prowess of eastern Plateau women. See his illustrations of women hunting and warring on horseback in Peterson, *Sacred Encounters*, 58 and 72, and fig. 2 here.

68. D.3/2, fol. 91. Re skills with horses, see, e.g., B.146/e/2, fol. 4; Work, Journal No. 4, fol. 31.

69. B.146/e/2, fol. 4.

70. Re horse stealing, see, e.g., B.146/a/1, entries for 3, 5 April 1831, re Babine Fendu. See general discussions in John Ewers, "Horse in Blackfoot Culture," 305, 308–16; Fowler, *Shared Symbols*, 26, 34, 36–37.

71. See, e.g., B.146/a/1, passim; B.146/e/1,2, passim; B.223/b/1–6, passim, Black's correspondence with McLoughlin; B.223/b/2, fol. 22; D.5/3, fol. 326. The energy devoted to the horse trade is revealed in the extent of coverage it receives in Stern, *Chiefs and Chief Traders*.

72. B.223/b/2, fols. 9, 42–43.

73. B.97/a/2, fols. 13, 14.

74. B.97/a/2, fols. 13, 14.

75. Cox, *Columbia*, 136.

76. B.69/a/1, fol. 4; Thompson, *Narrative*, 462–63. Stern concurs, noting that Plateau buffalo parties travelled "under collective leadership" (*Chiefs and Chief Traders*, 43).

77. B.69/e/1, fol. 1; Work, Journal No. 4, fols. 65–66, 71–73.

78. B.69/a/1, fol. 3; B.146/e/2, fols. 8, 9; Ross, *Adventures*, 315. See Stern, *Chiefs and Chief Traders*, 61, on the possibility of greater centralization of leadership among the Cayuse and Nez Percé. See also his cautionary remarks regarding the limited nature of leadership, 62.

79. Cf. Fowler, *Shared Symbols*, chap. 1 re the Gros Ventre.

80. See especially Ruby and Brown, *Cayuse Indians*, 3–4, 8, and passim.

81. See *Chiefs and Chief Traders*, e.g., 55, 58. For a sharply contrasting view of the river dwellers, see Hunn et al., *Nch'i-Wana*.

82. Ross, *Adventures*, 318.

83. B.45/e/2, fols. 5–6.

84. B.69/a/1, fol. 3.

85. B.145/e/2, fol. 6.

86. Van Kirk, *"Many Tender Ties,"* 19.

87. Moore, *Feminism and Anthropology*, 30.

88. Point, "Journals," 124, 128; Alan Klein, "Political Economy of Gender," 155; Ewers, *Indian Life*, 150.

89. The most detailed contemporary source from the region is Point, "Journals," 128.

90. See Klein, "Political Economy of Gender"; Patricia Albers, "From Illusion to Illumination," 142; Margot Liberty, "Hell Came with Horses"; Fowler, *Shared Symbols*, 37; Weist, "Plains Indian Women" and "Beasts of Burden."

91. See the concise discussion in Peers, *Ojibwa of Western Canada*, 122.

92. Klein, "Political Economy of Gender," 156–58; Patricia Albers, "From Illusion to Illumination," 142; Fowler, *Shared Symbols*, 37.

93. Among many examples, see Alice Beck Kehoe, "Old Woman Had Great Power" and "Shackles of Tradition"; Marla Powers, *Oglala Women*; Beatrice Medicine, "'Warrior Women.'"

94. Alice Beck Kehoe, "Transcribing Insema, a Blackfoot 'Old Lady.'"

95. See, e.g., Work, Journal No. 6, fol. 20; B.146/a/1, entries for 16, 26 April 1831; B.223/b/2, fol. 41; B.97/a/3, fol. 14.

96. B.69/e/1, fol. 4. Re women's trade, see, e.g., Work, Journal No. 4, fols. 156, 163; B.45/a/1, fol. 29.

97. Ross, *Adventures*, 318, 324–25.

98. Cox, *Columbia*, 136–37, 142–43.

99. Robert Fulton and Steven Anderson argue that "berdache" originates in the Arabic *bardaj*, meaning "a boy slave kept for sexual purposes" ("Amerindian 'Man-Woman,'" 603.) This particular pejorative etymology does not fit well with fur-trade or later anthropological usages. The *Oxford English Dictionary* finds the root in the French fur trade in North America.

100. On the institution of the berdache and its specific expression in various societies, see Walter Williams, *Spirit and the Flesh*; Evelyn Blackwood, "Sexuality and Gender," and other sources cited below.

101. This stance is taken in the interests of brevity, and is not without its problems. For discussion of the ways in which "berdache" and "amazon" roles differed, see Blackwood, "Sexuality and Gender," and Paula Gunn Allen, *Sacred Hoop*, 96.

102. A synthesis of historical and ethnographic evidence is presented in Charles Callender and Lee Kochems, "North American Berdache."

103. Will Roscoe, "We'Wha and Klah," 128–33; Williams, *Spirit and the Flesh*, 69.

104. Thompson, *Narrative*, 437, 512–13; Franchère, *Journal*, 85, 88; Ross, *Adventures*, 92, 111, 156–58.

105. Ross, *Adventures*, 156–58.

106. Cox, *Columbia*, 190–92.

107. Work, Journal No. 4, fols. 159–60. Cf. Claude Schaeffer, "Kutenai Female Berdache," 213–14.

108. B.146/a/1, fol. 4; B.223/b/9, fol. 23; Work, Journal No. 11, fol. 7. See also Stern, *Chiefs and Chief Traders*, 162. Stern points out that the Nez Percé word for men of transformed gender is *si'méec*.

109. See discussion in Albers, "From Illusion to Illumination," 133–39; Callender and Kochems, "North American Berdache"; Beatrice Medicine, "'Warrior Women,'" and in sources cited above.

110. See discussion in Williams, *Spirit and the Flesh*; Callender and Kochems, "North American Berdache," 451–53.

7. Traders and Hunters II: Images of Wealth and Manly Virtue

1. Vibert, "Real Men Hunt Buffalo" (*Gender & History*, 1996), provides a distinctive analysis of some of the documentary material in this chapter, including the interweaving of gender and class in the image of the buffalo hunter.

2. For an insightful and entertaining account of the Jesuit mission, see Peterson and Peers, *Sacred Encounters*.

3. Point, "Journals," 145–47, 121.

4. Point, "Journals," 121–24.

5. Point, "Journals," 124.

6. Point, "Journals," 125–28.

7. Point, "Journals," 120, 128.

8. Melman, *Women's Orients*, chap. 4.

9. Lavater quoted in Melman, *Women's Orients*, 113.

10. B.45/e/2, fol. 12; Thompson, *Narrative*, 435; Fraser, *Journal*, 145.

11. Himmelfarb, *Idea of Poverty*, 371.

12. It might, in fact, signify the ability to raise horses or produce other goods in surplus for trade with hunters. Traders, however, tended to equate leather clothing with hunting.

13. D.3/2, fols. 86, 98.

14. D.3/2, fol. 86.

15. Cox, *Columbia*, 88, 259–60.

16. Joseph McGillivray, Fort Alexandria District Report 1827, 212.

17. Ross, *Adventures*, 97, 99.

18. Ross, *Adventures*, 320; B.146/e/2, fol. 7; B.45/e/2, fol. 6.

19. Lawrence, "William Buchan," 25–26.

20. Thompson, *Narrative*, 415, 467, 488; Cox, *Columbia*, 111, 267; B.69/a/1, fol. 3.

21. B.146/e/2, fol. 7.

22. B.45/e/2, fol. 5.

23. Thompson, *Narrative*, 533.

24. Cox, *Columbia*, 264, 267.

25. Thompson, *Narrative*, 463.

26. Thompson, *Narrative*, 548–52.

27. Thompson, *Narrative*, 548–52.

28. D.3/1, fol. 11; D.3/2, fol. 93.

29. Ross, *Fur Hunters*, 243, 283.

30. Thompson, *Narrative*, 432; Ross, *Fur Hunters*, 243, 283.

31. Bhabha, *Location of Culture*, chaps. 3 and 4.

32. For more discussion of the conflicts between middle-class and aristocratic notions of manhood, see Vibert, "Real Men Hunt Buffalo."

33. For narratives of British sport hunters in Africa and India, see especially MacKenzie, *Empire of Nature*.

34. B.69/a/1, fols. 3, 6; Cox, *Columbia*, 134; B.45/e/3, fols. 12–13.

35. Thompson, *Narrative*, 411, 420, 424.

36. Thompson, *Narrative*, 411, 463.

37. See discussions in Ludmilla Jordanova, "Earth Science and Environmental Medicine" and *Sexual Visions*; Richard Grove, *Green Imperialism*; P. J. Marshall and Glyndwr Williams, *Great Map of Mankind*.

38. Thompson, *Narrative*, 411, 420, 424, 463, 549; Rollins, "Journey of Mr. Hunt and His Companions," 303.

39. Ross, *Fur Hunters*, 48–52, 114.

40. Ross's enthusiasm apparently got the better of him. Archaeological evidence indicates that the fort was rather smaller than he recalled. See Stern, *Chiefs and Chief Traders*, chap. 1.

41. For recent studies analyzing nineteenth-century British imperialism as a profound historical expression of British masculinity,

see Graham Dawson, "Blond Bedouin"; Catherine Hall, *White, Male, and Middle Class*; J. A. Mangan and James Walvin, eds., *Manliness and Morality*; Lynne Segal, *Slow Motion*, especially chap. 7; Mrinalini Sinha, "Gender and Imperialism." Also suggestive on this theme are Helen Callaway, *Gender, Culture, and Empire*; Chandra Talpade Mohanty, "Introduction: Cartographies of Struggle." See also additional sources cited in Vibert, "Real Men Hunt Buffalo."

42. Ross, *Fur Hunters*, 154–55; B.146/a/1, 2 passim; B.223/b/11, fol. 49.

43. Class aspects of trader discourse are developed more fully in Vibert, "Real Men Hunt Buffalo."

44. Rich, ed., *Ogden's Snake Country Journals, 1824–26*, 15.

45. Rich, ed., *Ogden's Snake Country Journals, 1824–26*, 15, 58.

46. See, e.g., Work, Journal No. 4, fols. 165–68; Work, Journal No. 10, Pt. II, fols. 11, 17, 18; Rich, ed., *Ogden's Snake Country Journal, 1824–26*, 9, 62, 63, 84; William Kittson, "Journal of . . . Trapping Party to and from the Snake Country," 210, 237–39, 244–45.

47. That Pocahontas remains a significant icon in at least the Hollywood imagination is revealed in the 1995 release of the blockbuster Disney animated film *Pocahontas*. Sacajawea was the Shoshone woman who, rather like Pocahontas, was reputed to have saved the men of the Lewis and Clark expedition from her hostile people and showed them the way through the Rockies to Oregon. For the discussion that follows I am indebted to a conversation with Rayna Green; see her "Tribe Called Wannabee," 34–39. For an interesting older treatment, see John Ewers, "Emergence of the Plains Indian."

48. Cooper, *Prairie*, especially chap. 18; the quotation is from Cooper, *Notions of the Americans*, 491.

49. Cooper, *Notions of the Americans*, 490–91.

50. See also Ewers, "Emergence of the Plains Indian," 531–33.

51. On Rindisbacher, see Susan Hopkins Stewart, "Hudson's Bay Company's Contribution to the Work of Three Important Artists," chap. 2; and Alvin Josephy, *Artist Was a Young Man*.

52. George Catlin, *Letters and Notes on the North American Indians*, 89.

53. Catlin, *Letters and Notes*, 97–98.

54. Francis, *Imaginary Indian*, 16–23; Paul Kane, *Wanderings of an Artist*.

55. Green, "Tribe Called Wannabee," 36.

56. Green, "Tribe Called Wannabe," 38.

57. Cox, *Columbia*, 264, 267; Ross, *Fur Hunters*, 166.

58. See, e.g., MacKenzie, *Empire of Nature*, and William Beinart's response in "Empire, Hunting, and Ecological Change"; see also Beinart, "Introduction," and other essays in the special issue "Colonial Conservation," *Journal of Southern African Studies* 15 (2) (1989); Mahesh Rangarajan, "Hunting and Conservation"; Richard Grove, "Scottish Missionaries, Evangelical Discourses."

59. See especially Mahesh Rangarajan, "Hunting and Conservation."

60. MacKenzie, *Empire of Nature*, 172–73.

61. Quoted in MacKenzie, *Empire of Nature*, 175.

62. See Rangarajan, "Hunting and Conservation," 155–58 and passim.

63. MacKenzie, *Empire of Nature*, 86–89.

64. J. M. Coetzee, *White Writings*, 32.

65. MacKenzie, *Empire of Nature*, 92, 95; Beinart, "Empire, Hunting," 163.

66. MacKenzie, *Empire of Nature*, 95.

67. Quoted in Beinart, "Empire, Hunting," 163.

68. Beinart, "Empire, Hunting," 167, 174; Rangarajan, "Hunting and Conservation"; Richard Grove, "Scottish Missionaries, Evangelical Discourses"; Terence Ranger, "Whose Heritage?"

8. Concluding Remarks

1. Representatives of the Canadian media speak routinely in the language of "concessions" and "capitulation." See, for example, a story on provincial party positions on land-settlement issues and treaties in *British Columbia Report*, June 6, 1994, p. 8.

2. See the special issue of *B.C. Studies* entitled "Anthropology and History in the Courts"; and Hamar Foster, "It Goes Without Saying: Precedent and the Doctrine of Extinguishment."

3. McEachern, "Reasons for Judgement," 48–49.

4. McEachern, "Reasons for Judgement," 52.

5. McEachern, "Reasons for Judgement," 13, 24, 25, 53, 73, 129.

6. McEachern, "Reasons for Judgement," 129.

Bibliography

Primary Sources

Unpublished

British Columbia Archives and Records Service (BCARS), Victoria
    Fur Trade Returns for Columbia and New Caledonia, 1825–57
    Donald Ross Papers
    John Stuart, Journal at the Rocky Mountain, 1805–6
    Thompson's River Post Journal, 1841–43
    John Work Journals, 1823–34
Hudson's Bay Company Archives (HBCA), Winnipeg
    Section A: Headquarters Records
    Section B: Post Records
    Section D: Governors' Papers
    Section E: Miscellaneous Records
    Section F: Records of Allied and Subsidiary Companies
    PP 1828-1 Queries Connected with Natural History
Public Archives of Canada, Ottawa (PAC)
    Edward Ermatinger Papers, 1820–74
    John McLeod Papers, 1823–49 (transcript in BCARS)
    Selkirk Papers (transcript in BCARS)
Rhodes House, Oxford, England
    Aborigines' Protection Society, Annual Reports
    Aborigines' Protection Society, Transactions
    Church Missionary Society, Reports of the Columbia Mission
University of British Columbia Library, Special Collections Division,
    Vancouver (UBC Sp.Coll.)
    Alexander Caulfield Anderson Papers

Edward Ermatinger Papers, 1820–74 (transcript)
Francis Ermatinger, Notes of Clallum Expedition, 1828
Archibald McDonald, Fort Langley Journal, 1827–28

Published

Catlin, George. *Letters and Notes on the North American Indians.* Edited by Michael Mooney. [London, 1841] New York: Clarkson N. Potter, 1970.

Colonial Intelligencer; or Aborigines' Friend (Rhodes House, Oxford, England).

Cooper, James Fenimore. *Notions of the Americans, Picked up by a Travelling Bachelor.* [1828] Edited by Gary Williams. Albany: State University of New York, 1991.

Coues, Elliott, ed. *New Light on the Early History of the Greater Northwest: The Manuscript Journals of Alexander Henry and David Thompson.* Vol.2, *Henry's Journal.* [1897] Minneapolis: Ross and Haines, 1965.

Cox, Ross. *The Columbia River, or Scenes and Adventures. . . .* Edited by E. I. Stewart and J. R. Stewart. [London, 1831] Norman: University of Oklahoma Press, 1957.

Davies, K. G., ed. *Peter Skene Ogden's Snake Country Journal, 1826–27.* London: Hudson's Bay Record Society, 1961.

Defoe, Daniel. *A Tour Thro' the Whole Island of Great Britain. . . .* Vol. 2. [1778] Edited by G. D. H. Cole. London: Peter Davies, 1927.

Douglas, David. "Excerpts from Journals, Letters from Travels on Columbia River, 1826; 1833–34." In "A Brief Memoir of the Life of Mr. David Douglas, with Extracts from his Letters," edited by W. J. Hooker. *Companion to the Botanical Magazine*, 2. London, 1836.

Elliott, T. C., ed. "Thompson's Journeys in the Spokane Country . . . 1811." *Washington Historical Quarterly* 9 (1910).

———, ed. "Journal of Alexander Ross, Snake Country Expedition, 1824," *Oregon Historical Quarterly* 14 (1913).

———, ed. "Thompson's Journal: Voyage to the Mouth of the Columbia . . . 1811." *Oregon Historical Quarterly* 15 (1914).

———, ed. "Thompson's Narrative of the Expedition to the Kootenae and Flat Bow Indian Countries . . . 1807." *Oregon Historical Quarterly* 26 (1925).

Ermatinger, Edward. "York Factory Express Journal ... 1827–1828." *Transactions of the Royal Society of Canada* 6 (1912), sec. 2.

Fleming, R. Harvey, ed. *Minutes of Council, Northern Department of Rupert Land, 1821–31.* Toronto: Champlain Society, 1940.

Franchère, Gabriel. *Journal.* In *Franchère's Journal of a Voyage on the North West Coast of North America During the Years 1811–14*, edited by W. Kaye Lamb. Translated by W. T. Lamb. Toronto: Champlain Society, 1969.

Fraser, Simon. *Journal.* In *The Letters and Journals of Simon Fraser, 1806–1808*, edited by W. Kaye Lamb. Toronto: Macmillan Company, 1960.

A Fur Trader. *Traits of American Indian Life and Character.* London: Smith, Elder and Co., 1853.

Glazebrook, G. P. de T., ed. *The Hargrave Correspondence, 1821–1843.* Toronto: Champlain Society, 1938.

Harmon, Daniel Williams. *Journal, 1800–1816.* In *Sixteen Years in the Indian Country: The Journal of Daniel Williams Harmon*, edited by W. Kaye Lamb. Toronto: Macmillan, 1957.

Henry, Alexander. *Journal.* [1897] In *New Light on the Early History of the Greater Northwest: The Manuscript Journals of Alexander Henry and David Thompson*, vol.2, *Henry's Journal*, edited by Elliott Coues. Minneapolis: Ross and Haines, 1965.

Johnson, Samuel. *A Journey to the Western Islands of Scotland.* [London, 1775] Edited by Mary Lascelles. New Haven: Yale University Press, 1971.

Kane, Paul. *Wanderings of an Artist Among the Indians of North America ... through the Hudson's Bay Company Territory and Back Again.* [1859] Edited by John Garvin. Toronto: Radisson Society, 1925.

Kittson, William. "Journal of Occurrences in a Trapping Party to and from the Snake Country in the Years 1824 and (25)." In *Peter Skene Ogden's Snake Country Journals, 1824–25 and 1825–26*, edited by E. E. Rich. London: Hudson's Bay Record Society, 1950.

Lamb, W. Kaye, ed. *Sixteen Years in the Indian Country: The Journal of Daniel Williams Harmon.* Toronto: Macmillan, 1957.

———, ed. *The Letters and Journals of Simon Fraser, 1806–1808.* Toronto: Macmillan Company, 1960.

328 Bibliography

———, ed. *Franchère's Journal of a Voyage on the North West Coast of North America during the Years 1811–14.* Translated by W. T.Lamb. Toronto: Champlain Society, 1969.

———, ed. *The Journals and Letters of Sir Alexander Mackenzie.* Cambridge: Cambridge University Press for the Hakluyt Society, 1970.

McDonald, Archibald. "Journal." In *Peace River: A Canoe Voyage from Hudson's Bay to Pacific, by George Simpson,* edited by Malcolm McLeod. Edmonton: M. G. Hurtig, 1971.

McGillivray, William. "Some Account of the Trade Carried on by the North West Company." *Report of the Public Archives of Canada,* 1928.

McLean, John. *Notes of a Twenty-Five Years' Service in the Hudson's Bay Territories.* [1849] Edited by W. S. Wallace. Toronto: Champlain Society, 1932.

Mengarini, Gregory. *Recollections of the Flathead Mission.* Translated by Gloria Lothrop. Glendale, CA: Arthur H. Clark, 1977.

Merk, Frederick, ed. *Fur Trade and Empire: George Simpson's Journal . . . 1824–25.* [1931] Cambridge, MA: Harvard University Press, 1968.

Miller, Alfred J. *Braves and Buffalo: Plains Indian Life in 1837.* Edited by Michael Bell. Toronto: University of Toronto Press, 1973.

Point, Nicolas. "Journals." In *Wilderness Kingdom: Indian Life in the Rocky Mountains, 1840–1847: The Journals and Paintings of Nicolas Point, S.J.,* edited and translated by Joseph P. Donnelly. New York: Holt, Rinehart and Winston, 1967.

Rich, E. E., ed. *The Letters of John McLoughlin from Fort Vancouver to the Governor and Committee.* Vol.1. London: Hudson's Bay Record Society, 1941.

———, ed. *The Letters of John McLoughlin. . . .* Vol.2. London: Hudson's Bay Record Society, 1943.

———, ed. *Part of Dispatch from George Simpson Esqr . . . 1829.* London: Hudson's Bay Record Society, 1947.

———, ed. *Peter Skene Ogden's Snake Country Journals, 1824–25 and 1825–26.* London: Hudson's Bay Record Society, 1950.

Rollins, Phillip A., ed. "Robert Stuart's Narratives." In *The Discovery of the Oregon Trail.* New York: Edward Eberstadt, 1935.

———, ed. "Journey of Mr. Hunt and His Companions from Saint Louis to the Mouth of the Columbia by a New Route Across the Rocky

Mountains." In *The Discovery of the Oregon Trail*, edited by Phillip A. Rollins. New York: Edward Eberstadt, 1935.

Ross, Alexander. *Adventures of the First Settlers on the Oregon or Columbia River.* [London, 1849] Chicago: Lakeside Press, 1923.

———. *Fur Hunters of the Far West.* [London, 1855] Edited by Kenneth A. Spaulding. Norman: University of Oklahoma Press, 1956.

———. "Journal . . . Snake Country Expedition, 1824." Edited by T. C. Elliott. *Oregon Historical Quarterly* 14 (1913).

Shortt, A., and A. G. Doughty, eds. *Documents Relating to the Constitutional History of Canada, 1759–91.* Ottawa: Taché, 1918.

Simpson, George. *Journal 1824–25: Remarks Connected with the Fur Trade in the Course of a Voyage. . . .* [1931] In *Fur Trade and Empire: George Simpson's Journal . . . 1824–25*, edited by Frederick Merk. Cambridge, MA: Harvard University Press, 1968.

———. *Narrative of a Journey Around the World.* Vol. 1. London: Henry Colburn, 1847.

Thompson, David. *Narrative.* In *David Thompson's Narrative of his Explorations in Western America, 1784–1812*, edited by J. B. Tyrrell. Toronto: Champlain Society, 1916.

Thwaites, Reuben Gold, ed. *Original Journals of the Lewis and Clark Expedition 1804–06.* New York: Dodd, Mead and Co., 1905.

Tyrrell, J. B., ed. *David Thompson's Narrative of his Explorations in Western America, 1784–1812.* Toronto: Champlain Society, 1916.

Umfreville, Edward. *The Present State of Hudson's Bay.* London, 1790.

Wallace, W. Stewart. *Documents Relating to the North West Company.* Toronto: Champlain Society, 1934.

White, M. Catherine, ed. *David Thompson's Journals Relating to Montana and Adjacent Regions, 1808–1812.* Missoula: Montana State University Press, 1950.

Whitehouse, Joseph. "Journal." In *Original Journals of the Lewis and Clark Expedition 1804–06*, edited by Reuben Gold Thwaites. New York: Dodd, Mead and Co., 1905.

Williams, Glyndwr, ed. *Peter Skene Ogden's Snake Country Journals 1827–28 and 1828–29.* London: Hudson's Bay Record Society, 1971.

———, ed. *London Correspondence Inward from Sir George Simpson 1841–42.* London: Hudson's Bay Record Society, 1973.

————, ed. "The Character Book of George Simpson, 1832." In *Hudson's Bay Miscellany, 1670–1870*. Winnipeg: Hudson's Bay Record Society, 1975.

————, ed. *Andrew Graham's Observations on Hudson's Bay, 1767–91*. London: Hudson's Bay Record Society, 1969.

Secondary Sources

Aberle, David. "The Prophet Dance and Reactions to White Contact." *Southwestern Journal of Anthropology* 15 (1959).

Ackerman, Lillian. "Sexual Equality on the Colville Indian Reservation." In *Women in Pacific Northwest History*, edited by Karen Blair. Seattle: University of Washington, 1988.

Aguayo, Anna de. "On Power and Prophecy: A Nineteenth Century Prophet Movement Amongst the Carrier Indians." Master's thesis, London School of Economics, 1987.

Albers, Patricia. "From Illusion to Illumination: Anthropological Studies of American Indian Women." In *Gender and Anthropology*, edited by Sandra Morgen. New York: American Anthropological Association, 1989.

Albers, Patricia, and Beatrice Medicine, eds. *The Hidden Half: Studies of Plains Indian Women*. Washington, DC: University Press of America, 1983.

Allen, Paula Gunn. *The Sacred Hoop: Recovering the Feminine in American Indian Traditions*. Boston: Beacon Press, 1986.

Anastasio, Angelo. "The Southern Plateau: An Ecological Analysis of Intergroup Relations." *Northwest Anthropological Research Notes* 6 (2) (1972).

Anderson, David, and Richard Grove. "Introduction: The Scramble for Eden." In *Conservation in Africa: People, Policies, and Practice*, edited by Anderson and Grove. Cambridge: Cambridge University Press, 1987.

"Anthropology and History in the Courts." *B.C. Studies* 95 (1992), special issue.

Arthur, George. *An Introduction to the Ecology of Early Historic Communal Bison Hunting Among the Northern Plains Indians*. National Museum of Man, Archaeological Survey of Canada Paper 37. Ottawa: Supply and Services, Canada, 1975.

Axtell, James. *After Columbus: Essays in the Ethnohistory of Colonial North America.* New York: Oxford University Press, 1988.

Baker, James. "Archaeological Research Concerning the Origins of the Okanagan People." In *Okanagan Sources*, edited by Jean Webber and the En'owkin Centre. Penticton, BC: Theytus Books, 1990.

Balf, Mary. *The Dispossessed: Interior Indians in the 1800s.* Kamloops, BC: Kamloops Museum, n.d.

Barnes, Trevor J., and James S. Duncan, eds. *Writing Worlds: Discourse, Text, and Metaphor in the Representation of Landscape.* London: Routledge, 1992.

Barrett, Stephen, and Stephen Arno. "Indian Fires as an Ecological Influence in the Northern Rockies." *Journal of Forestry* 80 (10) (1982).

Bataille, Gretchen, and Kathleen Mullen Sands. *American Indian Women: Telling their Lives.* Lincoln: University of Nebraska Press, 1984.

Beinart, William. "Introduction." In "Special Issue on Colonial Conservation." *Journal of Southern African Studies* 15 (1989).

———. "Empire, Hunting, and Ecological Change in Southern and Central Africa." *Past and Present* 128 (1990).

Belich, James. *The New Zealand Wars and the Victorian Interpretation of Racial Conflict.* Auckland: Auckland University Press, 1986.

Berkhofer, Robert. *The White Man's Indian.* New York: Vantage, 1978.

Bermingham, Ann. *Landscape and Ideology: The English Rustic Tradition, 1740–1860.* Berkeley: University of California Press, 1986.

Bhabha, Homi. "The Other Question." In *The Sexual Subject: A Screen Reader in Sexuality*, edited by M. Merck. London: Routledge, 1992.

———. *The Location of Culture.* London: Routledge, 1994.

Biersack, Aletta. "Local Knowledge, Local History: Geertz and Beyond." In *The New Cultural History*, edited by Lynn Hunt. Berkeley: University of California Press, 1989.

Bishop, Charles. "The First Century: Adaptive Changes Among the Western James Bay Cree." In *The Subarctic Fur Trade: Native Social and Economic Adaptations*, edited by Shepard Krech. Vancouver: University of British Columbia Press, 1983.

Black-Rogers, Mary. "Varieties of 'Starving': Semantics and Survival in the Subarctic Fur Trade." *Ethnohistory* 33 (4) (1986).

Blackwood, Evelyn. "Sexuality and Gender in Certain Native American Tribes: The Case of Cross-Gender Females." *Signs* 10 (1984): 27–42.

Bourdieu, Pierre. *Outline of a Theory of Practice*. Cambridge: Cambridge University Press, 1977.

Boyd, Robert. "The Introduction of Infectious Diseases Among the Indians of the Pacific Northwest, 1774–1874." Ph.D. diss., University of Washington, 1985.

———. "Demographic History, 1774–1874." In *Northwest Coast*, edited by Wayne Suttles. Vol. 7, *Handbook of North American Indians*, edited by W. C. Sturtevant. Washington, DC: Smithsonian Institution, 1990.

Brent, Marie. "Indian Lore: My Life." *Okanagan Historical Society Report* 30 (1966).

Brettell, Caroline. "Nineteenth-Century Travellers' Accounts of the Mediterranean Peasant." *Ethnohistory* 33 (2) (1986).

Briggs, Asa. *The Age of Improvement*. [1959] London: Longman, 1979.

Brody, Hugh. *Maps and Dreams: Indians and the British Columbia Frontier*. London: Faber and Faber, 1981.

———. *Living Arctic: Hunters of the Canadian North*. Vancouver: Douglas and McIntyre, 1987.

Brown, Jennifer S. H. *Strangers in Blood: Fur Trade Company Families in Indian Country*. Vancouver: University of British Columbia Press, 1980.

———. "The Blind Men and the Elephant: Fur Trade History Revisited." In *Proceedings of the Fort Chipewyan and Fort Vermilion Bicentennial Conference*, edited by Patricia McCormack and Geoffrey Ironside. Edmonton: Boreal Institute for Northern Studies, 1990.

Brown, Jennifer S. H., and Robert Brightman. *"The Orders of the Dreamed": George Nelson on Cree and Northern Ojibwa Religion and Myth, 1823*. Winnipeg: University of Manitoba Press, 1988.

Brown, Jennifer S. H., and Elizabeth Vibert, eds. *Reading Beyond Words: Contexts for Native History*. Peterborough, ON: Broadview Press, 1996.

Brown, Jennifer S. H., and Laura Peers. "The Chippewa and Their Neighbours: A Critical Review." In *The Chippewa and Their Neighbours: A Study in Ethnohistory*, edited by Harold Hickerson. Rev. ed. Prospect Heights, IL: Waveland, 1988.

Brown, Kathleen M. "The Anglo-Algonquian Gender Frontier." In *Negotiators of Change: Historical Perspectives on Native American Women*, edited by Nancy Shoemaker. New York and London: Routledge, 1995.

Brumberg, Joan Jacobs. *Fasting Girls: The Emergence of Anorexia Nervosa as a Modern Disease*. Cambridge, MA: Harvard University Press, 1988.

Buchan, William. *The New Domestic Medicine; or A Treatise on the Prevention and Cure of Diseases, by Regimen and Simple Medicines*. London: Thomas Kelly, 1827.

Burgner, Robert. "Life History of Sockeye Salmon." In *Pacific Salmon Life Histories*, edited by C. Groot and L. Margolis. Vancouver: University of British Columbia Press, 1991.

Burnett, John. *A History of the Cost of Living*. London: Pelican Books, 1969.

Callaway, Helen. *Gender, Culture, and Empire: European Women in Colonial Nigeria*. Urbana: University of Illinois Press, 1987.

Callender, Charles, and Lee Kochems. "The North American Berdache." *Current Anthropology* 24 (4) (1983).

Campbell, Marjorie Wilkins. *The North West Company*. Vancouver: Douglas and McIntyre, 1983.

Campbell, Sarah. *PostColumbian Culture History in the Northern Columbia Plateau: A.D. 1500–1900*. New York: Garland, 1990.

Carstens, Peter. *The Queen's People: A Study of Hegemony, Coercion, and Accommodation Among the Okanagan*. Toronto: University of Toronto Press, 1991.

Carter, Paul. *The Road to Botany Bay: An Essay in Spatial History*. London: Faber and Faber, 1987.

Chalfant, Stuart. "Ethnological Field Investigation . . . Relative to Coeur d'Alene Indian Aboriginal Distribution." In *Historical Material Relative to Coeur d'Alene Indian Aboriginal Distribution*, edited by Stuart Chalfant. New York: Garland Publishing, Inc., 1974.

Chance, David. *Influences of the Hudson's Bay Company on the Native Cultures of the Colvile District. Northwest Anthropological Research Notes*, Memoir 2. 1973.

Chartier, Roger. "Texts, Printing, Readings." In *The New Cultural History*, edited by Lynn Hunt. Berkeley: University of California Press, 1989.

Chatwin, Bruce. *The Songlines*. London: Penguin Books, 1987.

Chiapelli, Fredi, ed. *First Images of America: The Impact of the New World on the Old*. 2 vols. Berkeley: University of California Press, 1976.

Chittenden, Hiram M. [1902] *The American Fur Trade of the Far West*. Lincoln: University of Nebraska Press, 1986.

Clayton, Daniel. "Captain Cook and the Spaces of Contact at 'Nootka Sound.'" In *Reading Beyond Words: Contexts for Native History*, edited by Jennifer S. H. Brown and Elizabeth Vibert. Peterborough, ON: Broadview Press, 1996.

Clifford, James. *The Predicament of Culture: Twentieth-Century Ethnography, Literature, and Art*. Cambridge, MA: Harvard University Press, 1988.

Clifton, James A. *Being and Becoming Indian: Biographical Studies of North American Frontiers*. Chicago: Dorsey Press, 1989.

Cline, Walter. "Religion and World View." In *The Sinkaietk or Southern Okanagon of Washington*, edited by Leslie Spier. Menasha, WI: George Banta, 1938.

Coates, Colin M. "Like 'The Thames towards Putney': The Appropriation of Landscape in Lower Canada." *Canadian Historical Review* 74 (3) (1993).

Coetzee, J. M. *White Writings: On the Culture of Letters in South Africa*. New Haven: Yale University Press, 1988.

Coffey, John, et.al. *Shuswap History: The First 100 Years of Contact*. Kamloops, BC: Secwepemc Cultural Education Society, 1990.

Cohen, David W. "The Undefining of Oral Tradition." *Ethnohistory* 36 (1) (1989).

Collier, Jane, and Michelle Rosaldo. "Politics and Gender in Simple Societies." In *Sexual Meanings: The Cultural Construction of Gender and Sexuality*, edited by Sherry Ortner and Harriet Whitehead. Cambridge: Cambridge University Press, 1981.

Cooper, James Fenimore. *The Prairie*. [1827] New York: Dodd, Mead, 1954.

Cowan, Ian, and Charles Guiguet. *The Mammals of British Columbia*. Victoria: British Columbia Provincial Museum, 1956.

Cowdrey, Albert. *This Land, This South: An Environmental History*. Kentucky: University of Kentucky Press, 1983.

Cronon, William. *Changes in the Land: Indians, Colonists, and the Ecology of New England*. New York: Hill and Wang, 1983.

————. "Modes of Prophecy and Production: Placing Nature in History." *Journal of American History* 76 (4) (1990).

————. "A Place for Stories: Nature, History, and Narrative." *Journal of American History* 78 (4) (1992).

Crosby, Alfred. "Virgin Soil Epidemics in the Aboriginal Depopulation of America." *William and Mary Quarterly* 33 (2) (1976).

————. *Ecological Imperialism: The Biological Expansion of Europe, 900–1900*. Cambridge: Cambridge University Press, 1986.

————. "Summary on Population Size Before and After Contact." In *Disease and Demography in the Americas*, edited by John W. Verano and Douglas Ubelaker. Washington, DC: Smithsonian Institution Press, 1992.

Cruikshank, Julie. "Introduction: Life History and Life Stories." In *Life Lived Like a Story*, by Julie Cruikshank with Angela Sidney, Kitty Smith, and Annie Ned. Vancouver: University of British Columbia Press, 1991.

————. "Oral Tradition and Oral History: Reviewing Some Issues." *Canadian Historical Review* 85 (3) (1995).

————. "Discovering Gold on the Klondike: Perspectives from Oral Tradition." In *Reading Beyond Words: Contexts for Native History*, edited by Jennifer S. H. Brown and Elizabeth Vibert. Peterborough, ON: Broadview Press, 1996.

Cruikshank, Julie, with Angela Sidney, Kitty Smith, and Annie Ned. *Life Lived Like a Story*. Vancouver: University of British Columbia Press, 1991.

Dahlberg, Frances. *Woman the Gatherer*. New Haven: Yale University Press, 1981.

Dalton, George. "The Impact of Colonization on Aboriginal Economies in Stateless Societies." *Research in Economic Anthropology* 1 (1) (1978).

Daniels, Stephen. "The Political Iconography of Woodland in Later Georgian England." In *The Iconography of Landscape: Essays on the Symbolic Representation, Design, and Use of Past Environments*, edited by Denis Cosgrove and Stephen Daniels. Cambridge: Cambridge University Press, 1988.

Daniels, Stephen, and Denis Cosgrove. "Introduction: Iconography and Landscape." In *The Iconography of Landscape: Essays on the Symbolic Representation, Design, and Use of Past Environments*, edited by Denis Cosgrove and Stephen Daniels. Cambridge: Cambridge University Press, 1988.

Davidoff, Leonore, and Catherine Hall. *Family Fortunes: Men and Women of the English Middle Class, 1780–1850*. Chicago: University of Chicago Press, 1987.

Dawson, Graham. "The Blond Bedouin: Lawrence of Arabia, Imperial Adventure, and the Imagining of English-British Masculinity." In *Manful Assertions: Masculinities in Britain since 1800*, edited by Michael Roper and John Tosh. London and New York: Routledge, London, 1991.

DeMallie, Raymond. "The Lakota Ghost Dance: An Ethnohistorical Account." *Pacific Historical Review* 51 (1982): 385–405.

Deneven, William. "Native American Populations in 1492: Recent Research and Revised Hemispheric Estimate." In *The Native Population of the Americas in 1492*, edited by William Deneven. 2nd ed. Madison: University of Wisconsin Press, 1992.

Desmond, Gerald. *Gambling Among the Yakima*. Catholic University of America Anthropological Series, no. 14. Washington, DC, 1952.

Dickason, Olive P. *The Myth of the Savage, and the Beginnings of French Colonialism in the Americas*. Edmonton: University of Alberta Press, 1984.

Dirks, Nicholas, Geoff Eley, and Sherry Ortner, eds. *Culture/Power/History: A Reader in Contemporary Social Theory*. Princeton: Princeton University Press, 1994.

Dobyns, Henry. "Estimating Aboriginal American Populations: An Appraisal of Techniques with a New Hemispheric Estimate." *Current Anthropology* 7 (1966).

———. "Disease Transfer at Contact," *Annual Review of Anthropology* 22 (1993).

Dominguez, Virginia. "Invoking Culture: The Messy Side of 'Cultural Politics.'" *South Atlantic Quarterly* 91 (1) (1992).

Douglas, Mary. *Natural Symbols: Explorations in Cosmology.* New York: Vintage Books, 1973.

———. *Implicit Meanings: Essays in Anthropology.* London: Routledge and Kegan Paul, 1975.

Drury, Clifford H., ed. *The Diaries and Letters of Henry H. Spaulding and Asa Bowen Smith.* Glendale, CA: Arthur H. Clark, 1958.

Du Bois, Cora. *The 1870 Ghost Dance.* Publications in Anthropological Records, no. 3. Berkeley and Los Angeles: University of California Press, 1939.

Duff, Wilson. *The Indian History of British Columbia.* Vol. 1, *The Impact of the White Man.* Victoria: University of British Columbia Provincial Museum, 1964.

Elliott, John H. "Renaissance Europe and America: A Blunted Impact?." In *First Images of America: The Impact of the New World on the Old,* edited by Fredi Chiapelli. 2 vols. Berkeley: University of California Press, 1976.

Elliott, T. C. "The Fur Trade in the Columbia River Basin Prior to 1811." *Oregon Historical Quarterly* 15 (1914): 43–63.

———. "In the Land of the Kootenai." *OHQ* 27 (3) (1926): 106–25.

Elmendorf, William. "Linguistic and Geographic Relations in the Northern Plateau Area." *Southwestern Journal of Anthropology* 21 (1965): 63–78.

Etienne, Mona, and Eleanor Leacock, eds. *Women and Colonization.* New York: Praeger, 1980.

Ewers, John. *The Horse in Blackfoot Culture, with Comparative Material from other Western Tribes.* Bureau of American Ethnology Bulletin 159. Washington, DC: Government Printing Office, 1955.

———. "The Emergence of the Plains Indian as the Symbol of the North American Indian." *Annual Report of the . . . Smithsonian Institution, 1964.* Washington, DC, 1965.

———. *Indian Life on the Upper Missouri.* Norman: University of Oklahoma Press, 1968.

Fiddes, Nick. *Meat: A Natural Symbol.* London and New York: Routledge, 1991.

Fisher, Robin. "Indian Warfare and Two Frontiers: A Comparison of British Columbia and Washington Territory During the Early Years of Settlement." *Pacific Historical Review* 50 (1) (1981).

————. *Contact and Conflict: Indian-European Relations in British Columbia, 1774–1890.* 2nd ed. Vancouver: University of British Columbia Press, 1992.

————. "Judging History: Reflections on the Reasons for Judgement in Delgamuukw v. B.C." *B.C. Studies* 95 (Autumn 1992).

Fiske, Jo-Anne. "Carrier Women and the Politics of Mothering." In *British Columbia Reconsidered: Essays on Women*, edited by Gillian Creese and Veronica Strong-Boag. Vancouver: Press Gang Publishers, 1992.

Foster, Hamar. "It Goes Without Saying: Precedent and the Doctrine of Extinguishment by Implication in Delgamuukw et al v. The Queen." *The Advocate* 49 (May 1991).

Fowler, Loretta. *Shared Symbols, Contested Meanings: Gros Ventre Culture and History, 1778–1984.* Ithaca: Cornell University Press, 1987.

Francis, Daniel. *The Imaginary Indian: The Image of the Indian in Canadian Culture.* Vancouver, BC: Pulp Press, 1992.

Francis, Daniel, and Toby Morantz. *Partners in Furs: A History of the Fur Trade in Eastern James Bay, 1600–1870.* Kingston, ON: McGill-Queen's University Press, 1983.

Fulton, Robert, and Steven Anderson. "The Amerindian 'Man-Woman': Gender, Liminality, and Cultural Continuity." *Current Anthropology* 33 (1992).

Galbraith, John S. *The Hudson's Bay Company as an Imperial Factor.* Toronto: University of Toronto Press, 1957.

Geertz, Clifford. *The Interpretation of Cultures.* New York: Basic Books, 1973.

Gerbi, Antonello. *The Dispute of the New World: The History of a Polemic, 1750–1900.* Pittsburgh: University of Pittsburgh Press, 1973.

Gibson, A., and T. C. Smout. "Food and Hierarchy in Scotland, 1550–1650." In *Perspectives in Scottish Social History*, edited by Rosalind Michison. Aberdeen. Scotland: Aberdeen University Press, 1988.

Gibson, James. *Farming the Frontier: The Agricultural Opening of the Oregon Country, 1786–1846.* Vancouver: University of British Columbia Press, 1985.

Godelier, Maurice. *The Mental and the Material.* London: Verso, 1986.

Green, Rayna. "The Tribe Called Wannabee: Playing Indian in America and Europe." *Folklore* 99 (1) (1988).

Greer, Allan. *Fur Trade Labour and Lower Canadian Agrarian Structures.* Historical Papers, Canadian Historical Association. Toronto, 1981.

Groot, C., and L. Margolis, eds. *Pacific Salmon Life Histories*. Vancouver: University of British Columbia Press, 1991.

Grove, Richard. "Scottish Missionaries, Evangelical Discourses, and the Origins of Conservation Thinking." *Journal of Southern African Studies* 15 (2) (1989).

———. "Origins of Western Environmentalism." *Scientific American* 267 (1) (July 1992).

———. *Green Imperialism: Colonial Expansion, Tropical Island Edens, and the Origins of Environmentalism, 1600–1860*. Cambridge and New York: Cambridge University Press, 1995.

Guha, Ranajit, ed. *Selected Subaltern Studies*. New York: Oxford University Press, 1988.

Guilmet, George, et al. "The Legacy of Introduced Disease: The Southern Coast Salish." *American Indian Culture and Research Journal* 15 (1) (1991).

Gunther, Erna. "The Westward Movement of Some Plains Traits." *American Anthropologist* 52 (2) (1950).

Haines, Francis. "The Northward Spread of Horses Among the Plains Indians." *American Anthropologist* 40 (3) (1938).

Hajda, Yvonne. "Regional Social Organization in the Greater Lower Columbia." Ph.D. diss., University of Washington, 1984.

Hall, Catherine. *White, Male, and Middle Class: Explorations in Feminism and History*. London and New York: Polity and Routledge, 1992.

Hamell, George. "Strawberries, Floating Islands, and Rabbit Captains: Mythical Realities and European Contact in the Northeast During the Sixteenth and Seventeenth Centuries." *Journal of Canadian Studies* 21 (1986–87):72–94.

Hammond, Lorne. "'Any Ordinary Degree of System': The Columbia Department of the Hudson's Bay Company and the Harvesting of Wildlife, 1825–1849." Master's thesis, University of Victoria, 1988.

Harley, J. B. "Deconstructing the Map." In *Writing Worlds: Discourse, Text, and Metaphor in the Representation of Landscape*, edited by Trevor J. Barnes and James S. Duncan. London: Routledge, 1992.

Harris, Bob; Harley Hatfield; and Peter Tassie, *The Okanagan Brigade Trail in the South Okanagan, 1811–1849*. Penticton, BC: Okanagan Historical Society, 1989.

Harris, R. Cole. *Historical Atlas of Canada*. Vol. 1. Toronto: University of Toronto Press, 1987.

———. "Voices of Disaster: Smallpox Around the Strait of Georgia in 1782. *Ethnohistory* 41 (4) (1994).

Harris, Marvin. *The Sacred Cow and the Abominable Pig*. New York: Viking Books, 1985.

Hayden, Brian, ed. *A Complex Culture of the British Columbia Plateau: Traditional Stl'atl'imx Resource Use*. Vancouver: University of British Columbia Press, 1992.

Himmelfarb, Gertrude. *The Idea of Poverty: England in the Early Industrial Age*. New York: Knopf, 1984.

Hobsbawm, Eric, and Terence Ranger, eds. *The Invention of Tradition*. Cambridge: Cambridge University Press, 1983.

Holt, Roberta; Alfred Jahnke; and Peter Tassie. *The Okanagan Brigade Trail*. Vernon, BC: Okanagan Historical Society, 1986.

Honour, Hugh. *The New Golden Land: European Images of America from the Discoveries to the Present Time*. New York: Pantheon Books, 1975.

Houston, R. A., and I. D. Whyte, eds. *Scottish Society, 1500–1800*. Cambridge: Cambridge University Press, 1989.

Hulme, Peter. *Colonial Encounters*. Cambridge: Cambridge University Press, 1987.

Humes, W. M., and H. M. Paterson, eds. *Scottish Culture and Scottish Education, 1800–1980*. Edinburgh: John Donald, 1983.

Hunn, Eugene. "Mobility as a Factor Limiting Resource Use in the Columbia Plateau." In *Resource Managers: North American and Australian Hunter-Gatherers*, edited by Nancy Williams and Eugene Hunn. Boulder: American Association for the Advancement of Science, 1982.

Hunn, Eugene, with James Selam and family. *Nch'i-Wana, "The Big River": Middle Columbia Indians and Their Land*. Seattle: University of Washington Press, 1990.

Hunn, Eugene, and David French. "Lomatium: A Key Resource for Columbia Plateau Native Subsistence." *Northwest Science* 55 (2) (1981).

Hunt, Lynn, ed. *The New Cultural History*. Berkeley: University of California Press, 1989.

Ingold, Tim; David Riches; and James Woodburn, eds. *Hunters and Gatherers I: History, Evolution, and Social Change*. Oxford, England: Berg, 1988.

Innis, Harold A. *The Fur Trade in Canada*. Toronto: University of Toronto Press, 1962.

Jaenen, Cornelius. "Amerindian Views of French Culture in the Seventeenth Century." *Canadian Historical Review* 55 (1974): 261–91.

Janzen, John. "The Tradition of Renewal in Kongo Religion." In *African Religions: A Symposium*, edited by Newell S. Booth. New York: NOK Publishers, 1977.

Johnson, Douglas, and David Anderson, eds. *The Ecology of Survival: Case Studies from Northeast African History*. London: Lester Crook, 1988.

Josephy, Alvin. *The Artist Was a Young Man*. Fort Worth: Amon Carter Museum, 1970.

Jordanova, Ludmilla. "Earth Science and Environmental Medicine: The Synthesis of the Late Enlightenment." In *Images of the Earth: Essays in the History of the Environmental Sciences*, edited by Ludmilla Jordanova and Roy Porter. Chalfont St. Giles: British Society for the History of Science, 1979.

———. *Sexual Visions: Images of Gender in Science and Medicine*. Hemel Hempstead, England: Harvester Wheatsheaf, 1989.

Judd, Carol, and A. J. Ray, eds. *Old Trails and New Directions: Papers of the Third North American Fur Trade Conference*. Toronto: University of Toronto Press, 1980.

Karamanski, Theodore. *Fur Trade and Exploration: Opening the Far Northwest, 1821–1852*. Norman: University of Oklahoma Press, 1983.

Kehoe, Alice Bece Beck. "Old Woman Had Great Power." *Western Canadian Journal of Anthropology* 6 (1976).

———. "The Shackles of Tradition." In *The Hidden Half: Studies of Plains Indian Women*, edited by Patricia Albers and Beatrice Medicine. Lanham Park, MD: University Press of America, 1983.

———. *The Ghost Dance: Ethnohistory and Revitalization*. New York: Holt, Rinehart and Winston, 1989.

———. "Transcribing Insema, a Blackfoot 'Old Lady.'" In *Reading Beyond Words: Contexts for Native History*, edited by Jennifer S. H. Brown and Elizabeth Vibert. Peterborough, ON: Broadview Press, 1996.

Kelly, M. T. "The Land Before Time." *Saturday Night* 104 (July 1989).

Kew, Michael. "Salmon Availability, Technology, and Cultural Adaptation in the Fraser River Watershed." In *A Complex Culture of the*

British Columbia Plateau: Traditional Stl'atl'imx Resource Use, edited by Brian Hayden. Vancouver: University of British Columbia Press, 1992.

Klein, Alan. "The Political Economy of Gender: A Nineteenth Century Plains Indian Case Study." In *The Hidden Half: Studies of Plains Indian Women,* edited by Patricia Albers and Beatrice Medicine. Lanham, MD: University Press of America, 1983.

Knox, H. M. *Two Hundred and Fifty Years of Scottish Education, 1696–1946.* Edinburgh and London: Oliver and Boyd, 1953.

Koponen, Juhani. *People and Production in Late Precolonial Tanzania: History and Structures.* Helsinki: Finnish Society for Development Studies, 1988.

Kracht, Benjamin. "The Kiowa Ghost Dance, 1894–1916: An Unheralded Revitalization Movement." *Ethnohistory* 39 (4) (1992).

Krech, Shepard, ed. *The Subarctic Fur Trade: Native Social and Economic Adaptations.* Vancouver: University of British Columbia Press, 1983.

———. "The State of Ethnohistory." *Annual Review of Anthropology* 20 (1991).

———, ed. *Native Canadian Anthropology and History: A Selected Bibliography.* Norman: University of Oklahoma Press, 1993.

Kroeber, A. L. *Cultural and Natural Areas of Native North America.* Berkeley: University of California Press, 1947.

Lang, Samuel. "Cultural Ecology and the Horse in Flathead Culture." In *Lifeways of Intermontane and Plains Montana Indians,* edited by Leslie Davis. Occasional Papers of the Museum of the Rockies, no. 1. Bozeman: Montana State University, 1979.

Lanternari, Vittorio. *The Religions of the Oppressed: A Study of Modern Messianic Cults.* New York: Knopf, 1963.

———. "Revolution and/or Integration in African Socio-religious Movements." In *Religion, Rebellion, Revolution: An Interdisciplinary and Cross-Cultural Collection of Essays,* edited by B. Lincoln. Basingstoke, England: Macmillan, 1985.

Lawrence, C. J. "William Buchan: Medicine Laid Open." *Medical History* 19 (1975): 20–35.

Leacock, Eleanor. *The Montagnais 'Hunting Territory' and the Fur Trade.* American Anthropological Association Memoir 78. Menasha, WI, 1954.

———. "Women's Status in Egalitarian Society," *Current Anthropology* 19 (2) (1978).

———. "Relations of Production in Band Society." In *Politics and History in Band Societies*, edited by Eleanor Leacock and Richard Lee. Cambridge: Cambridge University Press, 1982.

Leacock, Eleanor, and Richard Lee, eds. *Politics and History in Band Societies*. Cambridge: Cambridge University Press, 1982.

Lee, Richard. "What Hunters do for a Living." In *Man the Hunter*, edited by Richard Lee and Irven De Vore. New York: Aldine, 1968.

Lee, Richard, and Irven De Vore, eds. *Man the Hunter*. New York: Aldine, 1968.

Liberty, Margot. "Hell Came with Horses: Plains Indian Women in the Equestrian Era." *Montana: The Magazine of Western History* 32 (3) (1982).

Lincoln, Bruce. *Discourse and the Construction of Society: Comparative Studies of Myth, Ritual, and Classification*. Oxford: Oxford University Press, 1989.

Linton, Ralph. "Nativistic Movements." *American Anthropologist* 45 (1943): 230–41.

Loo, Tina. *Making Law, Order, and Authority in British Columbia, 1821–1871*. Toronto: University of Toronto Press, 1994.

McEachern, Allan. "Reasons for Judgement: Delgamuukw v. B.C." Smithers, BC: Supreme Court of British Columbia, 1991.

McGinnis, Anthony. *Counting Coup and Cutting Horses: Intertribal Warfare on the Northern Plains, 1738–1889*. Evergreen, CO: Cordillera Press, 1990.

McGrane, Bernard. *Beyond Anthropology: Society and the Other*. New York: Columbia University Press, 1989.

McKenney, Thomas L., and James Hall. *The Indian Tribes of North America, with Biographical Sketches and Anecdotes of the Principal Chiefs*. Vol. 2. [Rev. ed. 1844] Edinburgh: John Grant, 1934.

MacKenzie, John. *Empire of Nature: Hunting, Conservation, and British Imperialism*. Manchester, England: Manchester University Press, 1988.

Mackie, Richard. "The Hudson's Bay Company on the Pacific, 1821–1843." Ph.D. diss., University of British Columbia, 1993.

MacLaren, I. S. "Alexander Mackenzie and Landscapes of Commerce." *Studies in Canadian Literature* 7 (2) (1982).

———. "The Aesthetic Mapping of Nature in the Second Franklin Expedition." *Journal of Canadian Studies* 20 (1) (1985).

———. "Exploration/Travel Literature and the Evolution of the Author." *International Journal of Canadian Studies* 5 (1992): 39–68.

MacLeod, Carol. *The Fur Trade on the Southern Pacific Slope, 1779–1858.* National Historic Parks and Sites Branch, Manuscript Report 163. Ottawa: Parks Canada, n.d.

McNeill, W. H. *Plagues and Peoples.* Anchor City, NY: Anchor/Doubleday, 1976.

Malthus, Thomas. *On Population.* Edited by Gertrude Himmelfarb. New York: Modern Library, 1960.

Mangan, J. A., and James Walvin, eds. *Manliness and Morality: Middle Class Masculinity in Britain and America, 1800–1940.* Manchester, England: Manchester University Press, 1987.

Marks, Shula, and Anthony Atmore, eds. *Economy and Society in Pre-Industrial South Africa.* London: Longman, 1980.

Marshall, Alan. "Nez Percé Subsistence." Paper presented at Forty-fourth Annual Northwest Anthropological Conference, 1991.

Marshall, P. J., and Glyndwr Williams. *The Great Map of Mankind: British Perceptions of the World in the Age of Enlightenment.* London: J. M. Dent, 1982.

Martin, Calvin. *Keepers of the Game: Indian-Animal Relationships and the Fur Trade.* Berkeley: University of California Press, 1978.

Martin, Christopher. *A Short History of English Schools, 1750–1965.* Hove, England: Wayland Publishers, 1979.

Marx, Karl. *Capital.* Vol.1. *Extracted in Karl Marx: Selected Writings,* edited by David McLellan. Oxford: Oxford University Press, 1977.

Mauss, Marcel. *The Gift: Forms and Functions of Exchange in Archaic Societies.* [1925] New York: W. W. Norton, 1967.

Medicine, Beatrice. "'Warrior Women': Sex Role Alternatives for Plains Indian Women." In *The Hidden Half: Studies of Plains Indian Women,* edited by Patricia Albers and Beatrice Medicine. Lanham, MD: University Press of America, 1983.

Meek, R. L. *Social Science and the Ignoble Savage.* Cambridge: Cambridge University Press, 1982.

Meinig, D. W. *The Great Columbia Plain: A Historical Geography, 1805–1910.* Seattle: University of Washington Press, 1968.

Melman, Billie. *Women's Orients: English Women and the Middle East, 1718–1918: Sexuality, Religion, and Work.* Ann Arbor: University of Michigan Press, 1992.

Mennell, Stephen. *All Manners of Food: Eating and Taste in England and France from the Middle Ages to the Present.* Oxford, England: Basil Blackwell, 1985.

Merchant, Carolyn. "Gender and Environmental History." *Journal of American History* 76 (4) (1990).

Miller, Christopher. *Prophetic Worlds: Indians and Whites on the Columbia Plateau.* New Brunswick, NJ: Rutgers University Press, 1985.

Miller, Christopher, and George Hamell. "A New Perspective on Indian-White Contact: Cultural Symbols and Colonial Trade." *Journal of American History* 73 (1986): 311–28.

Miquelon, Dale. *New France, 1701–1744: "A Supplement to Europe."* Toronto: McClelland and Stewart, 1987.

Mohanty, Chandra Talpade. "Introduction: Cartographies of Struggle." In *Third World Women and the Politics of Feminism,* edited by Chandra Talpade Mohanty, Ann Russo, and Lourdes Torres. Bloomington: Indiana University Press, 1991.

Mooney, James. *The Ghost-Dance Religion and the Sioux Outbreak of 1890." Fourteenth Annual Report of the Bureau of Ethnology,* Part 2. Washington, DC: Government Printing Office, 1896.

Moore, Henrietta. *Feminism and Anthropology.* Cambridge, England: Polity Press, 1988.

Morantz, Toby. "The Probability of Family Hunting Territories in Eighteenth Century James Bay." In *Papers of the 9th Algonquian Conference,* edited by William Cowan. Ottawa: Carleton University Press, 1978.

———. "The Fur Trade and the Cree of James Bay." In *Old Trails and New Directions: Papers of the Third North American Fur Trade Conference,* edited by Carol Judd and Arthur Ray. Toronto: University of Toronto Press, 1980.

———. "Economic and Social Accommodations of the James Bay Inlanders to the Fur Trade." In *The Subarctic Fur Trade: Native Social and Economic Adaptations,* edited by Shepard Krech. Vancouver: University of British Columbia Press, 1983.

———. "'Gift Offerings to their Own Importance and Superiority': Fur Trade Relations, 1700–1940." In *Papers of the 19th Algonquian*

    Conference, edited by William Cowan. Ottawa: Carleton University
        Press, 1988.
Mukhopadhyay, Carol, and Patricia Higgins. "Anthropological Studies of
    Women's Status Revisited: 1977–1987." *Annual Review of
    Anthropology* 17 (1988).
Murphy, Robert, and Yolanda Murphy. "Northern Shoshone and Bannock."
    In *Great Basin*, edited by Warren L. D'Azevedo. Vol. 11, *Handbook
    of North American Indians*, edited by W. C. Sturtevant. Wash-
    ington, DC: Smithsonian Institution, 1986.
Murray, J. A. H., ed. *A New English Dictionary on Historical Principles*.
    Oxford, England: Clarendon Press, 1888.
Nash, Gary B. "The Image of the Indian in the Southern Colonial Mind."
    In *The Wild Man Within: An Image in Western Thought from the
    Renaissance to Romanticism*, edited by Edward Dudley and M.
    E. Novak. Pittsburgh: University of Pittsburgh Press, 1972.
Newman, Peter C. *Company of Adventurers*. Markham, ON: Viking, 1985.
Nicks, John. "David Thompson." In *Dictionary of Canadian Biography*,
    vol. 8.
Nicks, Trudy. "The Iroquois and the Fur Trade in Western Canada." In
    *Old Trails and New Directions: Papers of the Third North American
    Fur Trade Conference*, edited by Carol Judd and A. J. Ray. Toronto:
    University of Toronto Press, 1980.
Obeyesekere, Gananath. *The Apotheosis of Captain Cook: European
    Mythmaking in the Pacific*. Princeton: Princeton University Press,
    1992.
Orr, Willie. *Deer Forests, Landlords, and Crofters: The Western Highlands
    in Victorian and Edwardian Times*. Edinburgh: John Donald, 1982.
Ortner, Sherry, and Harriet Whitehead, eds. *Sexual Meanings: The Cultural
    Construction of Gender and Sexuality*. Cambridge: Cambridge
    University Press, 1981.
Pagden, Anthony. *The Fall of Natural Man: The American Indian and the
    Origins of Comparative Ethnology*. Cambridge: Cambridge
    University Press, 1986.
Palmer, Gary. "Cultural Ecology in the Canadian Plateau." *Northwest
    Anthropological Research Notes* 9 (2) (1975).
Payne, Michael. "Daily Life on Western Hudson Bay, 1714 to 1870: A Social
    History of York Factory and Churchill." Ph.D. diss., Carleton
    University, 1989.

Payne, Michael, and Gregory Thomas. "Literacy, Literature, and Libraries in the Fur Trade." *The Beaver* 313 (4) (1983).

Peers, Laura. "Rich Man, Poor Man, Beggarman, Chief: Saulteaux in the Red River Settlement." In *Papers of the 18th Algonquian Conference*, edited by William Cowan. Ottawa: Carleton University Press, 1987.

———. *The Ojibwa of Western Canada, 1780–1870*. Winnipeg: University of Manitoba Press, 1994.

———. "Trade and Change in the Plateau." N. d. Essay in possession of author.

Peires, J. B. *The Dead Will Arise: Nongqawuse and the Great Xhosa Cattle-Killing Movement of 1856—7*. London: James Currey, 1989.

Peterson, Jacqueline. "Prophetic Worlds." *Ethnohistory* 35 (2) (1988).

Peterson, Jacqueline, and John Anfinson. "The Indian and the Fur Trade: A Review of Recent Literature." In *Scholars and the Indian Experience*, edited by W. R. Swagerty. Bloomington: Indiana University Press, 1984.

Peterson, Jacqueline, and Jennifer S. H. Brown, eds. *The New Peoples: Being and Becoming Mtis in North America*. Winnipeg: University of Manitoba Press, 1985.

Peterson, Jacqueline, with Laura Peers. *Sacred Encounters: Father DeSmet and the Indians of the Rocky Mountain West*. Norman: University of Oklahoma Press, 1993.

Poovey, Mary. *Uneven Developments: The Ideological Work of Gender in Mid-Victorian England*. Chicago: University of Chicago Press, 1988.

Porter, Roy. "Mixed Feelings: The Enlightenment and Sexuality in Eighteenth-Century Britain." In *Sexuality in Eighteenth-Century Britain*, edited by Paul-Gabriel Bouc. Manchester, England: Manchester University Press, 1982.

———. "Review Article: Man, Animals and Nature." *Historical Journal* 28 (1) (1985).

Post, Richard. "The Subsistence Quest." In *The Sinkaietk or Southern Okanagon of Washington*, edited by Leslie Spier. General Series in Anthropology, no. 6. Menasha, WI: George Banta, 1938.

Powers, Marla. *Oglala Women*. Chicago: University of Chicago Press, 1986.

Prakash, Gyan. "Introduction: After Colonialism." In *After Colonialism: Imperial Histories and Postcolonial Displacements*, edited by Gyan Prakash. Princeton: Princeton University Press, 1995.

Pratt, Mary Louise. *Imperial Eyes: Travel Writing and Transculturation*. London: Routledge, 1992.

Pyne, Stephen. *Fire in America: A Cultural History of Wildland and Rural Fire*. Princeton: Princeton University Press, 1982.

Ramenofsky, Ann. *Vectors of Death: The Archaeology of European Contact*. Albuquerque: University of New Mexico Press, 1987.

———. "Loss of Innocence: Explanations of Differential Persistence in the Sixteenth-Century Southeast." In *Columbian Consequences*, edited by David Hurst Thomas. Vol. 2, *Archaeological and Historical Perspectives on the Spanish Borderlands East*. Washington, DC: Smithsonian Institution Press, 1991.

Ramsey, Jarold. "Simon Fraser's Canoe; or, Capsizing into Myth." In *Reading the Fire: Essays in the Traditional Indian Literature of the Far West*, edited by Jarold Ramsey. Lincoln: University of Nebraska Press, 1983.

Rangarajan, Mahesh. "Hunting and Conservation in India." D. Phil. thesis, Oxford University, 1992.

Ranger, Terence. "The Invention of Tribalism in Zimbabwe." Gweru, Zimbabwe: Mambo Press, 1985.

———. "Religious Movements and Politics in Sub-Saharan Africa." *African Studies Review* 29 (2) (1986).

———. "Whose Heritage? The Case of Matobo National Park." *Journal of Southern African Studies* 15 (2) (1989).

———. "Plagues of Beasts and Men: Prophetic Responses to Epidemic in Eastern and Southern Africa." In *Epidemics and Ideas*, edited by T. O. Ranger and Paul Slack. Cambridge: Cambridge University Press, 1992.

Ray, Arthur J. *Indians in the Fur Trade: Their Role as Trappers, Hunters, and Middlemen in the Lands Southwest of Hudson Bay, 1660–1870*. Toronto: University of Toronto Press, 1974.

———. "Periodic Shortages, Native Welfare, and the Hudson's Bay Company, 1670–1930." In *The Subarctic Fur Trade: Native Social and Economic Adaptations*, edited by Shepard Krech. Vancouver: University of British Columbia Press, 1983.

Ray, Arthur J., and Donald Freeman. *"Give Us Good Measure."* Toronto: University of Toronto Press, 1978.

Ray, Verne. *The Sanpoil and Nespelem*. Seattle: University of Washington Press, 1933.

————. *Cultural Relations in the Plateau of Northwestern North America.* Los Angeles: Southwest Museum, 1939.

Reff, Daniel T. *Disease, Depopulation, and Culture Change in Northwestern New Spain, 1518–1764.* Salt Lake City: University of Utah Press, 1991.

Reynolds, Henry. *The Other Side of the Frontier: Aboriginal Resistance to the European Invasion of Australia.* Sydney: Penguin, 1982.

Rich, E. E. "Trade Habits and Economic Motivation Among the Indians of North America." *Canadian Journal of Economics and Political Science* 26 (1) (1960).

————. *The Fur Trade and the Northwest to 1857.* Toronto: McClelland and Stewart, 1967.

Ridington, Robin. *Swan People: A Study of the Dunne-za Prophet Dance.* Canadian Ethnology Service Paper 38. Ottawa: National Museum of Man, 1978.

————. *Trail to Heaven: Knowledge and Narrative in a Northern Community.* Iowa City: University of Iowa Press, 1988.

Robinson, Harry. *Write It on Your Heart: The Epic World of an Okanagan Storyteller.* Edited by Wendy Wickwire. Vancouver: Talonbooks/Theytus, 1989.

Romanoff, Steven. "Fraser Lillooet Salmon Fishing." *Northwest Anthropological Research Notes* 19 (2) (1985).

Ronda, James P. *Lewis and Clark Among the Indians.* Lincoln: University of Nebraska Press, 1984.

Rousseau, Jean-Jacques. *A Discourse on Inequality.* Translated by Maurice Cranston. London: Penguin Books, 1984.

Ruby, Robert H., and John A. Brown. *The Cayuse Indians: Imperial Tribesmen of Old Oregon.* Norman: University of Oklahoma Press, 1972.

Sahlins, Marshall. *Stone Age Economics.* Chicago: Aldine-Atherton, 1972.

————. *Culture and Practical Reason.* Chicago: University of Chicago Press, 1976.

————. *Islands of History.* Chicago: University of Chicago Press, 1985.

Said, Edward W. *Orientalism.* New York: Pantheon Books, 1978.

————. "On Palestinian Identity: A Conversation with Salman Rushdie." *New Left Review* 160 (November–December 1986).

————. "Representing the Colonized: Anthropology's Interlocuters." *Critical Inquiry* 15 (2) (1989).

Sass, Louis. "Anthropology's Native Problems: Revisionism in the Field."
    Harpers, May 1986.
Saum, Lewis. *The Fur Trader and the Indian.* Seattle: University of
    Washington Press, 1965.
Schaeffer, Claude. "The Kutenai Female Berdache: Courier, Guide,
    Prophetess, and Warrior." *Ethnohistory* 12 (3) (1965).
Schama, Simon. *Landscape and Memory.* New York: Harper Collins, 1995.
Scotland, James. *The History of Scottish Education.* London: University
    of London Press, 1969.
Segal, Lynne. *Slow Motion: Changing Masculinities, Changing Men.*
    London: Virago, 1990.
Shoemaker, Nancy. "Introduction." In *Negotiators of Change: Historical
    Perspectives on Native American Women,* edited by Nancy
    Shoemaker. New York and London: Routledge, 1995.
————, ed. *Negotiators of Change: Historical Perspectives on Native
    American Women.* New York and London: Routledge, 1995.
Sinha, Mrinalini. "Gender and Imperialism: Colonial Policy and the
    Ideology of Moral Imperialism in Late Nineteenth-Century
    Bengal." In *Changing Men: New Directions in Research on Men
    and Masculinity,* edited by Michael S. Kimmel. London: Sage, 1987.
Smith, Adam. *Lectures on Jurisprudence.* Edited by R. L. Meek et al. Oxford:
    Clarendon Press, 1978.
Smith, Bernard. *European Vision and the South Pacific.* 2nd. ed. New
    Haven: Yale University Press, 1985.
Smith, Jonathan. "The Slightly Different Thing That Is Said: Writing the
    Aesthetic Experience." In *Writing Worlds: Discourse, Text, and
    Metaphor in the Representation of Landscape,* edited by Trevor
    J. Barnes and James S. Duncan. London: Routledge, 1992.
Smith, J. V. "Manners, Morals and Mentalities." In *Scottish Culture and
    Scottish Education, 1800–1980,* edited by W. M. Humes and H.
    M. Paterson. Edinburgh: John Donald, 1983.
Smits, David. "'The Squaw Drudge': A Prime Index of Savagism."
    Ethnohistory 29 (1982): 281–306.
Spier, Leslie. *The Prophet Dance of the Northwest and Its Derivatives.*
    General Series in Anthropology, no. 1. Menasha, WI: George Banta,
    1935.
Spivak, Gayatri Chakravorty. *In Other Worlds: Essays in Cultural Politics.*
    New York: Methuen, 1987.

Stannard, David. "The Consequences of Contact: Toward an Interdisci-
    plinary Theory of Native Responses to Biological and Cultural
    Invasion." In *Columbian Consequences*, edited by David Hurst
    Thomas. Vol. 3, *The Spanish Borderlands in Pan-American
    Perspective*. Washington, DC: Smithsonian Institution Press, 1991.
Stern, Theodore. *Chiefs and Chief Traders: Indian Relations at Fort Nez
    Percés, 1818–1855.* Vol. 1. Corvallis: Oregon State University Press,
    1993.
Stewart, Edgar I., and Jane R. Stewart. "Introduction." In *The Columbia
    River, Or Scenes and Adventures* . . . , by Ross Cox. Norman:
    University of Oklahoma Press, 1957.
Stewart, Susan Hopkins. "The Hudson's Bay Company's Contribution to
    the Work of Three Important Artists in Their Territory." Master's
    thesis, University of British Columbia, 1979.
Stocking, George W. *History of Anthropology*. Vol. 1, *Observers Observed:
    Essays on Ethnographic Fieldwork*. Madison: University of
    Wisconsin Press, 1983.
Sturtevant, W. C., ed. *Handbook of North American Indians*. Washington:
    Smithsonian Institution, 1984–.
Suttles, Wayne. "The Plateau Prophet Dance Among the Coast Salish."
    Southwestern Journal of Anthropology 13 (1957): 352–96.
————. *Coast Salish Essays*. Vancouver: University of British Columbia
    Press, 1987.
Swagerty, William R. "Indian Trade in the Trans-Mississippi West to 1870."
    In *History of Indian-White Relations*, edited by Wilcomb E. Wash-
    burn. Vol. 4, *Handbook of North American Indians*, edited by W. C.
    Sturtevant. Washington, DC: Smithsonian Institution, 1988.
————. "Protohistoric Trade in Western North America: Archaeological
    and Ethnohistorical Considerations." In *Columbian Consequences*,
    edited by David Hurst Thomas. Vol. 3, *The Spanish Borderlands
    in Pan-American Perspective*. Washington, DC: Smithsonian
    Institution Press, 1991.
Taussig, Michael. *Shamanism, Colonialism, and the Wild Man: A Study
    in Terror and Healing*. Chicago: University of Chicago Press, 1987.
Teit, James. "The Thompson Indians of British Columbia." *Memoirs of the
    American Museum of Natural History* 2 (4) (1900).
————. "The Shuswap." *Memoirs of the American Museum of Natural
    History* 2 (7) (1909).

———. "The Salishan Tribes of the Western Plateaus." *45th Annual Report of the Bureau of American Ethnology . . . 1927–28.* Washington, DC: Governtment Printing Office, 1930.

Tennant, Paul. *Aboriginal Peoples and Politics: The British Columbia Land Question, 1850–1988.* Vancouver: University of British Columbia Press, 1990.

Thomas, David H., ed. *Columbian Consequences.* 3 vols. Washington, DC: Smithsonian Institution, 1989–91.

Thomas, Keith. *Man and the Natural World: Changing Attitudes in England, 1500–1800.* London: Allen Lane, 1983.

Thompson, E. P. *The Making of the English Working Class.* London: Victor Gollancz, 1963.

———. *Whigs and Hunters: The Origin of the Black Act.* London: Allen Lane, 1977.

Thomson, Duncan Duane. "A History of the Okanagan: Indians and Whites in the Settlement Era, 1860–1920." Ph.D. diss., University of British Columbia, 1985.

Thornton, Russell. *We Shall Live Again: The 1870 and 1890 Ghost Dance Movements as Demographic Revitalization.* Cambridge: Cambridge University Press, 1986.

———. *American Indian Holocaust and Survival: A Population History Since 1492.* Norman: University of Oklahoma Press, 1987.

———. "Boundary Dissolution and Revitalization Movements; The Case of the Nineteenth-Century Cherokees." *Ethnohistory* 40 (1993).

Thornton, Russell; Jonathan Warren; and Tim Miller. "Depopulation in the Southeast After 1492." In *Disease and Demography in the Americas*, edited by John W. Verano and Douglas Ubelaker. Washington, DC: Smithsonian Institution Press, 1992.

Todorov, Tzvetan. *The Conquest of America: The Question of the Other.* New York: Harper and Row, 1984.

Townsend, Joan. "Firearms Against Native Arms: A Study in Comparative Efficiencies." *Arctic Anthropology* 20 (2) (1983).

Trigger, Bruce. *The Children of Aataentsic: A History of the Huron People to 1660.* Montreal: McGill-Queen's University Press, 1976.

———. *Natives and Newcomers: Canada's 'Heroic' Age Reconsidered.* Montreal: McGill-Queen's University Press, 1985.

————. "Early Native North American Responses to European Contact: Romantic Versus Rationalistic Interpretations." *Journal of American History* 77 (1991): 1195–1215.

Trigger, Bruce; Toby Morantz; and Louise Dechne, eds. *Le castor fait tout: Selected Papers of the 5th North American Fur Trade Conference, 1985.* Montreal: Lake St. Louis Historical Society, 1987.

Turner, Frederick Jackson. *The Frontier in American History.* New York: Holt, Rinehart and Winston, 1920.

Turner, Nancy; Randy Bouchard; and Dorothy Kennedy. *Ethnobotany of the Okanagan-Colville Indians.* Victoria: Royal British Columbia Museum, 1980.

Turner, Nancy, et.al. *Thompson Ethnobotany.* Victoria: Royal British Columbia Museum, 1990.

Turney-High, H. H. *The Flathead Indians of Montana.* Memoirs of the American Anthropological Association, no. 48. Menasha, WI, 1937.

————. *Ethnography of the Kutenai.* Memoirs of the American Anthropological Association, no. 56. Menasha, WI, 1941.

Twigg, Julia. "Vegetarianism and the Meanings of Meat." In *The Sociology of Food and Eating,* edited by Anne Murcott. Aldershot, England: Gower, 1983.

Van Kirk, Sylvia. *Many Tender Ties: Women in Fur Trade Society in Western Canada, 1670–1870.* Winnipeg: Watson and Dwyer, 1980.

————. "'What if Mama Is an Indian?': The Cultural Ambivalence of the Alexander Ross Family." In *The Developing West,* edited by John Foster. Edmonton: University of Alberta Press, 1983.

————. "Donald McKenzie." In *Dictionary of Canadian Biography,* vol. 8.

Vaughan, Megan. *The Story of an African Famine: Gender and Famine in Twentieth-Century Malawi.* Cambridge: Cambridge University Press, 1989.

————. *Curing Their Ills: Colonial Power and African Illness.* Cambridge, England: Polity Press, 1991.

Verano, John W., and Douglas Ubelaker, eds. *Disease and Demography in the Americas.* Washington, DC: Smithsonian Institution Press, 1992.

Vibert, Elizabeth. "'Traders' Tales: British Fur Traders' Narratives of the Encounter with Plateau Peoples, 1807–1846." D. Phil. diss., Oxford University, 1993.

———. "'The Natives Were Strong to Live': Re-interpreting Early Nineteenth-Century Prophetic Movements in the Columbia Plateau." *Ethnohistory* 42 (2) (1995).

———. "Real Men Hunt Buffalo: Masculinity, Race, and Class in British Fur Traders' Narratives," *Gender & History* 8 (1) (1996).

Visser, Margaret. *Much Depends on Dinner.* Toronto: McClelland and Stewart, 1986.

Walker, Deward. *Conflict and Schism in Nez Percé Acculturation.* Pullman: Washington State University Press, 1967.

———. "Nez Percé Sorcery." *Ethnology* 6 (1967): 66–96.

———. "New Light on the Prophet Dance Controversy." *Ethnohistory* 16 (1969): 245–55.

Wallace, Anthony F. C. "Revitalization Movements." *American Anthropologist* 58 (1956): 264–81.

———. *The Death and Rebirth of the Seneca.* New York: Knopf, 1970.

Warkentin, Germaine, ed. *Canadian Exploration Literature: An Anthology.* Oxford: Oxford University Press, 1993.

Washburn, Wilcomb E. "Symbol, Utility, and Aesthetics in the Indian Fur Trade." In *Aspects of the Fur Trade: Selected Papers of the 1965 North American Fur Trade Conference.* St. Paul: Minnesota Historical Society, 1967.

Webber, Jean, and the En'owkin Centre, eds. *Okanagan Sources.* Penticton, BC: Theytus Books, 1990.

Weist, Katherine. "Beasts of Burden and Menial Slaves." In *The Hidden Half: Studies of Plains Indian Women*, edited by Patricia Albers and Beatrice Medicine. Lanham, MD: University Press of America, 1983.

———. "Plains Indian Women: An Assessment." In *Anthropology on the Great Plains: The State of the Art*, edited by W. R. Wood and M. Liberty. Lincoln: University of Nebraska Press, 1980.

White, Bruce. "Give Us a Little Milk": The Social and Cultural Significance of Gift Giving in the Lake Superior Fur Trade." In *Rendezvous: Selected Papers of the 4th North American Fur Trade Conference*, edited by T. C. Buckley. St. Paul, MN: North American Fur Trade Conference, 1981.

———. "Encounters with Spirits: Ojibwa and Dakota Theories About the French and Their Merchandise." *Ethnohistory* 41 (3) (1994).

White, Hayden. "The Forms of Wildness: Archaeology of an Idea." In *The Wild Man Within: An Image in Western Thought from the Renaissance to Romanticism*, edited by Edward Dudley and M. E. Novak. Pittsburgh: University of Pittsburgh Press, 1972.

White, Richard. *The Roots of Dependency: Subsistence, Environment, and Social Change Among the Choctaws, Pawnees, and Navajos.* Lincoln: University of Nebraska Press, 1983.

———. "Ecological Change and Indian-White Relations." In *History of Indian-White Relations*, edited by Wilcomb E. Washburn. Vol. 4, *Handbook of North American Indians*, edited by W. C. Sturtevant. Washington, DC: Smithsonian Institution, 1988.

———. *"It's Your Misfortune and None of My Own": A History of the American West.* Norman: University of Oklahoma Press, 1991.

———. *The Middle Ground: Indians, Empires, and Republics in the Great Lakes Region.* Cambridge: Cambridge University Press, 1991.

Whitney, Stephen, ed. *Western Forests.* New York: Alfred A. Knopf, 1985.

Wickwire, Wendy. "Cultures in Contact: Music, the Plateau Indian, and the Western Encounter." Ph.D. diss., Wesleyan University, 1982.

———. "Women in Ethnography: The Research of James A. Teit." Paper presented at B.C. Studies Conference, Vancouver, November 1990.

Williams, Glyndwr. "The Hudson's Bay Company and the Fur Trade, 1670–1870." *The Beaver* 314 (2) (Autumn 1983).

Williams, Nancy, and Eugene Hunn, eds. *Resource Managers: North American and Australian Hunter-Gatherers.* Boulder: American Association for the Advancement of Science, 1982.

Williams, Raymond. *The Country and the City.* New York: Oxford University Press, 1973.

———. *Keywords.* New York: Harper and Row, 1976.

Williams, Walter. *The Spirit and the Flesh: Sexual Diversity in American Indian Culture.* Boston: Beacon Press, 1986.

Wolf, Eric. *Europe and the People Without History.* Berkeley: University of California Press, 1982.

Wolfenden, Madge. "John Tod." In *Dictionary of Canadian Biography*, vol. 11.

Wood, W. R. "Plains Trade in Prehistoric and Protohistoric Intertribal Relations." In *Anthropology on the Great Plains: The State of* the Art, edited by W. R. Wood and M. Liberty. Lincoln: University of Nebraska Press, 1980.

Worster, Donald. *Nature's Economy: The Roots of Ecology.* San Francisco: Sierra Club Books, 1977.

Wyatt, Victoria. *Shapes of Their Thoughts: Reflections of Culture Contact in Northwest Coast Indian Art.* New Haven: Yale University Press, 1984.

————. "Art and Exploration." Paper presented at the Vancouver Conference on Exploration and Discovery, Vancouver, 1992.

Index